24th December 2007

Darling,

Our eighth Christmas together - and this one is no less special than the previous Christmases. I love you very much and value your love, support, generosity, kindness - and Bond type quips. Happy travelling Darling - I'm amazed about our future travel together, and hope this will be of some use in that direction.

With love hugs & Christmas blessings

Amanda & a (Bondess)

THE TRAVEL BOOK

THE TRAVEL BOOK

A JOURNEY THROUGH EVERY COUNTRY IN THE WORLD

MELBOURNE · OAKLAND · LONDON

THE STORY OF THE TRAVEL BOOK

This book contains some 1200 images and 100,000 words, and covers 230 countries. Every country, large or small, is featured and we have sought to evoke each destination through a unique mix of images and original text. The effect is a series of tantalising glimpses, which somehow gather their own momentum with every page turned and combine to present an awesome picture of our vast and kaleidoscopic world.

We started this book with a seemingly simple proposition – *to represent every country in the world in amazing images and inspirational text in an accessible A to Z format*. A few obstacles soon stood in our way. Firstly, the possible answers to the question 'what is a country?' Secondly, the fact that we set out to create a travel book, not an exhaustive reference book of the world. We viewed the world through the lens of the traveller, focusing on places to visit for their beauty, fascination or singularity, even if this sometimes conflicted with the world as it is defined by political or geographical borders. And lastly, sheer logistics – the world is a breathtakingly big place, and to cover it all in one book is a big ambition.

What is a Country?

Our first port of call was the United Nations' list of defined countries – all 192 of these had an automatic ticket for entry into this book. The UN list does not include the foreign dependencies of these countries, whether self-governing or Crown colony, but we wanted to feature some of these places because they are ever-popular traveller hang-outs. In this category we included some, but not all, Caribbean islands and groups, as well as Bermuda, New Caledonia, the Cayman Islands and French Polynesia, all dependencies of geographically far-flung entities.

We decided, based on traveller interest more than political correctness, to feature the component parts of Britain – England, Scotland and Wales – as separate entities. Arch enemies and old friends, England, Scotland and Wales all have rich and distinctive histories and cultures, which hold enduring appeal for travellers, and we wanted to reflect that in this book. Other destinations, such as vibrant and colourful Hong Kong, Macau and Taiwan, which are all parts of China, have historic identities that separate them from their present-day political situation. For the traveller, they are often experienced as separate and different, and so we featured them that way.

Antarctica and Greenland are not countries, strictly speaking, but these vast lands are not only extremely photogenic, they are also fascinating to visit, a fact not lost on adventure travellers who make tracks there in ever-increasing numbers.

At the end of the book, you will find 12 'bonus' destinations that we couldn't bear to leave out, but could not justify as full entries. These places were selected because they are fascinating, often beautiful and remote places that are fast gathering focus on the insatiable explorer's map. Visit these places and you may find yourself competing with our illustrious founder, Tony Wheeler, for recognition as Lonely Planet's best-travelled person.

Lonely Planet's Perspective

In spite of our dilemmas about what to include and what not to include, the structure and organisation of the book was never in doubt. The A to Z format allowed us to view the world with a pleasing kind of egalitarianism, giving equal weight to superpowers like the United States of America and less high-profile nations like Burkina Faso or Belarus. It creates a sense of exhilaration and wonderment as such dramatically diverse and different places follow one after another – Afghanistan, Albania, Algeria, Andorra, Angola – the arbitrary linking of countries by letters of the alphabet belying the deeper connections that are shared across nations and humanity.

Having finally selected our official list of countries, we sent out the call to everyone at Lonely Planet to help us compile text and images for each destination. We had an amazing response from the avid travellers among our own staff, all of whom are passionate about the world and their favourite parts of it.

The guiding philosophy for us in writing this book was to present a subjective 'Lonely Planet' view of the world which gets under the skin of the place, showing a slice of life in every single country in the world. With just two pages per country, we could never hope to cover everything, so we chose instead to evoke the spirit of the place by focusing on the senses – what might you expect to see, what might you hear people say in conversation or greeting, what kind of food or drink can you expect to taste, and what sort of music, books or film would help open up your imagination to each country? In this sense, the book is much more about impressions than dry statistics – impressions that we hope will whet your appetite to find out more.

The same applied to image selection: we could never illustrate every aspect of every country in this book, so we again focused on capturing the spirit of a place and its people. Our image researchers avoided clichéd icons and picture-postcard views, beautiful as they often are, in favour of the icons of everyday life – people together and alone relaxing, eating, walking, reading, praying, working, sleeping, laughing and living.

The Whole World in Your Hands

Hundreds of Lonely Planet staff gave their time to be involved in this book, from writing text and selecting images to editing, checking, proofing and scanning pictures. It is their passion and their perspectives on our world which make for the wonderful, vibrant and breathtakingly BIG book which you now hold in your hands.

We hope that you will enjoy using this book to rediscover your favourite places, plan your next adventure, or dream about the places you may never go…

Roz Hopkins
Trade and Reference Publisher
Lonely Planet Publications

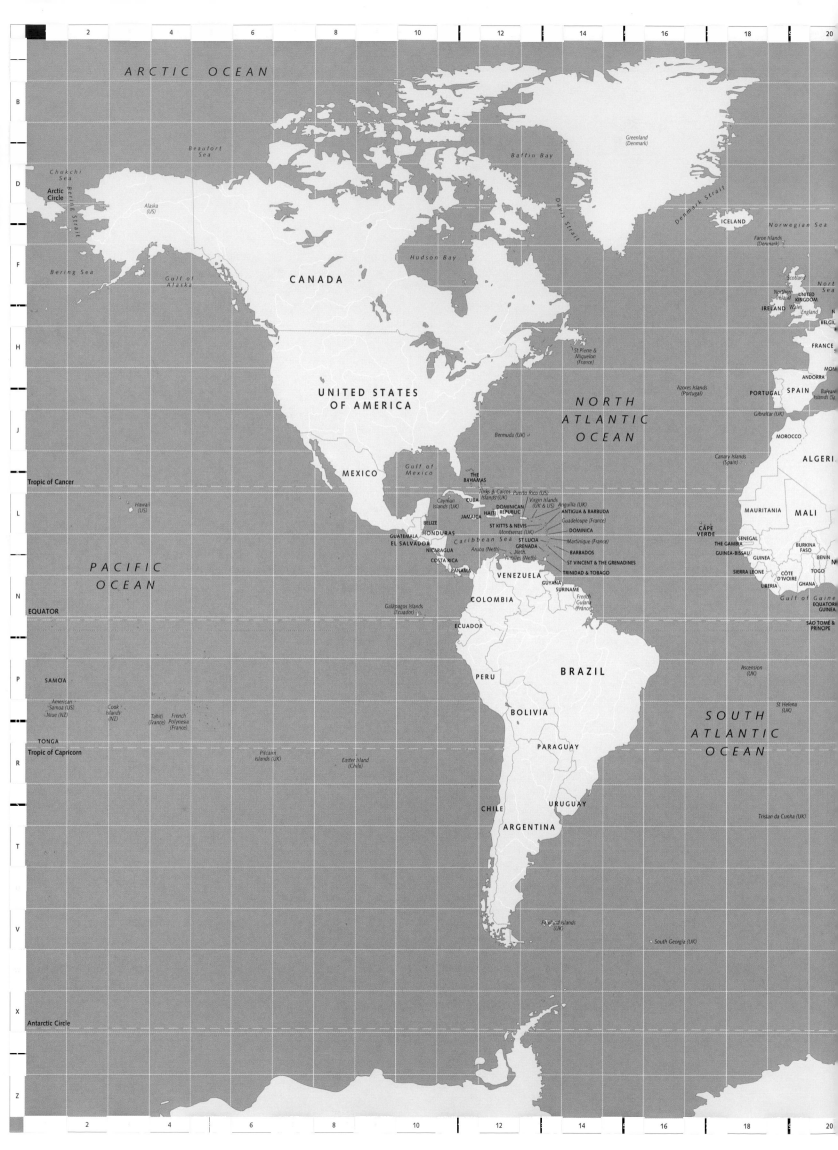

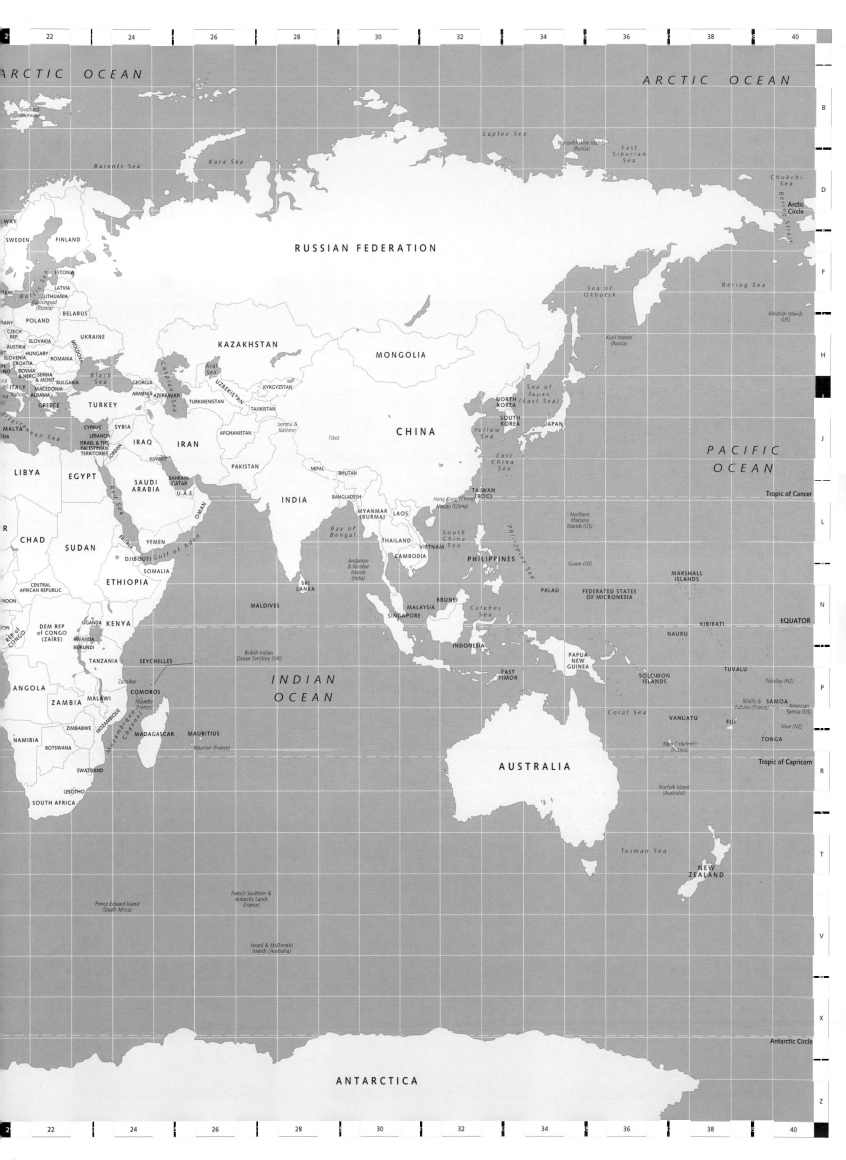

2. Curious children stand above a cultivated valley in Ghor Province Stephane Victor

3. The last of the sunlight glows on a house in the riverside town of Chaghcheran Stephane Victor

4. Lost for words, a man sits in front of a heavily inscribed marble wall in Mazar-e Sharif Stephane Victor

5. A widow wearing a burkha begs at the Shrine of Hazrat Ali (Blue Mosque) in Mazar-e Sharif Stephane Victor

1. Men stroll in front of the majestic Shrine of Hazrat Ali (Blue Mosque) in Mazar-e Sharif Stephane Victor

Blessed with a stark natural beauty, venerable history and rich and diverse culture, Afghanistan has of late been blighted with more than its share of troubles. This landlocked country, at the crossroads of Central Asia, has seen armies and empires, merchants and mendicants, poets and prophets come and go over millennia. Images of a war-blighted landscape do not do justice to a country that once hosted Silk Road caravans and was once the ultimate destination on the hippy trail.

BEST TIME TO VISIT
April to June for clement weather — or the 1380s, the artistic zenith of the Timurids

ESSENTIAL EXPERIENCES
Shopping for bargains in the bazaar in Herat, seat of Persian culture

Climbing the Chihil Zina (40 steps) carved into the hillside near Kandahar

Gazing at the dizzyingly high Minaret of Jam — what's it doing in the middle of nowhere?

Joining the pilgrims flocking around the blue domes of the Shrine of Hazrat Ali in Mazar-e Sharif

Soaking in the deep-blue, mineral-rich waters of the Band-e Amir lakes

GETTING UNDER THE SKIN
Read Robert Byron's *The Road to Oxiana* or Eric Newby's *A Short Walk in the Hindu Kush*, both all-time travel classics; Idris Shah's *Afghan Caravan* — a compendium of spellbinding Afghan tales, full of heroism, adventure and wisdom

Watch *Osama*, directed by Sidiq Barmak, a poignant tale of a young girl forced to assume a male identity to survive, and one of Afghanistan's first post-Taliban movies

Eat *qabli pulao* (seasoned rice with mutton, almonds, grated carrots and raisins); apricots dried in mountain villages

Drink green tea scented with cardamom

IN A WORD
Salām alekum (peace be with you), a ubiquitous greeting and blessing; *Borou bekheir* (travel well)

TRADEMARKS
Men with moustaches and turbans; women in head-to-toe veils; opium poppies; snow-topped mountain vistas; intricate weaves of tribal rugs; horseborne swashbucklers playing polo with a headless goat carcass instead of a ball; oasis cities looming on the horizon

SURPRISES
Overwhelming hospitality and spontaneous generosity; historical treasures; skies as perfectly blue as azure tiles; melons and mulberries

A marvellous, crazy country — vast empty deserts, historic old towns and best of all the proud and noble Afghanis. How else can you describe them? They clearly realise that no amount of money or capital possessions could ever compensate you for the unfortunate handicap of not being born in their country.

— Lonely Planet's *Across Asia on the Cheap* (1973)

6. Destroyed buildings loom above a road in Kabul Stephane Victor

MAP REF: J,27

2. Farmers fill baskets with olives bound for the free market in Berat Michel Setboun

3. An artillery bunker in Gjirokastra, one of many similar structures dotted around the country Paul Hellander

1. An apartment building catches the sun Catherine Karnow

This pint-sized, sunny slice of Adriatic coast has been ground down for years by poverty and blood vendettas, but Albania now manages to pack a wild punch of traditional Mediterranean charm and Soviet-style inefficiency. It's a giddy blend of religions, styles, cultures and landscapes, from Sunni Muslim to Albanian Orthodox, and from idyllic beach or rocky mountain to cultivated field. Relics from one of the longest dictatorships in Eastern Europe rub shoulders with citrus orchards, olive groves and vineyards.

BEST TIME TO VISIT
May to September

ESSENTIAL EXPERIENCES
Admiring the beauty and mystique of Albania's mountains

Getting lost in the ancient city of Durrës, founded in 627 BC by the Greeks

Visiting the stunning and well-preserved Roman ruins at Butrint

Beach-hopping from one gorgeous sun-soaked spot to another

Being overwhelmed by the strikingly picturesque museum town of Gjirokastra, perched on the side of a mountain above the Drino River

Wandering around Berat — sometimes called 'the city of a thousand windows' for the many windows in its red-roofed houses

GETTING UNDER THE SKIN
Read *Broken April* by Albania's best-known contemporary writer, Ismail Kadare, which deals with the blood vendettas of the northern highlands before the 1939 Italian invasion. *Biografi* by Lloyd Jones is a fanciful story set in the immediate post-communist era, involving the search for Albanian dictator Enver Hoxha's alleged double

Listen to *Albania, Vocal and Instrumental Polyphony*, an outstanding recording of traditional Albanian music

Watch *Lamerica*, a brilliant and stark look at Albanian post-communist culture

Eat *fërgës* (a rich beef stew), or *rosto me salcë kosi* (roast beef with sour cream)

Drink the excellent red wine *Shesi e Zi* from either Librazhd or Berat, or *raki* (a clear brandy distilled from grapes), taken as an aperitif

IN A WORD
Tungjatjeta (hello)

TRADEMARKS
Polyphony; shish kebabs; a former communist state; baggy pants and colourful scarves

SURPRISES
As much as 20% of the labour force currently works abroad, mainly in Greece and Italy; Albanians shake their heads to say 'yes' and usually nod to say 'no'

The Kanun *is an ancient social law, which outlines most aspects of social behaviour, including the treatment of guests. This has meant that Albanians can be hospitable in the extreme and will often offer travellers lodging and food free of charge. Travellers must be wary of exploiting this tradition and, while payment may well be acceptable in some cases, a small gift of a book or a memento from home will often suffice.*

— Lonely Planet's *Eastern Europe*

4. Albanian Muslims pray to celebrate the Eid al-Adha festival at Tirana's Skanderberg Square Arben Celi

MAP REF: 1,22

2. Sisters cast sibling shadows on a wall in Algiers Frank Carter

3. A man leads a train of pack camels over rocky ground Jean Robert

4. The tall figure of a Tuareg man stands out in the gloom Frank Carter

5. A stone dwelling in Assekrem blends into the surrounding landscape Peter Ptschelinzew

6. A group of desert travellers break their journey for a drink and a chat Jean Robert

LEFT 1 The dignified bearing of a local man dressed for the desert Jean Robert

Despite continued political violence and a history of instability, Algeria is beginning to show signs of a more secure, positive environment. Independent travel can be difficult here, so outside the cities travellers are better off joining an organised tour to see such sights as the dunes of the Sahara and the majestic Atlas ranges. In Algiers there are French-influenced buildings and the majestic Turkish palaces of the medina to explore, while the nearby mountain villages and oasis towns are rich in Berber culture.

BEST TIME TO VISIT
March to April or October to November; Saharan temperatures can be ferocious in the summer months

ESSENTIAL EXPERIENCES
Taking in the views over Algiers from the edge of the medina

Exploring the exceptional Roman ruins at Timgad

Drinking the sweetest water of the Sahara, specific to the oasis town of El-Goléa

Shopping for carpets amid the bustle of the daily market in Ghardaïa

Catching a sunrise in the scenic mountains of Assekrem

Enjoying magic moonlit views over the salt lake at Timimoun

GETTING UNDER THE SKIN
Read *Between Sea and Sahara: An Algerian Journal* by Eugene Fromentin, Blake Robinson and Valeria Crlando, a mix of travel writing and history; or *Nedjma* by the Algerian writer Kateb Yacine, an autobiographical account of childhood, love and Algerian history

Listen to *Algeria: The Diwan of Biskra*, a collection of traditional Algerian rhythms

Watch Brigitte Rouan's *Outremer* (Overseas), a story of revolution and the social change that disrupts the privileged life of three sisters in French-colonial Algeria

Eat chickpea fritters, couscous in both savoury and sweet dishes, and lamb *tajine* spiced with cinnamon

Drink rejuvenating fresh mint tea or robust Turkish coffee

IN A WORD
Marhaba or *salam* (hello)

TRADEMARKS
Sand dunes; the Atlas Mountains; Berber people and traditions; magnificent views; searing heat; colourful carpets; mosques; breathtaking scenery; desert nomads; Tuareg swords; the old quarter in Algiers

SURPRISES
The museum overflowing with mosaics at Djemila; soft drinks made from the inescapable salty water at In Salah

As very few people depend on tourism for their income, the constant Moroccan-style street hassle you might expect to find is very rare in Algeria, and anyone who does accost you will usually be genuinely interested in where you come from and what you're doing. Invitations to tea can be regarded with far less suspicion than elsewhere!

– Lonely Planet's *Africa*

MAP REF: K,20

2. Mountain goats cling to the dizzy heights of Estany de Sisquero Ingrid Roddis

3. Old meets new – a modern steel sculpture and an ancient watchtower outside Parliament House in Andorra la Vella Hugh Watts

All but lost between France and Spain, like the fairytale pea in the mattresses, Andorra comprises just a handful of mountainous landscapes and meandering rivers. Though it is tiny, it contains some of the most dramatic scenery – and the best skiing – in the Pyrenees. There are plenty of good hiking opportunities in the high, remote parts of the country, away from the overdevelopment and heavy traffic that plague Andorra's towns.

BEST TIME TO VISIT
The ski season is from December to March

ESSENTIAL EXPERIENCES
Skiing at Pas de la Casa-Grau Roig or Soldeu-El Tarter, La Massana

Wandering the narrow cobblestone streets between stone houses in the Barri Antic (Historic Quarter), in Andorra la Vella

Relaxing at Caldea – an enormous complex of pools, hot tubs and saunas fed by natural thermal springs, enclosed in what looks like a futuristic cathedral

Hiking in the hamlet of Llorts, set amid fields of tobacco and backed by near-pristine mountains

GETTING UNDER THE SKIN
Read *Andorra* by Peter Cameron, a darkly comic novel set in a fictitious Andorran mountain town. *Approach to the History of Andorra* by Lídia Armengol Vila is a solid work published by the Institut d'Estudis Andorrans.

Listen to classical violinist Gérard Claret

Watch *Dies d'Hivern* (Days of Winter) directed by Andorran Josep Duran, about a band of young delinquents on a voyage of self-discovery

Eat *trinxat* (bacon, potatoes and cabbage) or *escudella* (a stew of chicken, sausage and meatballs)

Drink mulled red wine to which lemon, apple, cinnamon, raisins and cognac are added

IN A WORD
Hola (hello)

TRADEMARKS
Ski resorts; duty-free shopping; the Pyrenees; a pocket-sized princedom; tax haven

SURPRISES
True to logic-defying form, Andorrans are a minority in their own country, forming only about a quarter of the total population of 69,000, the majority of whom are Spaniards. Democratic Andorra is a 'parliamentary co-princedom' – the bishop and president are joint, but largely nominal, heads of state. Until the 1950s, Andorra's population hovered around 6000.

The town of Andorra la Vella is squeezed into the Riu Gran Valira Valley and is mainly engaged in retailing electronic and luxury goods. With the constant din of jackhammers and shopping-mall architecture, you might be in Hong Kong – but for the snowcapped peaks and an absence of noodle shops!

– Lonely Planet's *Western Europe*

1. A snowy landscape in the mountainous province of La Massana Richard Nebeský

4. A streetlamp casts a shadow on a stone wall in the old quarter of Andorra la Vella Hugh Watts

Parish of Ordino

FRANCE

● El Serrat

Llorts ●

Parish of Canillo

● Arinsal

● Soldeu

Parish of La Massana

● Canillo

● Ordino

● La Massana

Parish of Encamp

SPAIN

⊙ Andorra La Vella

Parish of Andorra La Vella

Santa Coloma ●

Parish of Escaldes-Engordany

Parish of Sant Julià de Lòria

● Sant Julià de Lòria

SPAIN

MAP REF: I,20

2. An African initiation costume transmogrifies this participant into the persona of an old man Charles Lenars

3. The explorer Benedict Allen parks his camels at the Cunene River Adrian Arbib

For most outsiders this Sub-Saharan giant means bloody war, bloodier diamonds and bubbling crude – oil, that is. This, with its long, nasty marriage and messy split from Portugal has had more than a few labelling it an African basket case. But this land and its people are not to be underestimated. Angolans are unshockable, resilient and resourceful. They're fighters – but they're lovers too. Portuguese is a great language for singing about love, which is perfect for these music-mad romantics.

BEST TIME TO VISIT
June to August during the dry season, or any time in peace time

ESSENTIAL EXPERIENCES

Weaving your way through Luanda's potholed, palm-fringed streets alongside Rastas, streetkids, flash wheeler-dealer types and fashion-obsessed girls

Going wild in Kissama's grassland park among giraffes, ostriches, and the antelope unique to Angola, the palanca

Dancing in the wake of a fast-moving *kizomba* dancer, or busting a move to accordion-fuelled dance music, *rebita*

Soaking it up on your own stretch of beach in Namibe

Taking in the dizzing heights at Tunda-Vala volcanic fissure, 2600km above sea level

GETTING UNDER THE SKIN

Read *Angola Beloved* by T Ernest Wilson, the story of a pioneering Christian missionary's struggle to bring the gospel to an Angola steeped in witchcraft

Listen to anything by Bonga Kwenda, former world-record holding runner and star soccer player who became an African musical legend

Watch *Rostov-Luanda*, which documents the journey of a returning refugee across Angola in search of an old friend

Eat *calulu de peixe* (fish stew)

Drink local coffee: Angola was one of the largest producers of coffee worldwide prior to the civil war

IN A WORD
Tudo bom? (how's things?)

TRADEMARKS
Mass population displacement, starvation, landmines – all the trophies of war; sparkling beaches; mineral wealth; poverty

SURPRISES
Luanda is the fourth-most expensive city in the world (all that imported food); much of the large national park areas are devoid of animals, because most have been eaten by starving people during recent periods of conflict

In this post-war period, relief is tempered with continuing difficulties and the reality of dislocation. The answer is escapism and spirituality, and the vehicle is love. Angolans love going to church and they love romance. They go nuts for Valentine's Day and soap operas. But their favourite means of removal from reality is shaking their well-shaped and sexily clad booties at all-night parties. No wonder they have the highest fertility rate in the world!

— Lonely Planet's *Africa*

ANGOLA CAPITAL LUANDA POPULATION 10,766,471 AREA 1 246,700 SQ KM OFFICIAL LANGUAGE PORTUGUESE, ENGLISH

1. A tight cluster of thatched-roof housing provides distinctive architectural rhythm Volkmar Wentzel

4. An Angolan woman wears a decorative headscarf James F Housel

MAP REF: P.21

13

2. A house of many colours Timothy O'Keefe

3. Beachside, a wooden fishing boat waits for its next excursion to sea Mark & Audrey Gibson

4. Ouch! A young man belly flops into the Caribbean Sea Layne Kennedy

1. Fishermen enjoying Anguilla's lush aquatic delights Catherine Karnow

Anguilla, the most northerly of the British Leeward Islands, retains the laid-back character of a sleepy backwater. It's small and lightly populated, but the islanders are friendly and easy-going. It also has some of the finest beaches in the Caribbean. The interior of the island is flat, dry and scrubby, pockmarked with salt ponds and devoid of dramatic scenery, but it is fringed by beautiful beaches, aquamarine waters and nearby coral-encrusted islets, which offer great swimming, snorkelling and diving.

BEST TIME TO VISIT
December to February

ESSENTIAL EXPERIENCES
Lazing on Shoal Bay, one of the finest beaches in the Eastern Caribbean

Snorkelling and having a picnic on Prickly Pear Cays

Taking a sunset stroll along Meads Bay – a lovely mile-long sweep of white sand with calm turquoise waters

Diving one of Anguilla's many shipwrecks

Hanging out in Sandy Ground, with its casual beach bars and old saltworks

Riding around the island on a scooter and checking out the numerous salt ponds

GETTING UNDER THE SKIN
Read *Green Cane and Juicy Flotsam: Short Stories by Caribbean Women*, or check out the island's history in Donald E Westlake's *Under an English Heaven*

Listen to Bankie Banx, a celebrated Anguillan singer-songwriter

Watch *Pirates of the Caribbean* – it has nothing to do with Anguilla, but you can pretend. There is no local film industry.

Eat a local crayfish or lobster – don't forget to suck out the tasty brains

Drink Guinness or rum

IN A WORD
Limin' (hanging out with friends and passing the time)

TRADEMARKS
Tranquil; crystal-clear water and white-sand beaches; wild goats running amok; ganja; snorkelling

SURPRISES
During the two-year rebellion against the British there were no fatalities; Anguillans are fanatic boat racers and on Sunday you'll see plenty of boats cutting up the ocean

The island's top archaeological site is the Fountain, a huge underground cave along a rocky pathway a few hundred yards southeast of what used to be the Fountain Beach Hotel. The cave, which draws its name from its former importance as a freshwater spring, contains scores of Amerindian petroglyphs, including a rare stalagmite carving of Jocahu, the Arawak god of creation. The Fountain is thought to have been a major regional worshipping site and a place of pilgrimage for Amerindians.

– Lonely Planet's *Eastern Caribbean*

5. An Anguillan woman regards the camera Dave G. Houser

MAP REF: L.13

3. A friendly Weddell seal surfaces from an opening in the ice
Jonathan Chester

2. Exploring the Antarctic Plateau David Tipling

4. A courtship ritual at the Dawson Lambton Glacier, Weddell Sea David Tipling

5. Passengers witness the *Kapitan Khlebnikov* ice-cutter at work in the Ross Sea Kerry Lorimer

1. A lone figure walks across the icy terrain of Coats Land David Tipling

6. Emperor penguins hunched beneath a wave of ice at Dawson-Lambton Glacier, Weddell Sea David Tipling

Antarctica is spectacular, a wilderness of landscapes reduced to a pure haiku of ice, rock, water and sky, filled with wildlife still unafraid of humans. A land of extremes, it is described by a bevy of superlatives – the driest, coldest, most inhospitable and isolated continent on Earth. Vast and ownerless, Antarctica is unique, and a journey here is like no other.

BEST TIME TO VISIT
November to February for 'summer' – or in time for a solar eclipse

ESSENTIAL EXPERIENCES
Bathing in Deception Island's thermally heated Pendulum Cove

Taking a cruise on an inflatable rubber dinghy among the icebergs

Scuba diving in McMurdo Sound

Visiting the historic explorers' huts in the Ross Sea region for a taste of the Heroic Era

Having postcards stamped at the Dome, South Pole

GETTING UNDER THE SKIN
Read Ernest Shackleton's *Aurora Australis*, the only book ever published in Antarctica, and a personal account of Shackleton's 1907–09 *Nimrod* expedition; Nikki Gemmell's *Shiver*, the story of a young journalist who finds love and tragedy on an Antarctic journey

Listen to Doug Quin's *Antarctica* – a collection of nature recordings, including seals, penguins and creaking glaciers. Icestock is an annual rock festival held by staff at McMurdo station, and recordings are often available online.

Watch Koreyoshi Kurahara's *Antarctica*, the story of sled dogs on a 1958 Japanese expedition. David Attenborough's *Life in the Freezer* is a BBC documentary series with excellent wildlife footage

Eat an Antarctic barbecue, set up on deck or even on the ice; early explorers had to make do with penguin and seal

Drink an Antarctic Old Fashion, a blend of bourbon, LifeSavers sweets and snow; travellers may prefer to stick to adding a little glacier ice to their whisky

IN A WORD
The 'A-factor' (the local term for the unexpected difficulties caused by the Antarctic environment)

TRADEMARKS
Icebergs; penguins; freezing cold; geologists; explorers; the South Pole; glaciers; seals; 24-hour sunlight

SURPRISES
No polar bears (that's the Arctic); penguins smell terrible; dehydration and sunburn are real risks

One day, it was announced that the temperature was steadying at around -101°F (-73.9°C). We crowded into the sauna – cranked up to 200°F (93°C). About 15 minutes later we burst through the door. I wore nothing but socks, tennis shoes and a neck gaiter over my nose and mouth so my lungs wouldn't get frostbitten while I ran...I'm glad I did it, though I did get a touch of frostbite on my thumbs (of all places) – nothing serious. Better my thumbs than somewhere more important!

– Ricardo Ramos on his entry to the '300 Club', Lonely Planet's *Antarctica*

● *Bouvetoya*

Zavodovski Island

South Georgia

SOUTHERN OCEAN

South Orkney Islands

Deception Island
Paradise Harbor
Lemaire Channel
Antarctic Peninsula *Weddell Sea*

Vinson Massif 4897m

Geographic South Pole

● Amundsen-Scott Station

SOUTHERN OCEAN

Ross Ice Shelf

McMurdo Station

The Dry Valleys

Wilkes Land

● South Magnetic Pole
64°42'S - 138°36'E

MAP REF: Y,30

2. Taxi drivers wait for their next passenger, killing time with a few rounds of Island Wari Bob Krist

3. Sarongs and caps for sale sway gently on line Walter Bibikow

1. School children links hands on a field trip, St John's Bob Krist

4. A local girl in a yellow hat sports the ultimate accessory: a matching house James Davis

Antigua's tourist office boasts that the island has 365 beaches, 'one for each day of the year'. It has great reefs and wrecks for diving and snorkelling. On neighbouring Barbuda you can track the island's fabled frigate birds and visit the Caribbean's largest rookery. Barbuda is a quiet, single-village island that gets very few independent visitors, mainly ardent bird-watchers and a few yachties enjoying its clear waters and tranquil beaches. Antigua is a touch more happening, but the pace is still deliciously slow.

BEST TIME TO VISIT
December to mid-April

ESSENTIAL EXPERIENCES
Exploring colonial-era sights, including a working sugar mill at Betty's Hope and the 18th-century Nelson's Dockyard

Kicking back on the island's white-sand beaches

Diving coral canyons, wall drops and sea caves with marine life such as turtles, sharks and barracuda

Touring the Caribbean's largest rookery, in Barbuda

Taking the scenic route along Fig Tree Drive

Snorkelling the coral-encrusted wreck of the *Andes*, lying in the middle of Deep Bay, its mast poking up above the water

Poking around the overgrown churchyard of Antigua's first church, St Paul's Anglican Church — one of the island's oldest buildings, dating to 1676

GETTING UNDER THE SKIN
Read Jamaica Kincaid's novel *Annie John*, which recounts growing up in Antigua. Desmond Nicholson, president of the Antigua historical society, has published several works on the country's history, including *Antigua, Barbuda and Redonda: A Historical Sketch*

Listen to steel band, calypso and reggae music

Watch *No Seed* by Antiguan husband-and-wife team, director Howard Allen and producer Mitzi Allen

Eat *duckanoo* (a dessert made with cornmeal, coconut, spices and brown sugar) or black pineapple, purported to be the sweetest of them all

Drink the island's locally brewed rum Cavalier or English Habour, or try the local lager, Wadadli

IN A WORD
Fire a grog (drink rum)

TRADEMARKS
Cricket players; rum; endless pristine white-sand beaches; dancing; calypso music; black pineapples

SURPRISES
Barbuda has less than 2% of the nation's population, the black pineapple is not black, most of Barbuda's 1100 people share half a dozen surnames and can trace their lineage to a small group of slaves brought to the island in the late 1600s

One of the best things that the British did for the West Indies was introduce the local population to cricket. It soon became the national passion of Antigua and is played everywhere — on beaches, in backyards or anywhere there's some flat, open ground.

— Lonely Planet's *Eastern Caribbean*

MAP REF: L,13

2. A cardon cactus in the arid landscape of San Juan John Hay

3. Setting sun casts long shadows over Diagonal Roque Sáenz Peña, Buenos Aires Tom Smallman

4. Street musicians inspire spontaneous dancing in Buenos Aires Donald & Priscilla Alexander Eastman

5. Thundering falls form a curtain of mist above the grasslands Jason Edwards

6. Works of art for sale beneath the brightly painted houses of La Boca, Buenos Aires John Hay
LEFT 1. The dazzling Perito Moreno Glacier in Los Glaciares National Park Wes Walker

From its tropical north to its glacial south, Argentina boasts more diversity and beauty than its fair share, and it takes time to grasp the multitude of environments and experiences on offer. Despite the country's tumultuous political heritage, the people of Argentina remain friendly, open and willing to share a laugh with a new amigo. Do as the Argentines do – accept the concept of time as fluid, and draw in all that life brings to greet you.

BEST TIME TO VISIT
March to May (spring) – or before 1516 when Spanish navigator Juan Díaz de Solís first probed the region

ESSENTIAL EXPERIENCES
Being enchanted by street tango at the Sunday antique market in San Telmo

Listening to the deafening roar of the spectacular Iguazú Falls

Indulging your chocolate cravings in Bariloche

Taking in the dizzy heights of Cristo Redentor in the Central Andes

Getting friendly with a Magellanic penguin at the Península Valdés wildlife sanctuary

Staying at a *gaucho* ranch in Las Pampas

GETTING UNDER THE SKIN
Read Patricia Sagastizabal's *A Secret for Julia*, which won Argentina's equivalent to the Pulitzer Prize in 2000. For a humorous account of Buenos Aires life, pick up Miranda France's *Bad Times in Buenos Aires*

Listen to the legendary tangos of Carlos Gardel and the contemporary folk music of Mercedes Sosa of Tucumán

Watch the magic realism of Luis César D'Angiolillo's *Killing Grandpa*

Eat *empanadas* (turnovers stuffed with savoury fillings), *alfajores* (a popular sweet) and *facturas* (sweet pastries)

Drink *maté* (pronounced mah-tay), *licuados* (milk-blended fruit drinks) and *chopp* (lager)

IN A WORD
¿Qué tal? (how are things?)

TRADEMARKS
Tango; *maté-drinking* rituals; Spanish colonial architecture; the Péróns; glaciers; the Andes; *gauchos*; charmingly inflated egos; hearty steaks; wine; *cumbia* music

SURPRISES
Delicious *helado* (ice cream); locals enjoying *maté* on the bus (and just about everywhere!); *gauchos* still in traditional dress

Because of their country's ability to produce enormous quantities of beef, Argentines tend to eat a lot of the stuff. The average intake is around 60kg per person per year, or almost 133lbs, though in the past they ate even more. Most of the consuming takes place at the family asado, *often held on Sundays in the backyards of houses all over the country. (If you are lucky enough to be invited to one, make sure you attend.)*

— Lonely Planet's *Argentina, Uruguay & Paraguay*

MAP REF: S,12

ARGENTINA CAPITAL BUENOS AIRES POPULATION 38,740,807 AREA 2,766,890 SQ KM OFFICIAL LANGUAGE SPANISH

21

2. Shoppers at the entrance to the indoor Hayastan Market in Yerevan Bill Wassman

3. The mysterious Sanahin Monastery rising above the surrounding woodlands Bill Wassman

4. Inside the home of a Kurdish family in Ararat Bill Wassman

Fate placed Armenia at the point where the European and Middle Eastern continental plates collide, with a resulting mix in fortunes. Geography has brought the natural beauty of the Caucasus – majestic mountain ranges, snowy peaks, alpine lakes and forests. History, however, has seen Armenia suffer at the hands of conquering armies passing through – Roman, Persian, Arab, Ottoman Turk and Russian. These factors define the Armenians, a nation of artists, merchants, poets and stonemasons, who are fiercely proud of their language, culture and homeland.

BEST TIME TO VISIT
March to June – or the 10th century, the golden age of Armenian literature and art

ESSENTIAL EXPERIENCES
Photographing the domes and cupolas of the national treasury in Echmiadzin
Enjoying cosmopolitan Yerevan's choice of opera, concerts, museums and dining
Visiting the reconstructed temple to Helios, Roman god of the sun, Garni
Imagining life on the ancient Silk Road at Selim Caravanserai
Travelling to dramatic Tatev Monastery, rising high above the Vorotan Canyon

GETTING UNDER THE SKIN
Read Phillip Marsden's *The Crossing Place* – a thought-provoking journey through the Armenian diaspora

Listen to *Black Rock* by Djivan Gasparian, master of the *duduk* (traditional reed flute), the quintessential Armenian sound

Watch Sergei Paradjanov's *The Colour of Pomegranates*, a visually striking Armenian epic, dizzy with colour and symbolism

Eat *khoravatz* (lamb or pork, skewered and barbecued) and *lavash*, the wafer-thin bread that accompanies every meal

Drink strong and gritty coffee; vodka; Armenian cognac – a national speciality

IN A WORD
Genats! (cheers!)

TRADEMARKS
Solitary churches on rocky peaks; intricate stonemasonry; medieval manuscripts; bracing breezes from snow-capped mountains; rich vestments on bearded priests; vital people said to have their minds in the West but their hearts in the East

SURPRISES
Toasts (lots of them) before, during and after every meal; a culture imbued with literature and poetry; the delights of summer fruits

Armenians remember the denials and unanswered prayers of their long history (a local form of 'good to see you' is 'tsavoot danem' – 'let me take your pain'), but they always put on a good face for visitors. If you're ever someone's guest at home, watch how quickly a table of fresh produce, snacks, cognac, fruit vodkas and wine appears. Carrying on, rebuilding stone by stone, is how the centuries pass in Armenia.

— Lonely Planet's *Georgia, Armenia & Azerbaijan*

1. Friends enjoy an outdoor meal and plenty of wine Bill Wassman

5. An elderly woman from Yerevan enjoys a quiet moment Bill Wassman

MAP REF: I,24

2. A man splitting bananas on the floating market in Willemstad Jerry Alexander

3. The architecture of Curaçao's towns reflects Dutch, Spanish and Portuguese colonial styles Jerry Alexander

It's possible that the Dutch Antilles is the most concentrated area of multiculturalism in the world. Papiamento, spoken throughout the Netherlands Antilles, is testament to this fact – the language is derived from every culture that has impacted on the region, including traces of Spanish, Portuguese, Dutch, French and local Indian languages. The islands are diverse – there are the cutesy houses of Curaçao, ruggedly steep Saba, Sint Maarten with its large resorts and casinos, and the delightfully slow pace of Sint Eustatius.

BEST TIME TO VISIT
Year-round

ESSENTIAL EXPERIENCES
Hiking to the top of Mt Scenery on Saba, for a close-up view of an elfin forest with its lush growth of ferns, tropical flowers and mahogany trees, and a panoramic view of Saba and neighbouring islands

Diving in Bonaire with hawksbill turtles, peacock flounders, stingrays and seahorses

Exploring the strange volcanic Hooiberg ('haystack') on Aruba – the parched scrub and cacti landscape are classic Spaghetti Western country

Kicking back in Sint Eustatius, a tranquil little Dutch outpost where islanders strike up conversations and stray chickens and goats mosey in the streets

Cycling around Simpson Bay Lagoon on Sint Maarten

Wandering around Willemstad on Curaçao – the maze of streets and lanes wiggling back from the waterfront are lined with houses running the gamut from pastel and spruce to crumbling and spooky

GETTING UNDER THE SKIN
Read *Nights in Aruba* by Andrew Holleran, which tells the story of a gay man who spends his early years on Aruba before heading to the USA

Listen to lyric-heavy calypso, beat-based soca, or reggae

Eat cornmeal johnny cakes and *yambo* (green soup of okra, salt pork, onions, celery and sometimes fish)

Drink Saba Spice (a rum-based liqueur spiced with a 'secret concoction') or Amstel beer on Aruban beaches

IN A WORD
Bon bini ('welcome' in Papiamento)

TRADEMARKS
Palm-fringed white-sand beaches; tourism; diving; Dutch colonialism

SURPRISES
Only about 20% of all residents were born on Sint Maarten; the town of Willemstad on Curaçao is one of a select number of urban areas on Unesco's World Heritage List

...demand for tender iguana flesh is high, not only for its taste (which is a bit like chicken) but also due to the widespread belief that iguana flesh has a positive affect on your sex life, both in terms of desire and performance. In fact, there was a time on Curaçao when doctors prescribed iguana as a cure for any number of strength-sapping maladies.

– Lonely Planet's *World Food Caribbean*

1. The Alto Vista chapel, one of the first missionary buildings to be established in the Caribbean Angelo Cavalli

4. A portrait of a young Caribbean girl Wayne Walton

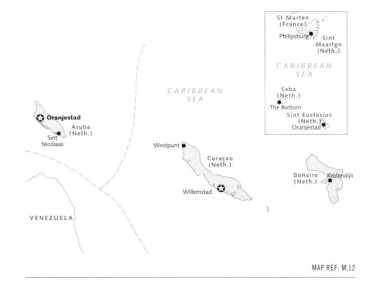

MAP REF: M,12

2. Two Queensland boys enjoy a cool-down swim Oliver Strewe

3. The station boss at Bow River Station in the eastern Kimberly region relaxes with a rollie Richard I'Anson

4. An architectural feature of Federation Square, Melbourne Juliet Coombe

5. The Hills Hoist clothesline, an iconic Australian invention, in Cape York Peninsula Oliver Strewe

6. A herd of cautious kangaroos, on the alert for whizzing golf balls at the ninth hole of the Anglesea Golf Club, Victoria Bernard Napthine

LEFT 1. Uluru at sunrise, Northern Territory Richard I'Anson

From endless sunbaked horizons to dense tropical rainforest and wild southern beaches, Australia's biggest attraction is its natural beauty. Scattered along the coasts, its cities blend a European enthusiasm for art and food with a passionate love of sport and the outdoors. Visitors expecting to see an opera in Sydney one night and meet Crocodile Dundee the next day will have to re-think their grasp of geography in this huge country. It is its sheer vastness that gives Australia – and its diverse population – much of its character.

BEST TIME TO VISIT
Any time is a fine time – and definitely before 1788 when Europeans arrived

ESSENTIAL EXPERIENCES
Watching the dramatic changing colours of sunrise or sunset over Uluru (Ayers Rock)

Exploring the underwater world of the Great Barrier Reef, the world's largest coral reef

Sampling the exquisite wines of the Barossa Valley

Discovering the natural beauty of tropical Fraser Island by 4WD

Viewing Sydney Harbour after climbing to the top of the "coathanger", Sydney Harbour Bridge

Meeting the native wildlife on Kangaroo Island

GETTING UNDER THE SKIN
Read *Remembering Babylon* by David Malouf, a compelling insight into the social dynamics of early-colonial Australia; Bruce Chatwin's controversial *Songlines* for a look at the Aboriginal lay of the land

Listen to Slim Dusty's 'Pub with No Beer', a classic Australian country tune; Paul Kelly's *Songs from the South* greatest hits compilation

Watch *The Castle*, about an 'Aussie battler' who takes on the big guys and wins

Eat kangaroo or emu – if you can bring yourself to eat the animals represented on Australia's coat of arms! Try the fresh seafood – local specialities are always your best choice

Drink ice-cold beer; Australia's superb wines, in particular shiraz and chardonnay

IN A WORD
G'day mate!

TRADEMARKS
Bronzed Aussies; dangerous creatures; endless beaches; friendly locals; Outback pubs; sizzling barbecues; Aussie Rules football

SURPRISES
Kangaroos don't hop down city streets; it isn't always hot and sunny; it has the oldest continuing culture in the world

Few people who visit the Northern Territory (NT) leave untouched by the experience – it's that sort of place. While it's the most barren and least-populated area of Australia, this is where many people find the country's soul. It is in the Centre – the Red Heart – that the picture-book, untamed and sometimes surreal Australia exists.

– Lonely Planet's *Australia*

MAP REF: R.34

2. View of St Michael's dome from Kohlmarkt, Vienna Jon Davison

3. The mighty Grossglockner flanks the Pasterze Glacier in Salzburg province Gareth McCormack

1. Julie Andrews appears at any moment, Tirol Chris Mellor

Austria is an environmentally responsible land of mountains and impressive architecture with an unrivalled musical tradition that even *The Sound of Music* couldn't sully. Vienna is the capital, hub of the country's musical life and littered with beautiful buildings. Music, art and architecture reach baroque perfection in Salzburg, Mozart's birthplace. Innsbruck's snow-capped peaks frame its fascinating historic buildings. The rhythm of daily life throughout Austria has a musical beat and music festivals fill its calendar.

BEST TIME TO VISIT
Year-round

ESSENTIAL EXPERIENCES
Enjoying the wine in a Heurigen or an evening of high culture in the Staatsoper
Wandering your way through Vienna's *Christkindlmarkt* (Christmas markets)
Strolling through Salzburg — one perfect view after another
Sipping coffee in a *Kaffeehaus*
Gawking at the oddities of the Josephinum, Vienna's medical history museum
Marvelling at the unfolding scenic magnificence of the Grossglockner Road
Hobnobbing with jetsetter skiers in upmarket Lech
Gorging at the Giant Chocolate Festival of Bludenz

GETTING UNDER THE SKIN
Read *The Left-Handed Woman* by Peter Handke; the *Nibelungenlied*, an epic poem of passion, faithfulness and revenge in the Burgundian court at Worms; or Wittgenstein's *Tractatus*, a seminal book in the field of linguistic philosophy

Listen to Beethoven, Mozart, Haydn, Schubert, the Vienna Boys' Choir and Falco

Watch *The Third Man*, set in postwar Vienna

Eat *Wiener Schnitzel* with *Knödel* (dumplings) followed by *Mohr im Hemd* for dessert (chocolate pudding with whipped cream and chocolate sauce)

Drink *Sturm* (new wine) in autumn, and *Glühwein* (hot, spiced mulled wine) at Christmas

IN A WORD
It is customary to greet people, even shop assistants, with the salute *Grüss Gott* and to say *Auf Wiedersehen* when departing

TRADEMARKS
Strauss waltzes; strudel; *Inspector Rex* (or *Commisar Rex* as it's known in Austria); edelweiss; Sigmund Freud; dirndls (traditional peasant dresses)

SURPRISES
The *Föhn*, a hot, dry wind that sweeps down the mountains in early spring and autumn, which causes — according to folk wisdom — restless animals, increased car crashes and suicides

Klimt became the most celebrated artist in Vienna at the turn of the century. His works were renowned then, as now, for their sexuality and decadence. However, his femmes fatales exuded an eroticism and power too explicit for their time. Klimt was accused of ugliness, pornography and perverted excess. His response was typical: a work entitled Goldfish *or* To My Critics, *portraying a voluptuous flame-haired maiden baring her bottom to the world.*

— Lonely Planet's *Austria*

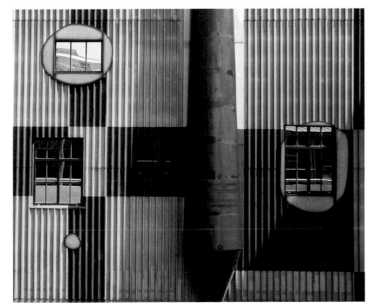

4. Detail of the abstract façade of the Spittelau incinerator, decorated by Friedensreich Hundertwasser, Vienna Diana Mayfield

MAP REF: H,21

2. It's a tight fit as a family stops at a gas station near Baku
Ami Vitale

3. Geese have all the fun – villagers take their birds for a ride
Ami Vitale

4. Refugees from the war with Armenia play dominoes outside the abandoned train car that serves as their home   Ami Vitale

1. A sheep herder leads his flock through an oil field outside Baku Ami Vitale

Azerbaijan is exotic by the standards of its more European neighbours. The click of *nard* (backgammon) through the hot summer nights; the endless sweet tea, jam and cigarettes; the entire herds of cattle wandering aimlessly across motorways – it's clear that while Georgia and Armenia look to Europe, Azerbaijan is very much part of Asia. This ancient land of Zoroastrianism displays a history and scenery that are equally dramatic – from Albanian churches and Baku's old walled city to the extraordinary beauty of the High Caucasus Mountains and the lush plantations of tea covering the gentle hills of the south.

BEST TIME TO VISIT
May to June and September to October, to avoid the extremes of summer and winter

ESSENTIAL EXPERIENCES
Visiting Xınalıq, a remote village high in the Caucasus Mountains with a unique language and culture that has changed little since the Middle Ages

Exploring Baku, Azerbaijan's cosmopolitan capital, packed full of crumbling oil-boom mansions and Soviet and Islamic architecture, and with an impressive walled city

Hiking near the ancient Persian mountain hamlet of Lahıc and exploring its pretty village

Strolling around the hunter gatherers' caves of Qubustan, home to a unique reserve of Stone- and Bronze-Age petroglyphs

GETTING UNDER THE SKIN
Read Mehmed bin Suleyman Fuzuli's sensitive rendition of the classic *Lcyli* and *Majnun*, which influenced many Azeri writers right up to the 19th century

Listen to *mugam* jazz pianist and composer Aziza Mustafazade

Watch *The Bat*, directed by Ayaz Salayev, and Samil Aliyev's *The Accidental Meeting*

Eat *shashlyk* (lamb kebab) or *dograma* (a cold soup made with sour milk, potato, onion and cucumber)

Drink a traditional restorative cup of tea at a *çayxana* (teahouse)

IN A WORD
Salam (hello)

TRADEMARKS
Oil; carpets; wine; Zoroastrianism; tea plantations; saffron; caviar; kebabs

SURPRISES
Noruz Bayramı (New Year Festival) marks the return of spring and the start of the New Year, according to the Persian solar calendar; traditions associated with Noruz Bayramı include spring-cleaning the house, preparing special rice dishes and jumping over bonfires to cleanse the spirit

Knowing how to play nard *(backgammon) will hugely enhance your social interaction with Azeris. No matter whether or not you speak any Azeri or Russian, a challenge to a* nard *match at a çayxana anywhere between Astara and Nabran will win you instant friends.*

– Lonely Planet's *Georgia, Armenia & Azerbaijan*

5. Oil workers take a break from pumping black gold in miserable weather conditions Ami Vitale

MAP REF: I,25

2. Sailing the spectacular seas off Eleuthera Michael Lawrence

3. A pink flamingo preens itself with contortionate expertise
Michael Lawrence

4. A young woman from Nassau Juliet Coombe

5. A local girl sits in a colourful window sill at the straw
market on Harbour Island Greg Johnston

1. A local woman sells straw hats and bags from her house on Cat Island Greg Johnston

6. An old church overlooks the fields of Cat Island Greg Johnston

The Bahamas has successfully promoted itself as a destination for US jet-setters, and a lot of it is Americanised. Yet there are still places among its 700 islands and 2500 cays to disappear into a mangrove forest, explore a coral reef and escape the high-rise hotels and package-tour hype. The 18th-century Privateers' Republic has become the 21st-century banker's paradise, at least on New Providence and Grand Bahama. On the other islands – once known as the Out Islands but now euphemistically called the Family Islands – the atmosphere is more truly West Indian.

BEST TIME TO VISIT
June to August when it's hottest and wettest

ESSENTIAL EXPERIENCES
Listening to a rake 'n' scrape band in a bar on a backwater cay

Hiking in Abaco National Park

Watching flocks of flamingos in Inagua National Park

Journeying by mail boat

Swimming with sharks while they feed at Stella Maris and Walker's Cay

Staying at Pink Sands on Harbour Island and enjoying the charming historic village of Dunmore Town, with a pink-sand beach and great nightspots

GETTING UNDER THE SKIN
Read Brian Antoni's *Paradise Overdose*, about the 1980s drug- and sex-addled Bahamian highlife

Listen to Tony Mackay's 'Natty Bon Dey' on his *Canaan Lane* album. The Obeah Man, alias Tony Mackay, is a flamboyant performer and musical superhero from Cat Island (he now lives in Miami) His music is pure *goombay*

Watch James Bond in action in *For Your Eyes Only*, *The Spy Who Loved Me* and *Never Say Never Again* for the Bahamas backdrop

Eat conch (a mollusc served pounded, minced and frittered; marinated and grilled; or even raw as a ceviche) or, for something sweet, try duff (a fruit-filled jelly pudding served with sauce made of sugar, egg, butter and rum)

Drink Kalik (a light, sweet, lager-style beer perfect for hot days) or Bacardi rum

IN A WORD
Hey man, what happ'nin'?

TRADEMARKS
Casinos; luxury yachts; golf courses; rum; drug trading; sun, sand and 'sin'

SURPRISES
Many Bahamians believe that if you take the 'bibby' (mucus) from a dog's or horse's eye and put it in your own, you can actually see a spirit; conch is considered an aphrodisiac capable of 'givin' men a strong back'

Isolation and the small scale of things have fostered another integral component of Bahamian culture: gossip, called 'sip-sip', incorporating everything from political events to who's sleeping with whom. Everybody knows everyone else's business. And they're sure to share it. The more salacious, the better.

– Lonely Planet's *Bahamas, Turks & Caicos*

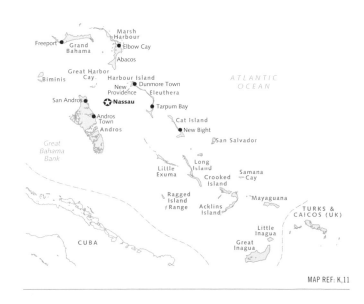

MAP REF: K,11

2. A potter in his workshop in the small village of A'ali Clint Lucas

3. The ornately engraved wooden doors of Manama's old High Court building Phil Weymouth

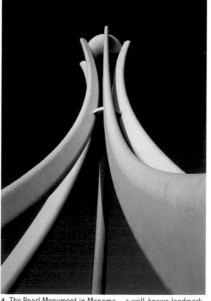

4. The Pearl Monument in Manama – a well-known landmark of Bahrain Tony Wheeler

5. A smiling resident of Manama Clint Lucas

1. A large mosque near Beit Sheikh Isa bin Ali Phil Weymouth

6. An incongruous billboard on the wall of the Beit al-Quran (the House of the Koran) in Manama Phil Weymouth

The only island-state in the Arab world, Bahrain comprises 33 islands and was once the seat of one of the ancient world's great trading empires. It's a fascinating and diverse place, offering travellers an easy and hassle-free introduction to the Persian Gulf. There are alleys to explore, coffeehouses in which to sit and watch the world go by, magnificent desert landscapes, basket weaving with palm leaves and every kind of *souk* (market) your shopping heart could wish for.

BEST TIME TO VISIT
November to February (for warm days and cool nights)

ESSENTIAL EXPERIENCES
Absorbing 7000 years of Bahrain's history at its excellent National Museum in Manama

Entering the Al-Fatih Mosque in Manama, a rare opportunity for non-Muslims

Spotting an Arabian oryx at the Al-'Areen Wildlife Sanctuary

Visiting the seven layers of excavated material at the Qala'at al-Bahrain archaeological site

Watching the local weavers at work in the village of Bani Jamrah

Sipping Arabic coffee in the funky *souk* and viewing the traditional houses on Muharraq Island

Wandering through the impressive Royal Tombs at A'ali

GETTING UNDER THE SKIN
Read Geoffrey Bibby's *Looking for Dilmun*, an archaeologist's account of early excavations on Bahrain. It also paints a fascinating picture of life there in the 1950s and 1960s.

Listen to *Desert Beat*, an album of ambient rhythms and Arabic songs by the young Bahraini musician and composer Hashim al-Alawi

Watch *Al Za'ir* (Visitor), Bahrain's first ever thriller, directed by Bassam Al Thawadi

Eat *machbous* (rice served with meat or fish), *shawarma* (spit-roasted lamb or chicken wrapped in pita bread) or *sambousak* (cheese or meat filled filo pastry)

Drink coffee, coffee and more coffee – cardamom-infused Arabic-style

IN A WORD
Salām 'alaykum (common greeting; literally, 'peace be upon you')

TRADEMARKS
Amazing archaeological excavations; palm trees; dates; carpet weaving; embroidered ceremonial gowns; ancient temples and forts; colourful *souks*; burial mounds; drinking tiny cups of tea at the teahouses; *dhows* (fishing boats); baklava

SURPRISES
Scuba diving in the shallow, warm waters, which offer over 200 species of fish; snorkelling among Bahrain's coral reefs

In Arabic, bahrain means 'two seas'. Since the dawn of history Bahrain has been a trading centre, and until about a generation ago, virtually all trade came and went by sea. Occupying a strategic position on the great trade routes of antiquity, with good harbours and abundant fresh water, the Bahrainis are natural traders.

— Lonely Planet's *Bahrain, Kuwait and Qatar*

THE GULF

Muharraq
Karbabad   Al-Hidd
Al-Budayyi   Jidd Hafis   ✪ **Manama**
   Mina Sulman
Al-Janabiya
Al-Jasra   Isa Town
Umm al-Na'san   Hamad
Gulf of Bahrain   Awali
Al-Zallaq   'Askar
   Ad-Dur
Al-Mamtalah   Ar-Rumaythah
THE GULF

MAP REF: K,25

35

2. A farmer harvests jute in Tangail Richard l'Anson

3. Sacrificial Eid ul-Adha cows in Dhaka Felicity Volk

4. A passenger peeks through the back window of a gaudy rickshaw in Dhaka Richard l'Anson

5. Rickshaws and baby taxis fight for space on the streets of Dhaka Richard l'Anson

Bangladesh may have had its share of floods, famines and cyclones but this visually stunning destination has much to offer. The world's most crowded country has friendly people, luxuriously fertile land, rich history, a broad mix of cultures and a tropical atmosphere that's unique to Bangladesh. Away from the noise and bustle of the capital, Dhaka, there are magnificently lush rural hill regions just waiting to be explored, plus archaeological sites, the longest beach on the planet and cruises along the country's countless rivers.

BEST TIME TO VISIT
October to February (winter) – or the 16th century, when this region was the wealthiest part of the subcontinent

ESSENTIAL EXPERIENCES
Wandering through the dilapidated 19th-century mansions of the maharajas

Watching the panorama of river-life in Dhaka's old city

Taking a ride in one of Dhaka's 600,000-plus rickshaws

Visiting Sompapuri Vihara – a Buddhist monastery covering 11 hectares

Spotting a Royal Bengal tiger in Sundarbans National Park

Enjoying a refreshing dip in Kaptai Lake in the Chittagong Hill Tract

GETTING UNDER THE SKIN
Read *Gitanjali* by Rabindranath Tagore, the great Bengali poet and winner of the 1913 Nobel Prize for Literature; James J. Novak's *Bangladesh: Reflections on the Water*, a good all-round introduction to the country

Listen to *Garo of the Madhupur Forest*, a collection of traditional Bengali music

Watch the *Apu-Trilogy* by Satyajit Ray, one of the fathers of Bengali cinema

Eat *dal* (yellow lentils) and rice; fish or meat with vegetables cooked in a spicy, mustard-oil spiked sauce; crispy *bhaja*, fried morsels of vegetables dipped in spicy chick-pea batter

Drink yoghurt *sharbat*, a chilled spicy yoghurt drink flavoured with chilli, mint, coriander and cumin

IN A WORD
No-mosh-kar (hello)

TRADEMARKS
Green rice fields; rivers; manicured tea plantations; palm trees; rickshaws; stupas; mosques; Hindu temples; tribal villages; forests full of monkeys and spectacular bird life; terracotta sculpture; Royal Bengal tigers; Asiatic elephants

SURPRISES
The Bangladeshi habit of staring at the unusual means that foreigners can draw a fixed gaze just by walking out on the street

Despite being the world's most crowded country, rural Bangladesh feels relaxed, spacious and friendly: travellers from India have been agreeably surprised to find border officials offering them cups of tea rather than reams of forms to fill in.

– Lonely Planet's *Bangladesh*

1. A group of women stand with their cattle in Pabna   Jerry Galea

6. A neglected *rajbari* in Painam Nagar village, Sonargaon   Tony Wheeler

MAP REF: K.29

2. Children keep an eye on things from the balcony Annie Fox

3. You definitely need a hat to play at this table Michael Lawrence

1. A bright beer mural on a wall in Bridgetown Richard Cummins

4. Now where did I moor my boat? Herb Schmitz

Barbados is the 'Little England' of the Caribbean, but not to the point where the locals have given up rotis for kidney pies, or rum for bitter ale. Bajans, as the islanders call themselves, are as West Indian as any of their neighbours, and have tended to appropriate rather than adopt English customs. You'll notice this the first time you check out a local cricket match, since the gentlemanly English game has a totally different rhythm here. Nonetheless, there are old stone Anglican churches in every parish, horse races on Saturdays and portraits of Queen Liz hanging on plenty of walls.

BEST TIME TO VISIT
February to May

ESSENTIAL EXPERIENCES
Taking a tram ride through Harrison's Cave, an astonishing network of limestone caverns and subterranean waterfalls

Revelling in lush tropical plants in the natural wilderness of Welchman Hall Gully or the cultivated botanical gardens of the Flower Forest

Exploring the Barbados Museum and the adjacent history-laden Garrison area

Wandering around grand 17th-century plantation homes and estate gardens

Bodysurfing at Crane Beach, a scenic stretch of pink-tinged sand

Encountering local fauna at the Barbados Wildlife Reserve, which features green monkeys, red-footed turtles, caimans, brocket deer, iguanas and agoutis

GETTING UNDER THE SKIN
Read the acclaimed novel *In the Castle of My Skin* by Bajan author George Lamming, in which he tells what is was like growing up black in colonial Barbados

Listen to calypso artist the Mighty Gabby, whose songs on cultural identity and political protest speak for emerging black pride throughout the Caribbean

Watch *The Tamarind Seed* starring Omar Sharif and Julie Andrews, a romance cum spy thriller set partly in Barbados

Eat *cou-cou* (a creamy cornmeal and okra mash, often served with saltfish) or *souse* (a dish made out of pickled pig's head and belly, spices and a few vegetables, commonly served with a pig-blood sausage called 'pudding')

Drink Mount Gay rum or Banks, which is a good locally brewed beer

IN A WORD
Workin' up (dancing)

TRADEMARKS
Cricket fanatics; elderly women in prim hats; calypso music; rum; nightlife

SURPRISES
Barbados boasts more international cricket players on a per capita basis than any other nation; women are the head of the household in many families, and a majority of children are born outside of wedlock

In 1751, at age 19 – some 38 years before he would become the first US president – George Washington visited Barbados as a companion to his half brother Lawrence, who suffered from tuberculosis. It was hoped that the tropical climate would prove therapeutic…The six-week Barbados trip was the only overseas journey George Washington ever made.

– Lonely Planet's *Eastern Caribbean*

ATLANTIC OCEAN

Speightstown

Bathsheba

Holetown

Boarded Hall

Bridgetown

Oistins

CARIBBEAN SEA

Silver Sands

MAP REF: M,13

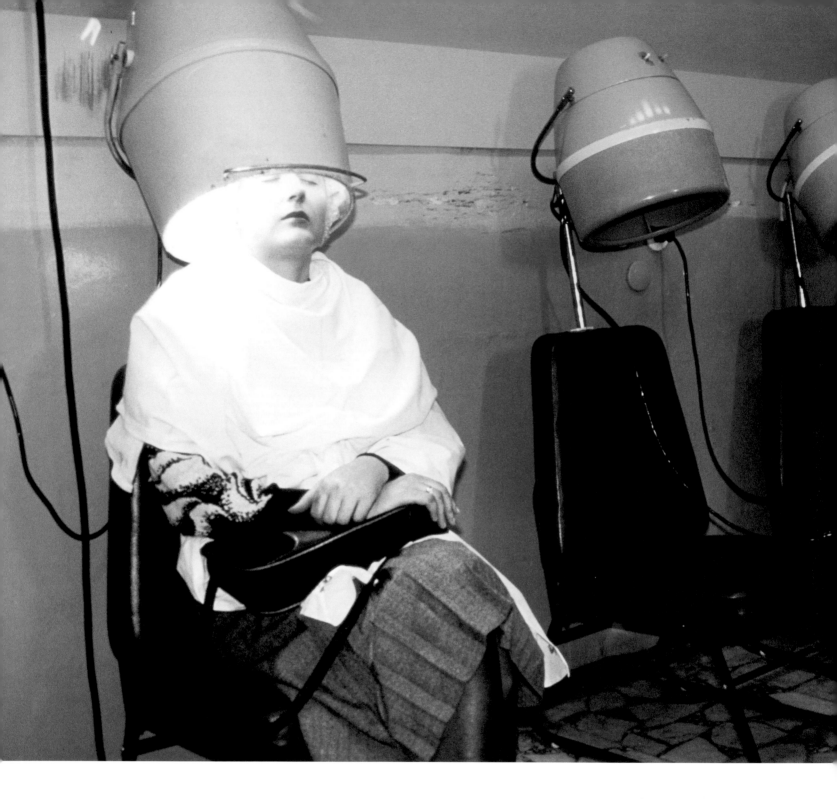

2. The Victory Obelisk in Victory Square, Minsk Steve Kokker

3. A devotee lights candles beneath an icon in a Russian orthodox church Jeff Greenberg

4. The dramatic star-shaped entrance to the Brest Fortress WWII Memorial Jonathan Smith

5. A farm worker tosses hay with a pitchfork Jeff Greenberg

1. Pausing for pleasure in a Minsk beauty salon Jeff Greenberg

Geography has played a major role in the history of Belarus, as the low-lying country straddles the shortest route between Moscow and the Polish border. The land has consequently been ravaged by war and controlled by Soviet dictatorship, but has emerged a survivor. A welcome detour from the madding tourist trail, there's more to see in Belarus than you might suspect. Wide stretches of unbroken birch groves, vast forested marshlands, and wooden villages amid rolling green fields give it a haunting beauty; and the friendly hospitality of the Belarusian people is legendary.

BEST TIME TO VISIT
It's always low season in Belarus but best from April to May (spring) or September (late summer) – but not during the 1930s when Stalin ruled

ESSENTIAL EXPERIENCES
Downing a Belarusian pint in the shadow of the KGB building in Minsk

Being bowled over by the monumental scale of the Brest Fortress WWII memorial

Catching a glimpse of European bison, the continent's largest mammal, at the Belavezhskaja Pushcha National Park

Walking in Marc Chagall's footsteps through the charming old sectors of Vitsebsk

Eating and drinking with friendly locals in cosmopolitan Brest, the lively, bustling bordertown

Marvelling at Minsk, a shining testament to neoclassical Stalinist architecture

GETTING UNDER THE SKIN
Read Maxim Haradsky's *Two Souls*, a poignant expression of the repressed state of Belarus after WWI

Listen to *Kupalinka: Folk Music of Belarus*

Watch *Kojak: The Belarus File*, conspiracy-theory intrigue where Kojak investigates the deaths of Russian émigrés

Eat mushrooms – mushrooming is a traditional expedition in Belarus. Try the mushroom and barley *hribnoy sup* (soup) and *kotleta pokrestyansky* (pork cutlet smothered with mushroom sauce).

Drink *kvas*, an elixir made of malt, flour, sugar, mint and fruit

IN A WORD
Dob-ree dzhen Добры дзень (hello)

TRADEMARKS
Onion dome architecture; the last dictatorship in Europe; splendid isolation; mountain villages; hearty peasant food and sweet, strong liqueurs; freezing cold temperatures; furry hats; monasteries, churches and cathedrals

SURPRISES
Belarus beat the Swedes in the 2002 Winter Olympics hockey tournament; there are still some working collective farms in the Belarusian countryside

One of the first things foreigners notice in Belarus, especially those familiar with Russia, is the cleanliness of the cities and towns. Even in Soviet times, Belarusians had the reputation of being exceptionally neat and tidy. Central streets are kept immaculate – by the swarms of overnight street sweepers but also by citizens. Even tipsy teens assiduously use rubbish bins for their beer bottles.

– Lonely Planet's *Russia & Belarus*

6. Reconstructed 10th- and 13th- century Russian Orthodox churches near the Dzvina River Jonathan Smith

MAP REF: G,23

2. The Carnival of Binche where a posse of costumed performers known as *Gilles* energises the crowd with a display of clog stomping Geert Cole

3. Delicious chocolate pralines await consumption Leanne Logan

4. The still waters of a canal in Ghent depict the buildings above in impressionist brush strokes Mark Daffey

5. Pride of the kingdom, the Grand Place in Brussels Jean-Bernard Carillet

1. Crimson doors and window frames adorn the façade of an appealing triangular barn Esbin Anderson Photography

Despite being home of the EU, Belgium's spotlight on the European stage remains a little dim, but only because its people are rarely boastful. Belgium has more history, art and architecture packed inside its tiny borders than many of its bigger, louder neighbours. For a start, it claims some of Europe's finest medieval cities: Antwerp, Brussels, Bruges, Ghent and Leuven. Festivals and celebrations keep the locals occupied year-round, and eating well or lingering over a beer in good company are national pastimes.

BEST TIME TO VISIT
May to September (summer), Christmas and Carnival (January–February)

ESSENTIAL EXPERIENCES
Stepping back in time in dreamlike Bruges

Sampling the country's 800-odd beers and world-renowned chocolates

Creeping through corridors and dungeons at the Château de Bouillon

Visiting Ypres' poppy-clad WWI battlegrounds

Wining, dining and indulging in lively and atmospheric Antwerp

Warming up on hot wine at a Christmas market

GETTING UNDER THE SKIN
Read *A Tall Man in a Low Land* by Englishman Harry Pearson for a humorous look at the country; Hugo Claus' *The Sorrow of Belgium* — wartime Belgium through the eyes of a Flemish adolescent

Listen to Jacques Brel's poetic oeuvre or tunes from dEUS, Arno, Vaya con Dios and K's Choice

Watch Van Dormael's charming *Le Huitième Jour* and *Toto le Héros*, or the Dardenne frères' *Rosetta* – they're all shot locally

Eat *mosselen/moules* (mussels), *gegratineerd witloof/gratin au chicon* (chicory au gratin), grey North Sea *garnalen/crevettes* (shrimps), *waterzooi* (a chicken or fish stew)

Drink Duvel, Westmalle, Hoegaarden or even Kriek (cherry) *bieren/bières* (beers), or some excellent 'young' or 'old' *jenevers/genièvres* (gin) from distilleries like Smeets and Filliers

IN A WORD
Schol!/santé! (cheers!)

TRADEMARKS
Beer; chocolates; lace; the linguistic divide; the European Union; Rubens, Breugel & Van Eyck; kisses on the cheek; Tintin; *frites* (hot chips) with mayonnaise; pigeon-racing; confusing placenames; Manneken Pis; elegant town squares; waffles; Hercule Poirot

SURPRISES
Alcohol-free beer does exist; the saxophone was invented in Belgium

The Belgians swear they invented frieten/frites, *and judging by the availability it's a claim few would contest. The popularity of this snack cannot be understated. Every Belgian village has at least one* frituur/friture *where* frites *are served in a paper cone or dish, smothered with large blobs of thick mayonnaise until almost unrecognisable and eaten with a small wooden fork in a mostly futile attempt to keep your fingers clean.*

— Lonely Planet's *Belgium & Luxembourg*

MAP REF: G,20

6. Pedestrians in the psychedelic St Anna tunnel built under the Schelde river in the 1930s, Antwerp Martin Moos

2. A young girl from the Maya Mountains shows off her teeth and her Sunday best Jeffrey Becom

3. Nose first, a tamandua (three-toed anteater) eats his way up a sapling Tom Boyden

4. A Caye Caulker islander keeps the hair out of his eyes Belize-style Doug McKinlay

5. A sailing vessel glides through the glassy waters off Glover's Atoll, the southernmost of Belize's triad of atolls Susan Rimerman

6. A hieroglyphic frieze adorns the imposing Mayan structure known as El Castillo in Xunantunich, rediscovered in the late 19th century Wayne Walton

LEFT 1. Arms outstretched, an Atlantean statue of Jesus welcomes a diver in the mysterious depths off Ambergris Caye Mark Webster

Belize embraces a beguiling mix of Caribbean and Latin cultures, infused with a colonial history brought to its shores by British settlers. English-speaking, Creole-dominated and with a thoroughly coup-free history, this tiny country has an atmosphere that couldn't be more laid-back. Tourism may be unashamedly big business, but visitors rarely feel commodified. The local people are friendly, open and relaxed, and everyone here seems to know how to have a good time.

BEST TIME TO VISIT
It rains less in the first half of the year, but you'll probably be too relaxed to care either way

ESSENTIAL EXPERIENCES
Flying into Belize City, then hightailing it out to the beaches as quickly as possible

Ordering a Belikin beer, then ordering another one

Riding the bus into Belmopan, Belize's capital city, still wondering if you've arrived as you drive out the other side

Snorkelling in the impossibly warm waters of the Caribbean Sea

Exploring Belize's many beautiful Mayan ruins

GETTING UNDER THE SKIN
Read *Belizious Cuisine*, a collection of 200 dishes that demonstrate the richness of Belize's multicultural past

Listen to the Garifuna rhythms, culture and politics of Andy Palacio's *Til Da Mawnin*

Watch *The Mosquito Coast*, starring Harrison Ford and River Phoenix, which flaunts the lush beauty of Belize's interior (though the setting is supposed to be neighbouring Honduras)

Eat the two main dishes on a Belizean menu: 'rice and beans' and 'beans and rice' – either way, it tastes great with a dash of Marie Sharp's famous hot sauce

Drink Belize's famous Belikin beer, which always goes down a treat

IN A WORD
You better Belize it! (cringeworthy but ubiquitous)

TRADEMARKS
Mayan ruins; 'surf-and-turf'; diving the Blue Hole; Marie Sharp's famous hot sauce

SURPRISES
Listening in on a conversation in a curious language, only to realise the language is English; it is actually possible to fill an entire day doing absolutely nothing

Those looking for relaxation, adventure and wildlife in a small, easy-to-get-around package will be enamoured by Belize, and indeed, many travellers return year after year. You'll get the best of both worlds here – there's a well-trodden tourist trail, and all the amenities that come with it, but step off the trail and you'll find that you're in a Central American country with unlimited opportunities for adventure.

– Lonely Planet's *Belize*

MAP REF: L.10

2. A *tata somba* house of Kuaba Craig Pershouse

3. The tide scales the palm-lined beach of Grand Popo
Jane Sweeney

4. A woman strolls past a mosque in Porto Novo Craig Pershousex

5. A girl carries her snoozing baby brother on her back
Craig Pershouse

As the birthplace of voodoo and the seat of one of West Africa's most powerful kingdoms, Benin once had a historical renown that extended far beyond its borders. More recently the country has shrugged off Marxism to embrace democracy and capitalism with characteristic fervour. Visitors to surprising Benin will find remnants of the vast palaces of the formidable Dahomey empire, take boat rides through villages built entirely on stilts, see hippos eyeballing them from murky rivers, stop off at deserted beaches where slave ships once sailed and see stunning indigenous architecture.

BEST TIME TO VISIT
January and February (the dry season)

ESSENTIAL EXPERIENCES
Witnessing the life-affirming ceremonies of traditional Beninese dance

Visiting the ancient capital of Abomey, home to one of West Africa's largest palaces

Bowing before Legba upon entering the Sacred Forest of Ouidah

Boating to Ganvié, an extraordinary stilt village in the middle of Lake Nokoué

Spying elephants, hippos and lions at Parc National de la Pendjari

Relaxing on the long, palm-fringed beaches of Grand Popo

GETTING UNDER THE SKIN
Read Bruce Chatwin's *The Viceroy of Ouidah*, which tells the story of a Brazilian trader stranded on the 'Slave Coast' in the 17th century

Listen to Angélique Kidjo, Gnonnas Pedro, Nel Olivier and Yelouassi Adolphe

Watch *Globe Trekker: West Africa - Mali, Benin and Burkina Faso* for a visual tour of the region

Eat *pâte de maïs* (mashed maize) with either meat, cheese or *gombo* (okra) sauce

Drink La Béninoise, the local beer, or *sodabe*, the local rocket fuel

IN A WORD
Neh-àh-dèh-gbòhng? (how are you? in the local language, Fon)

TRADEMARKS
Voodoo fetishes; smiling faces; fishing villages on stilts; poachers; multiple coups; elephants and hippos

SURPRISES
The name of the de facto capital, Cotonou, means 'mouth of the river of death' in Fon, referring to the role the town played in the exportation of slaves; on Voodoo Day (10 January) people meet on Ouidah's beaches to pray for good health

Temple Sémassou is dedicated to the wife of Dahomey King Aglongo, and to gynaecological deformations. Sémassou is said to have given birth to a fetish instead of a child; the fetish was buried here and the temple built above it. Nearby is a large white fetish sans penis. It is believed that a female tourist broke off the oversized erect penis and kept it as a souvenir. Previously local women would straddle it to ensure their future productivity.

— Lonely Planet's *West Africa*

1. Women and girls in costume at Easter Day Parade in Porto Novo Jane Sweeney

6. A boy clambers amongst the huts of Koko village, Atakora Jane Sweeney

MAP REF: M,20

2. Empty deck chairs on Elbow Beach await the midday influx of sun worshippers David Sanger

3. The bleached walls of a church in the city of Hamilton Nicholas Pavloff

4. The bells and bellows of St George's town crier Greg Johnston

5. A croquet player casts long shadows over a manicured lawn Chris Sanders
LEFT 1. Businessmen in Bermuda like to keep it cool and casual Doug Wilson

Visitors from the USA find this most isolated of island groups to be quaintly English with its cricket matches and afternoon teas. Brits, on the other hand, find it has an American flavour. Whatever your point of origin, you can't fail to appreciate that subtropical Bermuda is far enough from urban pollution to offer clear skies and clean turquoise waters. Bermuda is sometimes erroneously associated with the Caribbean, which lies nearly 1000 miles to its south.

BEST TIME TO VISIT
Year-round

ESSENTIAL EXPERIENCES
Strolling along the crooked streets in Town of St George and poking into its churches, museums and historic sites

Watching the boats cross the harbour from Hamilton's Front St, a harbourfront road lined with turn-of-the-century Victorian buildings in bright pastel lemon, lime, apricot and sky blue

Visiting the Royal Naval Dockyard, where the inner fort has been turned into the island's leading historic museum, the Bermuda Maritime Museum

Lazing in the sun on the dazzling pink-sand beaches at South Shore Park

Splashing about in the turquoise waters of Horseshoe Bay

GETTING UNDER THE SKIN
Read *Bermuda's Story* by Terry Tucker, the island's most highly regarded historian

Listen to reggae, calypso and Bermuda's most rocking band, the Kennel Boys

Watch *The Deep*, an underwater thriller of drug lords and treasure set off the coast of Bermuda

Eat fish chowder (a tasty reddish-brown chowder commonly made with rockfish or snapper and flavoured with local black rum and sherry peppers sauce) or a traditional Sunday codfish breakfast (codfish, eggs, boiled Irish potatoes, bananas and avocado, with a sauce of onions and tomatoes)

Drink Gosling's Black Seal Rum (a dark rum) or dark 'n' stormy (a two-to-one mix of carbonated ginger beer with Black Seal Rum)

IN A WORD
De rock – the rock (meaning Bermuda)

TRADEMARKS
Bermuda shorts; tidy pastel cottages; pink-sand beaches; the Bermuda Triangle

SURPRISES
Bermuda held 'witch' trials in the 17th century; Bermuda has the world's northernmost coral reefs

A Gombey group traditionally consists of men and boys, referred to as a 'crowd'. The young boys are called 'warriors' and wear short capes and carry wooden tomahawks. The older boys are called 'Indians' and carry bows and arrows, and the head males, or 'chiefs', wear long capes, carry whips and command the show. The capes of all the dancers are brightly coloured and decorated with sequins, yarn fringe and trailing ribbons. Their tall headdresses are elaborately ornamented with glitter and peacock feathers, and long sleeves, gloves, scarves and masks keep their bodies covered from head to toe.

– Lonely Planet's *Bermuda*

MAP REF: J,13

2. Rice fields on the way to Paro and Thimphu Izzet Keribar

3. School children vie for attention in Thimphu
Richard I'Anson

4. One of the temples of Kurjey Lhakhang in the Choskhor Valley Julia Wilkinson

5. The monk's room at the National Memorial Chorten in Thimphu Izzet Keribar

6. Dancers in brilliant silk re-enact legendary religious stories in front of the National Library, Thimphu
Stan Armington

LEFT 1. A young Bhutanese boy from Paro in traditional dress Alison Wright

The Kingdom of Bhutan teeters between contemporary and medieval: monks transcribe ancient Buddhist texts into laptop computers, traditionally dressed archers use alloy-steel bows and arrows, and its farsighted leaders maintain Bhutan's pristine environment and unique culture. The king is supposed to have said, 'I am not as much concerned about the Gross National Product as I am about the Gross National Happiness'. Since Bhutan's doors opened in 1974, visitors have been mesmerised by spectacular Himalayan scenery, impressive architecture and hospitable people.

BEST TIME TO VISIT
September to November when skies are clear and the high mountain peaks visible

ESSENTIAL EXPERIENCES
Experiencing the extraordinary friendliness and warm hospitality of the Bhutanese people

River-rafting down remote, stunningly beautiful rivers, from small alpine runs like the Paro Chhu to the big water Puna Tsang Chhu

Exploring ancient and precious Buddhist sites at Bumthang, Bhutan's spiritual heartland

Marvelling at the imposing Trashi Chhoe Dzong (Fortress of the Glorious Religion) at Thimphu and visiting 'the painting school' below it

Spotting black-necked cranes at the glacial valley of Phobjika on the western slopes of the Black Mountains

GETTING UNDER THE SKIN
Read *A Baby in a Backpack to Bhutan*, an engaging, amusing adventure by Bunty Avieson, who quit her job and travelled with her newborn baby to Bhutan

Listen to *Music to Meditate By: Tibetan Buddhist Rites From the Monasteries of Bhutan, Vol. 1: Rituals of the Drukpa* by the Thimphu Monastic Orchestra

Watch *Little Buddha*, directed by Bernardo Bertolucci and starring Keanu Reeves — partly set and filmed in Bhutan. *The Other Final*, a documentary about a football match between Bhutan and Montserrat, the world's worst soccer teams in 2002.

Eat Tibetan-style *momos* (filled steamed dumplings), yak meat, and *ema datse* (chillies and cheese) — but not all at once!

Drink XXX Bhutan Rum

IN A WORD
Dzong (the iconic white, fortress-style monastery)

TRADEMARKS
The last Himalayan Buddhist kingdom; colourful, hand-woven textiles; unsurpassed beauty; ancient myths and legends; a hair-raising descent into Paro airport; a place for inspiration and solitude; prayer flags, beads and wheels; *datse* (archery) enthusiasts

SURPRISES
Thimphu is the only world capital without traffic lights. One set was installed, but residents complained that it was too impersonal.

In a mountain village named Laya, I was standing in a schoolhouse and staring at a document entitled Manual for Teachers of Mathematics. What caught my eye is something that is offered as a 'first rule': 'Always remember that you are a human being as well as a teacher, that your students are also human beings, and that you are here because you have something important to give them that they need.'

— Lonely Planet's *Bhutan*

MAP REF: K,29

2. An Aymara woman and her dog take a break in colourful La Paz Eric Wheater

3. The shoreline of Lake Verde with the majestic volcano Licancabur in the background Woods Wheatcroft

4. A shy llama peeks between the cacti on the Isla de los Pescadores Edward Snijders

5. A local takes a walk in downtown La Paz Jane Sweeney

6. The aridly beautiful, high-terrain landscape is reflected in a saline lake in in the far southwest Grant Dixon

LEFT 1. Between Potosi and Sucre, a young girl stops at the roadside Chris Beall

Bolivia isn't called the Tibet of the Americas for nothing: it's the western hemisphere's highest, most isolated and most rugged nation. It's also South America's most traditional realm: the majority of the population claim pure Amerindian blood, and many maintain the cultural values and belief systems of their forebears. The geography of this landlocked, Andean country runs the gamut from jagged peaks and hallucinogenic salt flats to steamy jungles and wildlife-rich pampas. Bolivia is often left off travellers' itineraries, making it the perfect off-the-beaten-track destination.

BEST TIME TO VISIT
May to October (winter)

ESSENTIAL EXPERIENCES
Strolling along the cobblestoned streets surrounding Iglesia de San Francisco in La Paz

Visiting the spectacular ice caves and turquoise lakes of the Zongo Valley

Choosing one of Lake Titicaca's 36 islands and sailing through the clear sapphire-blue waters to get there

Taking a jungle trip to the rainforest surrounding Rurrenabaque, on the Río Beni

Finding out that seeing is believing – Salar de Uyuni, the southwest's salt deserts, have spurting geysers and eerie lagoons

GETTING UNDER THE SKIN
Read *The Fat Man from La Paz: Contemporary Fiction from Bolivia*, a collection of 20 short stories edited by Rosario Santos. Sir Arthur Conan Doyle's memorable *The Lost World* was inspired by tales of the northeastern Bolivian plateaux.

Listen to *Charango* masters Celestino Campos, Ernesto Cavour and Mauro Núñez, or local pop outfit Azul Azul

Watch *Sexual Dependency*, directed by Bolivian Rodrigo Bellott, dealing with the loss of sexual innocence

Eat *salteña* (a pastie filled with meat and vegetables); *surubí* (catfish), the lowlands' most delicious freshwater fish

Drink the favourite alcoholic drink *chicha cochabambina*, obtained by fermenting corn. *Mate de coca* (coca leaf tea) is the most common boiled drink

IN A WORD
Buenos días sopita. ¿Qué tal? (good day, how are you?)

TRADEMARKS
Bowler hats; altitude sickness; Lake Titicaca; La Paz; cocaine guerrillas; colourful hand-woven shawls; llamas; chewing coca

SURPRISES
Legendary outlaws Butch Cassidy and the Sundance Kid supposedly met their demise in San Vicente

Bolivians invited to lunch on a Tuesday might arrive on a Wednesday and, by their understanding of time, may regard themselves as only a little late. You should not adopt local habits to this extent, but arriving a bit late is normal. If you're invited to a party at, say, 8pm and you turn up at 9pm, you're likely to be the first guest to arrive.

– Lonely Planet's *South America*

MAP REF: Q,12

2. In Bosnia, not even snow and sleet gets in the way of a good old kickabout Damir Sagolj

3. A brave soul indulges in a local tradition: jumping off the remains of the Old Mostar Bridge Danilo Krstanovic

4. Pigeons rise in the morning light over Sarajevo's old town Danilo Krstanovic

5. A Bosnian Muslim prays at a cemetery Danilo Krstanovic

6. Two women walk down a war-scarred street in Sarajevo Dan Herrick
LEFT 1. An old man bathed in Sarajevo's golden dawn Nic Lehman

Sandwiched between Croatia and Serbia, the small mountainous country of Bosnia and Hercegovina has been a zone of contention since Occident and Orient first began arm-wrestling for it nearly two millennia ago. It's been through Christian, Muslim and Orthodox hands, and for a while its people seemed to enjoy their multicultural milieu. Then came the devastating war of the 1990s. Despite the destruction of much of its heritage, progress since then has been substantial and Bosnia and Hercegovina shows proud resilience through its scars. Gorgeous Sarajevo is coming back to life and a drive through the craggy, dramatic countryside is unforgettable.

BEST TIME TO VISIT
Year-round – the weather is agreeable except for summer and winter extremes

ESSENTIAL EXPERIENCES
Taking a tram ride and drinking Turkish coffee in the streets of Sarajevo

Clambering among the cobblestones in the ancient walled city of Jajce

Visiting the medieval castle, Many-Coloured Mosque and natural springs at Travnik

Discovering Islamic culture and Turkish souvenir shops in Mostar, nestled in the valley of the aqua-green Neretva River

Making a pilgrimage to Međugorje to search for an apparition of the Virgin Mary

Skiing on quaint Mt Jahorina, site of the 1984 Winter Olympics

GETTING UNDER THE SKIN
Read Misha Glenny's *The Fall of Yugoslavia: The Third Balkan War*, a British journalist's first-hand account of the disintegration of the former Yugoslavia

Listen to *Bosnian Breakdown: the Unpronounceable Beat of Sarajevo (Yugoslavia)* by Kalesijki Zvuci – a mix of pop and folk tunes featuring drums and *sargija* (lute)

Watch *No Man's Land* by Sarajevo-born Danis Tanović, depicting the relationship between a Serb and a Muslim soldier during the time of siege in Sarajevo

Eat *sirnica* (cheese pie) or *tufahije* (apple cake topped with walnuts and cream)

Drink *šljivovica* (plum brandy) or *loza* (grape brandy)

IN A WORD
ivjeli ('cheers!' when toasting)

TRADEMARKS
Old cobbled streets; medieval forts and castles; mountain villages; excellent Turkish food; war memorials; sniper-pocked façades; hilly countryside and forests; bronze artisans; beautiful natural springs

SURPRISES
Rafting the excellent and varied rapids of the Una River at Bihać; the Dervish monastery *(tekija)* at Blagaj; homemade wines for sale at Cevrići

Sarajevo, Bosnia and Hercegovina's capital, is tucked in the peaceful Miljacka river valley. Before the war, the city was an ethnic microcosm of Yugoslavia, where Muslims, Serbs, Croats, Turks, Jews and others had peacefully coexisted for hundreds of years. Despite the highly visible scars of war, Sarajevo is again bursting with energy. Colorful trams run down the road once called 'Sniper's Alley', innumerable cafés line the streets, and locals spend leisurely evenings strolling down the main pedestrian street, Ferhadija.

— Lonely Planet's *Eastern Europe*

CROATIA

• Bosanski Novi   • Derventa   Bijeljina •

• Bihać   Banja Luka •   Doboj •

Tuzla •   SERBIA & MONTENEGRO

Zvornik •

CROATIA   Jajce •   Zenica •

• Kupres   **Sarajevo** ✪   Višegrad •

Jablanica •   Foča •

• Mostar

• Međugorje   SERBIA & MONTENEGRO

ADRIATIC SEA   • Neum

Trebinje •

MAP REF: H,21

2. A red-billed oxpecker helps maintain a zebra's coat ABI

3. A female cheetah surveys her surroundings Dave Hamman

4. A Ngambiland local enjoys a pipe Richard l'Anson

5. Known as the Sleeping Sisters, these baobabs in Makgadikgadi were immortalised in paintings by Thomas Baines in 1862 ABI

An African success story, Botswana achieved independence from Britain in 1966 and immediately thereafter, in a mad stroke of luck, discovered three of the world's richest diamond mines. And just like a good mystery story, it takes time to unravel the country's secrets. Beyond the narrow eastern corridor, where the majority of the population is concentrated, Botswana is a largely roadless wilderness of savannas, deserts, wetlands and salt pans. As freedom of speech and equality are all guaranteed under the country's constitution, the greatest threat to Botswana's stability is posed by the AIDS virus.

BEST TIME TO VISIT
April to August (the dry season), for wildlife viewing

ESSENTIAL EXPERIENCES
Travelling by *mokoro* (traditional canoe) on the Okavango River

Seeing the incredible gallery of ancient San paintings in the remote and mystical Tsodilo Hills

Wildlife spotting in Chobe National Park – take your pick of lions, cheetahs, hippos, giraffes, antelopes, zebras and any number of species of birds

Camping with the wild things at Moremi Game Reserve

Keeping a lookout for buried treasure in the Gcwihaba Caverns, with their gargantuan stalagmites and stalactites

GETTING UNDER THE SKIN
Read *Bayeyi & Hambukushu: Tales from the Okavango* (edited by Thomas J Larson), a compilation of oral poetry and stories from the Okavango Panhandle region; or Alexander McCall Smith's popular mystery series, *The No 1 Ladies' Detective Agency*

Listen to Nick Nkosanah Ndaba's *Dawn of Bojazz* and Rastafarian Ras Baxton's 'Tswana reggae'

Watch *The Gods Must Be Crazy* and *March of the Flame Birds* for the Botswana landscape

Eat *mabele* (sorghum) or *bogobe* (porridge made from sorghum), which form the basis of most Batswana meals

Drink *bojalwa*, a sprouted-sorghum beer that's brewed commercially as Chibuku

IN A WORD
Dumêla ('hello' in Tswana)

TRADEMARKS
National parks; poaching; the San people; the Kalahari desert; salt pans

SURPRISES
Okavango is the world's largest inland delta; baobab trees with a circumference of ...... 4000 years old; Botswana has the highest rate of HIV/AIDS infection in the world

The Batswana staple was beef, but each of the several Batswana groups had its own food taboos. No-one ate fish or crocodile – the latter being the totem of the tribe as a whole – and other groups were forbidden to eat their own totems. Some tribes relied upon different food staples: the Yei of the Okavango were dependent upon fish, the Bakalanga ate mainly sorghum, millet and maize, while the Baherero (Herero) subsisted mostly on thickened, soured milk.

– Lonely Planet's *Botswana*

1. Ostriches await an approaching thunderstorm in Savute marsh, Chobe National Park ABI

6. Travelling along the Delta river in a *mokoro* boat hollowed from a tree trunk Juliet Coombe

MAP REF: Q,22

2. A capoeira dancer pulls a stunt on the cobbled streets of Salvador da Bahia Tom Cockrem

3. Soft-drink vendors help beachgoers cool off in Rio de Janeiro Andrew Draffen

4. One of the many colourful houses in Rio's Jardim Botanico (Botanical Gardens) district John Pennock

5. A sunny clearing in the Atlantic rainforest, Ipiranga Robyn Jones

From the frenzied passion of Carnaval to the immensity of the dark Amazon, Brazil is a country of mythic proportions. Encompassing half the continent, South America's giant has stretches of unexplored rainforest, islands with pristine tropical beaches and endless rivers. After decades of internal migration and population growth, Brazil is also an urban country; more than two out of every three Brazilians live in a city, and São Paulo is among the world's most populous metropolises.

BEST TIME TO VISIT
There is no bad time to visit Brazil

ESSENTIAL EXPERIENCES
Dancing through the cobblestone streets of Salvador da Bahia during Carnaval

Escaping to Ilha Grande, the perfect island getaway, blending tropical beach and Atlantic rainforest

Experiencing the mad spectacle of football at Maracanã

Partying till dawn at sexy samba clubs in Lapa

Watching *capoeira* (an Afro-Brazilian martial art) on the beach

Taking a jungle tour into the heart of the Amazon

GETTING UNDER THE SKIN
Read *The Alchemist* by novelist Paulo Coelho, or *The Masters and the Slaves: A Study in the Development of Brazilian Civilization* by Gilberto Freyre, the most famous book on Brazil's colonial past

Listen to bossa nova's founding father, guitarist João Gilberto; for something more contemporary, the punk-driven Legião Urbana

Watch Hector Babenco's *Pixote*, the tale of a street kid in Rio that won the best film award at Cannes in 1981. *Cidade de Deus* (City of God) gives an honest and disturbing portrayal of life in a Rio *favela* (slum).

Eat *feijoada* (pork stew served with rice and a bowl of beans) or *acarajé* (peeled brown beans, mashed in salt and onions, and then fried – inside is dried shrimp, pepper and tomato sauce)

Drink *cafezinho* (coffee, served as an espresso-sized shot with plenty of sugar and without milk) and *sucos* (juice from the incredible variety of Brazilian fruits)

IN A WORD
Bacana (cool)

TRADEMARKS
Carmen Miranda; 'The Girl from Ipanema'; Carnaval; the Amazon; soccer; beaches; bossa nova

SURPRISES
Candomblé gods are known as *orixás* and each person is believed to be protected for life by one of them. Millions of Brazilians go to the beach at New Year to pay homage to Iemanjá, the sea goddess, whose alter ego is the Virgin Mary.

Brazilians love to celebrate, and parties happen year-round. But it isn't all samba and beaches in the land of the tropics. At times, Brazilians suffer from saudade, a nostalgic, often deeply melancholic longing for something. Saudade manifests itself in many forms – from the dull ache of homesickness to the deep regret over past mistakes.

— Lonely Planet's South America

1. The sun sets over Ipanema Beach with its dramatic backdrop of the Dois Irmãos (Two Brothers) mountain John Pennock

6. A family from the Amazonas region John Maier Jr

MAP REF: P.14

2. Boats speed through the floating villages of Kampung Ayer Jane Sweeney

3. Children play on the verandah of their home in Bandar Seri Begawan Liz Barry

4. Backed by the Jame' Asr Hassanal Bolkiah Mosque, girls chat by a fountain Jane Sweeney

5. The Sultan of Brunei's magnificent palace Graham Tween
LEFT 1. A fisherman paddles along the mangrove swamps beside the Brunei River Liz Barry

The Islamic sultanate of Brunei is one of the world's smallest countries – and richest, thanks to its treasure trove of oil. It's known chiefly for the astounding wealth of its sultan and for its tax-free, subsidised society. The country's full name is Negara Brunei Darussalam, translated as 'Brunei – the Abode of Peace', and with alcohol virtually unobtainable, no nightlife or active political culture, it's certainly peaceful. The capital, Bandar Seri Begawan, has retained its fringe of traditional, river-dwelling stilt villages as an enduring vision of the past, and away from the coast the landscape is taken over by largely pristine tropical forest.

BEST TIME TO VISIT
March to October – or 1929 when oil was discovered, Brunei's most memorable payday

ESSENTIAL EXPERIENCES
Racing through the waterways of Sungai Brunei in a sleek longboat

Contemplating the shadows and light on the capital's Omar Ali Saifuddien Mosque as the sun goes down

Getting lost in the maze of plank-walks linking the water villages of Kampung Ayer

Trekking though Brunei's Peradayan Forest Reserve

Feasting on an abundance of satay, barbecued fish, and sweet pancakes filled with peanuts, raisins and sugar at a local food market

GETTING UNDER THE SKIN
Read *Time and the River* by Prince Mohamed Bolkiah, penned by the sultan's youngest brother

Listen to the Brunei national anthem, a cheery tribute to the sultan and to prosperity

Watch any number of pirated DVDs – Brunei's film industry is virtually nonexistent and censorship is entrenched, but video piracy is booming

Eat *roti chanai* for breakfast – flaky flat bread accompanied by coconut curry dipping sauce

Drink fresh fruit juices and luridly coloured soy drinks

IN A WORD
Panas (hot)

TRADEMARKS
Flamboyant sultans; exotic waterways; excellent medical and education services; a place for your liver to recuperate; strict drug laws; a tax haven

SURPRISES
Daily oil production: 163,000 barrels; the oil supply is predicted to run out in 2030

Brunei has a cattle station in Australia that is larger than the sultanate itself. The 5986 sq km station in Willaroo, in Australia's Northern Territory, supplies Brunei with beef and other meat products. The live cattle are brought direct to Brunei from Darwin and slaughtered according to halal practices.

– Lonely Planet's *Southeast Asia on a Shoestring*

MAP REF: N,32

2. The majestic Hrelyu Tower and church domes of the Rila Monastery, Sofia Tom Cockrem

3. Ranks of umbrellas line the popular beach front at Sozopol Paul Greenway

4. Women in a donkey and trap clatter their way into the town of Veliko Târnovo, Lovech Chris Mellor
LEFT 1. Wistful and contemplative, two elderly women observe the street from the steps of a house in rural southwest Bulgaria Tom Cockrem

Since the early 1990s Bulgaria has morphed into a more modern version of itself, attracting tourists with its cheap skiing, beach holidays on the Black Sea coast, bustling capital Sofia, dramatic mountains, havenlike monasteries, Roman and Byzantine ruins, and excellent coffee. In the villages you can still find folk who ride a donkey to work, eat homegrown potatoes and make their own cheese – the difference now is that dinner is eaten in front of a satellite TV.

BEST TIME TO VISIT
April to mid-June (spring) – and in 863 to help saints Kiril and Metodii create the Cyrillic alphabet

ESSENTIAL EXPERIENCES
Skiing down Bulgaria's affordable snowy peaks

Sipping full-bodied aromatic coffee in a Sofia café

Walking through the strikingly beautiful Rila Mountains, encountering deers, wild goats, eagles and falcons among the forests of fir trees and beechwoods

Basking on the beach at Burgas on the Black Sea coast

Sampling a glass of dark red wine at Melnik in a centuries-old wine bar cut into the rocks

Reflecting and contemplating life at revered Rila Monastery, a significant symbol of national identity

GETTING UNDER THE SKIN
Read *Bulgarian Rhapsody: The Best of Balkan Cuisine* by Linda J. Forristal – an informative cookbook with delicious recipes and snippets of Bulgarian culture and history

Listen to Orthodox chants sung by a 100-strong choir at the Aleksander Nevski Church, Sofia

Watch *Under the Same Sky,* an award-winning film of the Sofia International Film Festival directed by Krasimir Krumov, about a 15-year-old girl who goes in search of her father

Eat *kyopolou,* baked eggplant with garlic and walnuts, a Varna speciality

Drink a glass of red wine, a tradition in Bulgaria since 6th century BC

IN A WORD
Blagodarya, mersi (thank you)

TRADEMARKS
Monasteries; feta; rose petals; ancient ruins; hearty meat and vegetable stews; kooky festivals; traditional fire-dancing

SURPRISES
There are over 160 monasteries; rose oil is a major export; Bulgaria is the world's fifth-largest exporter of wine

Since 1998, the Beautiful Bulgaria Project has been renovating homes and beautifying public buildings in dozens of villages in 42 municipalities including Belogradchik, Elena and Chepelare and the old town of Veliko Târnovo. The BBP ostensibly started as an employment project for the longterm unemployed in rural Bulgaria and is now rated by the EU as the most successful employment initiative in Eastern Europe.

– Lonely Planet's *Bulgaria*

MAP REF: I,22

2. Burkinabé lads play table soccer, a popular pastime in Burkina Faso Carl Drury

3. A young herdsman squints at the sun from beneath a traditional straw hat Eric Wheater

4. The Grande Mosquée of Bobo-Dioulasso, a classic example of traditional mud architecture Anthony Ham

5. The thoughtful stare of a young Burkinabé boy Eric Wheater

6. A street scene of downtown Ouagadougou, the nation's capital Anthony Ham

LEFT 1. Peul women wearing bright colours and brighter smiles gather at the Gorom-Gorom market, Oudalan Ingrid Roddis

Between Sahelian empires and coastal kingdoms, between Muslim and animist Africa, between Saharan desertscapes and southern waterfalls, Burkina Faso weaves many of Africa's diverging strands into a fascinating and thoroughly seductive fabric. In the markets, turbaned traders on camels mix with farmers on donkey-drawn carts in a colourful swirl of diverse ethnic groups. The Burkinabé are descended from a long line of regal emperors who have suffered the plebeian indignities of colonialism and blackbirding, but this has only served to strengthen and preserve their cultural identity.

BEST TIME TO VISIT
November to February

ESSENTIAL EXPERIENCES
Strolling through Ouagadougou by day and then dancing the night away

Marvelling at the intricate decoration of Bani's seven mosques

Kicking back in the languid charm of Bobo-Dioulasso, with its old quarter and distinctive Grande Mosquée

Exploring the other-worldly landscapes of the Sindou Peaks near Banfora

Wandering amid the colour of Gorom-Gorom's Thursday market

Swimming in the Karfiguéla waterfalls in the dry season

GETTING UNDER THE SKIN
Read *The Maxims, Thoughts and Riddles of the Mossi* by Dim-Dolobsom Ouedraogo, which offers a glimpse of Burkina Faso barely 30 years after the French colonised it

Listen to Idak Bassave's *Les Mêmes Problèmes*

Watch *Les Etrangers* by Mamadou Kola Djim, or *Samba Traoré* by Idrissa Ouedraogo – both are excellent Burkinabé directors

Eat *pintade grillé* (grilled guinea fowl) or *riz sauce* (rice with sauce)

Drink *Brakina* or *So.b.bra* – popular lager-type beers

IN A WORD
Start the day with some Moré (the language of the Mossi): *yee-bay-roh* (good morning)

TRADEMARKS
The Pan-African Film Festival; a 'don't worry be happy' attitude; one of the world's poorest countries

SURPRISES
Burkina Faso literally translates as 'Homeland of the Incorruptible', or 'Country of Honest Men'. As a means of fostering unity among an ethnically diverse people, the name was coined from two of the country's most widely spoken languages: the Moré word for 'pure' and the Dioula word for 'homeland'

Artistically, the Mossi are best known for their tall wooden antelope masks, often more than 2m high and painted red and white. Male and female antelope masks are distinguished from each other by their top sections. Female masks feature a human female figure, while male masks consist of a nonhuman planklike structure. At the bottom of these masks is a small, oval face bisected by a serrated vertical strip, with triangular eyeholes on either side. The masks were originally worn primarily at funerals.

— Lonely Planet's *West Africa*

MALI
- Djibo
- Dori
NIGER
- Ouahigouya
- Yako
- Kaya
- Dédougou
- Koudougou
- ✪ Ouagadougou
- Fada N'Gourma
- Bobo-Dioulasso
- Léo
- Pô
- Banfora
- Gaoua
BENIN
GHANA
TOGO
CÔTE D'IVOIRE

MAP REF: M,20

2. A dome-shaped, thatched rondavel hut   Kennan Ward

3. Huge horns dominate the thin body of the Longhorn Bull
Kennan Ward

4. A fisherman carefully threads his net   Bruno De Hogues

Wedged between Tanzania, Rwanda and Congo is the tiny mountainous nation of Burundi. A turbulent history of tribal wars and factional struggles has left its scars on the beautiful landscape, and colonisation has only complicated the conflict. Civil war is synonymous with the nation and gunfire not uncommon in the capital, Bujumbura.

BEST TIME TO VISIT
Avoid the extremes of the wet season (May to September) and dry season (June to August and December to January)

ESSENTIAL EXPERIENCES
Going on safari to spot monkeys and chimpanzees in Parc National de la Kibira, the largest rainforest in Burundi

Getting in before the curfew after a night drinking in Bujumbura's vibrant restaurants and bars

Cruising across Lake Tanganyika all the way to Tanzania

Lazing by the lake at Plage des Cocotiers (Coconut Beach)

Investigating Source du Nil, the country's claim to the origin of Africa's celebrated river

Getting historical at La Pierre de Livingstone et Stanley — the alleged site of the legendary 'Dr Livingstone, I presume?' encounter

GETTING UNDER THE SKIN
Read Ahmedou Ould-Abdallah's *Burundi on the Brink 1993–95*, a heartrending account by the former UN ambassador about his efforts to bring peace

Listen to *Drummers of Burundi: Live at Real World*, a truly skin-splitting performance

Watch *Gito the Ungrateful*, the story of a cosmopolitan young Burundian's return to his homeland

Eat *busoma*, a cereal made from corn, soybeans and sorghum

Drink *impeke*, a beer brewed from sorghum, which is commonly served at family gatherings

IN A WORD
Bwa ('hello' in Kirundi)

TRADEMARKS
Safaris through dense jungle; civil war raging through the streets; Lake Tanganyika dwarfed by surrounding mountains; colonial explorers in pith helmets; the 'Heart of Africa' nickname; abundant chimps and gorillas

SURPRISES
Secluded in the mountains and forests, the Twa tribal group still live an uninterrupted hunter-gatherer lifestyle just as their ancestors have for thousands of years

Burundi is famous for its athletic and acrobatic dances. Les Tambourinaires du Burundi are the country's most famous troupe and have performed in Berlin and New York. Their performances are a high-adrenaline mix of drumming and dancing that drowns the audience in a wave of sound and movement.

— Lonely Planet's *Africa*

1. Drummers accompany Gitaga dancers who make spectacular flying leaps in the air Kennan Ward

5. The curious faces of Hutu children Howard Davies

MAP REF: 0,23

2. Angkor Wat at dawn John Banagan

3. Massive roots frame the entrance to the mysterious Ta Prohm Temple Anders Blomqvist

4. Sunlight illuminates the face of an elderly man holding incense, Angkor Bernard Napthine

1. Traditional Khmer dancing taught in a Siem Reap classroom for both boys and girls Juliet Coombe

The spectres of Pol Pot and the Khmer Rouge still haunt Cambodia, but peace and optimism are slowly returning and there's a frontier-style excitement and entrepreneurial zing to the place.

Take saffron-robed monks, lichen-covered ruins, hard-core *moto* traffic and clouds of dragonflies, and mix with jasmine-scented sunsets, gracious colonial boulevards, gorgeous silks and rioting bougainvilleas, garnish with the zest of Buddhism and serve at steaming temperatures.

BEST TIME TO VISIT
November to January, when humidity levels are low

ESSENTIAL EXPERIENCES
Gliding down the Mekong River past houseboats and villages

Gazing at the mysteriously beautiful temples of Angkor, among the foremost architectural wonders of the world, at sunset or sunrise

Trekking through Bokor National Park and swimming in its waterfall

Joining in the mayhem of the Water Festival in Phnom Penh

Taking a *moto* trip through the capital in the jasmine-and-pepper scented air of sunset, taking you past the Royal Palace and down to the waterfront

GETTING UNDER THE SKIN
Read *The River of Time*, by John Swain – a journalistic memoir of the Khmer Rouge and the tragedy of people who find themselves in situations beyond their control

Listen to the unmistakable sound of monks chanting

Watch *The Killing Fields* – the gut-wrenching account of the reign of the Khmer Rouge, and of ordinary Cambodians caught up in the madness

Eat sticky banana – a baked banana wrapped in rice, inside a banana leaf; fish *amok* – a coconut fish curry, served in a coconut; fried spiders – by all accounts they taste like…chicken

Drink soda and fresh lime – nothing beats the heat quite as well; Angkor beer, the award-winning local beer

IN A WORD
Niak teuv naa? (where are you going?)

TRADEMARKS
Monks in saffron robes with yellow umbrellas; manic traffic; classic Apsara dancers; street urchins; ceiling fans; meticulously clean cyclos; beautiful silks; the Mekong; trucks crowded with people from the provinces; rice paddies; coconut palms; the smell of jasmine

SURPRISES
Cambodia is not as cheap as other destinations in the region; the sun goes down between 5 and 6pm regardless of the time of year; luxury items such as French wines are available in supermarkets

The Bayon was especially enchanting right after dawn, when the rainforest was shrouded in mist and the air was filled with the songs of invisible birds and the sound of giant dew drops bursting on the vegetation of the jungle floor. The only other people around were a few monks in light yellow robes – survivors of Pol Pot's concerted effort to exterminate the Buddhist clergy…

– 'An Angkor Odyssey', *Unpacked Again*, Lonely Planet Travel Literature

5. Saffron-robed monks queuing during an event at the ancient site of Angkor Frank Carter

MAP REF: M,31

2. A Rumsiki man known as the Crab Sorcerer displays some of the tools of his trade David Wall

3. Crowds gather at the entrance to the Maroua market Anthony Ham

1. Pipers play in front of the Sultan's Palace in Foumban David Wall

At the crossroads of West and Central Africa, Cameroon is one of the most culturally diverse countries on the continent – rich in indigenous cultures, vibrant artistic and musical traditions, and wonderful Cameroonian hospitality. The country is made up of a network of ancient tribal kingdoms, and offers visitors the choice of rainforests and relaxing beaches in the south; rocky outcrops, terraced hillsides and hobbit-like villages in the north; and the wildlife of Parc National de Waza.

BEST TIME TO VISIT
March and April, for wildlife viewing before the rains come

ESSENTIAL EXPERIENCES
Bargaining for local crafts at Foumban's artisans market

Dining on grilled fish on the beaches around Limbe and Kribi

Exploring the mountains and picturesque villages around Maroua

Climbing Mt Cameroon, West Africa's highest peak

Watching wildlife at Parc National de Waza

Hiking among ancient tribal kingdoms and striking mountain scenery in the Ring Road area near Bamenda

GETTING UNDER THE SKIN
Read *The Poor Christ of Bomb*, Mongo Beti's cynical recounting of the failure of a missionary to convert the people of a small village, or Kenjo Jumban's novel *The White Man of God*, which deals with the country's colonial experience

Listen to Manu Dibango's hit album *Soul Makossa*

Watch *Afrique, Je Te Plumerai* (Africa, I Will Fleece You), directed by Jean-Marie Teno, an outstanding documentary about modern Cameroon life

Eat delicious sauces accompanied by *riz* (rice), or with *pâte* or *fufu*, both thick mashed potato-like staples made from corn, manioc, plantains or bananas; *feuille* (manioc leaves)

Drink tea served with loads of sugar in a small glass or, if you're feeling brave, tackle a white *mimbo* (local brew)

IN A WORD
No ngoolu daa (hello)

TRADEMARKS
Tribal kingdoms; Pygmies; black rhinos; trekking; great food; *makossa* music

SURPRISES
When travelling to areas that see few outsiders, it's always best to announce your presence to the local chief (known as the *fon* in western Cameroon, and *lamido* in parts of the north). The ruler of the Bamoun is known as the sultan, and the Bamoun can trace the lineage of their sultan back to 1394.

Most Pygmies follow traditional religions, which typically centre around a powerful forest spirit, with the forest viewed as mother, father and guardian. Among the Baka, this forest god is known as Jengi. Jengi is also the name given to celebrations marking the rite of passage of young Baka men into adulthood.

– Lonely Planet's *West Africa*

4. Giant volcanic plugs in Rhumsiki David Wall

MAP REF: N,21

2. Grain silos in the early morning light, Denholm, Saskatchewan Deanna Swaney

3. Families stroll through the sea mists of Long Beach, Pacific Rim National Park Reserve Frank Carter

4. Morning light dapples the old shop fronts along Rue de la Commune O, Montréal Chris Mellor

5. A picnic table bedecked with snow and autumn leaves, Waterton Lakes National Park Lawrence Worcester

1. Detail of dancer in traditional Ojibwa Nation costume, Wanuskewin Heritage Park Jeff Greenberg

Canada's wild northern frontier has etched itself into the national psyche, and its distinct patchwork of peoples has created a country that is decidedly different from its southern neighbour. It's the sovereignty of Canada's indigenous, French and British traditions that gives the nation its complex three-dimensional character. Add to this a constant infusion of US culture and a plethora of traditions brought by immigrants, and you have a thriving multicultural society.

BEST TIME TO VISIT
March to November — spring, summer and autumn

ESSENTIAL EXPERIENCES
Gorging on a whopping big lobster supper on the delectable Prince Edward Island

Checking out fog-bound Halifax, one of the world's largest natural harbours

Chilling out in the old town of Montréal — the streets are filled with musicians, restaurants, groovy shops and a general atmosphere of *bonhomie*

Spotting arctic wildlife in Churchill — from polar bears and beluga whales to caribou and arctic foxes

Hiking in Auyuittuq National Park, a pristine wilderness of mountains, valleys, fjords and meadows

Visiting the historic Viking settlement at L'Anse aux Meadows

Canoeing in Algonquin Provincial Park

GETTING UNDER THE SKIN
Read Margaret Atwood's Booker Prize–winning *Blind Assassin*, and Michael Ondaatje's *In the Skin of a Lion*, both set in 1930s Canada

Listen to Leonard Cohen, Neil Young, Ron Sexsmith and the Cowboy Junkies

Watch Bruce Macdonald's *Dance Me Outside* about contemporary Native Indian life

Eat Oka cheese from Quebec or maple syrup (best served on pancakes with ice cream)

Drink VO ('Very Own') rye whisky, or a cherry cider

IN A WORD
Parlez-vous anglais? (do you speak English?)

TRADEMARKS
Moose and bears; the Rockies; smoked salmon; Bryan Adams; maple trees

SURPRISES
Halifax was the base of rescue operations for the *Titanic* tragedy. The plains people, such as the Cree and Blackfoot, were forced into the Europeans' world by the virtual extinction of the buffalo.

Canadians can lay claim to quite an assortment of the products of human ingenuity, a real mixed bag of inventions and firsts...Greenpeace, one of the world's predominant environmental groups, was founded in Vancouver. On the other hand, the green plastic garbage bag was also created in Canada. Two Canadians devised that 1980s classic, Trivial Pursuit, a board game that outsold Monopoly. The inexpensive Laser sailboat, globally popular, was designed by Canadians. Ice hockey was developed in the mid-1800s. And, to the chagrin of the country's US friends, it should be noted that the game of basketball was created by a Canadian.

— Lonely Planet's *Canada*

6. Young baseball players watch a game unfold in Calgary Rick Rudnicki

MAP REF: G,9

2. Children play table football in Ponta do Sol   Jean Robert

3. The small town of Paul on Santo Antão island, perched on the tip of the Atlantic   Frances Linzee Gordon

4. A Cape Verde local gives a wry smile   Jean Robert

5. Colourful boats line the beaches   Jean Robert

1. The imposing Mt Fogo volcano (last eruption 1995), Ilhas do Sotavento region Frances Linzee Gordon

On the islands of Cape Verde you can find lush valleys and mountains, long stretches of white sand, smoking volcanoes and dusty deserts, and pretty towns with cobbled streets. Additionally, there are Portuguese wine and local liquor, songs that are sad alongside those with a frenetic Latin beat, and exciting diving and windsurfing, hiking and fishing. Islanders mix up African, Portuguese, Mediterranean and Latin influences and come out with a flavour that's distinctly 'Cabo'.

BEST TIME TO VISIT
August to October

ESSENTIAL EXPERIENCES
Vanishing into the verdant valleys and forests of beautiful Santo Antão island

Gorging on Cape Verde's delicious fresh fish or famous lobsters

Losing yourself in the colour and chaos of Mindelo's Mardi Gras, the country's most vibrant festival

Plunging into the open waters of the Atlantic and seeking out sharks, manta rays and whale

Huffing and puffing to the top of Mt Fogo, an active volcano, still spouting its stuff

Cooing over a *coladeira* or two sung by a talented local singer

GETTING UNDER THE SKIN
Read poet Jorge Barbosa's *Arquipélago*, which is laden with melancholic reflections on the sea, and longings for liberation

Listen to the undisputed star of *mornas* and *coladeiras* Cesária Évora

Watch *O Testamento do Senhor Napumoceno* (Napumoceno's Will), a comedy about social and sexual mores among Cape Verde's bourgeoisie

Eat the national dish, *cachupa* (a tasty stew of several kinds of beans plus corn and various kinds of meat, often sausage or bacon, or fish). Or try a tasty *pastel com diablo dentro* (pastry with the devil inside) – a mix of fresh tuna, onions and tomatoes, wrapped in a pastry blended from boiled potatoes and corn flour, deep fried and served hot

Drink *grogue* (grog), the local sugar-cane spirit; *ponch* (rum, lemonade and honey), or Ceris, a decent bottled local beer

IN A WORD
Bom-dee-ah ('good morning' in Crioulo, a Portuguese-based Creole)

TRADEMARKS
Portuguese cultural legacy; volcanic islands; high literacy rate; *mornas*; *coladeiras* and *funaná* music

SURPRISES
The razo lark *(Alauda razae)* is one of the rarest birds in the world (only 250 specimens are thought to remain). Many indigenous inhabitants have left Cape Verde and now expats outnumber the islanders.

Despite the islands' name (meaning 'green cape'), when Charles Darwin visited them more than 100 years ago, he noted that such 'an utterly sterile land possesses a grandeur which more vegetation might spoil'.

— Lonely Planet's *West Africa*

6. Every man and his dog help launch a fishing boat in Sao Pedro village Jean Robert

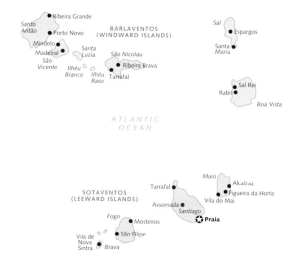

MAP REF: L,17

2. The pastel-coloured door and balcony of a house in George Town David Tomlinson

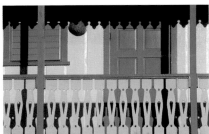

3. A magnificent green turtle finds its way through the coral labyrinth of The Maze on Grand Cayman Steve Rosenberg

4. A craft shop vendor in East End posing beneath coconut bird feeders Jeff Greenberg

The Cayman Islands are dotted with deal-cutting characters with briefcases and mobile phones, scuba divers in wetsuits and English folk checking the cricket scores. The islands are colourful: coral reefs, bright orange frogfish, sociable stingrays and reggae beats on the street. As a result of the islands' mellow charms, resorts and condos have sprung up all over. But if you want to get away from it all there are lots of places to escape satellite dishes and slickness, not least of them underwater.

BEST TIME TO VISIT
June to October to avoid the peak season

ESSENTIAL EXPERIENCES
Diving famous dive spots such as the Bloody Bay Wall and Jackson Point on the northwestern coast of Little Cayman

Strolling the mile-long trail that winds through the Queen Elizabeth II Botanic Park – lush terrain, orchids, iguanas and parrots

Treasure-hunting on Cayman Brac – spelunkers can go caving along the northern shore, where legend has it pirates used to stow away their loot

Meandering through Mastic Trail – the old-growth forest that once supplied early settlers with timber

Sightseeing on Cayman Brac, which is covered in fruit trees, orchids and cacti, and surrounded by good beaches

GETTING UNDER THE SKIN
Read *The Cayman Islands: The Beach and Beyond* by Martha K Smith – excellent for those who think being a beach bunny is boring

Listen to West Indian soca, calypso and reggae

Watch the action beneath the waves if you happen to be in the Caymans for the annual International Underwater Film Festival

Eat local specialties at the annual cooking festival, known simply as The Cook Off, in May, or the Taste of Cayman festival in June

Drink a cold beer after a day's diving, or sip on a gin and tonic

IN A WORD
Brac (actually a Gaelic word meaning bluff)

TRADEMARKS
Shipwrecks; pirate history; condos; resorts; snorkelling and diving, diving, diving

SURPRISES
The Booby Pond Nature Reserve is home to one of the hemisphere's largest breeding populations of red-footed boobies. Cayman Turtle Farm is the only one of its kind in the world. This government-run operation raises green turtles to increase their population in the wild and – slightly more disturbing – sell their meat and shells.

A number of curious fish use the Oro Verde *as their home, a phenomenon we find on wrecks around the world. Fish that know the labyrinth of a wreck are safer from predators than they would be on a reef because passing predators don't know the structure and find it strange, perhaps even threatening.*

– Lonely Planet's *Diving & Snorkeling Cayman Islands*

1. An empty jetty awaits the threatening approach a hurricane Wade Eakle

5. A studious school of schoolmaster snapper Steve Rosenberg

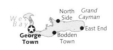

Caribbean Sea

MAP REF: L,11

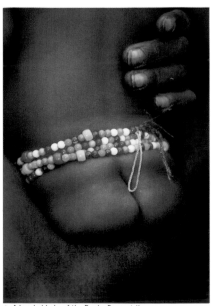

2. A beaded baby of the Baaka Pygmy tribe Martin Harvey

3. Fishermen cast their nets into the Dzanga River Martin Harvey

A country of rare natural beauty, with some of the world's most amazing wildlife, Central African Republic (CAR) nonetheless remains underdeveloped, fragmented and poverty-stricken. It's a country that has important mineral deposits and great natural resources, yet precious little of the wealth generated seeps down to the population. For centuries CAR has endured rapacity, first from invaders, later from its own leaders, and the situation doesn't look like changing any time soon. True to the spirit of 'real' Africa, however, the people of this plundered nation are open, friendly and generous.

BEST TIME TO VISIT
November to April (dry season)

ESSENTIAL EXPERIENCES
Buying ebony sculptures, leathergoods and batiks at Bangui's artisans centre

Taking a guided tour of 'Emperor' Bokassa's former palace outside the capital, past lion cages and other gruesome relics of his time in power

Spotting wildlife at St Floris and Bamingui-Bangoran parks

Visiting the spectacular Chutes de Boali (Boali Waterfalls) during the rainy season

Trekking through the Dzanga-Sangha Reserve

GETTING UNDER THE SKIN
Read *The Central African Republic: The Continent's Hidden Heart*, a social history by Thomas E O'Toole

Listen to *Aka Pygmy Music*, a Unesco recording

Eat the staples: rice, fermented cassava (manioc root) and bananas

Drink a jug of home-brewed palm or banana wine

IN A WORD
Bara ala kwe (hello in the Sango language)

TRADEMARKS
Forest elephants; lowland gorillas; Pygmies; dictators; political chaos

SURPRISES
Hunting safaris are still huge business in CAR, and have been ever since the French arrived a century ago and began parcelling up the land into hunting estates. Big-game hunting grounds near the Sudanese border were personally sponsored by former French president, Giscard d'Estaing.

The national psyche has taken a battering due to ongoing political instability in the countryside, and to protracted moves by governments and rebels to force people from their homes (an act that perpetuates the poverty). And so like all humans, the people of CAR are glad for a release. They like to drink banana and palm wine or beer and dance the gbadoumba, *mambo and* lououdou.

— Lonely Planet's *Africa*

1. An African forest elephant calf runs between two adults in Dzanga Bai clearing, Dzanga-Sangha National Park Martin Harvey

4. A young girl of the Baaka Pygmy tribe Martin Harvey

MAP REF: M,22

2. A man waits outside a mud-brick building in Gaoui village, N'Djaména Anthony Ham

3. Harvested cotton piled high in a southern Chad village
Anthony Ham

4. Herdsmen drive their sheep between Abéché and Adré in the dry season Rebecca Donaldson

With one of the most painful histories in Africa, Chad is a nation with its foundations built on conflict. The harsh climate, geographic remoteness, poor resource endowment and lack of infrastructure have combined to create a weak economy susceptible to political turmoil. There's the promise of a more optimistic future though – Chad's position as one of the world's poorest nations may change if the country's oil industry takes off.

BEST TIME TO VISIT
December to mid-February, when the days are dry and warm and the nights quite cool

ESSENTIAL EXPERIENCES
Living it up in Chad's capital, N'Djaména, with markets, bars and a thriving live-music scene

Photographing the country's best wildlife in Zakouma National Park

Chilling out in Moundou's riverside bars with an icy beer

Haggling yourself hoarse in the frontier markets of Mao

Witnessing the cultural clash of the old town of Abéché, the gateway to exploring the Sudan

Dancing the night away in Sarh, the capital of the south

GETTING UNDER THE SKIN
Read *Chad: A Nation in Search of Its Future* by Mario J Azevedo and Emmanuel U Nnadozie, presenting an economic, political and social view of the nation

Listen to the lute, a long-necked guitar popular in Chad and heard on *Africa: Anthology of the Music of Chad*

Watch *Abouna* (Our Father), a heart-rending feature filmed in Chad in which two boys search for their lost father

Eat a hearty dish of *nachif* (finely minced meat in sauce)

Drink a Gala beer in Moundou, straight from the brewery

IN A WORD
Harmattan (dry, dusty Saharan wind)

TRADEMARKS
Desert expanses; unpaved roads; unsettled relationship with Libya; impoverished citizens; mud-brick architecture

SURPRISES
To (legally) take photos in Chad, visitors need a permit from the Ministry of Information; an estimated one billion barrels of oil could be extracted from the Doba Basin

Physically you couldn't mistake Chad for anything except a Sahel country, though in the south the dusty expanses of the landscape are interspersed with incongruously green villages fed by small rivers, giving a welcome quasi-tropical break from the rigours of the road.

– Lonely Planet's *Africa on a Shoestring*

1. Children fetch water and women wash clothes as their herds drink from the waters of the lake at Adré , Ouaddai   Rebecca Donaldson

5. A young herdsman rides his water-laden donkey between Abéché and Adré   Rebecca Donaldson

MAP REF: L,22

2. El Tatio Geysers on the Chilean north plains in the light of dawn Woods Wheatcroft

3. Fishing boats packed like sardines at the harbour in Antofagasta David Ryan

4. Sisters in Temuco share a favourite doll Eric Wheater

5. The benign face of a hardcore rodeo competitor in Rancagua Brent Winebrenner

It may look like a long string bean but Chile is among South America's richest countries, both economically and culturally. For years exploited internally by unsavoury leadership and externally by the great powers of the northern continent, Chile has surfaced as vibrant, economically stable and resilient. It boasts a myriad of sights and cultures – from post-Columbian architecture to ancient sites in Easter Island – and is well recognised as a safe destination for travellers, who feel right at home thanks to the Chileans' warmth and generosity.

BEST TIME TO VISIT
September to December (spring)

ESSENTIAL EXPERIENCES
Driving a 4WD across the sand dunes of the Atacama desert

Watching cosmopolitan life in Santiago go by from the Terraza Neptuno on Cerro Santa Lucia

Skiing the slopes of the high Cordillera in Middle Chile

Standing next to one of the colossal *moai* of Easter Island (Rapa Nui), and wondering how the heck they got there

Travelling to Chile's rugged southern tip, considered to be 'the end of the world', to watch the breaching whales

GETTING UNDER THE SKIN
Read Isabel Allende's *House of the Spirits*, the story of a Chilean family depicted with modern-day realism and a dose of the supernatural

Listen to Victor Jara, murdered after Pinochet's 1973 coup, who sang about political issues of the time. Local singer Nicole has recently signed to Madonna's Latin music label.

Watch Cristián Galaz's *El Chacotero Sentimental* (The Sentimental Teaser), a popular and highly awarded film about love stories on the radio

Eat *empanadas fritas* (fried pasties with ground beef and spices)

Drink Mistral beer or try a foamy pisco sour (brandy with lemon juice, powdered sugar and egg white)

IN A WORD
Ah, que rico(a) – normally used when describing a good-tasting dish (but just as applicable when referring to a good-looking person)

TRADEMARKS
The Andean condor; cowboys; the Allendes; Pinochet; micro buses; magic realism; street vendors; great wine

SURPRISES
Reality TV is an unexpected hit in Chile; Chileans often work six days a week, but are always ready for a *carrete* (party)

Cheek kissing is an art form in Chile, often exchanged between men and women upon leaving and greeting. It's a lovely way of breaking the ice but remember if that kiss turns into something more, Chile still doesn't have a divorce law.

– Lonely Planet's *Chile & Easter Island*

1. Lush marshlands carpet the foreground of Parinacota volcano in Lauca National Park Woods Wheatcroft

6. The mysterious *moai* of Ahu Akivi wait under brooding sky on Easter Island Jan Stromme

MAP REF: S,12

2. School children prepare to clean the streets of Shenyang
Keren Su

3. The sun touches the ancient Great Wall of China and surrounding hills Nicholas Pavloff

4. A Zhuang girl works in the water-soaked rice terraces of Long Ji, Guangxi Keren Su

5. Bicycles flood Beijing's streets during rush hour
Nicholas Pavloff

1. The spice markets come to life at night in Guangzhou Ray Laskowitz

Recent times have seen a ceaseless drama of energetic development and economic contortions unfold in China. Emerging from the austerities and craziness of the Mao era, the country is now a full member of the World Trade Organization, and is home to the 2008 Beijing Olympics. Massive investment has radically improved transport quality, and travel has become steadily speedier and more comfortable. China has never been so transformed, except perhaps when the Mongols passed through with their own blueprints for change.

BEST TIME TO VISIT
March to May and September to November are best, avoiding the extremes of winter and summer

ESSENTIAL EXPERIENCES
Adding the Great Wall sites near Beijing to your have-seen must-sees

Paying a mandatory visit to the ancient Forbidden City and Summer Palace in Beijing

Parading through the Army of Terracotta Warriors, grand reminders of China's imperial past

Enjoying the more-familiar Western atmosphere of Shanghai

Chilling out in Xishuangbanna's lush, subtropical rainforest

GETTING UNDER THE SKIN
Read *The Search for Modern China* by Jonathan D Spence – probably the most readable attempt to encompass Chinese modern history in a single volume; the novels of Pearl S Buck, including *The Good Earth* and *Imperial Woman*

Listen to *Moon Rising in the Rosy Clouds*, a selection of classical and modern works featuring traditional instruments by the Chinese National Orchestra

Watch the gorgeous films of Zhang Yimou, of the 'Fifth Generation' film movement, including *Shanghai Triad* and *Raise the Red Lantern*

Eat Peking duck in Beijing; anything with four legs (bar your table) in Guangzhou

Drink *chá* (tea). As political surveillance is relaxed, China's teahouses, traditional centres of gossip and intrigue, are making a comeback

IN A WORD
Tài guì le! (too expensive!)

TRADEMARKS
Pandas; unchecked development; students practising English on tourists; edgy modern art scene; Tiananmen Square; noodles; the Great Wall

SURPRISES
Not all Chinese 'look' Chinese: the majority, Han Chinese (92%), are only one of 56 officially recognised ethnic groups in China

China has a thriving music industry, but has been sluggish at developing a market for Western music – largely due to limited airings of tame Western songs on the radio. Generations of Chinese are still convinced that Western music is the Carpenters, Richard Clayderman, Kenny G and Lionel Richie.

– Lonely Planet's *China*

6. Monks ascend stairs in the Dongcheng district of Beijing Phil Weymouth

MAP REF: J,30

2. Bathers transform themselves into living statues in the mud of the Volcán de Lodo El Totumo near Cartagena Krzysztof Dydyński

3. Gruesome fangs bared, a leering megalithic statue guards the entrance to San Agustín Archaeological Park Jane Sweeney

4. High-stepping street performers entertain crowds in Plaza de Bolivar, Bogotá Krzysztof Dydyński

1. The primary colours and vacant streets of Raquira lend this important craft centre the atmosphere of a model village Krzysztof Dydyński

For most travellers, Colombia is unknown territory – a place of cocaine barons, guerrillas and mysterious lost cities. It is the land of Gabriel García Márquez and his *One Hundred Years of Solitude* – a tale as magical as the country itself. Far from being a place to avoid, complex and hospitable Colombia offers some of South America's most varied landscapes, flora and fauna. As you travel through this diverse country, you'll discover a changing panorama of climate, architecture, topography, wildlife, crafts and music.

BEST TIME TO VISIT
January to March (the dry season)

ESSENTIAL EXPERIENCES
Visiting Cartagena – a living museum of Spanish colonial architecture

Beachcombing at Parque Nacional Tayrona, on the Caribbean coast

Photographing the enigmatic stone statues at San Agustín – a pre-Hispanic ceremonial funeral site

Hanging out in the great cosmopolitan metropolis of Bogotá

Hiking to Ciudad Perdida, one of the greatest pre-Hispanic cities found in the Americas, hidden in a lush rainforest

GETTING UNDER THE SKIN
Read *One Hundred Years of Solitude* by Nobel prize winner Gabriel García Márquez, or anything by José Asunción Silva, perhaps the country's best poet

Listen to Colombia's most famous musical export Shakira, whose album *Laundry Service* stormed charts in 2002. For some traditional Afro-Caribbean tunes check out *Totó La Momposina*.

Watch *Ilona Arrives with the Rain* or *Time Out* by Colombian film director Sergio Cabrera

Eat *ajiaco* (soup made with chicken and potato); or, for the more adventurous, *hormiga culona* (a dish unique to Santander consisting largely of fried ants)

Drink coffee, the number one drink – *tinto* (a small cup of black coffee) is served everywhere. Other coffee drinks are *perico or pintado*, a small milk coffee, and *café con leche*, which is larger and uses more milk.

IN A WORD
Chévere (cool)

TRADEMARKS
Coffee; Gabriel García Márquez; emeralds; lost cities; El Dorado; football

SURPRISES
Colombia claims to have the highest number of species of plants and animals per unit area of any country in the world; Laguna de Guatavita, the sacred lake and ritual centre of the indigenous Muiscas, is where the myth of El Dorado originated

Trying to adapt to the generations-long violence, many Colombians have developed a sort of siege mentality. In cities particularly, children and teenagers are often under strict supervision, residential buildings have 24-hour security guards and sniffer dogs are omnipresent. Many people will travel intercity only under the umbrella of the caravanas turísticas organised during holiday peaks (which involve placing an enormous number of soldiers along major roads in order to discourage robberies and kidnappings).

– Lonely Planet's *South America*

MAP REF: N,12

5. The spiny trunks of Colombia's national tree, La Palma de Cera, protrude from a hillside in Quindío Krzysztof Dydyński

2. The crater lake of Dziani Dzaha, Mayotte Olivier Cirendini

3. A man displays a rural mosque made of corrugated iron
Christine Osborne

4. Markets burst with colour on Grande Comore island
Thor Vaz de Leon

5. Children share a joke in Moroni Thor Vaz de Leon

COMOROS & MAYOTTE

CAPITAL MORONI (C), MAMOUTZOU (M) POPULATION 632,948 (C), 178,437 (M) AREA 2170 SQ KM (C), 374 SQ KM (M) OFFICIAL LANGUAGES ARABIC, FRENCH (C), FRENCH (M)

1. A Muslim boy catches the evening rays outside a mosque in Mitsamiouli Christine Osborne

6. A Comoran woman with a painted face Thor Vaz de Leon

Studding the Indian Ocean between the African mainland and Madagascar, the islands of Comoros and Mayotte offer an amazing diversity of people and cultures. Despite a succession of political coups and civilian riots, the islands boast cobblestoned medinas, ports bustling with dhows, tropical moonrises over white-sand beaches and blazing ocean sunsets that set the sky on fire. All this is wrapped in the fragrant aroma of ylang-ylang oil, African warmth, French chic and Arabic aesthetics and a colourful history of sultans, eloping princesses and plantation owners.

BEST TIME TO VISIT
May to October (dry season) – or in the 15th and 16th centuries when Shirazi Arab royal clans arrived building mosques and royal houses

ESSENTIAL EXPERIENCES
Discovering the coral reefs and white sandy beaches at Chiroroni

Breathing in the scents of the ylang-ylang distillery at Bamboa

Walking through the crumbling, decaying palaces at Hari ya Moudji

Wandering the maze-like lanes of the medina at Moroni

Fishing, diving and boating in the waters of Mayotte

Finding the perfect hand-crafted souvenir at Mitsoudjé

Green sea turtle–watching at Chissioua Ouénéfou

Hiking past majestic waterfalls and beautiful deserted beaches

Swimming in the pristine waters on Anjouan

GETTING UNDER THE SKIN
Read *The Comoros Islands: Struggle Against Dependency in the Indian Ocean*, by Malyn Newitt, which outlines the turbulent recent history of the region

Listen to a performance by the Maalesh Group, a group of musicians led by Comoran born Maalesh who sing songs of injustice and hope in Comoran, Swahili and Arabic

Eat *langouste à la vanille* (lobster cooked in vanilla sauce) or rice and meat infused with cardamom, vanilla, cinnamon, cloves and nutmeg, or fish with coconut

IN A WORD
Habari or *salama* ('Hello' in Comoran)

TRADEMARKS
Magnificent blue-green clear ocean waters; fields of ylang-ylang, jasmine, cassis and orange flower; blazing sunsets; long, white beaches; beautiful rainforests; political turmoil; excellent seafood; mosques; scuba diving; big-game fishing

SURPRISES
Swahili-inspired architecture with arcades; balustrades and carved wooden latticework; Comoran women with faces applied with a yellowish paste of sandalwood and coral *(m'sidzanou)*

A unique Comoran tradition is the grande marriage *which translates as, yes, the Big Wedding. But we're talking more than just yards of frou-frou and taffeta, and a ten-tier wedding cake here. We're talking big. We're talking bigger than Ben Hur. It's usually a prearranged union between an older man and a younger woman, and the man must pay for the two- to nine-day public festivity* (toirab) *that caters for the entire village.*

— World Guide, www.lonelyplanet.com

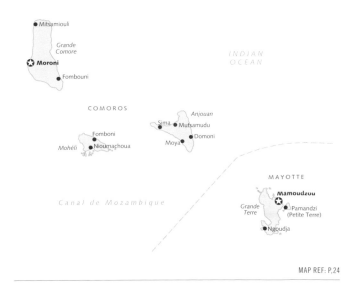

MAP REF: P.24

2. A bread vendor of Kinshasa plies his trade on the streets
Peter Andrews

3. Families get together to collect water during a power failure in the capital Peter Andrews

1. Hands free, a pipe-smoking woman trudges home in the foothills of Sabinyo volcano Martin Harvey

Almost as large as Western Europe, the Democratic Republic of Congo is a sprawling mass of rainforest, fast-running rivers, red clay and dust – the epitome of Joseph Conrad's *Heart of Darkness*. Formerly called Zaïre, and now often shortened to DRC, it remains intoxicatingly mysterious and largely cut off to visitors, thanks to civil war, lamentable lack of development, and naturally impenetrable terrain. The country clings to a fragile ceasefire after decades of brutal civil war and neglect, but if the situation stabilises it has the potential to reclaim its mantle as Africa's most adventurous destination.

BEST TIME TO VISIT
December to February (north of the equator), April to October (south of the equator)

ESSENTIAL EXPERIENCES
Experiencing hectic, confusing and colourful Kinshasa

Playing with bonobos (pygmy chimps) and enjoying the lakes at Chutes de Lukia

Perusing the fish market at Kinkole – constructed by Mobutu to honour the country's fishermen

Travelling by barge from Kinshasa to Kisangani along the Congo River – the real highway of Central Africa

GETTING UNDER THE SKIN
Read about Mobutu's looting as a form of government in Michaela Wrong's *In The Footsteps of Mr Kurtz*; or *The Catastrophist* by Ronan Bennett, a novel built around Patrice Lumumba, the charismatic leader of the fight for independence from Belgium

Listen to the *soukous* of Africa's Elvis Presley, Papa Wemba

Watch Ngangura Mweze's *Life is Rosy* – a celebration of Congolese culture and folklore, starring Papa Wemba

Eat barbecued goat and manioc from street vendors, and *liboke* (fish stewed in manioc leaves)

Drink beer from a roadside stall

IN A WORD
Mbóte (hello)

TRADEMARKS
Virgin jungle; bustling rivers; primates; political and military strife; *Heart of Darkness*

SURPRISES
Bonobos are the closest relatives to humans; the current civil war being fought between rival Congolese militias (the proxy armies of Uganda and Rwanda) has caused the death of an estimated 2.5 million people

Worshipping is a noisy business. A neighbourhood is far more likely to complain when a new church moves in (complete with sound system and huge speakers) than a brothel, which at least shuts down at 4am on a Sunday morning. Devout worship at one of the country's many imported churches – be it Protestant, Catholic or evangelical – is invariably accompanied by a strong belief in fetishisme *or witchcraft. The two often meet in exorcisms, which are practically a national pastime and can be seen on TV, acted out like an alternative soap opera. It makes for surprisingly compelling viewing.*

– Lonely Planet's *Africa*

4. Women gathering firewood form a Congolese congo line Gallo Images

MAP REF: O,22

2. Homeward bound, villagers pass beneath the menacing Nyiragongo volcano Ulli Michel

3. A mother prepares the morning meal for her family in the town of Goma Jacky Naegelen

4. Children at play in an orphanage at Minova George Mulala
LEFT 1. A Kota man sports a striking blue paint job Daniel Lainé

The Republic of Congo is a former French colony on the west Atlantic coast of central Africa. The countryside around Brazzaville is all rolling hills and lush green trees; further north, there's bright orange earth and untamed tropical rainforest bristling with wildlife – the Congo boasts Africa's largest lowland gorilla population. After three devastating civil wars in less than a decade, this is a nation of people eager for a laugh and luckily, as the country slowly regains its stability, there's something to smile about.

BEST TIME TO VISIT
June to September, when the season is dry and temperatures uniform

ESSENTIAL EXPERIENCES
Being inspired by the intoxicating blend of Congolese food, culture and music

Trawling Brazzaville's colourful markets where you can pick up useful items such as caterpillars, bats, palm wine and aphrodisiacs

Eating croissants in a Brazzaville café while watching water hyacinths float down the Congo River and black marketeers paddle their pirogues (traditional canoes)

Retaining your cool after spotting a lowland gorilla at Odzala National Park

Playing a rowdy game of *babyfoot* (table football) with friendly Congolese locals

GETTING UNDER THE SKIN
Read *Congo Journey* by naturalist Redmond O'Hanlon, who explores the swamplands of the Congo with descriptive style

Listen to *Brazzaville*, an atmospheric compilation of jazz, samba and soul fusion tracks

Watch *Congo*, directed by Frank Marshall and based on a Michael Crichton novel about an unknown race of killer apes – certainly not to be taken seriously

Eat *maboke*, river fish cooked with chilli and wrapped in manioc (cassava) leaves

Drink a huge bottle of refreshing Ngok ('crocodile') beer

IN A WORD
Bonjour (hello)

TRADEMARKS
A nation of lively, enthusiastic conversationalists; riotous colour and glorious chaos; beaches; Denis Sassou Nguesso; gorillas, chimps and all things monkey; baguettes; a country in recovery; candlelit night markets; Congo River; elephants; civil war; towering office blocks housing foreign oil companies

SURPRISES
Even Brazzavillois don't know the street names of their city! Instead, everyone makes reference to landmarks

Dress and manners are a sacred cow in the Congolese psyche and you will be judged on what you wear. A Congolese man will sleep on the floor rather than buy a mattress if it means he can save enough for a three-piece suit with hand stitching on the lapels... If you are lucky enough to be invited into a Congolese home, take a carton of Spanish table wine. It's champagne to the Congolese and will be seen as properly respectful in a country obsessed with manners.

– Lonely Planet's *Africa*

MAP REF: 0,21

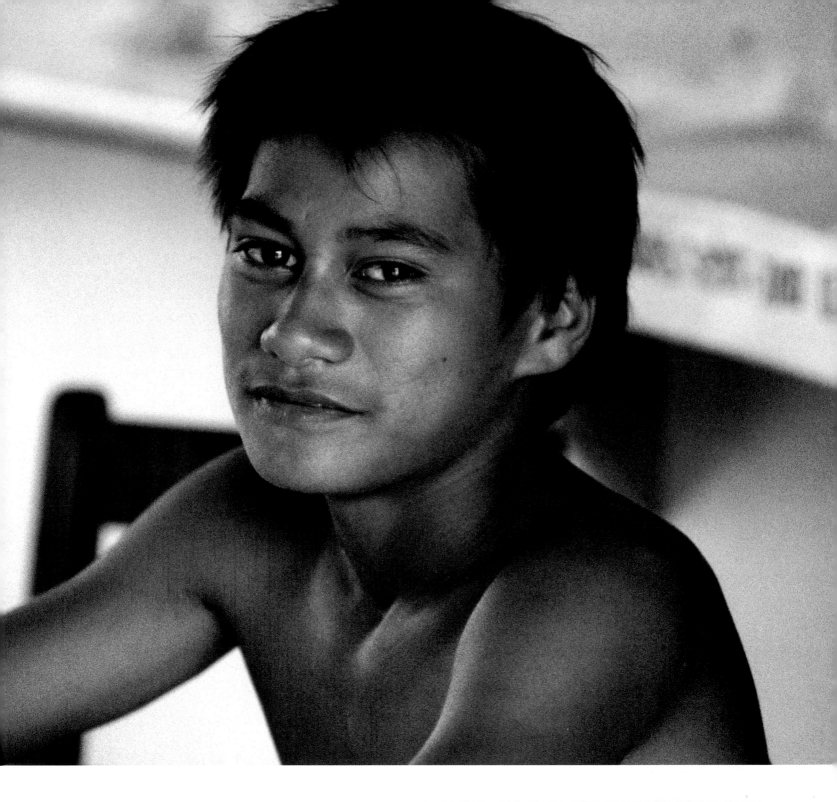

2. The tropical frangipani flower, native to the Cook Islands
Jean-Bernard Carillet

3. Flower-clad school children from Rarotonga Jean-Bernard Carillet

4. A cloud hovers over the island of Rarotonga and Muri lagoon Manfred Gottschalk

1. A student on Rarotonga Dallas Stribley

Wafer-thin cays and farflung atolls, blue lagoons and superb reef snorkelling, white-sand beaches and verdant volcanic mountains, a slow pace and friendly people – what's not to like about the Cook Islands? Lascivious dancing and beer bashes in the bush have survived years of missionary zeal. Rarotonga, the gorgeous main island, has been a Maori hang-out for at least 1500 years and it's easy to see why. Get yourself stranded on an outer island and hope your return-trip freighter doesn't come back any time soon.

BEST TIME TO VISIT
April to November (the dry season)

ESSENTIAL EXPERIENCES
Hiking the lush, craggy mountains of Rarotonga

Taking a dip in the turquoise lagoon of Aitutaki

Dancing and feasting the night away at an 'island night' theme party on Rarotonga or Aitutaki

Whale-watching from any of the main islands

Spelunking the caves of 'Atiu, Ma'uke, Mitiaro and Mangaia

Photographing the island from Rangimotia, the highest point on Mangaia

GETTING UNDER THE SKIN
Read *An Island to Oneself,* the account of hermit Tom Neale, who lived on Suwarrow Atoll

Listen to *Drums, Songs and Chants of the Cook Islands,* a great sampler of local music

Watch *The Other Side of Heaven,* a delightful coming-of-age tale that was mostly filmed on Rarotonga

Eat island fare such as *ika mata* (raw fish in coconut sauce) or *anga kuru akaki ia* (stuffed breadfruit)

Drink at a *tumunu* (or bush beer-drinking session), akin to the ancient Polynesian *kava*-drinking ceremonies in Fiji or Samoa

IN A WORD
Kia orana! (may you live long!) – a greeting

TRADEMARKS
Saucy traditional dancing; pandanus-thatched roofs; rich Maori culture; deserted atolls ripe for diving; breadfruit served at every meal; tax haven for well-tanned fat cats

SURPRISES
The stunning black pearl jewellery for sale; soulful Christian hymns sung in churches everywhere

Beneath a Western veneer, layers of Cook Islands culture survive. Every native Cook Islander is part of a family clan, and each clan is connected to the ancient system of chiefs. Rarotonga's six ariki *clans are based on the original land divisions from when Maori first arrived on the island many centuries ago.*

— Lonely Planet's *South Pacific*

5. A local fisherman displays his catch on the island of Aitutaki Peter Hendrie

Pukapuka

Nassau

Northern Group

SOUTH PACIFIC OCEAN

Aitutaki

Mitiaro

Southern Group

'Atiu Ma'uke

Rarotonga Avarua

Mangaia

MAP REF: Q,3

2. A carnival-coloured keel-billed toucan Alfredo Maiquez

3. A white-faced capuchin monkey reclines on a branch in his rainforest home Ralph Lee Hopkins

4. Mother and child walk past a run-down wooden church near Puerto Limón Eric Wheater

5. A family gather in the doorway of their home in Fray Casiano Eric Wheater

1. Three boys playing with a football on the pavement outside a row of painted buildings, Puerto Limón
Eric Wheater

For decades, Costa Rica was a forgotten backwater, a country so laconic it couldn't be bothered having an army, even though it was sandwiched between war-torn Nicaragua and Canal-plagued Panama. Then North American retirees discovered its charms and its *poco a poco* ('little by little') life style, and Costa Rica became hot property. With its luxuriant rainforests, pristine white beaches, diverse wildlife, to-die-for coffee, relaxed hospitality and full-on eco-tourist trade, Costa Rica is definitely one of the destinations *de jour*.

BEST TIME TO VISIT
December to April (the dry season)

ESSENTIAL EXPERIENCES
Soaring across the jungle canopy on a flying fox at Monteverde

Taking time out to sit and ponder the majestic rainforest at Parque Nacional Manuel Antonio

Making a nocturnal visit to Arenal volcano, followed by a soak in a hot spa

Learning to surf at Witch's Rock

Ignoring the bus and doing the Fortuna to Saint Elena route by jeep and horseback

GETTING UNDER THE SKIN
Read *Costa Rica: A Traveler's Literary Companion*, 26 short stories that capture the soul of the county

Listen to *Costa Rica: Calypso*, happy calypso tunes for the road, from rootsy trad to pop

Watch *1492: Conquest of Paradise*. This Hollywood version of Colombus' discovery of the New Americas was always going to be problematic – a Frenchman playing an Italian-born employee of the Spanish army interacting with Mayans is asking for trouble. The location shots are stunning though.

Eat *la olla*, a stew of potatoes, beef, onions, maize, beans and tomatoes

Drink coffee – Costa Rica is possibly the only country in the world where even a take-away coffee in a Styrofoam cup from a fast-food burger joint tastes like ambrosia

IN A WORD
Pura vida (literally 'pure life', a national expression that sums up the desire to live the best and most pure existence)

TRADEMARKS
Dripping rainforests; toucans and macaws; erupting volcanoes; La Negrita (or the Black Madonna); dead-keen soccer fans; foaming waterfalls; the aroma of coffee

SURPRISES
A former president (Oscar Arias Sánchez) is the winner of a Nobel Peace Prize; there are great surfing beaches, but hordes of sharks

Apart from hiking and camping in rainforests and mountains and on beaches, you can snorkel on tropical reefs, surf the best waves in South America, and raft some of the most thrilling white water in the tropics. Pristine rivers tumble down the lower slopes of the mountains and the riverbanks are clothed with curtains of rainforest – a truly unique white-water experience.

– Lonely Planet's *Costa Rica*

6. The dry bed of El Limbo lagoon in Parque Nacional Santa Rosa Luke Hunter

MAP REF: M,11

2. Women enter a small *banco* (baked mud) mosque in Kong Craig Pershouse

3. A young girl carries her baby sister in Sassandra Craig Pershouse

4. A woman carries her load past the mosque in Korhogo Craig Pershouse

5. Fishermen mend their nets on a lazy afternoon in Sassandra Craig Pershouse

LEFT 1. Two performers from La Troupe Artistique Sangbe in Grand Bassam Craig Pershouse

Côte d'Ivoire's most powerful attraction is its people, so if you're interested in African history, art or music, this is the place to be. There's also a whole lot of physical beauty, from towering mountains to fishing villages. For many years Côte d'Ivoire was the jewel of West Africa. Its strong economy attracted thousands of workers from neighbouring countries, and sizeable French and Lebanese communities established themselves in Abidjan. In recent times, the country has been rocked by huge debts and a military coup.

BEST TIME TO VISIT
November to February

ESSENTIAL EXPERIENCES
Exploring Grand Bassam's faded colonial charm

Experiencing the warmth and friendliness of Ivoirians

Taking in a live performance of exhilarating music and masked dance in the Man area

Goggling at Yamoussoukro's colossal basilica

Soaking up the sun at rainforest-clad beaches, such as Monogaga, Grand Béréby or Grand Lahou

Communing with chimpanzees in the Parc National de Taï or with hippos at Parc National de la Comoë

GETTING UNDER THE SKIN
Read Bernard Dadié's *Climbié*, an autobiographical account of his childhood, or Maurice Bandaman's novel *Le Fils de la Femme Mâle*

Listen to *Apartheid is Nazism* by Côte d'Ivoire's best-known reggae star, Alpha Blondy

Watch *Visages des Femmes* (Faces of Women), directed by Côte d'Ivoire's Désiré Ecaré

Eat *kedjenou* (chicken, or sometimes guineafowl, simmered with vegetables in a mild sauce), or snack on *aloco* (ripe bananas fried with chilli in palm oil – it's a popular street food)

Drink *bangui* (a local palm wine), or try it distilled as *koutoukou* (a skull-shattering spirit)

IN A WORD
I-ni-cheh. I-kah-kéné ('Hello. How are you?' in Dioula, the market language)

TRADEMARKS
Violence-plagued elections; eating out in *maquis*; coups; Korhogo cloth, Dan masks

SURPRISES
Côte d'Ivoire lost 42% of its forest and woodland from 1977 to 1987 – the highest rate of loss in the world; Côte d'Ivoire is the largest producer of cocoa in the world

Every day some 375 fanicos (washermen), mostly Burkinabé and none Ivoirian, jam together in the middle of a small stream near the Parc du Banco, frantically rubbing clothes on huge stones held in place by old car tyres. Afterwards, they spread the clothes over rocks and grass for at least 500m (never getting them mixed up) and then iron them. Any washer not respecting the strict rules imposed by the washers' trade union, which allocates positions, is immediately excluded. The soap is black and sold by women who make it from palm oil.

– Lonely Planet's *West Africa*

MAP REF: N,19

2. A view of the terracotta rooftops of Dubrovnik Jon Davison

3. Fans of the all-over tan, sunbathers in Cavtat set to work on their complexions Jon Davison

4. An old sea dog presides over the harbour in Split Wayne Walton

5. The famed walls of Lovrjenac Fort, Dubrovnik, newly repaired since the Balkan conflict Wayne Walton

6. The crenellated walls of the 11th-century church of St Nicholas in Nin, rise imposingly above an ancient burial mound Wayne Walton

LEFT 1. The sun comes out for washing day in the old town of Rovinj, Istria Damien Simonis

Croatia has the best that Eastern Europe has to offer in a nutshell: forested hills, rustic villages, idyllic islands, walled medieval cities, Roman ruins, Adriatic coastline and a vibrant culture. Sitting on the fault line where Western and Eastern Europe meet, Croatia has weathered its share of difficulties, but has absorbed Latin, Venetian, Hapsburg and Slavic influences to create its own distinctive whole.

BEST TIME TO VISIT
April to September for the good weather – or the 15th century in independent Ragusa (Dubrovnik)

ESSENTIAL EXPERIENCES
Wandering through the walled medieval city of Dubrovnik – a rhapsody in limestone, cobbled streets and terracotta tiles

Fossicking in Split, a city built around Roman Emperor Diocletian's palace

Sunning yourself in the Venetian harbour town of Hvar, where the sun shines 300 days a year

Visiting the country's surprisingly cosmopolitan capital, Zagreb

Watching the tumbling cascades at Plitvice Lakes National Park

GETTING UNDER THE SKIN
Read Rebecca West's *Black Lamb and Grey Falcon*, a classic account of a 1930s trip through the region; Slavenka Drakulić's *Café Europa*, an insightful series of essays on Croatia and Eastern Europe

Watch *How the War Started on My Island* by Vinko Brešan, a contemporary black comedy

Eat *čevapčići* (grilled, spiced meatballs), a Balkan classic; *pašticada* (beef stuffed and roasted in wine and spices)

Drink *šljivovica*, plum brandy with a kick; wines from Istria or Kvarner

IN A WORD
Na zdravlje (to your health)

TRADEMARKS
Untouched fishing villages on the Dalmatian coast; European café culture; terracotta rooftops and baroque cathedrals; paprika and garlic; crystal-clear seas and beachside promenades; al fresco dining – meat on the grill

SURPRISES
Shakespeare's *Twelfth Night* is set in Dalmatia; cravats and ballpoint pens were invented by Croatians; there are few spotted dogs in Dalmatia

The Kvarner coast and its offshore islands are a microcosm of the many influences that have formed Croatian culture. Rijeka, Croatia's third largest city, owes its architecture to Hungary, which ruled the city in the late 19th century. The opening of a rail link to Vienna in 1857 made Opatija the resort of choice for the Austrian aristocracy. Venetian influence pervades the islands of Cres, Lošinj and Rab, while Krk was the seat of Croatia's native nobility, the Frankopan dukes.

– Lonely Planet's *Croatia*

MAP REF: H,21

2. Trinidad street scene, Sancti Spiritus Doug McKinlay

3. A simple advertisement for Cuban rum adorns a wall in Old Havana Martin Lladó

4. Dressed to impress, two gentlemen hit the streets of Old Havana Dominic Bonuccelli

5. A gracefully decaying car blends into the peeling wall of a colonial building in Havana Alfredo Maiquez

6. In the late afternoon, a denizen of the capital takes time out Martin Lladó
LEFT 1. Fidelity to Fidel – a Havana local smokes on his doorstep Doug McKinlay

In an amazing balancing act, Cuba is at once poor and broken, and rich and thriving. From the beat of the music echoing through towns and villages to the hustle of Havana's glorious, crumbling streets, Cuba challenges and enchants all who venture in. Its political isolation has prevented a tourist flood, and locals are sincerely friendly to visitors. While Fidel's infrastructure has seen better decades and the food is, well, best not spoken about, the last great bastion of communism enchants with its intoxicating human spirit. Or was that the rum?

BEST TIME TO VISIT
November to May to avoid the heat and hurricanes – or before Fidel goes, and whenever you want to shake your booty

ESSENTIAL EXPERIENCES
Walking along Havana's Malecón on a warm night

Pretending you can salsa in a nightclub

Taking a photo of a '50s Cadillac on your first day

Speaking Spanish to the locals – even if you can't!

Taking in a baseball game in Cuba's Major League – Go Industriales!

Smoking a cigar…just because

Drinking *mojitos*…just because

GETTING UNDER THE SKIN
Read *Trading with the Enemy: A Yankee Travels Through Castro's Cuba* by Tom Miller – it's a rich feast of Cuban lore, and a great travel book about Cuba

Listen to Polo Montañez's *Guajiro Natural*. Montañcz died tragically in 2002, but the raspy, mellow strains of this album will leave you feeling full of life

Watch everyone's favourite, *Fresa y Chocolate*, 1995's hit Havana comedy directed by Tomás Gutiérrez and Juan Carlos Tabío

Eat something home-cooked, especially an *ajiaco* stew, featuring potatoes, meat, plantains, corn, old beer and anything else lying around

Drink a minty, sweet rum *mojito* as the sun goes down

IN A WORD
No es fácil ('it's not easy', applied to virtually everything)

TRADEMARKS
Cigars; communists; rum; salsa; Fidel; poverty; sex; the *Buena Vista Social Club*

SURPRISES
Even if you *know* the food is bad, it's actually much worse; many people actually like communism; everything is priced in US dollars, and more expensive than you'd think; TV soap operas are the biggest show in town

Cubans drive how they want, where they want. It seems chaotic at first, but has its rhythm. Seatbelts are supposedly required and maximum speed limits are technically 50km per hour in the city and 90km per hour on highways, but some cars can't even go that fast and those that can go faster still.

– Lonely Planet's *Cuba*

MAP REF: L.11

2. The Byzantine stones of Kantara Castle gaze from the Kyrenia mountain range Paul Hellander

3. Limpid waters reveal a wealth of gleaming pebbles near Aphrodite's Rock Chris Christo

4. Distinguished only by its architecture, a mosque stands adjacent to a Christian orthodox church Izzet Keribar

1. A goat herder near Agia Marina protects his flock with a big stick and an intent look Stella Hellander

Culturally European but geographically almost Middle Eastern, Cyprus is a blend of Turkish and Greek, Muslim and Christian influences, viewed through the perspective of 9000 years of constant invasion. Crusader castles rub shoulders with ancient vineyards, frescoed monasteries overlook citrus orchards, and sandy, sun-soaked feet tread Roman mosaic floors. Politically, Cyprus has remained a divided island since 1974 and, although unity is now on the EU's agenda, the wounds caused by 30 years of division will not be easily healed.

BEST TIME TO VISIT
April to May and September to October to avoid the heat and crowds

ESSENTIAL EXPERIENCES
Visiting the Byzantine frescoed churches of the Troödos Mountains
Cycling through the almost-deserted Karpas Peninsula
Wandering around the castles of the Girne (Kyrenia) Range
Skin diving at Cape Greco and swimming at deserted beaches
Hiking the Mt Olympus trails in the Troödos Mountains

GETTING UNDER THE SKIN
Read *Journey Into Cyprus* by Colin Thubron, a classic Cyprus travelogue

Listen to Pelagia Kyriakou's *Paralimnitika* recordings, a superb collection of Cypriot demotic songs from the beginning of the 19th century and sung in the original Cypriot dialect

Watch *The Wing of the Fly*, directed by Hristos Siopahas, or *The Slaughter of the Cock*, directed by Andreas Pantazis – both deal with the Turkish invasion of Cyprus in 1974

Eat *kleftiko* (oven-baked lamb) or *mezedes* (dips, salads and other appetisers)

Drink *raki* (Turkish) or *zivania* (Greek), the local firewater made from distilling the leftovers of grape crushings

IN A WORD
Yasas (hello) for Greek Cypriots; *merhaba* (hello) for Turkish Cypriots

TRADEMARKS
Strong, thick coffee; Turkish and British military camps; British pubs at Agia Napa; the Green Line; citrus orchards

SURPRISES
Richard the Lionheart married Berengaria at Lemesos Castle in the 12th century; there was once a rail system in Cyprus that ran the length of the island

The bouzouki, which you will hear all over Cyprus, is a mandolin-like instrument similar to the Turkish saz and baglama. It is one of the main instruments of rembetika music – the Greek equivalent of American blues. The name rembetika may come from the Turkish word rembet, which means outlaw. Opinions differ as to the origins of rembetika, but it is probably a hybrid of several different types of music. One source was the music that emerged in the 1870s in the 'low-life' cafés, called tekedes (hashish dens).

– Lonely Planet's *Cyprus*

5. We all knead each other – a family gets together to make bread Stella Hellander

MAP REF: J,23

2. Snow and silence fall in a bright corner of Český Krumlov
Simon Bracken

3. Speed and light streak the ultra-modern Můstek station,
Nové Město, Prague   Richard Nebeský

4. A rainbow emerges from a gilded field of mustard seed
plants   Richard Nebeský

5. Roof and façade of the Town Hall, Prague   Jonathan Smith

1. Under the baleful gaze of vigilant statues, early-morning commuters pace across Charles Bridge, Prague
Martin Moos

6. Heavenly light illuminates a pub in Kampa, Prague   Richard Nebeský

Most visitors to the Czech Republic spend their time in its near-mythical capital, Prague. Granted, the Golden City does exert a siren pull, and you could spend endless hours there – roaming through the maze of its Old Town, discovering its back-street secrets, getting to know each stone saint on the Charles Bridge. But don't miss out on the rest of the country, with its stately old spa towns, fanciful castles, spruce forests and subterranean caves. The Czech Republic is a feast of art, history and heart-attack food – abandon your vowels and tuck in.

BEST TIME TO VISIT
April to June (spring) – or during the halcyon Prague Spring of 1968 (preferably before the Soviet tanks rolled in)

ESSENTIAL EXPERIENCES
Getting up early to cross Prague's Charles Bridge at dawn

Drinking *slivovice* at an all-night bonfire party on the Day of the Witches

Hiking through the crenellated sandstone pinnacles of the Adršpach-Teplice Rocks

Contemplating your mortality under the bone chandelier in the Ossuary Chapel of All Saints in Sedlec

Catching a classical music concert in the underground caves of the Moravian Karst

GETTING UNDER THE SKIN
Read Milan Kundera's *The Book of Laughter and Forgetting*, in which the absurdity of the communist era is deftly woven with themes of love, memory and music; or Bruce Chatwin's *Utz*, a novella about porcelain and alchemy set in Prague's Jewish quarter

Listen to Dvořák, everyone's favourite Czech classical composer; or *The Plastic People of the Universe*, the psychedelic but oppressed heroes of the Prague Spring

Watch *Divided We Fall*, Jan Hrebejk's uneasily funny film about a Czech couple who hide a Jewish man in their apartment during the Nazi occupation; Jan Sverák's *Kolya*, about an aging Czech musician who has to care for a small Russian boy

Eat *sma ený květák s bramborem* (cauliflower fried in breadcrumbs, served with boiled potatoes and tartar sauce); *svíčková na smetaně* (beef in cream sauce with dumplings and lemon or cranberries)

Drink Budvar (the original version of Budweiser and one of the most famous of the Czech Republic's famous beers) or absinthe (very green – very mean)

IN A WORD
Ahoj (hello, informal)

TRADEMARKS
Beer; castles; crystal; dumplings; folk art; acid rain; American students; impenetrable language

SURPRISES
The word 'defenestration' is derived from incidents in Czech history where Catholic and Hapsburg councillors were flung out of windows during disputes in Prague; Czechs love the sun; it *is* possible to eat vegetarian

…it's not just about sights, sounds and splendour. It's also about people, and it's about connection. Strike up a conversation at a bar (over a pint of the best beer in the world) and you'll find an intelligent, engaging and friendly person at the other end.

— Lonely Planet's *Czech & Slovak Republics*

MAP REF: G,21

107

2. The dim light of streetlamps glistens on the dark surface of a canal in Nyhavn, Copenhagen Jon Davison

3. A mantle of frost transforms a woodland in northwest Zealand into a frozen tableau Martín Lladó

4. Yellow flowers blaze in a dazzling rape seed plantation in west Zealand Martín Lladó

5. Shielding the sun from his eyes, a bewildered tourist inadvertently salutes an indifferent Royal Palace Guard, Copenhagen Jon Davison

1. The Tilsandede Kirke (Buried Church) smoulders in the glow of sunset in Skagen, North Jutland
Jon Davison

Cute and compact, Denmark is a harmonious blend of the old and the new. Ancient castles and Viking ring forts exist side-by-side with lively cities and the sleekest modern design you'll ever see. Over a millennium ago Danish Vikings brought the country to the world's attention when they took to the seas and ravaged half of Europe, but these days they've filed down their horns and forged a society that stands as a benchmark of civilisation, with progressive policies, widespread tolerance and a liberal social-welfare system.

BEST TIME TO VISIT
May and June or AD 900 if pillaging is your thing

ESSENTIAL EXPERIENCES
Knocking back a local beer while enjoying a summer evening on Nyhavn canal

Letting your hair down at northern Europe's largest rock festival, Roskilde Festival

Being charmed by the cobbled streets and well-preserved buildings of Ribe, Denmark's oldest town

Building (and destroying) your own mini-empire at Legoland

Dipping a toe at Skagen, where the waters of Kattegat and Skagerrak clash

Cycling from end to end of this flat landscape on the extensive bike routes

Exploring a Viking ring fortress at Trelleborg

GETTING UNDER THE SKIN
Read *Miss Smilla*'s *Feeling for Snow* by Peter Høeg, a suspense set in Copenhagen; or for a change of pace, Kierkegaard's philosophical works or Hans Christian Andersen's fairy tales

Listen to the pop of Aqua, dance beats of Junior Senior, or raw rock of D-A-D

Watch anything by Lars Von Trier, particularly *The Idiots*, a black comedy set in Denmark

Eat *smørrebrød* (the famous Danish open-faced sandwich), *frikadeller* (Danish meatballs of pork mince, served with potatoes and gravy), *sild* (pickled herring), and of course Danish pastries, known locally as *wienerbrød* (literally, Vienna bread)

Drink *øl* (beer), or *akvavit* (schnapps) - but you have to swallow it in one swig

IN A WORD
Det var hyggeligt! (that was cosy!)

TRADEMARKS
Butter cookies; brightly coloured plastic bricks; social progressiveness; 'The Little Mermaid'; Bang & Olufsen stereos; Royal Copenhagen plates and Georg Jensen jewellery; Arne Jacobsen's egg chair

SURPRISES
Denmark has virtually no downhill skiing because its highest 'mountain' is 147m; not all Danes are blond and blue-eyed

Perhaps nothing captures the Danish perspective more than the concept of hygge *which, roughly translated, means cosy and snug. It implies shutting out the turmoil and troubles of the outside world and striving instead for a warm, intimate mood. Hygge affects how Danes approach many aspects of their personal lives, from the design of their homes to their fondness for small cafés and pubs. There's no greater compliment that a Dane can give their host than to thank them for a cosy evening.*

— Lonely Planet's *Denmark*

6. Mummy gets delivered to the headquarters of a major travel agency in Copenhagen Martin Lladó

MAP REF: G,21

2. Unforgiving terrain surrounding the Bay of Ghoubbet shimmers in the midday heat Frances Linzee Gordon

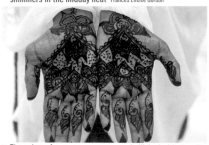

3. The palms of a young woman are embellished with stunning henna tattoos to celebrate a festival in Djibouti City Frances Linzee Gordon

4. Two elegant Somali women, displaced from their neighbouring homeland, observe the proceedings of a wedding in Hol Hol, Ali Sabieh Frances Linzee Gordon

5. Fishermen drag in their ropes Frances Linzee Gordon

Djibouti's strangely seductive blend of African, Arab, Indian and European influences is seasoned with a hefty dose of *qat*, the mildly intoxicating herb that is chewed by most males and sets the country's pace to unhurried. The capital may be little more than a minor port filled with peeling colonial buildings, but its streets are unforgettable, shared by traditionally robed tribesmen and French legionnaires, hennaed women and Somali refugees, and filled with the aromas of French cuisine and seedy bars. Away from the coast, the hinterland is a bizarre treat of eerie volcanic landscapes and vast salt lakes. Djibouti could just well be one of East Africa's best-kept secrets.

BEST TIME TO VISIT
November to mid-April, when the weather is coolest

ESSENTIAL EXPERIENCES
Exploring the great salt lake of Lac Assal

Visiting the weird, lunar landscape of Lac Abbé at dawn

Snorkelling the stunning coral reefs off Djibouti's Red Sea coast

Spotting birds and animals in the Fôret du Day national park

Trekking behind the Afar nomads and their caravans along the ancient salt route

Sharing a *poisson yéménite* (fish supper) with the locals

GETTING UNDER THE SKIN
Read *Khamsine*, a collection of lyrical, sometimes semi-erotic, poems by Djiboutian poet William JF Syad

Listen to solo guitarist Aïdarous and Guux musician Taha Nahari

Watch *Total Eclipse*, which was made in part in Djibouti

Eat local *foie* (liver) for breakfast and *cabri farci* (stuffed kid) for lunch

Drink the fizzy and slightly salty local bottled water or tea

IN A WORD
Salam 'alekum (greetings)

TRADEMARKS
Nomads; men chewing *qat*; arid deserts; the Red Sea; the civil war; camels

SURPRISES
Many Afar nomads still file their front teeth into ferocious-looking points; Afar huts are usually spherical, while Somali huts are more quadrangular in design

Without a hint of a written record, hotel receptionists effortlessly recall complicated telephone messages, and operators recall long international numbers. Waiters and taxi drivers wax lyrical at the slightest provocation, and any inhabitant can, on demand, recite the entire family tree, and in conversation retell hundreds if not thousands of proverbs and traditional tales. Such gifts are considered the product of a nomadic culture, in which the spoken word has always been more important than the written one. Individuals carry in their heads their nation's culture and their ancestors' artistry; great memories are developed and a remarkable diction learnt.

— Lonely Planet's *Ethiopia, Eritrea & Djibouti*

1. An Afar tribesman awakens beside his mobile dwelling on the stony banks of Lac Abbe Frances Linzee Gordon

6. Afar tribesmen gather natural salt from Lac Assal Frances Linzee Gordon

MAP REF: M,24

2. Infernal vapours issue from the craters of Boiling Lake, St Patrick Jean-Bernard Carillet

3. A declaration of devotion emblazoned on a beachside banner, Scott's Head Michael Lawrence

4. With stripes in his stride a policeman marches past a vivid building Michael Lawrence

5. Dusk light captures three boys at play Michael Lawrence

1. Nestled amongst the greenery, a house overlooks the Roseau Valley Michael Lawrence

Dominica is largely rural, uncrowded and unspoiled. It has a lush mountainous interior of rainforests, waterfalls, lakes, hot springs and rivers, many of which cascade over steep cliff faces en route to the coast. Apart from its natural splendours, including the highest mountains in the Eastern Caribbean, the island has an interesting fusion of British, French and West Indian cultural traditions, and is home to the Eastern Caribbean's largest Carib Indian community.

BEST TIME TO VISIT
December to February

ESSENTIAL EXPERIENCES
Enjoying scenic Roseau, with its colonial architecture and Creole food and culture

Exploring Cabrits National Park, with fine views from the ruins of Fort Shirley

Taking in the unsurpassed mountain and rainforest scenery

Hiking to Boiling Lake, the world's second-largest natural boiling lake

Kicking around Scotts Head, a tiny fishing village of only 800 souls on the gently curving shoreline of Soufrière Bay (the rim of a sunken volcanic crater)

Diving at Scotts Head Drop, a shallow coral ledge that drops abruptly to a depth of over 50m (160ft) and has a wall of tube sponges and soft corals

GETTING UNDER THE SKIN
Read *Voyage in the Dark* by Dominica's most celebrated author, Jean Rhys, or Dominica's other noted novelist, Phyllis Shand Allfrey, who is best known for *The Orchid House*

Listen to African *soukous*, Louisiana zydeco and a variety of local bands at the World Creole Music Festival held in the last week of October in Roseau

Watch Dominican filmmaker Pauline Marcelle's animation films *Burn, The Snake Steps* or *Paradogs*

Eat callaloo soup (a creamy soup made with dasheen leaves) and mountains of delicious fresh fruit

Drink fruit punch made with fresh fruit and rum, or the locally brewed beer Kubuli

IN A WORD
Lime about (lazing about).

TRADEMARKS
Diving; Rasta colours; rainforests; cricket; Creole culture

SURPRISES
Dominica's national bird, the Sisserou parrot, is the largest of all the Amazon parrots; there are more than 200 rivers in Dominica

Dominica's national dish is the mountain chicken, which is not a chicken at all but rather the legs of a giant frog called the crapaud (Leptodactylus fallax), which is endemic to Dominica and Montserrat. Found at higher elevations, it's a protected species and can only be caught between autumn and February. Crapaud meat is white and tastes like chicken.

— Lonely Planet's *Eastern Caribbean*

6. A young fisherman casts his line into shallow waters Michael Lawrence

Guadeloupe Channel

ATLANTIC OCEAN

Portsmouth

Marigot

Salisbury

Castle Bruce

St Joseph

Massacre

Roseau

CARIBBEAN SEA

Soufriere

Martinique Channel

MAP REF: L,13

2. All grins and giggles, cheeky children peer from a shuttered window Andrew Marshall & Leanne Walker

3. A local of Bayahibe, La Romana, enjoys her relaxation equipment with matching house Greg Johnston

4. Cruising for customers, ice-cream vendors ply their trade along the scorching streets
Pascale Beroujon

5. Relaxation is obligatory at Balneario Los Platos, a river-fed public pool in Paraíso Scott Doggett

6. Eyes on the prize, a soldier checks his slip outside a betting shop in Santo Domingo Alfredo Maiquez
LEFT 1. A boy carries a heavy load through Duarte Street, Santo Domingo Alfredo Maiquez

Is there are better definition of paradise than palm-fringed white-sand beaches, turquoise waters and rum-and-merengue-soaked nights? Santo Domingo offers architectural charm and historical gravitas, while the rugged mountain interior pleases adventure-seekers with world-class rafting, trekking and wildlife-watching opportunities. Above all, however, it's Dominicans who make the DR tick: fun-seekers throw themselves wholeheartedly into all manner of neighbourhood parties, surfing and windsurfing contests, music festivals and not one but two annual Carnival celebrations.

BEST TIME TO VISIT
December to April

ESSENTIAL EXPERIENCES
Discovering the New World in Santo Domingo's Zona Colonial

Whale-watching on the Península de Samaná

Cheering for *beisbol* champions in San Pedro de Macorís

Windsurfing in Caberete, the DR's hippest beach town

Hiking, rafting and bird-watching in the interior's mountainous national parks

Taking part in a Dominican fiesta: one part rum, one part Presidente beer, one part *sancocho* and three parts dancing (salsa, merengue and the countryfied *bachata*)

GETTING UNDER THE SKIN
Read Julia Alvarez's *In the Time of the Butterflies*, the lyrical tale of 1960s political martyrs, the Mirabal sisters; or *Feast of the Goat* by Mario Vargas Llosa, about the Trujillo regime

Listen to 1960s and '70s tunes by merengue legend Johnny Ventura; Juan Luis Guerra's *Bachata Rosa*, a revolutionary album by the DR's most celebrated contemporary artist; anything by prolific *bachateros* Antony Santos and Raulín Rodriguez

Watch *1492: The Conquest of Paradise*, the lavish Columbus-meets-New World epic

Eat *sancocho de siete carnes*, hearty soup with manioc, plantain and seven (count 'em!) types of meat, *the* soup for a family gathering

Drink rum or Presidente, the country's beloved local beer

IN A WORD
¡Que chulo! (great!)

TRADEMARKS
Palm-lined beaches; plantains; merengue; rum; cigars that are better than but not as famous as those from Cuba; Sammy Sosa

SURPRISES
Dominicans are amazingly polite and tend to dress quite formally; Dominicans often refer to their island by its Taino name, Quisqueya

In the Dominican Republic, maintaining close family ties and cultivating friendships are top priorities, and music is a part of everyday life. Merengue, the quintessential Dominican beat, is more than just music; it is a tool for fostering those relationships. That is why you hear it everywhere – at the beach, on the bus, in the street. Dominicans need little excuse for a party …

– Lonely Planet's *Dominican Republic & Haiti*

MAP REF: L,12

2. In a flurry of feathers, men perform a Timorese dance John Banagan

3. A young traditional dancer from the mountain town of Ainaro Tony Wheeler

4. The iconic statue of the Virgin gazes from Mt Ramelau, the highest point in East Timor Tony Wheeler

5. Children scavenge for coral and other collectibles on the beach of Dili John Banagan

6. Peak hour traffic in the hill village of Maubisse John Banagan
LEFT 1. The afternoon sun gleams on playful children on the shores of Dili John Banagan

The world's newest nation is fast emerging from a dark past of violence, oppression and neglect. With pristine beaches, newly discovered reefs, superb diving and snorkelling just a paddle offshore, crumbling stone fortresses and elegant Portuguese buildings, you'd expect this place to be heaving with tourists. In fact East Timor is blissfully uncrowded – and a lack of infrastructure means your most important piece of luggage will be your adventurous spirit.

BEST TIME TO VISIT
May to November for the weather – since gaining official independence in 2002 there hasn't been a better time to visit in 400 years!

ESSENTIAL EXPERIENCES
Walking up to the towering Christ Statue at Cape Fatucama to take in the view over the bay to Dili

Diving the crystal waters off Atauro Island amid turtles, dugongs and colourful reef fish

Climbing lofty Mt Matebian (2315m), East Timor's holy mountain

Overnighting in the historic *pousada* (Portuguese inn) at Maubisse

Visiting the crumbling Portuguese garrison of Fatusuba in Pantemakassar

GETTING UNDER THE SKIN
Read Timothy Mo's *The Redundancy of Courage*, which uses the fictional country of Danu to depict East Timor's struggle during the Indonesian occupation. Luis Cardoso's *Crossing. A Story of East Timor* is a memoir of growing up in East Timor under Portuguese and Indonesian rule

Listen to *Liberdade Viva East Timor*, the benefit album for the newly created nation

Watch *Death of a Nation: The Timor Conspiracy*, John Pilger's exploration of the international abandonment of the tiny nation

Eat fresh seafood – East Timor's crystal-clear seas are teeming with gourmet goodies, which find their way onto restaurant tables cooked in various tempting Indonesian, Chinese and Portuguese styles

Drink rich, flavoursome Arabica coffee or *sopi*, a potent brew distilled from the pandanus plant

IN A WORD
Ba nebé? (where are you going?)

TRADEMARKS
Xanana Gusmão; José Ramos-Horta; UN convoys; freedom fighters; colourful woven lengths of *tais* (traditional cloth)

SURPRISES
A small patch of East Timor (the Oecussi Enclave) sits nearly 100km removed from the rest of the country, sharing all its land borders with Indonesian West Timor; the Greater Sunrise oilfield between Australia and East Timor is believed to be a rich source of both oil and gas and its bounty should provide the struggling nation with income for years to come

My travels around East Timor were dotted with magic moments...sitting on the veranda of the flamboyant Pousada de Baucau, sipping a sunset beer, marvelling at the view from the headland at Tutuala...my delight when our boat was surrounded first by dolphins and then by pilot whales on the way back to Dili from Atauro Island. Everywhere there was a feeling that this was a country which had seen tough times but was determined to move on.

— Tony Wheeler, Lonely Planet's *East Timor*

MAP REF: P.33

2. Marine iguanas let their tails down at Punta Suárez
Richard I'Anson

3. Ramshackle houses of the Las Peñas district, Guayaquil
Richard I'Anson

4. A vendor flashes a golden-toothed smile at the Otavalo
Indian Market Juliet Coombe

5. An unimpressed chicken takes a tour on the back of a local
girl in Otavalo Woods Wheatcroft

CAPITAL QUITO POPULATION 13,710,234 AREA 283,560 SQ KM OFFICIAL LANGUAGE SPANISH

A wealth of vibrant indigenous cultures, colonial architecture, otherworldly volcanic landscapes and dense rainforests are packed into the borders of tiny Ecuador, the smallest Andean country in South America. You can change your surroundings here as fast as you can change your mind – one day your cold fingers are picking through handwoven woollen sweaters at a chilly indigenous market in the Andean highlands, and the next they're slapping mosquitoes on a tropical beach. Then there are the Galápagos Islands, lauded as one of the world's greatest natural history treasures.

BEST TIME TO VISIT
From May to December on the mainland, or January to April for the Galápagos

ESSENTIAL EXPERIENCES
Travelling to the Galápagos Islands to snorkel with harmless sharks, stare at iguanas and scuba dive with manta rays

Wandering through the splendid colonial streets of Cuenca

Outdoor pursuits in the Oriente – where you can hike, visit indigenous communities, white-water raft, fish for piranhas and spot caimans

Bouncing around the spectacular high Andean road known as the Quilotoa loop, stopping to hike, buy indigenous crafts and visit Ecuador's most stunning crater lake, Laguna Quilotoa

Journeying down the Río Napo to the Amazon River by canoe and cargo boat from Coca In the Oriente to Iquitos Peru

GETTING UNDER THE SKIN
Read Jorge Icaza's *Huasipungo* (The Villagers), a naturalistic tale of the miserable conditions experienced on Andean haciendas in the early 20th century. *Galápagos* by Kurt Vonnegut is a comic, cautionary, evolutionary tale

Listen to Marco Villota, a singer-songwriter who plays with the band Pueblo Nuevo

Watch *Talking with Fish and Birds*, directed by Rainer Simon, documenting the life and death of a shaman

Eat *ceviche* (uncooked seafood marinated in lemon and served with popcorn and onion) or *patacones* (fried plantain chips)

Drink the good local *cervezas* (beer), or *aguardiente* (sugarcane alcohol) – a more acquired taste

IN A WORD
Bacán (cool)

TRADEMARKS
The Galápagos Islands; panama hats; panpipes; the Andes; eating roasted guinea-pigs

SURPRISES
Ecuador has one of the highest deforestation rates in Latin America; the oldest tools found in Ecuador date to 9000 BC

Most Ecuadorians have three things in common: pride in the natural wealth of their country (both its beauty and its resources); disdain for the corrupt politicians who promise to redistribute yet continue to pocket that wealth; and the presence of a relative in another country (over 10% of the population – some 1.3 million people – have left Ecuador in search of work elsewhere).

– Lonely Planet's *South America*

1. Herders follow a flock of sheep down the flanks of Cotopaxi Volcano Woods Wheatcroft

6. Dark clouds loom above a team of climbers descending Cotopaxi Volcano Grant Dixon

MAP REF: O.11

2. An easy rider of the Cuscatlan region prepares to hit the mean streets of Suchitoto on his pedal-powered chopper bike Margie Politzer

3. Rich colours form appealing contrasts on the wall of a house in Suchitoto Jeffrey Becom

4. How's it hanging? Cowboy-hatted characters shoot the breeze at a Suchitoto handicraft stall Alfredo Maiquez

1. Child leans against a gaudy turquoise wall   Lou Jones

El Salvador's name still evokes images of the brutal civil war fought throughout the 1980s in its tangle of mountains and farmlands. The war, however, is over and the volcanic landscape remains the most turbulent aspect of the country. Now El Salvador is making headlines once again, thanks to its degraded environment. The people of El Salvador are its richest resource, and the best reason to come: direct, friendly and unjaded by mass tourism.

BEST TIME TO VISIT
November to April (the dry season)

ESSENTIAL EXPERIENCES
Hiking in the mountains surrounding the former guerrilla stronghold of Perquín

Stepping off the Ruta de las Flores to visit the string of charming little towns in the cool western highlands

Visiting the weekend food fair at Juayúa

Checking out the laid-back vibe and happening arts scene in Suchitoto

Catching the bus from Metapán to El Poy through El Salvador's spectacular mountain scenery

GETTING UNDER THE SKIN
Read *Cuentos de Barro* (Tales of Mud) by Salarrué (one of El Salvador's most famous writers); the poetry of Manlio Argueta and Francisco Rodriguez

Listen to the underground movement of *canción popular* (folk music), which draws its inspiration from current events

Watch *Salvador*, the story of a war correspondent directed by Oliver Stone, for Hollywood's insights into the civil war

Eat *pupusas* (cornmeal dough stuffed with farmer's cheese, refried beans or fried pork fat) or *panes* (French breads sliced open and stuffed with chicken, salsa, salad and pickled vegetables)

Drink *licuados* (refreshing blended fruit and milk) or Torito (a vodka-like spirit made from sugar cane)

IN A WORD
Cheque (all right)

TRADEMARKS
Bitter civil war; liberation theology; coffee; surfing; volcanoes; circling vultures; lush cloud forest

SURPRISES
El Salvador enjoys the highest minimum wage in Central America; 9% of Salvadorans are considered of full European ancestry, while only 1% is indigenous

With the highest level of environmental damage in the Americas, El Salvador runs the risk of losing its beauty. Six percent of the country is forest or woodland, only 2% of that original growth. The Río Lempa, an important watershed, suffers from pollution, as do many other rivers and lakes. Uncontrolled vehicle emissions will test your respiratory functions in any metropolitan area.

– Lonely Planet's *Central America*

5. Fishermen haul their catch in Bahía de la Unión, once El Salvador's busiest port   Charlotte Hindle

MAP REF: M,10

2. How much is that doggy? Everything is for sale at the Brick Lane Market in London Juliet Coombe

3. The enigmatic Stonehenge in the Salisbury Plains Bryn Thomas

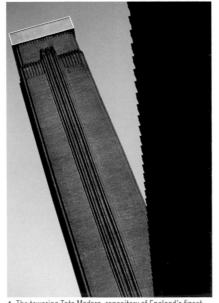

4. The towering Tate Modern, repository of England's finest collection of 20th-century art Neil Setchfield

5. A tube station sign marks the gateway to a subterranean world of speed, light and mute commuters Christopher Groenhout

England is where world-renowned institutions and symbols remain cherished and intact – from Big Ben at Westminster to Canterbury Cathedral, Eton College to the universities of Oxford and Cambridge, Wembley Stadium to Lord's Cricket Ground, Stonehenge to Tower Bridge. But the load is carried with panache as this tiny entity strides into the 21st century offering designer fashion, cutting-edge clubbing, and fine wining and dining as never before. England's presence on the global stage remains large, one of the many legacies of an empire long gone but not quite forgotten.

BEST TIME TO VISIT

May to September (summer) – or, for the free-spirited, the swinging 1960s

ESSENTIAL EXPERIENCES

Climbing to the top of St Paul's Cathedral for an alternative view of London

Marvelling at the prehistoric ruin of Stonehenge and the sheer effort involved in its creation

Revelling in the sense of achievement on reaching the peak of Scafell Pike in the Lake District, England's highest mountain

Mixing Roman and Georgian history in the elegant town of Bath

Eating fish and chips on a pebbly beach, and willing the sun to shine

Exploring Cornwall's coastline of cliffs and bays, dotted with picturesque harbours and villages

GETTING UNDER THE SKIN

Read *The English* by Jeremy Paxman, an exploration of the English psyche by one of the country's toughest TV interviewers

Listen to the Kinks' *Waterloo Sunset*, a great introduction to the many songs written about the capital; or anything by the Beatles

Watch *Sense and Sensibility*, a film of a thoroughly English novel in a thoroughly English setting

Eat Sunday roast dinner (typically beef with roast potatoes, Yorkshire pudding, carrots, peas and gravy) followed by a hearty apple crumble with custard and cream

Drink real ale – England is the home of proper beer

IN A WORD

'Oright?

TRADEMARKS

The weather; the Royal Family; Lords, Ladies and big hats at Ascot; Cockney rhyming slang; Brit Pop; jellied eels; warm beer; page three girls; fry-ups; football

SURPRISES

It doesn't actually rain that much; the English drink even more tea than you already think they do; most of the best things on offer in England are free

For visitors to England traditional pubs are a quintessential feature, and for the English themselves the pub is one of the country's finest social and cultural institutions. There are more than 50,000 pubs scattered across the country, in market towns and busy city centres, in picturesque villages and remote rural backwaters. They range from vast and ornate Victorian drinking-palaces to simple country inns with low beams and sloping flagstoned floors polished smooth by the passage of time and a thousand spilt pints.

— Lonely Planet's *England*

MAP REF: G,19

1. The pebbled shores of Brighton, the natural sunbathing habitat of Englishmen Christer Fredriksson

6. Cricketers enjoy a quiet game outside Warkworth Castle, Northumberland David Wall

2. This bean-counter takes his job extremely literally Giles Moberly

3. A crowded street in Malabo Giles Moberly

While most of Equatorial Guinea's two regions remain densely covered with the type of forest that made Tarzan swing, the recent discovery of underwater oil looks set to change the face of the country. Bioko Island has been thoroughly taken over by oil money and an influx of foreign workers, but a trip to the mainland (Rio Muni) is still like taking a step back in time. The only way to get from A to B is to hack and bribe and hold on tight to bush taxis making their way through the jungle. This is real adventure travel, with amazing rewards – rainforest, beaches, traditional African villages and, with some hard hiking and luck, you might get to spend some time with gorillas.

BEST TIME TO VISIT
December to February for slightly drier weather

ESSENTIAL EXPERIENCES
Hiking in search of gorillas, elephants, chimpanzees, crocodiles and whatever else turns up in the Monte Alen National Park

Beachcombing around Luba and other deserted beach towns on Bioko Island

Hanging around Bata, the mainland's biggest city, where the real action is

Taking a pirogue across the estuary between Gabon and Equatorial Guinea to the village of Cogo

Wandering around vibrant Malabo – a town in the heart of the African tropics – with its outdoor bars, thriving nightclubs and colourful markets

GETTING UNDER THE SKIN
Read Mary Kingsley's 1897 classic *Travels in West Africa*, which details her trip spent slogging through the rainforest to gather specimens for a natural history museum

Listen to a traditional orchestra of drums, wooden xylophones, *sanzas* (a small thumb piano made from bamboo), bow harps and even zithers

Eat wonderful seafood and fresh fruit

Drink beer, locally brewed palm wine and *malamba*, made from sugarcane

IN A WORD
Mbôlo (hello)

TRADEMARKS
Corrupt officials; oil; dense rainforest; hardcore travellers; small villages with mud-wattle houses; gorillas

SURPRISES
Sorcerers are still among the most important community members in Equatorial Guinea; among the country's most fascinating celebrations is the *abira*, a ceremony that helps cleanse the community of evil

The inhabitants of Equatorial Guinea have always been divided by geography. On Bioko Island people generally live in an urban environment, with jobs in government or the oil industry. On the mainland, outside the city of Bata, people live a very traditional African lifestyle, in small villages of mud-wattle houses, with agriculture the main occupation.

– Lonely Planet's *Africa*

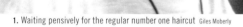
1. Waiting pensively for the regular number one haircut Giles Moberly

4. Hangin' tough down at the local aqueduct Giles Moberly

MAP REF: N.21

2. Young men strut down the main drag of Assab
Jean-Bernard Carillet

3. Two saltbushes stand watch over the empty waters of the
Red Sea Jean-Bernard Carillet

4. The striking face of a Tigre tribeswoman Oliver Strewe

5. Chilling out for a chat on the steps of the Khulafa Al
Rashidin (Great Mosque) in Asmara Patrick Syder

Perched on the horn of Africa, Eritrea is a tiny country with a strong sense of identity. Torrid deserts, fertile highlands and arid plains are all crowded together within the diminutive confines of its borders. Its richness and beauty did not escape the attention of the outside world and the country became a colony of Italy for more than fifty years. Evidence of Italy's imperial rule can still be seen in the magnificent architecture of the capital, Asmara. Modern Eritrea is a lively country with an exuberant and optimistic population.

BEST TIME TO VISIT
October to May, when the mercury settles at an agreeable temperature

ESSENTIAL EXPERIENCES
Strapping on a snorkel and marvelling at the unspoilt underwater treasures around the Dahlak Archipelago

Exploring Eritrea's remarkable archaeological ruins in Qohaito

Surveying war-torn Nakfa, once the heart of Eritrean resistance

Discovering the lunar landscape of Dankalia, one of the most desolate areas on earth

Hanging out in one of Asmara's Italian-style cafés and enjoying a coffee or a pastry

Climbing up to one of the isolated Orthodox monasteries, set amid spectacular scenery

GETTING UNDER THE SKIN
Read *Eritrea at a Glance*, edited by Mary Houdek and Leonardo Oriolo, for a fantastic introduction to the country, particularly the capital Asmara. For a gripping yarn of the struggle for independance read *Even the Stones Are Burning* by Roy Pateman

Eat *legamat*, a deep-fried dough sold hot in newspaper cones by little boys in the lowlands. A popular dish in the west is *sheia*, lamb drizzled with oil and herbs then barbecued on very hot stones until it sizzles

Drink excellent espresso or macchiato coffee, ginger coffee, fresh fruit juice or sweet black tea

IN A WORD
Selam (hello)

TRADEMARKS
Yellow Fiat taxis; politeness; excellent coffee; classic architecture; stark landscapes; relaxed attitudes

SURPRISES
Legend credits Eritrea as the El Dorado of Africa. The Egyptian pharaohs held the land comprising present-day Eritrea in awe, referring to it as The Land of Punt. From over its borders came a seemingly endless stream of gold, frankincense, myrrh, slaves, ostrich feathers, antelopes, ebony and ivory

The capital, Asmara, is like a film set from an early Italian movie. Old chrome espresso machines churn out cups of macchiato, Cinquecento taxis putt-putt about and all over town you can see outstanding examples of Art Deco architecture. Asmara is without doubt one of the safest, cleanest and most attractive capital cities in Africa.

— Lonely Planet's *Ethiopia & Eritrea*

1. A woman approaches her faithful donkey as a sandstorm brews in the bleak semi-desert near Keren, Anseba Patrick Horton

6. A novice monk at the Debre Libanos monastery beams a prayer across the valley Oliver Strewe

MAP REF: L,24

2. Empty rowing boats moored at a jetty in Triigi, Saaremaa John Noble

3. The domes of the Russian Orthodox Alexander Nevski Cathedral gleam in the sun Stephen Saks

4. Austere stone fortresses preside over the city walls of Tallinn Jane Sweeney

5. Gilded with snow, the rooftops of Tallinn present a picturesque winterscape Tiit Veermae

6. A young woman gazes at shifting scenery on a train journey Peter Turnley
LEFT 1. A stroller steps into the sunlight in the Old Town district of Tallinn Jonathan Smith

A forgotten gem strategically placed between Russia and Scandinavia, this former Soviet Republic has undergone a rapid transformation since independence. The internet and mobile phone revolutions in particular have taken the nation by storm. The influence of modern technology co-exists happily with a people that are strongly connected to nature, and whose land – almost half of which is forest – is home to countless traditions and folk tales.

BEST TIME TO VISIT
May to July for the good weather

ESSENTIAL EXPERIENCES
Rejuvenating in a mud bath at one of Pärnu's health spas

Trying to walk across the icy cobbled streets of wintry medieval Tallinn

Catching a ferry to the outlying island of Saaremaa

Collecting amber ('Baltic gold') washed up along the western coast

Seeking out brown bear, lynx, wolves and, if you're lucky, the rare European flying squirrel

GETTING UNDER THE SKIN
Read anything by Lydia Koidula – Estonia's first lady of poetry; or Jaan Kross's *The Czar's Madman*

Listen to *Miserere Litany* by Arvo Pärt

Watch animated films from Estonia such as the bizarre creations of Priit Pärn and Mati Kütt that verge on surreal and absurd

Eat *suitsukala* (smoked fish), *verivorst* (blood sausage), *verileib* (blood bread) and, for true vampires, *verikäkk* (balls of blood rolled in flour and eggs with pig fat thrown in for taste)

Drink Vana Tallinn (a syrupy liqueur) or Saku (beer)

IN A WORD
Ma olen taimetoitlane (I'm a vegetarian)

TRADEMARKS
Quiet, reserved people; mobile phone addicts; White Nights – midsummer evenings that remain in twilight till dawn; grand limestone buildings; open-air song festivals; stag night weekends

SURPRISES
Estonia received the attention of 160 million TV viewers when it hosted the 2002 Eurovision Song Contest; it is home to one of Europe's few accessible meteorite craters at Kaali on Saaremaa Island; it has a centuries-old shamanistic tradition

Bogs have historically provided isolation and protection to Estonians. Witches were said to live there. According to Estonian folklore, it is the evil will-o-the-wisp who leads people to the bog, where they are forced to stay until the bog gas catches fire, driving the grotesque bog inhabitants out for all to see. Closer to reality, bogs were also handy hiding places for partisans and anyone seeking to escape military invaders, who could not penetrate them as easily as forests.

– Lonely Planet's *Estonia, Latvia & Lithuania*

MAP REF: F,22

2. The verdant Rift Valley is known for its lush landscapes David Else

3. A proud woman of the nomadic Karo tribe is adorned with bright beaded necklaces Frances Linzee Gordon

4. First coat of the elaborate body painting that many tribal groups wear while dancing Frances Linzee Gordon

5. Raising a family – an Afar camel herder with his adult and child dromedaries Ariadne Van Zandbergen

6. Two men chat outside a rock-hewn church, one of 400 churches that date back to the 12th century Frances Linzee Gordon

LEFT 1. Amhara boy herders tending their flock in Simien Mountains National Park David Else

Rich in history, wildlife and cultural traditions, Ethiopia deserves the aura and fame of Egypt. To many it remains synonymous with famine and war, but the relative obscurity has its rewards, flavouring travel with a sense of adventure and discovery. The landscape is littered with rock-hewn churches, mighty castles and isolated monasteries. Nature lovers come away with memories of waterfalls, mountains and wildlife. Travel here can be tough but also hugely satisfying – and you won't have to worry about crowds of tourists, yet…

BEST TIME TO VISIT
October to January, when rains have turned the land into its lush, blooming best

ESSENTIAL EXPERIENCES
Walking around the rock-hewn churches at Lalibela at dawn

Trekking into the Bale Mountains in search of the elusive Ethiopian wolf

Exploring Gonder's castles and the colourful interior of Debre Beirhan Selassie Church

Visiting the ruins of Aksum, once home to a mysterious and mighty ancient civilisation

Taking a boat to Lake Tana's island monasteries

GETTING UNDER THE SKIN
Read Graham Hancock's *The Sign and the Seal*, a fascinating historical detective story which traces the Ark of the Covenant to Ethiopia, while providing an overview of the country's history and culture

Listen to anything by Mahmoud Ahmud, a legend of Ethiopian music with his soulful and funky Amharic sound. Start with his *Live in Paris* set.

Eat *injera*, a phenomenally bouncy bread that is found throughout the country. Try it with fiery *kai wat* sauce.

Drink the excellent Ethiopian beer, especially Harar. Delicious fruit juice mixtures known as *spris* shouldn't be missed.

IN A WORD
Denkenesh (you are wonderful), the Ethiopian Amharic name given to Lucy, the oldest complete hominid skeleton ever found, on display at the National Museum in Addis Ababa

TRADEMARKS
Ancient churches; Live Aid; Haile Selassie; Radio Ethiopia

SURPRISES
Ethiopia is home to one of the oldest Christian civilisations in the world; Ethiopians believe their country is the resting place of the Ark of the Covenant; the country is at peace

Though daunting at first, the ascents up rock faces required to reach some of the Tigrayan churches are not difficult if taken carefully. Just focus on the footholds, get a good grip, don't stop and don't look down. Sometimes the holds are very small, hewn by the bare feet of generations of priests. In which case, do as they do and take off your shoes. It's amazing the grip a toe can get!

— Lonely Planet's *Ethiopia & Eritrea*

MAP REF: M,24

2. An Antarctic cruise ship skirts the shoreline of Carcass Island where evergreen flowering gorse blooms in defiance of the icy Falkland weather Grant Dixon

3. The cheerful colours of a weatherboard house in East Falkland Tony Wheeler

4. A lovingly painted car parked in front of lovingly painted house in the well-decorated East Falkland region Tony Wheeler

5. A farmer drives his sheep along the dusty Port Howard-Fox Bay Road near Little Chartres Tony Wheeler

6. A retired anchor leans against a fence post on Westpoint Island Juliet Coombe
LEFT 1. King penguins greet one another in the grass Jonathan Chester

Just next door to South America and Antarctica, the Falklands are curiously British through and through, with peat fires burning in every hearth and jolly tea times to set your clock by. With only a scattering of inhabitants (most are British military personnel), it's hardly Touristville. The remote islands briefly rocketed to international importance during the 1980s, when Britain took them back after an invasion by Argentina and everyone learnt their alternative name: the Islas Malvinas.

BEST TIME TO VISIT
October to April – but not in April 1982 during Argentina's land grab

ESSENTIAL EXPERIENCES
Admiring ramshackle Stanley, a town that appears to have been pieced together from flotsam, local stone and a whole lot of bright paint

Wildlife-watching on the aptly named Sea Lion Island

Paying court to breeding pairs of king penguins at Volunteer Beach

Snacking on the South Sandwich Islands and seeing more than five million pairs of breeding chinstrap penguins

GETTING UNDER THE SKIN
Read *The Battle for the Falklands*, a cool assessment of the politics and strategy of the 1982 war by Max Hastings and Simon Jenkins

Listen to the Fighting Pig Band

Watch *Falklands – Taskforce South*, a gritty account of the British defence of the islands aboard a British naval vessel

Eat hydroponically grown vegetables in Stanley, but pack your own lunch anywhere else (British explorer Shackleton didn't and almost starved to death)

Drink a cup of tea during a regular smoko (traditional mid-morning tea break)

IN A WORD
Cuppa (usually a cup of tea, the most warming thing on a freezing-cold day)

TRADEMARKS
British-Argentine battlefield; penguin mating grounds; snow covered islands; near-dark winters; snow, snow and even more snow

SURPRISES
The Falklands War, for which the island is still best known, lasted only 72 days, but saw casualties of almost a thousand servicemen. Anywhere outside of Stanley is known as 'camp', from the Spanish word *campo*, countryside.

As in Japan, houses are shoe-free territory. It can be muddy outside so outdoor shoes are always removed at the front door. In places where unknowing outsiders may be regular visitors you may encounter warning signs, but whether it's signposted or not always take them off.

— Lonely Planet's *Falklands & South Georgia Island*

MAP REF: V.13

2. A thatched house of Navala village perched above the dramatic Nausori Highlands Robyn Jones

3. Sultry winds tease the fronds of immense palm trees on Yanuca Island Richard I'Anson

4. A parrot's-eye view of Qalito Island, known romantically as Castaway Island, in the Mamanuca archipelago David Wall

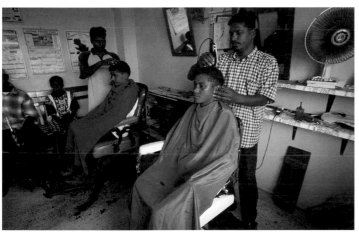

5. A close shave at a barber shop in Sigatoka David Wall

6. Noisy boys – traditional dancers leap to the beat on Denarau Island Peter Hendrie

LEFT 1. With a battledress of garlands and tattoos, a warrior dancer on Robinson Crusoe Island prepares an assault Robyn Jones

Lapped by warm azure waters, fringed with vibrant coral reefs and cloaked in the emerald green of the tropics, Fiji is a paradise-seeker's dream come true. Its sun-soaked, white-sand beaches and resorts are bliss, but only a slice of the country's allure. Fiji is an interesting blend of Melanesian, Polynesian, Micronesian, Indian, Chinese and European influences – which means visitors can feed on curries and chop suey, visit temples, churches and mosques, hear Urdu and Mandarin, and sip spiced chai or kava.

BEST TIME TO VISIT
May to October, during the 'Fijian winter' when humidity and rainfall are lower

ESSENTIAL EXPERIENCES
Exploring Suva's waterfront and market, with its exotic fruits and vegetables, seafood and spices

Snorkelling and diving in Fiji's extraordinary crystal-blue reefs

Experiencing the warmth and hospitality of Fiji's multiethnic inhabitants

Surfing the fantastic breaks of the southern Mamanucas

Admiring traditional *bure* (thatched dwelling) architecture in the highlands

Swimming through the dark chambers of the Sawa-i-Lau caves in the Yasawa group of islands

GETTING UNDER THE SKIN
Read Fiji's most popular coffee-table book, *Children of the Sun*, with photos by Glen Craig and poetry by Bryan McDonald

Listen to the guitar-strumming, crooning songs from *Bula Fiji Bula: Music of the Fiji Islands*

Watch Tom Hanks playing the modern-day Robinson Crusoe in *Cast Away*, featuring Monuriki Island

Eat traditional Fijian foods including *tavioka* (cassava) and *dalo* (taro) roots, and seafood in *lolo* (coconut cream)

Drink cloudy bowl of lip-numbing *yaqona* (also known as kava), a ritualistic drink prepared from the aromatic roots of the Pacific pepper shrub, originally drunk in honour of the ancestors

IN A WORD
Bula (hello)

TRADEMARKS
Surfers seeking the big break; honeymooners' paradise; grass skirts; *Blue Lagoon*; endless bowls of *yaqona*; hammocks; woven baskets; white-sand beaches

SURPRISES
Over 300 islands comprise Fiji's archipelago, and about two-thirds are uninhabited; boiled *beka* (bat) was once a popular indigenous Fijian dish

Snorkelling in Fiji's warm waters is a definite highlight. You are likely to see brilliant soft and hard corals, multitudes of colourful fish of various shapes and sizes, sponges, sea cucumbers, urchins, starfish, Christmas-tree worms and molluscs. Crustaceans are more difficult to spot and many only come out at night. Night snorkelling is a fantastic experience if you can overcome your fear of the unknown!

– Lonely Planet's *South Pacific*

MAP REF: Q,38

137

2. From trees to timber, a neat log pile stacked at the edge of a forest in northern Finland David Tipling

3. A row of identical wooden houses in Rovaniemi built in the architectural style typical of Lapland and the north John Borthwick

4. Reindeers wandering the streets of Vuotso, Lapland Craig Pershouse

1. Forest pines silhouetted against the supernatural glow of the aurora borealis (northern lights) near Kuusamo David Tipling

Finland is a quiet, laid-back place, where a ramshackle cottage by a lake and a properly stoked sauna are all that's required for happiness. It's a vast expanse of forests and lakes punctuated by small towns. During the months of the midnight sun, coastal regions are a sailing and fishing paradise; when the nights are cold and long (and they can be very, very long), you can huddle inside with a vodka.

BEST TIME TO VISIT
May to September to avoid the cold and dark

ESSENTIAL EXPERIENCES
Poking around the harbourside fish market in Helsinki – there's everything from salmon and sausages to handicrafts and all manner of reindeer-related souvenirs

Spending the afternoon among the ramparts of the historic fortress on Suomenlinna Island

Boating around the islands of Ekenäs Archipelago National Park

Staying overnight in one of Hanko's charming Russian villas

Dance your hear out at the annual festival of Finnish Tango, Tangomarkkinar

Seeing the aurora borealis – nature's Arctic light show

GETTING UNDER THE SKIN
Read anything by Aleksis Kivi, who founded modern Finnish literature with *Seven Brothers*, a story of brothers who try to escape civilisation in favour of the forest

Listen to Finnish jazz musician Raoul Björkenheim, or rock group The Flaming Sideburns

Watch Aki Kaurismäki's *The Man Without a Past*, the story of a man who loses his memory and becomes homeless, or the road film *Leningrad Cowboys Go America*

Eat snow grouse, reindeer stew or glowfired salmon

Drink *salmiakkikossu* (a home-made spirit combining dissolved liquorice-flavoured sweets with the abrasive Koskenkova vodka, or *sahti* – sweet, high-alcohol beer)

IN A WORD
Sisu (often translated as 'guts', epitomising Finnish resilience)

TRADEMARKS
Fish; beating oneself with a fragrant branch of birch leaves in a sauna; Nokia phones; the aurora borealis; reindeers; Sami; Moomin trolls

SURPRISES
The world's largest smoke sauna is in Kuopio; the world's most popular surf instrumentalists are Finnish band Laika & the Cosmonauts

Rarely do you get a chance to see such unadulterated commercialism in one neat little package. This, if Lapland's claims are true, is the home of Christmas and jolly ol' Saint Nick. The Santa Claus Main Post Office is here and it receives close to a million letters each year from children all over the world. As tacky and trite as this may sound, it's all good fun. You can send a postcard home with an official Santa stamp or have a photograph taken with Father Christmas himself (signs warn would-be photographers that Santa is a registered trademark and can only be photographed by his elves!).

– Lonely Planet's *Finland*

5. A sapling pokes its head from beneath a blanket of winter snow in Oulu David Tipling

MAP REF: E,22

2. Contrasting styles define the art and architecture of the Musée du Louvre, Paris Richard l'Anson

3. Cabaret any day – the windmill of the infamous Moulin Rouge is still turning since this burlesque beauty was established in 1889, Paris Manfred Gottschalk

4. Vineyards form quilted patterns of Van Gogh colours in the wine-growing region of Beaujolais Pascale Beroujon

5. A tourist photographs the Eiffel Tower, one of the most photographed structures in the world and icon of everything French Jan Stromme

1. Dancers pause for a breath of air at the tall windows of a Parisian studio Rodney Hyett

With a capital that's synonymous with romance, a culture that's richer than foie gras, and a gene pool of philosophers, revolutionaries and designers, it's no wonder France has status. Fantastic ski slopes, glamorous beach resorts and rural villages complete the picture, while the food and wine score a gastronomic A+. Passionately patriotic, the French believe they live in the best place on earth. And since they invented *joie de vivre*, they might just be right.

BEST TIME TO VISIT
April and May (spring) or September and October (autumn)

ESSENTIAL EXPERIENCES
Taking a boat down the Seine and marvelling at the Parisian architecture

Checking out the glitz and glamour of the Le Mans 24-Hour Race

Paying your respects at the evocative D-Day landing beaches in Normandy

Enjoying on-piste action and après-ski at Val d'Isère

Sipping a glass of Dom Perignon in Champagne

Visiting the imposing châteaux on the Loire

GETTING UNDER THE SKIN
Read Gustave Flaubert's *Madame Bovary*, a 19th-century classic about rural life and deluded passions

Listen to Serge Gainsbourg's 'Je t'aime...moi non plus' – it is impossible not to turn Francophile when you hear this song

Watch *À Bout de Souffle* (Breathless). Jump cuts, long takes, Jean Seberg's gamine look, Jean-Paul Belmondo's smouldering gaze – this is *nouvelle vague* cinema at its best.

Eat bloody steak, croissants, baguettes, Camembert

Drink red Bordeaux from Médoc, dessert wine from Sauternes

IN A WORD
Ooh la la!

TRADEMARKS
Café society; stinky cheese; the Eiffel Tower; garlic; la guillotine; stripy T-shirts; berets; Cartier; Chanel; Gaultier; Louis XIV; the impressionists; *boules*; red meat; red wine; Gauloises

SURPRISES
Attitudes can be conservative; bars close at 7pm in rural market towns

'The French think mainly about two things – their two main meals', a well-fed bon-vivant French friend once told us. 'Everything else is in parentheses'. And it's true. But don't suppose for a moment that this obsession with things culinary means dining out in France has to be a ceremonious occasion or one full of pitfalls for the uninitiated. Approach food and wine here with even half the enthusiasm les français *themselves do, and you will be warmly received, encouraged and very well fed.*

– Lonely Planet's *France*

6. The enchanting fortified abbey of Mont-Saint-Michel watches over a flock of sheep in Normandy John Elk III

MAP REF: H,20

141

2. The grim remains of the notorious convict prison on Devil's Island in the Îles du Salut James Lyon

3. Block rockin' beats on the streets of Cayenne
James Lyon

4. Pink defines the interior decoration of an old prison in the Îles du Salut Wayne Walton

5. Devil's Island caught in the natural frame of a rock formation Wayne Walton
LEFT 1. A contemplative young girl partially obscured by a swathe of cloth Adrien Vadrot

Modern French Guiana is a land of idiosyncrasies, where European Space Agency satellite launches rattle the market gardens of displaced Hmong farmers from Laos and thinly populated rainforests swallow nearly all but the country's coastline. Highly subsidised by Mother France, it boasts the highest standard of living of any 'country' in South America, but look beyond the capital city and you'll still find backwoods settlements of Maroons and Amerindians barely eking out a living.

BEST TIME TO VISIT
July to December, or in late February for Carnaval

ESSENTIAL EXPERIENCES
Observing by moonlight the amazing ritual of giant leatherback turtles storming the beach to lay eggs and their newborn offspring scuttling to the sea

Visiting the fascinating former penal-settlement islands of Îles du Salut by private catamaran or sailboat

Learning everything you always wanted to know about rockets but were afraid to ask at Centre Spatial Guyanais (French Guiana Space Center)

Hanging out in Cayenne and enjoying ethnic diversity, tropical ambience, gorgeous streetscapes and Creole cuisine

Being overwhelmed by the age-old virgin rainforest in the Trésor Nature Reserve (or just about anywhere in the interior)

GETTING UNDER THE SKIN
Read Henri Charrière's classic *Papillon* for a readable first-person account of the infamous penal colony on Devil's Island

Listen to Caribbean rhythms with a French accent

Watch the legendary Hollywood film *Papillon* starring Steve McQueen and Dustin Hoffman

Eat *crêpe forestière* (a savoury crepe of mushrooms and cheese), Vietnamese noodles or deliciously decadent pastries

Drink rum or fresh fruit juice

IN A WORD
Chébran (cool)

TRADEMARKS
Penal settlements (particularly Devil's Island); French space rockets; Francophiles; turtles

SURPRISES
French Guiana's rain forest is 90% intact; Plage Les Hattes contains the highest density of leatherback-turtle nesting sites in the world

Cayenne is one of the loveliest capital cities in South America. In lieu of soaring grandeur and modern urban vibrancy are bustling, colourful markets amid charming French colonial buildings ribbed with flowered balconies. The excellent Creole and Guianese food and the unique ethnic mix – locals, French expatriates, Brazilian fisherfolk, Surinamese Maroons and Hmong farmers – make this a fun place to spend a few days and eat, eat, eat while planning trips to the lush interior or along the populated coast.

— Lonely Planet's *South America*

MAP REF: N,14

143

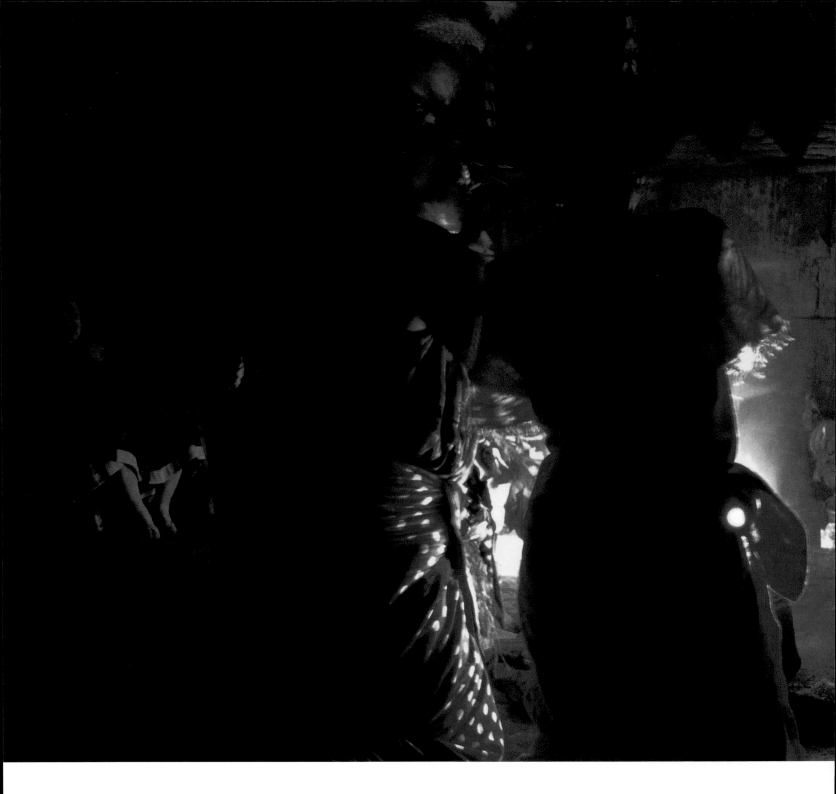

2. An orphaned gorilla hitches a ride back into the wild
Martin Harvey

3. Three women display initiatory face paint Sylvain Grandadam

Outside Libreville, its flashy air-conditioned capital, Gabon is a laid-back country of small villages, steamy rainforest, roaring rivers and imposing mountains. It's one of the richest and most stable countries in Africa, but also a place where people know the value of relaxation. The jungle is full of wildlife – elephants, leopards, gorillas, hippos, pythons – and new national parks are opening the forests to ecotourism, and closing them to loggers.

BEST TIME TO VISIT
May to September (dry season)

ESSENTIAL EXPERIENCES
Visiting Albert Schweitzer's jungle hospital in the wildlife-rich lakes region of Lambaréné

Swimming, exploring, eating and relaxing in Mayumba – an untouristed beach town

Walking through the forests of Réserve de la Lopé, Gabon's best wildlife park, with elephants, monkeys and, if you're lucky, gorillas

Camping at the Cirque de Leconi, a spectacular red-rock canyon on the Bateke Plateau

GETTING UNDER THE SKIN
Read *African Silences*, by Peter Matthiessen, which focuses on his journeys through Gabon and other parts of West Africa

Listen to Oliver N'Goma, the hottest Gabonese musician today

Watch *The Great White Man of Lambaréné*, a film about Albert Schweitzer from an African perspective

Eat manioc paste (or rice) served in a spicy sauce

Drink a Castel – or better yet, a Régab – beer from the Sobraga brewery, but never, ever the tap water

IN A WORD
Mbôlo (hello, in Fang)

TRADEMARKS
The wealthiest nation in sub-Saharan Africa; the slow pace of life; steamy rainforest; Albert Schweitzer

SURPRISES
The Pont de Liane south of Franceville is a bridge made of vines, which locals use to cross the river; Gabon has been ruled since 1967 by President El Hadj Omar Bongo

Glitzy and glamorous in some spots, ramshackle and anarchic in others, Libreville is very likely to give you culture shock, especially if you've been slogging your way through the jungles of Central Africa. High-rise hotels line the beaches, European expats fill the shops and restaurants, and flashy cars speed down the wide boulevards. Meanwhile on the other side of town garbage is piled high and traffic slows to a crawl in the narrow, noisy streets.

— Lonely Planet's *Africa*

1. Patients dance for redemption at all-night healing ceremony known as Bwiti in the village of Gamba Troy Inman

4. How's the serenity? A green-clad man blends into the Parc de la Lekedi rainforest Martin Harvey

MAP REF: 0,21

2. The mysterious Waasu Stone Circle, an enigmatic congregation of megalithic stones on MacCarthy Island David Else

3. A woman wearing a traditional head-wrap flashes her teeth and jewellery Ariadne Van Zandbergen

4. A man checks his salted fish at a Banjul market in the country's west Christine Osborne

5. At the close of day, traditional fishing pirogues retire in rows to Bakau beach Andrew Burke

6. Using their heads as counter-tops, women in Banjul sell refreshments to weary bus passengers David Else
LEFT 1. Musicians beat out traditional tunes at the Roots Homecoming Festival in Banjul Ariadne Van Zandbergen

Sunshine and golden beaches have long made the Gambia a winter getaway for Europeans. But beyond the European-flavoured resorts are African-style wildlife reserves and the ruins of long-abandoned slaving stations. The Gambia is blessed with so many species of birds in such a compact area that even those who would struggle to identify a pigeon can't fail to be impressed. Its size, people, language and food make the Gambia the perfect gateway to West Africa.

BEST TIME TO VISIT
November to April (dry season)

ESSENTIAL EXPERIENCES
Being surprised by the colonial elegance and unhurried pace of the capital, Banjul

Sunning in Serekunda, where there's a beach – and a beach bar – for every taste

Birdwatching in the Abuko Nature Reserve – home to 250 bird species

Relaxing in the southern fishing village of Gunjur, much quieter than neighbouring resorts to the north

Cruising down the Gambia River with an amazing array of birdlife for company

Soaking up the sleepy, crumbling, ex-colonial atmosphere of Georgetown

GETTING UNDER THE SKIN
Read *Chaff on the Wind* by Gambian author Ebou Dibba, which follows the fortunes of two rural boys who come to work in the city

Listen to ever-popular band Ifang Bondi's most recent effort, *Gis Gis*

Watch *Roots*, by Alex Haley, who traced his origins to Jufureh, a village on the lower Gambia River

Eat *domodah* (peanut stew with rice) or *benechin* (rice baked in a thick sauce of fish and vegetables)

Drink the refreshing local beer, JulBrew

IN A WORD
I be ñaading (hello)

TRADEMARKS
Beaches; birdwatching; riverboats; nightclubs; package tourism

SURPRISES
It's a taboo in the Gambia to whistle after dark; Banjul International Airport's main runway was partly built by NASA as an emergency runway for space shuttles

The apocryphal story of the country's origins help explain why its people are so laid-back: the borders were fixed when an English gunship sailed up the Gambia River and fired cannonballs port and starboard – the border was drawn where the cannonballs fell. Few countries better typify the artifice of the postcolonial nation-state. The grim realities of politics and economics, such as the ups and downs of tourism, are the ultimate theatre of the absurd – best taken with a fistful of salt.

– Lonely Planet's *Africa*

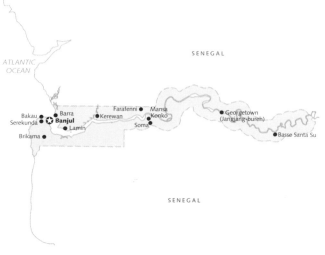

MAP REF: M,18

2. An oddly artistic look-out point on the Georgian Military Highway near Krestovy Pass Georgi Shablovsky

3. A candle illuminates the pious face of a worshipper at Kashveti Church, Tbilisi Paul Doyle

4. Lips pursed in concentration, a woman harvests grapes in the Kakheti wine region Paul Doyle

5. Wild flowers bloom beneath the ruins of Jvari, an early-seventh-century church in Mtskheta
Georgi Shablovsky

6. A villager keeps a careful grip on his chickens as he buses into town on market day Georgi Shablovsky
LEFT 1. The face of an elderly woman in Tbilisi etched with history and untold stories Paul Doyle

GEORGIA

CAPITAL TBILISI POPULATION 4,934,413 AREA 69,700 SQ KM OFFICIAL LANGUAGE GEORGIAN

Described variously as part of Europe, Central Asia or the Middle East, Georgia has long been a flash point for cultural and geographical collision. Tourist facilities in this newly independent nation are challenged by Western standards, but as a visitor you'll be fêted, fed, watered, and made to sing and dance, all in incomprehensible Georgian, one of the world's most unusual languages. Even if you can't understand much more than your hosts' smiles, the warmth you'll experience here will help you understand why Georgia remains a highlight of many people's travels.

BEST TIME TO VISIT
May, June and September for pleasant weather

ESSENTIAL EXPERIENCES
Hiking in the magnificent Caucasus Mountains
Taking a walk in Batumi's fragrant botanical gardens
Exploring the ancient cave monastery city at Vardzia
Strolling through the picturesque lanes of Tbilisi's Old Town
Discovering the religious architecture at Mtskheta
Chilling out at a pebble-beach resort on the Black Sea coast

GETTING UNDER THE SKIN
Read *Please Don't Call It Soviet Georgia* by Mary Russel, an entertaining travelogue describing the period of upheaval leading to independence

Listen to *Georgian Voices* by the Rustavi Choir, Georgian music performed by a collection of singers from various parts of the country showcasing different styles and brilliant harmonies

Watch *Keto and Kote* by respected Georgian filmmaker Siko Dolidze, shot in 1949

Eat *khachi* (a breakfast soup made from cow hoof, tripe and garlic), *pkhali* (beetroot or spinach paste mixed with garlic and walnuts), *lobio* (spiced red or green beans), *tkemali* (tasty wild plum sauce)

Drink delicious Georgian wines such as Guurdzaani, Tsinandali and Saperavi

IN A WORD
Didi madloba (many thanks)

TRADEMARKS
The stunning flora and fauna of the Caucasus; impressive cave complexes; elaborate toasting and revelry at a traditional dinner; cakes laden with cream, fruit and sugar; churches, monasteries and pagan temples

SURPRISES
Until you experience a full Georgian meal, complete with lengthy toasting ceremonies, you can't truthfully claim to have seen the real Georgia

Its weather and landscape are a meeting of east and west. Its history is a lengthy list of empires rising and falling. Its culture is ancient and built around a vast variety of influences; its people are a mix of traditional and very modern; and the food is legendary.

World Guide, www.lonelyplanet.com

MAP REF: I,24

2. The surreal architecture of Caligari Hall, part of the Filmpark Babelsburg in Brandenburg Andrea Schulte-Peevers

3. Dancers in Munich Dan Herrick

4. The striking Maxim Gorki Theatre in Berlin Jonathan Smith

5. A serene lookout over the Sylvenstein Reservoir, Lenggries
Thomas Winz

In the heart of Europe, Germany offers small picturesque towns, elegant big-city charm, fine wine and beer and a wealth of art and culture, plus the perennial pleasures of huge tracts of forest and castles along the Rhine. Germany also lies at the crossroads of Continental history. From Charlemagne and the Holy Roman Empire to Otto von Bismarck's German Reich, Nazism and the rise and fall of the Berlin Wall, no other nation has shaped Europe to the same extent as Germany.

BEST TIME TO VISIT
November to April for fewer tourists and surprisingly pleasant weather

ESSENTIAL EXPERIENCES
Hiking from *Gasthaus* (hotel) to *Gasthaus* in the Black Forest
Experiencing Dachau, Buchenwald, or another Holocaust memorial
Immersing yourself in the urban cultures of Berlin, Munich, Hamburg and Dresden
Taking a trip down the evocatively scenic Rhine Valley
Discovering the picturesque walled cities and towns along the Romantic Road
Enjoying a traditional meal in a *Ratskeller* (basement restaurant)
Viewing lofty cathedrals such as the Ulm Münster and the Dom in Köln
Summertime swimming at lakes and *Schwimbads* (swimming pools)

GETTING UNDER THE SKIN
Read Goethe's *Faust*, which tells of the classic deal with the devil, and nobel prize-winning author Günther Grass's novel *The Tin Drum*, which caused an uproar in Germany in the 1950s because of its depiction of the Nazis

Listen to Berlin-style punk symbol Nina Hagen, or tune in to Kraftwerk's '80s techno, and chanteuse Ute Lemper

Watch Wim Wenders' earthbound angels over divided Berlin in *Wings of Desire* or the fast-paced *Run Lola Run*

Eat *Wurst* (sausage) with mustard, sauerkraut and potato salad

Drink beer: with 80% of Europe's breweries in Germany, the choice is ample; or sample white wines such as Gewurtztraminer and Rieslings

IN A WORD
Auf Wiedersehen (goodbye/farewell/until we see each other again)

TRADEMARKS
Lederhosen; the legacy of WWII; good engineering; no speed limits; cuckoo clocks; Oktoberfest; the Berlin Wall; doing what is socially accepted (and expected); BMW, Volkswagen, Mercedes, Audi and Porsche

SURPRISES
German is a very pretty spoken language; Germans sometimes break the rules; Germans can play as hard as they work

From the claustrophobic beauty of its cathedrals to classical films from the silent era of cinema, from the most influential philosophers (try Kant, Hegel, Nietzsche and Marx for starters) to some of the world's great physicists (Einstein and Planck), from the cream of classical composers (Bach, Beethoven, Brahms, Handel and Wagner) to contemporary industrial-grunge music and Krautrock, from the genius of Goethe to the revolutionary theatre of Brecht, Germany has it all.

— Lonely Planet's *Germany*

1. The perfect fairytale, Neuschwanstein Castle perched 200m above the valley and nestled among trees
Greg Gawlowski

6. Berlin's new Jüdisches Museum (Jewish Museum) Guy Moberly

MAP REF: G.21

2. A musical mound of maraccas for sale at a market in Accra
Jane Sweeney

3. The setting sun heralds evening prayer at Larabanga mosque, the oldest religious building in Ghana Ariadne Van Zandbergen

4. A woman paddles her canoe between Benyin and the Nzulezu stilt village near Busua Ariadne Van Zandbergen

5. A devoted subject of the king bears a golden sceptre at Manhiya Palace in Kumasi Ariadne Van Zandbergen

1. Proud as a statue, a woman surveys her village from the flat roof of her mud house in Sirigu Ariadne Van Zandbergen

6. Nets at the ready, traditional fishing pirogues prepare to enter the waters off Cape Coast Ariadne Van Zandbergen

Ghanaians have plenty to be proud of. Their country was home to West Africa's mightiest, gold-dripping empire; it was the first to drop colonialism and go it alone; it built the biggest artificial lake in the world; and it produces some of Africa's best highlife music and most famous sculpture. Yet you won't find a more chilled-out and friendly people. So if you want to sample West Africa's modern and ancient cultures, explore its historic slave forts, toast yourself on its beautiful beaches – and do it all speaking English – it's got to be Ghana.

BEST TIME TO VISIT
October to March, when the weather is cooler and dryer

ESSENTIAL EXPERIENCES
Browsing Accra's Makola (batik and beads) and Kaneshie (food and spices) markets

Steeping yourself in Ashanti culture and history at the National Cultural Centre in Kumasi

Strolling through Accra's peaceful Aburi Botanical Gardens

Spending the night in an old fort or castle on the Atlantic coast

Lazing on the long white sandy beach at Busua

Hiking and wildlife watching at Kakum National Park

GETTING UNDER THE SKIN
Read *Asante: The Making of a Nation* by Nana Otamakuro Adubofour provides an insight into Ashanti history and culture

Listen to *Electric Highlife*, a taste of highlife that will really get you moving; *Master Drummer from Ghana* by Mustapha Tettey Addy, one of West Africa's greatest drumming performers

Watch *Heritage Africa* by the celebrated Ghanaian director Kwaw P Ansah – an exploration of the effects of colonialism in Ghana

Eat groundnut stew; *omo tuo* – mashed rice balls served with fish or meat soup; *kyemgbuma* – crabs with potatoes, meat and cassava dough; *ntomo krakro* – fried sweet potato cakes, a popular street food

Drink *askenkee* – a cool, milky-white non-alchoholic drink made from corn

IN A WORD
Hani wodzo (let's dance)

TRADEMARKS
Beautiful beaches; vibrant city nightlife; fishing villages; ruins of the slave trade; elephants and antelope; highlife music; ancient forts and castles

SURPRISES
It's possible to meet the current Ashanti king at Manhyia Palace in Kumasi – inquire politely and bring a gift

Ghanaians like to have fun. Accra and Kumasi on Saturday night are jumping. Ghana is, after all, the place where highlife music got its start. Ghanaian highlife was the most popular music in the region in the 1970s and you can still pick up recordings by ET Mensah, Nana Ampadu and The Sweet Talks. Highlife is still very big and there's a wide range of artists to choose from.

– Lonely Planet's *West Africa*

MAP REF: N,19

2. A row of octopus hanging up to dry on Lipsi island Paul Hellander

3. Pride of Athens, the ancient Parthenon of the Acropolis doesn't look a day older than two and a half thousand years Glenn Beanland

4. The picturesque village of Olymbos clings to the ridgeface below Mt Profitis Ilias, Karpathos George Tsafos

5. Well-dressed donkeys carefully pick their way down the cobbled steps leading from the old port of Fira Skala on Santorini Craig Pershouse

1. Sunnies are strictly orthodox for this hipster priest on Rhodes Bill Wassman

6. Inky clouds blot out the sky as a ferry approaches the coast of Santorini Greg Gawlowski

Having exported chaos, drama, tragedy and democracy before most nations stayed up late enough to want souvlaki, Greece boasts an unrivalled legacy. From smoggy Athens to the blindingly bright islands dotting the sea, ancient fragments abound – the belly button of the cosmos at Delphi, fallen columns galore on sacred Delos, frescoed Minoan palaces on Crete and even, quite possibly, the remnants of Atlantis at Santorini.

BEST TIME TO VISIT
Easter to mid-June for the weather and fewer crowds – or around 600 BC to witness the birth of democracy

ESSENTIAL EXPERIENCES
Dining out beneath the floodlit Acropolis in Athens

Taking a walk in spring through the Mani or Arcadia mountains in the Peloponnese

Island-hopping from Piraeus to Mykonos, Delos and Naxos

Hiking through Crete's dramatic Samaria Gorge

Wondering at the monasteries of Meteora, perched high on their pinnacles of rock

Catching that first glimpse of Santorini's sheer cliffs and whitewashed buildings

GETTING UNDER THE SKIN
Read *Zorba the Greek* by Nikos Kazantzakis – a tale about living life to the fullest by Greece's most celebrated contemporary author; *Captain Corelli's Mandolin* by Louis de Bernières – a captivating WW II-era love story set on Kefallonia

Listen to Demis Roussos – the larger than life singer who spent the 1980s strutting the world stage clad in his kaftan. Yanni is a US-based techno wizard who hails from Greece

Watch *Eternity and a Day*, directed by Theodoros Angelopoulos – traces the last days of a celebrated Greek writer; *Orgasmos tis Ageladas* (The Cow's Orgasm), directed by Olga Malea – a light-hearted comedy about two girls from Larissa who are frustrated by the restrictions of small-town society

Eat *spanakopita* (spinach pie), *moussaka* (layers of eggplant or zucchini, minced meat and potatoes topped with cheese and baked) or, for something sweet, *baklava* (layers of filo pastry filled with honey and nuts)

Drink Greek coffee, the national drink – it is served in a small cup with the grounds and no milk. Ouzo, the most popular aperitif in Greece, is distilled from grape stems and flavoured with anise

IN A WORD
Kalimera (good day)

TRADEMARKS
The Parthenon; ouzo; plate-smashing; package tourists; beautiful beaches; the birthplace of philosophy; inter-island hopping; olives

SURPRISES
Greeks wear blue trinkets to ward off the evil eye; gum mastic (from the lentisk bush) has been used since ancient times to cure ailments from stomach ache to snake bite

If you arrive in a Greek town in the early evening in summer, you could be forgiven for thinking you've arrived mid-festival. This is the time of the volta, *when everyone takes to the streets, refreshed from their siesta, dressed up and raring to go.*

– Lonely Planet's *Greece*

MAP REF: I,22

2. The setting sun gleams on houses both old and new in Qaqortoq Rich Prohaska

3. A home for gnomes – a traditional sod house in Nanortalik Deanna Swaney

4. A fishing boat slices through the freezing waters of Ilulissat Kangualua (Illulissat Icefjord), Disko Bay Graeme Cornwallis

Ever since 15th-century explorers returned from the distant north with wild and woolly tales of unicorns and citadels of ice, Greenland has been a semi-mythical destination. And it's still a fantasy land come to life, with the aurora borealis, the vast tundra, monstrous glaciers that calve icebergs into the sea, and a coastline of glacial ice and ancient rock – the oldest on the planet. Its far-flung villages are visited by Mercedes in summer and dogsled in winter, and though supermarkets these days offer pineapples from Hawaii and tomatoes from Mexico, you can still grab a seal steak from the frozen goods section.

BEST TIME TO VISIT
July to September during the thaw

ESSENTIAL EXPERIENCES
Hiking from Narsarsuaq to Kiattuut Sermiat's beautiful mountain lake

Soaking in the Uunartoq Hot Springs while watching icebergs floating past

Wandering around Hvalsey, the best-preserved Norse ruins in Greenland

Being awed by the soaring granite ramparts of Uiluit Qaaqa and Ulamertorsuaq at Tasermiut Fjord

Taking the ferry to Aappilattoq through sapphire-blue waters, past granite spires

Hanging out in Nanortalik – a relaxed and friendly town in scenic countryside

GETTING UNDER THE SKIN
Read The entertaining account of the country in *Last Places – A Journey in the North*, by Lawrence Millman

Listen to the melodic sounds of pop group Qulleq, or check out techno band Hap

Watch the Oscar-nominated classic *Qivitoq*, which is set in Greenland

Eat fresh *kapisillit* (salmon), or pick your own huckleberries (small blueberries)

Drink the local home-brew beer called *imiaq* – but you may need to gather some gumption first

IN A WORD
Brrrr!

TRADEMARKS
Whale steaks; seasonally affected depression ('SAD syndrome'); ice; Inuit people; fishing trawlers; glaciers

SURPRISES
Greenland has one of the world's lowest rates of cardiovascular disease due to the consumption of unsaturated fatty acids found in marine mammals; Greenlanders believe their children are born with the wisdom, survival instinct, magic and intelligence of their ancestors

One factor common to high latitudes in the long dark winters is a high incidence of depression, which the Inuit recognise and call perlerorneq *(the burden). Violent or other abnormal behaviour is often blamed on it but people don't try to explain it away or make excuses. Rather, they accept it as part of life.*

– Lonely Planet's *Iceland, Greenland & the Faroes*

1. Cheerful matchbox houses nest amongst the rocks of Uummannaq, one of the sunniest corners of Greenland Deanna Swaney

5. Pens, pencils and pennants– national dress is school uniform in Uummannaq Graeme Cornwallis

MAP REF: C,15

2. A woman carries fruit and flowers on her head Lee Foster

3. Boys playing with bicycle wheels, Hermitage Margie Politzer

Dubbed the 'Spice Island' because of its impressive production of nutmeg, mace, cinnamon, ginger and cloves, Grenada is a heady mix of idyllic tropical rainforests, fecund valleys, terraced gardens and rivers that fall away to white-sand beaches, bays and craggy cliffs. St George's, the beautiful capital, gives Grenada a small-town character, with a dash of dynamic sophistication. Its harbour, known as the Carenage, is one of the prettiest in the Caribbean.

BEST TIME TO VISIT
Temperatures are optimum year-round; Carnival, the second weekend in August, is hard to miss

ESSENTIAL EXPERIENCES
Swimming at glorious Grand Anse beach

Taking the ferry over to lazy Carriacou island

Walking around tiny Petit Martinique island

Driving through the Grand Etang National Park

Splashing about on the undeveloped sands of Bathways Beach

GETTING UNDER THE SKIN
Read native Grenadian Jean Buffong's *Under the Silk Cotton Tree: A Novel (Emerging Voices)*, a portrait of her Grenadian girlhood, religion and culture

Listen to local calypso, steel bands and reggae

Watch the documentary *Grenada: The Future Coming Towards Us*, which covers Grenada's early history and looks at contemporary Grenadian society

Eat pigeon peas and rice (pigeon peas are the brown, pea-like seeds of a tropical shrub) or curried *lambi* (conch)

Drink the nonalcoholic fruit juice *mauby* (a bittersweet drink made from the bark of the rhamnaceous tree), rum sprinkled with nutmeg, the locally brewed beer Carib

IN A WORD
Small is beautiful – a popular saying in the Caribbean

TRADEMARKS
'The Spice Islands'; the invasion led by former US president Ronald Reagan; Grand Anse beach; the *Bianca C* shipwreck; smuggling

SURPRISES
Grenada produces one third of the world's nutmeg; Scottish heritage on the island of Carriacou is evident in Highland-style cottages and Celtic methods of boat building

All-day spontaneous beach-cricket events are played on the water's edge with a wet tennis ball, a bat and three stick wickets in the sand. It's a Sunday afternoon tradition: families bring food and drinks in coolers down to the beach, and there's an easy carnival atmosphere as the people relax and swim and enjoy their day of rest. The orthodox high-paced crook-arm chuck, tacitly adjudged legal by all, is the preferred method of bowling.

— Lonely Planet's *Eastern Caribbean*

1. Out with the family, St George's Margie Politzer

4. Visitors kick back under thatched umbrellas on Grand Anse beach Margie Politzer

MAP REF: M,13

2. Terre-de-Haut clings to the coastline on the island of Les Santines Greg Gawlowski

3. Fishing boats return at sunset Greg Gawlowski

1. Local boys expressing sheer *joie de vivre* at the beach Bruno Morandi

4. The tropical Grand Etang lake Jean-Bernard Carillet

Guadeloupe's spirited blend of French and African influences goes straight to the heart of the Caribbean's Creole culture. As well known for its sugar and rum as for its beaches and resorts, the archipelago mixes modern cities and rural hamlets, rainforests and secluded beaches. There are nine inhabited islands to choose from, including Grande-Terre, Basse-Terre and Marie-Galant. Bustling Pointe-à-Pitre is the main hub, but the sleepy capital is on Basse-Terre's remote southwestern flank.

BEST TIME TO VISIT
February to April (dry season)

ESSENTIAL EXPERIENCES
Kicking back on the Frenchified island of Terre-de-Haut and checking out its grand 19th-century fort

Visiting the sleepy isles of La Désirade and Marie-Galante, with their uncrowded beaches and unspoilt scenery

Lazing on the beach at Anse à la Gourde, a gorgeous sweep of white coral sands

Exploring the rainforest in Parc National de la Guadeloupe, on Basse-Terre

Snorkelling the waters of the Réserve Cousteau

Hiking up the volcanic summit of Basse-Terre's La Soufrière

GETTING UNDER THE SKIN
Read *Anabase* by local poet Alexis Léger (translated by TS Eliot); *The Tree of Life* by Maryse Condé, centring around the life of a Guadeloupean family

Listen to local *zouk* group Malavoi or Gwo-ka master Guy Konket

Watch *Sucre Amer* directed by Christian Lara

Eat *crabes farci* (spicy stuffed land crabs) or *colombo cabri* (curried goat)

Drink *ti-punch* (white rum, cane sugar and fresh lime, mixed to your own proportions), or locally brewed Corsaire beer

IN A WORD
Bonjour! – best delivered with a big smile

TRADEMARKS
Sugar; rum; beaches; resorts; fishing villages; Creole food; women in traditional Creole costume

SURPRISES
Guadeloupe is a member of the EU; about two-thirds of all the bananas eaten in France are from Guadeloupe

Home to most of Terre-de-Haut's residents, Borg des Saints is a picturesque village with a decidedly Norman accent. Its narrow streets are lined with whitewashed, red-roofed houses with shuttered windows and yards of flowering hibiscus. The ferry is met by young girls peddling tourment d'amour *(agony of love) cakes with a sweet coconut filling – an almost painfully delicious island treat that makes a tasty light breakfast.*

– Lonely Planet's *Eastern Caribbean*

MAP REF: L,13

161

2. Mt Jumulong's slopes provide eternal pleasures for nature lovers Michael S. Yamashita

3. A girl in a Chamorro costume superimposed against a gaudy backdrop Joe Carini

Looking for tribal villages or ancient cultures untouched by the modern world? You won't find them in Guam, as this strategic US territory isn't in the 'Tropical Paradise' mould. You'll have more luck in the Northern Marianas, with their turquoise waters, white sands, fine diving, snorkelling and hiking. And if you really want to get away from it all, hop over to laid-back Tinian or rustic Rota. Guam and the Northern Marianas are inextricably linked by history and geography, sharing typhoons, an archipelago, Spanish and US influences, the Mariana Trench and Chamorro culture.

BEST TIME TO VISIT
December to March (the dry season)

ESSENTIAL EXPERIENCES
Dodging Saipan's golf courses to find that rare secluded beach

Slowing down to the village pace of Rota

Communing with monolithic latte stones or bodysurfing the beaches on Tinian

Whooping it up at a fiesta in Agana's Chamorro Village

Getting romantic at Guam's Two Lovers Point where two legendary lovers plunged to a precipitous death

GETTING UNDER THE SKIN
Read *Micronesia: Winds of Change*, spanning the history from 1521 to 1951 with accounts of early explorers, missionaries and locals

Listen to *It's Party Time in the Marianas* by the Castro Boyz for a funky mix of English and Chamorro tunes

Watch George Tweed's short film *Return to Guam*, which traces the journey back to the island by a former US serviceman

Eat anything with *finadene*, a hot sauce zinging with red peppers, soy sauce, lemon juice and onions that turns dishes into a real Chamorro meal

Drink a major American cola – they're all here

IN A WORD
Hafa adai (a catch-all greeting encompassing Hello, What's up and How are you?)'

TRADEMARKS
Crystal-clear blue waters and white-sand beaches; crusty American GIs comparing war wounds; package tourists ambling past centuries-old latte stones; beach bars pouring all day and night; spicy Spanish-inspired food

SURPRISES
The Marianas are at the edge of the deep-sea Mariana Trench, so if measured from their bases the islands are actually the world's highest mountains, dwarfing Mt Everest by 10,000 feet

Guam, an unincorporated US territory, is the metropolis of Micronesia. It is a haven for shoppers: the Japanese come by the planeload to scoop up the duty-free items available at innumerable malls, while locals from nearby islands haunt the enormous Kmart, which stocks US goods at the cheapest prices around.

— Lonely Planet's *Micronesia*

1. Palms frame a majestic cloud formation at sunset Michael S. Yamashita

4. An elderly woman from the Northern Marianas in traditional festival gear Anders Ryman

MAP REF: M,35

2. Mayan colours come out of the closet for market day in San Lucas Toliman Richard l'Anson

3. Hooded figures bless the streets of Antigua with incense during the Good Friday procession Jeffrey Becom

4. Look, no hands! Cheeky children carrying traditional embroidery in Antigua Aaron McCoy

5. The crown of Templo I in the lost city of Tikal materialises from the morning mist Ryan Fox

1. A Guinean woman deftly juggles brochettes in a frying pan Grazyna Bonati

Guinea was once ruled by one of the most oppressive regimes in Africa, but these days the country exudes a marked energy and growing economic vitality. High on the country's list of attractions is the vibrancy of its cultural traditions, particularly in music and dance, and its natural beauties include lush rainforests and breathtaking highland scenery. Visitors to Guinea can trek through the jungles of the southeast, watch an amazing dance performance in Conakry or browse through one of the many bustling markets.

BEST TIME TO VISIT
November to February (the dry season) – or between the 13th and 15th centuries when Guinea was part of the Empire of Mali

ESSENTIAL EXPERIENCES
Strolling the streets and taking in the vibrant neighbourhood life in Conakry

Hiking in the beautiful green hills of Fouta Djalon

Scouring the enormous Wednesday market at Guéckédou

Visiting the Grande Mosquée and sculpture workshop at Kankan

Viewing the Bridal Falls (during the rainy season) at Kindia

Lying in the sun on the beach at Cape Verga

GETTING UNDER THE SKIN
Read *L'Enfant Noir* by Guinean writer Camara Laye, full of fascinating insights into traditional daily life

Listen to *Bembeya Jazz National* by the popular Guinean group Bembeya Jazz, one of Africa's premier dance bands

Watch *Djembefola* by Laurent Chevallier, the story of Guinean drummer Mamady Keita's return to his remote native village

Eat *kulikuli* – peanut balls made with peanuts, onion and cayenne pepper; grilled fish; brochettes (kebabs)

Drink *café noir* – small cups of espresso-like coffee drunk with lots of sugar

IN A WORD
I be di (hello in Maninka)

TRADEMARKS
Indigo cloth; vibrant nightlife; gorgeous beaches; traditional music and dance; great street food; French colonial influences; mangrove swamps; rich wildlife

SURPRISES
The open-air cinema at Mamou; French-style pâtisseries in Conakry; chimpanzees and hippopotamii in the Parc Transfronalier Niokolo-Badier

Traditional music remains popular with most of the people in Guinea, despite the rise in popularity of more modern forms. National and international stars have blended western instruments with African rhythms and instruments, and the two types of music still exist side by side. Over 80 recordings have been made by Syliphone, the country's home-grown music label. They cover an enormous range of popular and traditional stylos.

– World Guide, www.lonelyplanet.com

4. All in a day's work! A young girl collects water from a well Graznya Bonati

MAP REF: M.18

2. A distinctly Mediterranean-influenced Christian church in Bissau David Else

3. Gone fishing – an ocean-going canoe tries its luck along the Guinea-Bissau coast David Else

Tiny, verdant and fractured by waterways, Guinea-Bissau is a gem for those prepared to seek it out. Sleepy towns, quiet beaches and sacred rainforests dot the mainland, while offshore the Arquipélago dos Bijagós has a unique culture and fantastic marine and animal life. Guinea-Bissau is not a well-developed nation – even by African standards it's gut-wrenchingly poor – and it's been badly served by its recent leaders. However, it remains peaceful and its people are some of the most unconditionally hospitable in West Africa.

BEST TIME TO VISIT
Late November to February, when it's dry and cool

ESSENTIAL EXPERIENCES
Viewing the flora and fauna of the Arquipélago dos Bijagós

Dancing at Bissau's February Carnival – music, papier-mâché masks and parades

Hiking and observing wildlife in the south's sacred forests

Checking out the Portuguese colonial architecture throughout the country

Relaxing on the archipelago's pristine beaches

GETTING UNDER THE SKIN
Read Susan Lowerre's *Under the Neem Tree*, which tells a vivid story of a Peace Corps volunteer's experiences in the region

Listen to Super Mama Djombo and popular singers Dulce Maria Neves, N'Kassa Cobra and Patcheco

Watch Flora Gomes' *The Blue Eyes of Yonta*, a film about dreams and revolution

Eat *riz gras* (rice with a greasy sauce) at rice bars, or grilled fish and salad at *barracas* (makeshift bar/restaurants)

Drink *caña de cajeu* (cashew rum) – made from the cashew fruit that surrounds the nuts

IN A WORD
Bom-dia (good morning)

TRADEMARKS
Monkeys; groundnuts; Portugese colonialism; the Arquipélago dos Bijagós

SURPRISES
Guinea-Bissau is the world's sixth-largest producer of cashew nuts; the Orango Islands National Park is home to a rare species of saltwater hippopotamus

While mainland Guinea-Bissau is not noted for the use of sculpted figures and masks, the Bijago people, due to their isolation, continue to maintain these traditions. Statues representing Iran, the great spirit, are used in connection with agricultural and initiation rituals. These are carved as seated figures, sometimes wearing a top hat. Initiation masks are also carved, the best known being the Dugn'be, a ferocious bull with real horns.

– Lonely Planet's *West Africa*

1. A jam-packed ship plies the waters around the Arquipélago dos Bijagós David Else

4. Brightly painted buildings showcase Bissau's Portugese colonial history David Else

MAP REF: M,18

2. A snapshot of the Guyanese way of life Philippe Giraud

3. This wooden cathedral in Georgetown is typical of the capital's 19th-century colonial architecture Genevieve Vallee

1. A foolhardy photographer descends into a green abyss Oliver Grunewald

4. A young Comopi Indian girl comes over all camera shy Robert Harding World Imagery

Dutch and British colonisation made an indelible mark on Guyana, leaving behind a now dilapidated colonial capital, a volatile mix of peoples and a curious political geography. The country's natural attractions, however, are impressive, unspoiled and on a scale that dwarfs human endeavour. Guyana has immense falls, vast tropical rainforest, and grasslands teeming with wildlife. If the government doesn't destroy the environment in a bid to pay off its huge foreign debt, it could be the ecotourism destination of the future.

BEST TIME TO VISIT
At the end of either rainy season: late January or late August

ESSENTIAL EXPERIENCES
Revelling in the spray of South America's most majestic waterfalls, Kaieteur Falls

Visiting Iwokrama, a rainforest conservation and development centre

Trucking on an unforgettable overland crossing from Georgetown to Lethem

Taking a wildlife-viewing excursion to a local ranch in the Rupununi Savanna, a vast area of grassland, termite mounds and forested hills

Exploring the gold and diamond fields near Bartica

GETTING UNDER THE SKIN
Read the country's best known work of literature, ER Braithwaite's *To Sir With Love*; or *Ninety-Two Days* which Evelyn Waugh wheezed his way through Guyana's rugged interior to write

Listen to Eddy Grant, who had a hit with 'Electric Avenue' in the early eighties

Watch *The Mighty Quinn* starring Guyanese-born Norman Beaton

Eat pepperpot (a spicy stew cooked in bitter cassava juice), souse (jellied cow's head) or try an East Indian curry and *roti*

Drink Banks beer, local rum El Dorado 5 Star, or delicious fruit punches

IN A WORD
Cat a ketch rat, but he a teef he massa fish (good and evil come from the same source)

TRADEMARKS
Crime; the Jim Jones tragedy; having the worst national football team in South America; internationally renowned cricketer Clive Lloyd

SURPRISES
An estimated 30% of Iwokrama's flora and fauna is still unidentified; the national indoor pursuit is dominoes

Nibbee fiber, extracted from forest vines, is the most distinctive and appealing local product and is used to make everything from hats to furniture. The Macushi of the southwest have developed a unique art form based on carving forest scenes and creatures from the hardened latex of the balata tree.

— Lonely Planet's *South America*

GUYANA CAPITAL GEORGETOWN POPULATION 702,100 AREA 214 970 SQ KM OFFICIAL LANGUAGE ENGLISH

MAP REF: N,13

2. Floating chefs take a catch of conch down to Lambi harbour where they will be cooked over hot coals for hungry customers Andrew Marshall & Leanne Walker

3. The sombre ruins of Sans Souci, a French Palace built by slaves in the nineteenth century and later destroyed by an earthquake Eric Wheater

4. The cautious eyes of a young girl carrying a tub-load of laundry in Artibonite Eric Wheater

5. A woman guards the doorway of her home in Les Cayes Eric Wheater

The modern world's first black-led republic, Haiti boasts a unique culture and an incredible artistic tradition. Its intensely spiritual people are known for their humour and passion, upheld in the face of poverty, civil strife, oppression and urban overpopulation. Their language, dance and music reflect a unique syncopation between the spiritual and material worlds. Haiti is not yet set up for the Club Med crowd, but the open-minded adventurer will find a country whose contradictions will linger in mind, heart and spirit.

BEST TIME TO VISIT
June to August (the dry season)

ESSENTIAL EXPERIENCES
Touring Jacmel's Victorian gingerbread homes

Visiting the Musée National in Port-au-Prince, housing King Christophe's suicide pistol and a rusty anchor reputed to have been salvaged from Columbus' *Santa Maria*

Strolling among the Spanish-influenced architecture of Cap-Haïtien

Shopping at Port-au-Prince's Marché de Fer (Iron Market) — packed with stalls, vendors and piles of fruit, baskets and religious totems

Taking the horseback trek to the Bassins Bleu — three cobalt-blue pools joined by spectacular cascades

GETTING UNDER THE SKIN
Read *Beast of the Haitian Hills* by Pierre Marcelin and Philippe Thoby Marcelin, a novel about life in the Haitian countryside; the historical novel *All Souls' Rising* by Madison Smartt Bell

Listen to Cuban-Haitian vocal group Desandann or Lody Auguste

Watch *Lumumba* by acclaimed Haitian director Raoul Peck, or for some classic Hollywood horror from 1932, *White Zombie*

Eat *grillot et banane pese* (pork chops with island bananas) or *diri et djondjon* (rice and black mushrooms)

Drink rum, the drink of choice

IN A WORD
Pas plus mal (no worse than before) — the standard answer to 'How are you?'

TRADEMARKS
Vodou; zombies; Papa Doc; slave history; racial discord; shanty towns

SURPRISES
Orange peels drying on sunny surfaces throughout Cap-Haïtien are destined to one day lend their flavour to luxury liqueurs Grand Marnier and Cointreau; actors in enormous papier-mâché masks act out parables of good versus evil during Jacmel's pre-Lent Mardi Gras festivities

Vodou ceremonies are highly developed rituals to pleasure, feed and ultimately summon the lwa through the possession of a human body. Once the drums start, the ceremony has begun. There are usually three drums, the mamman, the segon and the boula. The mamman is the largest drum, which the leading drummer beats fiercely with a single stick and one hand. The segon payer provides hypnotic counter-rhythms while the boula drummer plays an even rhythm holding all the others together.

— Lonely Planet's *Dominican Republic & Haiti*

1. Water, gossip and washing up — the market well is a one-stop shop for locals in Milot   Eric Wheater

6. Cheerful as a merry-go-round, an intercity bus in Port-au-Prince, welcomes passengers aboard
Eric Wheater

MAP REF: L,12

2. Stilt houses creep across the water on the island of Roatán David Behrens

3. The white façade of La Iglesia de l a Merced evinces old colonial glory in Gracias, Lempira Jeffrey N Becom

4. A pair of Scarlet Macaws perch on a carving at the archeological site of Copán Ruinas Ralph Hopkins

5. A young boy and his indignant reptiles pose for show-and-tell Jeffrey N Becom

6. Cowboy kids relax with snacks in the town of Copán Jonathan Selig
LEFT 1. A mermaid presides over an empty bar in Tela Jeffrey N Becom

Honduras' slow pace, natural beauty and low-profile tourism make it particularly appealing to travellers (well-armed with insect repellent) who enjoy getting off-the-beaten track. Take your pick from the spectacular Mayan ruins at Copán, the long and lazy Caribbean coastline, the idyllic Bay Islands, the tropical rainforest of the Mosquitia region, colonial mountain towns, the cool cloud forest of La Tigra National Park, and the manatees and birdlife in the country's protected coastlands, wetlands and lagoons.

BEST TIME TO VISIT
May to June for the festivals

ESSENTIAL EXPERIENCES
Diving in the warm, crystal-clear waters of Islas de la Bahía

Fossicking through the pyramids and temples of Copán Ruinas

Visiting the Spanish colonial mountain town of Gracias

Experiencing the spectacular cloud forest of Parque Nacional Celaque

Exploring the Río Plátano biosphere at La Mosquitia, where monkeys, toucans and jaguars roam the forests

Taking the eight-hour boat ride up the Río Plátano to Las Marías through virgin rainforest

GETTING UNDER THE SKIN
Read *El Gran Hotel* by Guillermo Yuscarán (one of Honduras' most celebrated writers) or *The Soccer War* by Ryszard Kapuscinski, which is about the 100-hour war between Honduras and El Salvador known as the Guerra de Fútbol (the Football War)

Listen to Garífuna band *Los Menudos*

Watch *El Espiritu de mi Mama* (Spirit of my Mother) directed by Ali Allie, about a young Garífuna woman

Eat coconut bread or *casabe* (a crispy flat bread common throughout the Caribbean)

Drink Port Royal or Salva Vida beer

IN A WORD
Buenos días (good day)

TRADEMARKS
The Mosquito Coast; inexpensive diving; Copán Ruinas; the brief Football War; howler monkeys

SURPRISES
Islas de la Bahía form part of the second-largest barrier reef in the world; Honduras is experiencing the most rapid urbanisation in Central America

The traditional Garífuna band is composed of three large drums, a turtle shell, some maracas and a big conch shell, producing throbbing, haunting rhythms and melodies. The chanted words are like a litany, to which the audience often responds. The dance is the punta, a Garífuna dance with a lot of hip movement.

– Lonely Planet's *Central America*

MAP REF: M,10

2. The beguiling smile of a fish farmer in the village of Sam Mum Chai, New Territories Oliver Strewe

3. Sweeping and gliding, a girl on rollerskates runs rings around Hong Kong Park Phil Weymouth

4. A rickshaw chauffeur catches his breath and the local news Richard I'Anson

5. Chinese banners jostle for airspace above the commercial sights and smells of Wet Market Ray Laskowitz

Hong Kong is like no other city on earth. It's a pulsating, densely populated fusion of East and West, lit by neon, fuelled by nonstop yum cha, dressed in faux Dior and serenaded by Cantopop. And just when you think it's all too much, it's a secluded sandy beach on Lantau or a visit to a Taoist temple in the New Territories. Despite its British colonial past, Hong Kong has always stuck to its roots, and the culture beneath the glitz is pure Chinese – with a vibrant twist.

BEST TIME TO VISIT
October to December (the dry season)

ESSENTIAL EXPERIENCES
Crossing the harbour on a crowded Star Ferry

Heading out for a night on Lamma Island by *san-pan* or night ferry

Sipping cocktails at sunset in a skyscraper bar overlooking the harbour

Hopping on the cable car at Ocean Park and enjoying the view of the cliffs down to Deep Water Bay

Riding the double-decker bus to Stanley market – try to get a seat in the front row on the upper deck

GETTING UNDER THE SKIN
Read *An Insular Possession* by Timothy Mo – a novel set in precolonial Hong Kong; *Fragrant Harbour* by John Lanchester – set in the more recent past

Listen to Canto-pop: treacly pop schmaltz, with stars including Sally Yip, Sammi Cheung and Andy Lau

Watch *Crime Story*, directed by Che Kirk Wong Chi Keung, a traditional Jackie Chan movie combining good comedy and kung fu; *Young and Dangerous*, directed by Andrew Lau Wai Keung, a film adaptation of a local comic series about Triad society

Eat *juk* (breakfast rice porridge), *cha siu bau* (steamed pork buns), *sinning jin yuen gain* (pan-fried lemon chicken), *she gang* (snake soup)

Drink *dong gafe* (chilled coffee soft drink), *bolei* (green tea), Tsingtao (a popular Chinese brand of beer), *mao tai* (Chinese wine)

IN A WORD
Nei ho ma? (hello; how are you?)

TRADEMARKS
Early morning bargains; crowds jostling for space; designer fakes; Jackie Chan; festivals all year around; expatriates; the Star Ferry; feng shui; dim sum

SURPRISES
Hong Kong consumes more oranges than anywhere else on earth; the frequently heard new year greeting '*kung hei fat choi*' literally means 'respectful wishes, get rich'

The Lunar New Year is the most important holiday of the Chinese year. Expect a lot of colourful decorations but not much public merry-making; for the most part, this is a festival for the family, though there is a parade on the first day, fantastic fireworks display over Victoria Harbour on the evening of the second day, and one of the largest horse races is held at Sha Tin on day three.

Lonely Planet's *Hong Kong & Macau*

1. Honk if you love Honkers – shoppers and businessmen cross paths at the bustling intersection of Queen's Road and D'Aguilar Street Andrew Burke

6. Villains and lovers take centre stage in a Cantonese opera performance Julia Wilkinson

MAP REF: K,32

2. A woman peers from the window of an elegant Art-Nouveau building in Szombathely Martin Moos

3. Fine buildings of Blaha Luiza Square on the Pest side of the capital Roberto Soncin Gerometta

4. Dusk brings an undersea atmosphere to the Danube where the famous Chain Bridge unites both halves of Budapest Stuart Wasserman

5. A man enjoys beer, sunflower seeds and warm light in a Csongrád pub David Greedy

1. Checkmates – playing chess is a steamy activity at the Széchényi Baths, Budapest David Greedy

As piquant as the paprika it's famous for, and romantic as the Roma music that inspired Béla Bartók, Hungary offers visitors a taste of Europe's heart and soul – but at half the price of anywhere in Western Europe. Budapest is the star attraction, fabulously located on the Danube and rich in Art Nouveau and baroque architecture. Outside the capital, there are ruined castles, rejuvenating spas, Roman and Turkish remnants, and exquisite lake and vine country. Now that Hungary has joined the EU, the time is more than ripe to experience Magyarország.

BEST TIME TO VISIT
May to September (summer) – or before 1526, and the devastating Battle of Mohács

ESSENTIAL EXPERIENCES
Soothing away those aches and pains in one of Budapest's thermal baths

Letting loose at a resort on Lake Balaton, Hungary's 'inland sea'

Strolling around the Castle District in Buda

Cycling along the Danube Bend, particularly around Szentendre

Birdwatching in the Hortobágy National Park

Caving in the Aggtelek Karst, a Unesco World Heritage site

GETTING UNDER THE SKIN
Read *Fateless*, by Imre Kertész, an autobiographical novel about the author's experiences in concentration camps in WWII; *Eclipse of the Crescent Moon*, by Géza Gárdonyi, a tale set in the 16th century during the Turkish siege

Listen to *Márta Sebestyén*, whose haunting voice appears on *The English Patient* soundtrack, or Hungarian folk ensembles such as Cifra

Watch *István a Király* (Stephen the King), written by Levente Szörényi and János Bródy, a stirring rock-opera about the life of the first king of Hungary. *6:3* is Péter Timár's account of the impact the 'football match of the century' between England and Hungary in 1953 had on people's lives

Eat *töltött káposzta*, cabbage leaves rolled and stuffed with meat and rice; *madártej* is a delicious custard-like dessert

Drink *Tokaji Aszú* – 'the wine of kings and the king of wines'; *pálinka*, a kick-like-a-mule brandy made from stone fruits such as pear, apricot or plum

IN A WORD
Szia (hello)

TRADEMARKS
Goulash; salami; Rubik's Cube; water polo; Nobel Prize winners; Zsa Zsa Gabor; Roma music

SURPRISES
Hungarian surnames appear before their Christian names, as in Asian cultures; the burial place of Attila the Hun and his lost treasure is said to be somewhere in Hungary

The national anthem calls Hungarians 'a people torn by fate' and the overall mood is one of honfibú (literally 'patriotic sorrow', but really a penchant for the blues with a sufficient amount of hope to keep most people going).

– Lonely Planet's *Hungary*

6. Swimmers paddle past magnificent columns in the opulent Gellért Thermal Baths, Budapest Martin Moos

MAP REF: H,22

179

2. Traditional turf-roofed farmhouses appear half-submerged in grass above the glacial sand plains of Sandur Paul Harding

3. Like castle ruins, the austere rim of an extinct volcano presides over Vestmannaeyjar Steve Hutton

4. Summer wildflowers bloom in defiance of the bleak landscape of Skeidararsandur Grant Dixon

1. The hills of Landmannalaugar marbled with gleaming snow, Fjallabak Nature Reserve Grant Dixon

The big island with the chilly name is becoming one of Europe's hottest properties, bursting with natural wonders: active volcanoes, valley glaciers, Europe's biggest waterfalls, lava fields, geysers, thermal pools and the aurora borealis. Reykjavík, the world's northernmost capital, is a cultural dynamo with live music, great restaurants and museums squeezed into a subtle small-town environment. Outside the capital there's puffin-watching, whale-gazing, white-water rafting and medieval relics that make those famous Icelandic sagas come to life.

BEST TIME TO VISIT
Early June to the end of August, when the country defrosts

ESSENTIAL EXPERIENCES
Enjoying Reykjavík's famously uninhibited nightlife

Swimming in the piping-hot waters of the geothermal field at Nesjavellir

Snapping a photo of the iceberg-filled Jökulsárlón lagoon

Checking out Vatnajökull – Europe's biggest icecap

Cooing over thousands of puffin chicks on Heimaey island

Dogsledding on the icecaps at Mýrdalsjökull

GETTING UNDER THE SKIN
Read *Independent People* by Halldór Laxness, one of half a dozen brilliant novels by the Nobel Prize winner, or the comic drama *Angels of the Universe*, by Einar Már Gudmundsson

Listen to Björk, Quarashi and Sigur Rós

Watch *Children of Nature* directed by Friðrik Thór Friðriksson, which tells the story of an elderly couple forced into a retirement home in Reykjavík. *101 Reykjavík*, directed by Baltasar Kormákur and based on the novel by Hallgrímur Helgason, is a dark comedy that explores sex, drugs and the life of a loafer in downtown Reykjavík.

Eat *harðfiskur* (haddock), which is cleaned and dried in the open air until dehydrated and brittle. For something sweet, try *pönnukökur* (Icelandic pancakes).

Drink *kaffi* (coffee), Icelandic beer or the traditional Icelandic brew *brennivín*, a sort of schnapps made from potatoes and flavoured with caraway

IN A WORD
Skál! (cheers!)

TRADEMARKS
Fire and ice; Björk; fish; volcanoes; the aurora borealis; beer guzzling; hot springs

SURPRISES
At weekends the whole of Reykjavík joins in the great Icelandic pub-crawl, which goes on till dawn; it's forbidden for parents to bestow non-Icelandic or foreign-sounding names on their children

Once you've seen some of the lava fields and eerie natural formations that characterise much of the Icelandic landscape, it will probably come as no surprise that Icelanders believe their country is populated by hidden races of wee people: jarðvergar (gnomes), álfar (elves), ljósálfar (fairies), dvergar (dwarves), ljúflingar (lovelings), tívar (mountain spirits), englar (angels) and huldufólk (hidden people).

– Lonely Planet's *Iceland*

5. A spontaneous game of volleyball in the steamy waters of Laugardalur outdoor pool in Reykjavík Juliet Coombe

MAP REF: E,18

2. Wanna lift? A taxi driver cruises the busy streets of Calcutta Richard I'Anson

3. All smiles, a young woman of Jaisalmer in a brilliant sari
David Hannah

4. Bollywood beauty emblazons a Kozhikode shopfront where a man relaxes to read the newspaper Greg Elms

5. Siblings compete for exposure in a family portrait, Udaipur
David Hannah

Everyone wants a piece of India. From Aryan, Afghani and Persian invasions to the British era, people from distant lands have sought to possess India's treasures for themselves. But a funny thing always happens: India takes these foreigners and makes them Indians. Defying the doctrine of 'us' and 'them', India weaves races, cultures and philosophies into a tapestry that grows richer and more intricate every day. To experience India is to share in the sorrows, dreams, tribulations and almost unbearable joy of a billion fellow human beings. Fear not: India will make you her own, too.

BEST TIME TO VISIT
November to March, when it's cooler

ESSENTIAL EXPERIENCES
Watching the sunrise at the Taj Mahal

Floating to Udaipur's Lake Palace

Kicking back on a Goan beach

Taking a camel safari in Rajasthan

Relaxing in a Shimla hill-station resort

GETTING UNDER THE SKIN
Read Jawaharlal Nehru's *Discovery of India*, tales from the Vedic era to WWII, or V S Naipaul's *India: A Million Mutinies Now*, a Trinidadian's take on India's tribulations and triumphs

Listen to Lata Mangeshkar's *The Greatest Film Songs* – the diva extraordinaire sings Bollywood hits, or to Ravi Shankar's *In Celebration* – the world's greatest sitarist plays classical and fusion

Watch *Mother India,* India's answer to *The Grapes of Wrath*; *Gandhi,* the epic film that made Ben Kingsley famous; or any Bollywood flick

Eat tandoori chicken, dhal, dosas, samosas, curries

Drink *lassi* (a sweet or savoury yogurt drink), or *toddy* (fermented palm sap)

IN A WORD
Are vah! (holy cow! – not literally)

TRADEMARKS
Cows in streets; snake charmers; world's largest slums; Bollywood; maharajahs in palaces; rickshaws; gods and goddesses; computer geeks

SURPRISES
Cities have killer nightlife scenes; most food isn't spicy hot; English is the de facto national language; for the most part Hindus and Muslims live together peacefully

Once we had arrived at the entrance to the cave, the crush to see the deity was tremendous. I had to protect my wife. I was so flabbergasted that I forgot to see the deities. My wife told me to go back to the viewing area, so again I had to face the crush. The deities were made of ice. Shiva was in the middle, Parvati on one side and their son Ganesh on the other. It was amazing, it was like I could see the whole of India from this small place on the mountain top.

— Hiten K Mitra, Lonely Planet's *Sacred India*

1. Whoever goes down to a river goes down to the Ganges, the sacred spring of India, Varanasi Sara-Jane Cleland

6. Bathers scrub themselves in the Yamuna river beneath the timeless majesty of the Taj Mahal Patrick Horton

MAP REF: L,28

2. Evening sun smoulders on tapered rooftops in West Sumatra   Paul Bigland

3. With a ceremonial sword strapped to his back a young boy observes a temple ceremony in Bali   Gregory Adams

4. Lush rice terraces at Ocking near Ubud offer a glimpse into the Garden of Eden   Richard I'Anson

5. A fisherman casts his net into the foam at the wild surf beach of Parangtritis in Central Java   Phil Weymouth

6. Buddha sits contemplatively among the bell-shaped stupas of Borobudur, an ancient Buddhist monument in Central Java   Bernard Napthine

LEFT 1.   Like Hindu dolls, a procession of finely robed girls makes its way back from a Balinese temple
Gregory Adams

The world's most expansive archipelago dips and rises across the equator from the Indian Ocean to the Pacific. There are around eighteen thousand islands to choose from, six thousand of which are uninhabited, offering adventure that's hard to find these days in the developed world. Indonesia is endowed with a phenomenal array of wildlife, including tigers and orang-utans, and its fine white-sand beaches, sublime rice fields and exotic temples continue to lure visitors from afar.

BEST TIME TO VISIT
May to September, during the dry season

ESSENTIAL EXPERIENCES
Climbing Bali's Gunung Batur for exceptional sunrises

Taking a Batik course in Yogyakarta, Java

Eating breakfast at the floating market in Benjarmasin, Kalimantan

Chilling out on Lombok's Gili Islands

Watching the Ramayana Ballet full story unfold at the outdoor theatre in Prambanan, Java

Catching a wave at Pantai Suluban, Bali's surfing Mecca

GETTING UNDER THE SKIN
Read Pramoedya Ananta Toer's *The Fugitive*, by the leader of a failed nationalist revolt against Japanese occupation during WWII. Ayu Utami's *Saman* is a story of political repression, extramarital sex and religious intolerance.

Listen to Iwan Fals, a rock idol who conveys society's sufferings, and Padi, the favourite group at the 2003 Indonesia MTV Video Awards

Watch Garin Nugroho's *Bulan Tertsuk Ilalang* (And the Moon Dances). Joko Anwar's *Arisan* is the first home-grown film showing two men kissing.

Eat *nasi goreng* (fried rice), the country's most common dish, and *sate* (skewered meats with spicy peanut sauce)

Drink *kopi* (coffee), as Indonesia is the world's third-largest coffee producer; black *teh* (tea); or *bir* (beer), especially the domestic Bintang and Anker

IN A WORD
Tidak apa-apa (no problem)

TRADEMARKS
Great surfing; komodo dragons; terraced ricescapes; woodcarvings, textiles, basketwork and beadwork; exotic fruits; political corruption

SURPRISES
The Balinese year is only 210 days long; snow is found two degrees south of the equator on 'Puncak Jaya' in Papua

Bali's roosters are the most spoiled animals of Indonesia. Preened, groomed and dined, they are as pampered as Queen Elizabeth's corgis. Their owners look after them with unerring devotion: take them to meet friends, save them the choicest feed, place them in baskets near roads so they are entertained by passing traffic.

— Lonely Planet's *World Food Indonesia*

MAP REF: 0.32

185

2. Village houses of Kandovan carved from eroded volcanic hillside Mark Daffey

3. The towering peaks of the Alborz Mountains cast deep shadows over the snowy valleys beneath Chris Mellor

4. The benevolent face of an Afghani refugee at the Shiraz Bazaar Phil Weymouth

5. Brilliant tiles grace the arches and porticos of the famed Masjed-e Emam in Esfahan Chris Mellor

1. A peacock soars sunward on a dazzling blue mural in Shiraz Clint Lucas

The Middle East's best-kept secret, Iran forms a footbridge between Europe and Asia, and has hosted some of the great invaders: Genghis Khan from the east, Alexander the Great from the west, and hippies from all over the world. A visit to Iran is a voyage of contrasts — women clad in black, mosques bejewelled and dazzling, desert towns with twisting laneways, formal gardens and snowcapped peaks. And wherever you go, you are welcomed with a warmth that is astounding.

BEST TIME TO VISIT
March to May or September to November — or during the reign of Shah Abbas, who, with an eye to international tourism, set up a vast network of caravanserais

ESSENTIAL EXPERIENCES
Sipping tea at sunset in Emam Khomeini Square, Esfahan, watching the shifting colours of the mosques

Trying to imagine what Persepolis was like during the time of Darius the Great

Getting lost in the twisting lanes of Yazd, feeling like you've stumbled onto a *Star Wars* set

Goggling at the fantastical exhibits of Tehran's National Jewel Museum, which have inspired war

Paying your respects to the dead poets of Shiraz by visiting their mausoleums

GETTING UNDER THE SKIN
Read *Moonlight on the Avenue of Faith* by Gina Nahai — magic realism set amongst the Jewish community of Tehran; *Persian Pilgrimages* by Afshin Molavi, an expat Iranian journalist who explores both history and current issues, by speaking to locals

Listen to *Night Silence Desert* by Kayhab Kalhor and Mohammad Reza Shajarian, a modern-day fusion of Iranian classical and folk music forms

Watch *The Circle*, Jafar Panahi's story of women who have fallen outside the law

Eat *ābgùsht*, a delicious meat soup stew, or *gaz* — nougat Esfahan style

Drink *chāy* tea, taken in conjunction with a puff on the hookah pipe. *Dùgh* is a popular cold drink made from yoghurt or sour milk and sparkling or still water.

IN A WORD
Masha'allah (God has willed it)

TRADEMARKS
Chadors, tiled mosques, mullahs, covered bazaars, Persian carpets, controlled borders; Paykan cars (*paykan* means 'arrow')

SURPRISES
The skiing season lasts through to May; women can pursue higher education; Iran is emphatically not Arabic

Esfahan is Iran's masterpiece, the jewel of ancient Persia and one of the finest cities in the Islamic world. The exquisite blue mosaic tiles of Esfahan's Islamic buildings, its expansive bazaar and the city's gorgeous bridges demand as much of your time as you can spare. It's a city for walking, getting lost in the bazaar, dozing in beautiful gardens, and drinking tea and chatting to locals in the marvellous teahouses.

— Lonely Planet's *Iran*

6. Sweet-toothed women from Tehran enjoy a cooling ice cream and each other's company John Borthwick

MAP REF: J,25

2. An evocative street in the old district Jane Sweeney

3. The doleful stare of a young girl from Uruk, Dhi Qar Jane Sweeney

4. Clinging to the walls, nervous adventurers scale the
vertiginous minaret of the Abu Duluf mosque in Samarra
Jane Sweeney

5. The faithful of Samarra flock beneath the golden dome of
the Ali El Hadi Mosque Jane Sweeney

1. Children linger outside their traditional Marsh Arab Reed house, tilting slowly in the stony earth Jane Sweeney

6. Gentlemen attend a civilised tea party outside the Holy Shrine of the Imam Ali Ibn Abi Talib Jane Sweeney

In its long and rich history Iraq has played host to great civilisations, such as the Mesopotamian, in which writing, mathematics and astronomy were developed, and the medieval Islamic period of great learning and beautiful architecture ruled over by the legendary city of Baghdad. But recent history has been less kind: the dictatorial reign of Sadaam Hussein, war with Iran and Kuwait, and trade embargoes after the Gulf War and the US-led invasion in 2003 have all taken severe tolls, resulting in food and medicine shortages and ongoing social and economic problems for the embattled country.

BEST TIME TO VISIT
April to September, depending on the political state of play and your tolerance to 35°C-plus days

ESSENTIAL EXPERIENCES
Visiting the Hanging Gardens of Babylon, one the Seven Wonders of the World and Iraq's most famous ancient site

Winding along mountain roads through dramatic scenery, pleasant towns, orchards and waterfalls in the Kurdish Autonomous Region

Experiencing the extreme and shimmering heat of the Anabar and Al Hajara deserts

Exploring a lively bazaar with people selling colourful rugs, jewellery and copperware

Taking a boat ride down the Euphrates River

GETTING UNDER THE SKIN
Read *The New Iraq: Rebuilding the Country for Its People, the Middle East, and the World* by Joseph Braude, a forward-looking and positive account of the country post-Saddam; or for a glimpse of the old Iraq, seek out a translation of the Sumerian epic of *Gilgamesh*, one of the world's oldest works of literature

Listen to Iraqi-born Kazem El-Saher singing 'love poetry' on his album *Abhathu Anki*

Watch *National Geographic – 21 Days to Baghdad*, an insider's look at Operation Iraqi Freedom; the eerie prologue of horror flick *The Exorcist*, filmed in Northern Iraq; and *Three Kings*, starring George Clooney and set in post–Desert Storm Iraq

Eat *masgouf*, a traditional dish made from Tigris River fish

Drink sweet, strong black tea; soft drinks made from rose petals or orange blossom

IN A WORD
Salām 'alaykum (peace be upon you)

TRADEMARKS
One of the world's most high-profile troubled spots; oil interests; arid desert; mosques; long-suffering people; marshes; dust storms

SURPRISES
The garden of Eden is said to have been located in Iraq; the country is a breeding centre for Arabian horses

Babylon lies 90km south of Baghdad. The ancient city reached its height during the reign of Nebuchadnezzar II (605–563 BC), and with its high walls and magnificent palaces and temples it was regarded as one of the most beautiful cities in the world. It was most renowned for its Hanging Gardens, one of the Seven Wonders of the World.

All that remains of the ruins of Babylon is a huge and magnificent lion, eroded by time and the weather.

—Lonely Planet's *Middle East*

MAP REF: J,24

2. Like mysterious fairy lines, the labyrinth at Dublin Castle weaves fabulous patterns over the lawn Corinne Humphrey

3. Twilight casts eerie colours over the ghostly ruins of Athassel Priory in County Tipperary Richard Cummins

4. Hook Head Lighthouse, the oldest in Europe, stands ever watchful over the stormy seas off County Wexford Richard Cummins

5. A farmer in Antrim herding his flock along a country lane Oliver Strewe

It's said that Ireland, once visited, is never forgotten, and for once the blarney rings true. The Irish landscape has a mythic resonance, the country's history is almost tangible, and a sustained period of investment and economic growth has injected a heady dose of confidence and energy. Thankfully, Ireland hasn't paid the ultimate price for this recent transition as the character, wit and hospitality of the people, the most successful of all Irish exports (except maybe the Irish pub), remains wonderfully intact.

BEST TIME TO VISIT
May to September, when the weather is warmer and the days are longer

ESSENTIAL EXPERIENCES
Enjoying Dublin's gorgeous old pubs and cutting-edge nightclubs

Visiting the ancient ring fort of Dún Aengus

Feeling history come alive at beautifully restored Kilkenny Castle

Exploring the country's past at County Offaly's Clonmacnoise monastery city

Checking out the murals in West Belfast for an insight into the history of the Troubles

Sampling the whiskey at Bushmills Distillery, County Antrim

GETTING UNDER THE SKIN
Read *McCarthy's Bar*, a terrifically funny account of the author's quest to explore his cultural heritage

Listen to anything by U2 and Sinead O'Connor, or more recent offerings by Damien Rice such as *O*

Watch *The Commitments* for good fun and *The Quiet Man* for an all-time classic family favourite

Eat soda bread, a fry-up, smoked salmon and Kimberly biscuits

Drink Guinness, whiskey and red lemonade

IN A WORD
What's the craic? (what's happening?)

TRADEMARKS
Potatoes; harps; shamrocks; Guinness; the good people (leprechauns); American tourists; shillelaghs; ceilidh; the Corrs; the Troubles; James Joyce

SURPRISES
The Irish drink more tea per capita than any other nation in the world; until the 19th century the national colour of the Emerald Isle was blue, as the flag of St Patrick featured a gold harp on a blue background

Ireland has not forsaken its stunning natural beauty and proud traditions. Slate-toned lakes, green pastures, tranquil mountain retreats, magnificent cliffs overlooking the wild Atlantic coast, remote sandy beaches, ancient offshore island villages and the friendliness of the people remain untarnished. Many traces of traditional culture survive, especially in remote western areas, and there are still communities in which Irish is the first language. Ireland remains one of the most beautiful and interesting countries in Europe.

— Lonely Planet's *Ireland*

1. The radiant Celtic features of a young Dubliner Oliver Strewe

6. Detail of a thatched roof, typical of the charming cottages of Dunmore East Greg Gawlowski

MAP REF: G,19

2. Two local gentlemen from the ultra orthodox Jewish community in Mea She'arim discuss anything and everything under a powder of snow Izzet Keribar

3. The oldest known harbour, frist mentioned by Hiram in conversation with Solomon, Tel Aviv
Anthony Pidgeon

4. An Arab man catches up the day's news
Leanne Logan

5. A Jewish man praying in Old Jerusalem Lee Foster

6. The Al-Aqsa Mosque and Dome of the Rock in the Old City of Jerusalem, the mosque houses up to 5000 praying supplicants at a time Oliver Strewe

LEFT 1. The sun sets over the restorative Dead Sea Eddie Gerald

Since its creation as a modern state in 1948 Israel has never been far from international attention. A combination of Promised Land, postcard beaches and political powder keg, everyone has their own perception of what Israel should be. The capital, Jerusalem, is a sacred place to Jews, Muslims and Christians, but it is as much a modern city as a concept, as full of living, breathing people as ghosts and biblical figures. And behind the political headlines is a bustling, noisy, modern country.

BEST TIME TO VISIT
The summer months are warm, but during major Jewish holidays the country fills up with pilgrims, accommodation prices double and travel between cities is impossible

ESSENTIAL EXPERIENCES
Admiring the magnificent Dome of the Rock, built on the spot where Mohammed ascended to heaven

Being dazzled by the golden view of Jerusalem's Old City at dawn

Hitting the clubs or shopping in Tel Aviv, Israel's most cosmopolitan city

Saying a prayer for peace at Jerusalem's Wailing Wall

Escaping to Hula Valley & Nature Reserve, a beautiful valley with unique wetlands wildlife

Splashing out at the water-sports capital of Eilat, with coral-fringed beaches for swimming, windsurfing, parasailing and water-skiing

Witnessing the many security fences and walls dividing Israel and Palestine

GETTING UNDER THE SKIN
Read the meditations of Israeli novelist, Amoz Oz, on his country and culture

Listen to pop princess Sarit Hadad, especially her Eurovision hit, 'Let's Light a Candle Together'

Watch *Promises*, an honest portrait of seven children from Israel and the Palestinian Territories by Justine Shapiro, BZ Goldbcrg and Carlos Bolado

Eat *malawach*, a buttery pastry served with fillings or spicy tomato salsa

Drink the ubiquitous *sahlab*, a milky, spicy concoction originally from Egypt, but drunk everywhere in Israel

IN A WORD
Shalom (hello, literally 'peace')

TRADEMARKS
Nobel Peace prize winner Shimon Peres; the Star of David adorning tanks; troubled war-zone; international kids on kibbutzim; dark-clothed Hasidics sweltering in the heat; diplomatic imbroglio

SURPRISES
A fifth of Israel's landmass is national parks — there are 300 of them

Israel is alone among the Mediterranean seaboard nations in allowing the free sale and export of its antiquities. What could earn you a stiff jail sentence in Greece or Egypt, can provide you with an unusual and often inexpensive memento from biblical times for your mantelpiece or your collection of travel artefacts.

— Lonely Planet's *Israel & the Palestinian Territories*

MAP REF: J,23

193

2. Thundering hooves announce the arrival of white-shirted jockeys at the S'Ardia horse race in Sedilo, Sardinia Dallas Stribley

3. A baker hits the pavements of Padova to deliver his pastries Alan Benson

4. The distinctive bumblebee behind of a yellow Fiat parked conveniently on a zebra crossing in Rome Jonathan Smith

5. The Leaning Tower of Pizza – a neon sign shares airspace with one of Italy's most recognisable monuments Jon Davison

6. Cyprus trees zig zag through a golden Tuscan landscape near La Foce Diana Mayfield

LEFT 1. Ranks of empty café tables bask in the glow of morning as Piazza San Marco prepares for its daily traffic of pigeons and pleasure-seekers, Venice Bethune Carmichael

La dolce vita, la Serenissima, il Belpaese...these phrases merely scratch the surface of a country that has beguiled visitors since the days of the Grand Tour and beyond. From design-conscious Milan, Renaissance-rich Florence, cosmopolitan Rome to the more-traditional south, Italy is a seductive mix of history, culture, fashion and cuisine. It's impossible not to fall in love with a country which is connected so strikingly to the ancient glories of yesteryear and the sophisticated pleasures of today.

BEST TIME TO VISIT
April to June, when it's not too crowded or hot

ESSENTIAL EXPERIENCES
Hiring a car and driving through the beautiful Tuscan countryside

Feeling history surround you in the ruins of Herculaneum or Pompeii

Queuing for hours to enter the Uffizi Gallery in Florence

Venturing offshore to the less-touristy islands of Sicily and Sardinia

Wandering along the canals of Venice and shelling out the euro for a gondola ride

Window shopping in Milan's Golden Quad or Rome's Via del Corso

GETTING UNDER THE SKIN
Read Umberto Eco's masterful *The Name of the Rose*, a medieval whodunnit with a difference. Giuseppe Tomasi di Lampedusa's *The Leopard* charts the demise of Sicilian royalty and rise of Italian nationhood

Listen to Pavarotti, one of the world's most beloved tenors; Andrea Bocelli, wildly popular for his renditions of popular classics; and Jovanotti, known for his wacky rap stylings

Watch *Roman Holiday* for a romantic fix or try Fellini's classic, *La Dolce Vita*; for a modern view, *L'Ultimo Bacio* explores issues affecting Italy's 30-somethings

Eat polenta (cornmeal), *baccalà* (salted cod), *risotto nero* (flavoured with squid ink), *sfogliatella* (pastry filled with ricotta), *panettone* (fruit bread eaten at Christmas)

Drink *espresso* (strong coffee), *Chianti* (Tuscan wine), *marsala* (sweet wine), *grappa* (grape-based liqueur)

IN A WORD
Ciao Bella! (hi beautiful!)

TRADEMARKS
Beeping Fiats and screeching Vespas; pizza by the slice; Roman ruins; Michelangelo and Leonardo; La Cosa Nostra, Prada, Gucci and Dolce and Gabbana

SURPRISES
Cappucinos are considered 'Americana' coffee; not every Italian has Mafia connections; pesto originally hailed from Genoa, in Liguria

The Italian character is to a degree conditioned by campanilismo (literally, an attachment to the local bell tower). An Italian is first and foremost a Sicilian or Tuscan, a Roman or Neapolitan, before being Italian. Confronted with a foreigner, however, Italians reveal a national pride difficult to detect in the cagey relationships they have with each other.

– Lonely Planet's *Italy*

MAP REF: I,21

2. Peanut soup? The owner of a roadside eatery offers the house special to passers-by Jerry Alexander

3. Hanging tuff outside the ghetto-fabulous Tuff Gong Studios in Kingston Christopher Baker

4. Pale colours adorn houses in Falmouth Jon Davison

5. Brisk trade at the Papin Market in the capital Jerry Alexander

6. A girl sells refreshing bunches of guinep fruit to bathers at Bluefields beach in the St Ann region Jerry Alexander

LEFT 1. A dreadlocked denizen of Kingston brandishes a rasta beard Jerry Alexander

Ever since Errol Flynn cavorted here with his Hollywood pals in the 1930s and '40s, travellers have regarded Jamaica as one of the most alluring of the Caribbean islands. Its beaches, mountains and carnal red sunsets regularly appear in tourist brochures promising paradise. Jamaica has a diversity that few other Caribbean islands can claim. Stray from the north coast resorts, and you'll discover radically different environments and terrain. Or throw yourself into the thick of the island's life and experience the three Rs: reggae, reefers and rum.

BEST TIME TO VISIT
May to November, during the off-season

ESSENTIAL EXPERIENCES
Spending the day in Alligator Pond, a deep blue bay backed by dunes

Clambering up tiers of limestone to get to Dunn's River Falls, which tumble down to the beach in a series of cascades and pools

Hiking in the Blue Mountains

Taking a helicopter excursion over the dramatic sculpted limestone plateau of Cockpit Country

Surfing at Long Bay in the northeast – a crescent-shaped bay with rose-coloured sand and deep turquoise waters

GETTING UNDER THE SKIN
Read Jean Rhys' *Wide Sargasso Sea*, a sultry tale of post-emancipation Jamaica

Listen to undisputed king of reggae Bob Marley and early pioneer of ska Tommy McCook

Watch *Bob Marley: Time Will Tell*, a documentary about Bob Marley & the Wailers

Eat *jerk* (meat smothered in tongue-searing marinade, and barbecued slowly in an outdoor pit over a fire of pimento wood, which gives the meat its distinctive flavour)

Drink the famous Jamaican Blue Mountain coffee or try a skyjuice, a cool drink made from shaved ice flavoured with syrup

IN A WORD
Evert'ing cool, mon? (a common greeting much like 'how are you?')

TRADEMARKS
Reggae, reefers and rum; Bob Marley; Rastafarianism; Kingston; palm-fringed beaches

SURPRISES
The national motto of Jamaica is 'Out of Many, One People'; once the major celebration on the slave calendar, Jonkanoo is a Christmas celebration in which revellers parade through the streets dressed in masquerade

Jamaicans' sarcastic and sardonic wit is legendary. The deprecating humour has evolved as an escape valve that hides their true feelings...Often Jamaican wit is laced with sexual undertones. Jamaicans like to make fun of others, often in the most subtle yet no-punches-pulled way, but they accept being the source of similar humour in good grace. Individual faults and physical abnormalities inspire many a knee-slapping jibe.

— Lonely Planet's *World Food Caribbean*

Caribbean Sea

Caribbean Sea

MAP REF: L,11

2. Following fashion, a kimono-clad woman walks Kyoto's streets Oliver Strewe

3. Autumn brings out rich hues in Kanto's maple trees
Chris Rowthorn

4. Cherry blossoms fringe the view of Mt Fuji from Kawaguchi
Bob Charlton

5. Sweet green *kusa mochi* rice cakes served up to celebrate the New Year Judy Bellah

1. Stepping out in style — geishas' kimonos and platform shoes Frank Carter

Whether you end up taking photos of a neon-lit skyline, surfing an indoor wave, musing in a Zen temple, shacking up in a love hotel or kipping down in a traditional inn, you'll do best to come to Japan with an open mind and be prepared to be surprised. Somewhere between the elegant formality of Japanese manners and the candid, sometimes boisterous exchanges that take place over a few drinks, between the sanitised shopping malls and the unexpected rural festivals, everyone finds their own vision of Japan.

BEST TIME TO VISIT
March and April; or before 1853, when Japan started opening up to foreigners

ESSENTIAL EXPERIENCES
Taking a relaxing dip in an *onsen* (hot bath) at Beppu or Asoyama

Admiring the cherry blossoms in Tokyo's Ueno Park in March

Drinking in the view of Tokyo from the top of Mt Fuji

Pretending you're a Samurai warlord at Himeji-jo castle

Having a zen experience at Kinkakuji temple, Kyoto

Finding out why war sucks at the Hiroshima or Nagasaki war museums

Riding on a slide made entirely of ice at the Sapporo Snow Festival

GETTING UNDER THE SKIN
Read *Inside Japan* by Peter Tasker, a fascinating foray into Japanese culture, society and the economy. *Kitchen* by Banana Yoshimoto is a hauntingly beautiful story set in contemporary Tokyo that shows a side of Japan not often seen.

Listen to 'Sukiyaki' by Kyu Sakamoto, a 1960s hit and classic Japanese tune, reminiscent of 1950s lounge music; or anything by Morning Musume, an all girl J-pop group of 13(!) members, where singing talent is optional

Watch Kurosawa's *Seven Samurai*, a classic 1954 film set in 17th-century rural Japan, or get a taste for Japan with *Tampopo*, a witty and insightful film set in a *ramen* (noodle) shop

Eat *ramen* noodles, Japan's fast food specialty – though you haven't 'done' Japan till you've experienced fresh raw fish

Drink *sake*, Japan's signature drink, commonly known as rice wine and served hot or cold

IN A WORD
Sugoi (used for surprise, wonder or horror and everything in between)

TRADEMARKS
Raw fish; Samurai swords; hard-working salary men; bowing; Hiroshima and the A-bomb; electronic gadgets; geisha girls; Mt Fuji; karaoke; manga comic books

SURPRISES
It's polite to slurp loudly when eating soup or noodles; shoes must be removed before entering any home; most home kitchens don't have ovens; Japan has over 1500 earthquakes a year

The synthesis of the modern and traditional is one of the things that makes travel in Japan such a fascinating experience. It also ensures that no matter what your taste, you'll find a side of Japan that suits your interests.

— Lonely Planet's *Japan*

6. Tokyo's 'CosPlay' culture can mean cross-dressing as your favourite *anime* character John Ashburne

MAP REF: J,34

199

2. A Bedouin woman herds a flock of sheep and goats across the arid terrain between Jebel Umm E'iil and Jebel Khazali Mark Daffey

3. The thoughtful face of an elderly Bedouin man, Petra Becca Posterino

4. A bejewelled Bedouin girl smiles beneath a florid headscarf Becca Posterino

5. The box-like buildings of Amman seen from the citadel John Elk III

6. Tourists enjoying the legendary buoyancy of the Dead Sea Patrick Syder

LEFT 1. A camel rests its haunches outside the majestic Treasury of Petra in Ma'an carved from the cliff face two thousand years ago Clint Lucas

Lawrence of Arabia, Bible stories and mysterious lost cities – Jordan is romantic and epic. Better yet, it's one of the most welcoming countries in the world. Where else do total strangers invite you into their homes for a heady brew of tea? It's also home to two of the most spectacular sights in the Middle East: Petra, the ancient Nabatean city, and the startling desert scenery of Wadi Rum that enraptured TE Lawrence.

BEST TIME TO VISIT
April to May or September to October, when you can dodge the baking sun of summer and the freezing winds of winter

ESSENTIAL EXPERIENCES
Visiting the ancient ruins of Petra

Pretending you're Julius Caesar at the preserved Roman city of Jerash

Lolling in the restorative salt, sea and mud of the Dead Sea

Diving into the scuba-friendly waters around Aqaba

Camping out under the stars at Wadi Rum

Finding your inner Richard the Lionheart at Karak, Jordan's best-preserved Crusader castle

GETTING UNDER THE SKIN
Read *Seven Pillars of Wisdom* by TE Lawrence – it's Lawrence of Arabia straight from the camel's mouth

Listen to *Khaliji*, a collection of tunes and belly dancing hits featuring Jordanian, Naser Musa

Watch *Indiana Jones and the Last Crusade* for the climactic scenes filmed in and around Petra

Eat *mensaf*, the Bedouin speciality – a whole lamb, head included, on rice and pine nuts

Drink tea, because you'll be offered it in bladder-bursting amounts by hospitable Jordanians

IN A WORD
Salam (hello)

TRADEMARKS
Bedouins in *keffiyah* (head robes); endless tea-drinking; windswept deserts; ancient ruins; bubbling *nargileh* (water pipes); peacemaking King Hussein

SURPRISES
Not everyone is a Bedouin in Jordan; there's a majority Palestinian population which arrived during times of war in their homeland

Amman's Queen Alia International Airport was bright, garish, modern, a 1970s disco film set leaping with so many orange-suited cleaners they almost had to clean each other for something to do.

– Kingdom of the Film Stars © Annie Caufield 1997; Lonely Planet Travel Literature

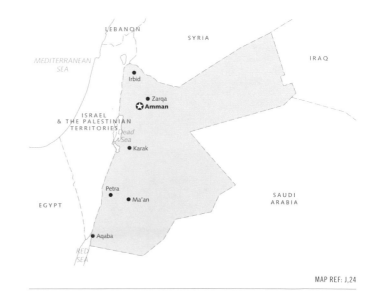

MAP REF: J,24

201

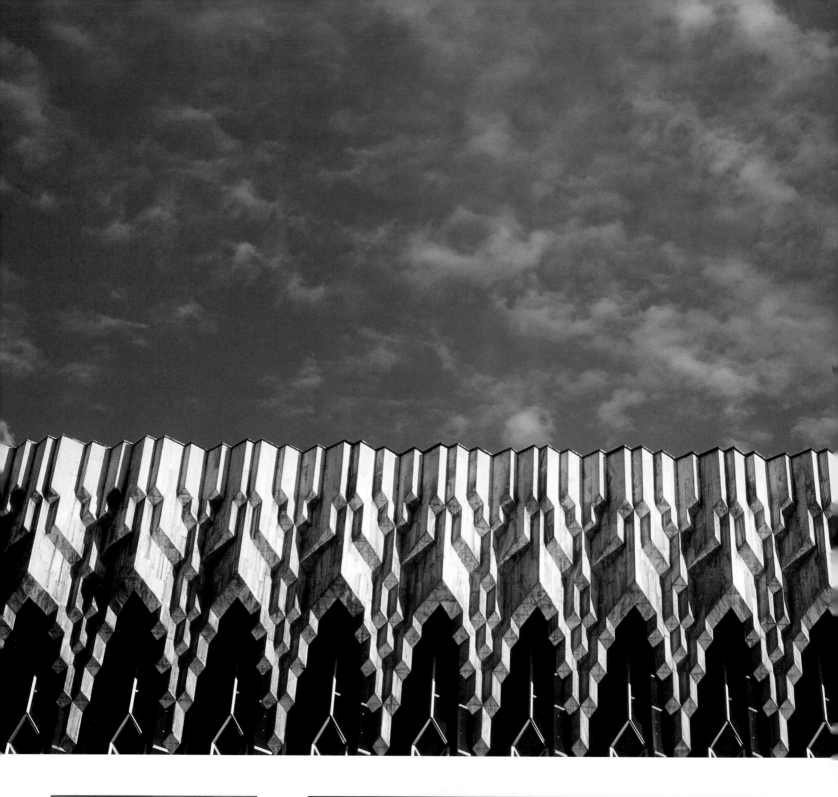

2. Old Russian houses line the deserted streets of Fort Shevchenko Simon Richmond

3. Cows recline beneath a yurt near the town of Shymbulak
Veronica Garbutt

4. The sheer hillsides around Nizhny Kol-Say with Alatau mountains in the distance Anthony Plummer

1. The imposing Soviet architecture of the television broadcasting centre in Almaty Andrew Peacock

If you love remoteness, wide open spaces, lunar landscapes, long hypnotic train rides and horse sausage (and who doesn't?), you'll be in your element in Kazakhstan. But it's not all barren steppes – there's also cosmopolitan Almaty and the spectacular spurs of the Tian Shan and Altay mountains to explore. And if it occasionally seems that the landscape has been bombarded by nuclear explosions, well, that's because Soviet rocket scientists began using Kazakhstan as a sandpit in the late 1940s.

BEST TIME TO VISIT
April to June (spring) and September to November (autumn)

ESSENTIAL EXPERIENCES
Market-hopping in Almaty, the mercantile city that gathers together Chinese, Uzbek, Russian and Turkish traders

Nature-spotting in Almatinsky Nature Reserve for the super-rare snow leopard and *arkhar* (big-horned wild sheep)

Gazing at the view across Lake Burabay, also seen on the 10 tenge banknote

Making the pilgrimage to Kazakhstan's greatest building, the mausoleum of Kozha Akhmed Yasaui

Trekking the mighty Altay mountains, border to both Russia and China

GETTING UNDER THE SKIN
Read *The Silk Road: A History* by Irene Frank and David Brownstone, a richly illustrated and mapped history of the legendary caravan routes

Listen to pop-folk fusionists Urker's *Made in Kazakhstan*, using the string instruments the *dombyra* and *kobyz*

Watch Ali G's mate Borat for cultural clashes when a supposed Kazakhstani visits the UK and US

Eat *qazy*, the smoked horsemeat sausage sometimes served sliced with cold noodles

Drink *shubat*, fermented camel's milk

IN A WORD
Asalam aleykum ('peace be with you' in Kazakh)

TRADEMARKS
Borat the travelling Kazakhstani TV celebrity; big furry hats; Silk Road traders haggling over a tenge; barren steppes spanning the horizon; Soviet-era service

SURPRISES
Ever-changing visa and border rules; enjoying a truly great local yogurt

The ninth largest country in the world, Kazakhstan lies at the heart of the great Eurasian steppe, the band of grassland stretching from Mongolia to Hungary, which has served for millennia as the highway and grazing ground of nomadic horseback peoples.

— Lonely Planet's *Central Asia*

5. Taking it up a notch, speed chess players race against time in Panfilov Park, Almaty Andrew Peacock

MAP REF: H,27

203

2. Clouds of dust billow over Aberdare National Park where Maasai cattle and native animals compete for grazing land Mitch Reardon

3. A Maasai woman loses herself in song Mitch Reardon

4. An afternoon chat in Watamu. Anders Blomqvist

5. If looks could kill – a Maasai warrior cuts an intimidating figure in the Rift Valley David Wall

Kenya beckons the traveller with a magical mix of incredible wildlife, rich cultural heritage, palm-fringed beaches and coastal towns seeped in Swahili history. Few places can rival Kenya for the safari experience, though these days your big-game hunting will (thankfully) be restricted to capturing trophies on film. Nothing can prepare you for the incredible sight of the annual migration of the wildebeest, and wherever you lay your head you'll be romanced by the star-studded night-sky and your imagination stirred by the noises of the African night.

BEST TIME TO VISIT
January to February, the hottest and driest months

ESSENTIAL EXPERIENCES
Taking a safari — by minibus, 4WD, truck, camel, small plane or hot-air balloon

Experiencing the wildebeest mass migration — the sight and sound of a million hoofs on the move with a host of eager predators in hot pursuit

Winding down a notch or ten with a lazy spell in other-worldly Lamu

Taking the Nairobi–Mombasa night-train for a taste of the old-colonial experience

GETTING UNDER THE SKIN
Read Isak Dinesen's epic settler account, *Out of Africa*

Listen to *benga*, the contemporary dance music of Kenya, by Shirati Jazz, Victoria Kings and Them Mushrooms

Watch Robert Redford and Meryl Streep in the big-screen version of *Out of Africa* or the equally tear-jerking screen-translation of Kiki Guillman's *I Dreamed of Africa*

Eat *nyama choma*, literally 'roasted meat' of any shape or form, but usually goat

Drink Tusker — the elephant beer

IN A WORD
Jambo (hello)

TRADEMARKS
Spear-bearing Maasai warriors; wiry marathon runners; strong-blend coffee; man-eating lions; gin-soaked old colonials; Nairobbery

SURPRISES
Nairobi's cosmopolitan population mix and its western-style skyscrapers and suburban sprawl; the shadowy, medieval architecture of spice-infused Swahili Lamu and old-town Mombasa and Malindi

If you've ever fantasised about Africa — sleeping in the bush, surrounded by wildlife or walking with tribespeople beneath the broad African sky — then Kenya is for you. You'll also encounter the everyday beauty of African life: the swerving Kenyan matatu (minibus), filled to bursting and careering through the streets of Nairobi; hawkers peddling their wares on the street corner; a truckload of women singing and dancing. This place is simply too good to ignore for long.

— Lonely Planet's *Kenya*

1. A bejewelled Maasai mother carries her baby past a village enclosure Alex Dissanayake

6. A herd of elephants meanders through the high grass of the savannah as Mt Kilimanjaro looms over the border in Tanzania David Else

MAP REF: N,24

2.No diving from the back door, living on the edge in a
thatched hut Thor Vaz de Leon

3.Chilling outside the local shop David Ryan

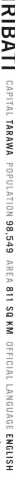

Blessed with billions of stunning fish swarming over myriad coral reefs and plenty of WWII wrecks, Kiribati (pronounced Kiri-Bahs) is a hidden island paradise. The atolls are scattered either side of the equator so the weather is dependably warm. Modernity is slowly rearing its head, but locals still welcome travellers as rarely seen curios. There are few organised activities on offer, though it's not hard to find diving and game fishing with local people, and the less adventurous will find idyllic beaches are never far away.

BEST TIME TO VISIT
March to October, to avoid the humidity and tropical downpours

ESSENTIAL EXPERIENCES
Taking part in a traditional dance in a *maneaba* (traditional meeting house)

Sipping fresh coconut milk in a stilt house over an aqua lagoon in North Tarawa

Being brought down to size by the enormous WWII guns at South Tarawa

Salting clams or weaving thatch with locals to enjoy the relaxed pace of the Outer Islands

Trying bonefishing or birdwatching on Christmas Island

GETTING UNDER THE SKIN
Read Gavin Bell's *In Search of Tusitala: Travels in the Pacific after Robert Louis Stevenson*, which follows Robert Louis Stevenson through Kiribati

Listen to anything by home-grown production company ND Teariki Music Productions, recording in Kiribati

Watch the documentaries of director Dennis O'Rourke, including *Atoll life in Kiribati*

Eat traditional islander fare like taro, sweet potato or coconuts

Drink the unfortunately named sour toddy, brewed from coconut palm

IN A WORD
Ko rabwa n rokom (thank you for your visit)

TRADEMARKS
Far-flung coral atolls; deep blue ocean; devout Catholics; coconut drinks by the beach; friendly locals; beachcombing the days away

SURPRISES
The International Date Line used to split Kiribati down the middle, until 1 January 1995 when Kiribati decided to have the same day nationwide

The passing centuries have had little impact on Kiribati's outer islands, where people subsist on coconuts, giant prawns, octopuses and fish. Even on Tarawa, most people live in thatched huts.

— Lonely Planet's *South Pacific*

1. Always keen on nautical sports, Gilbertese racing canoes compete in Tarawa Lagoon David Ryan

4. A Gilbertese boy hugs his dozing pig David Ryan

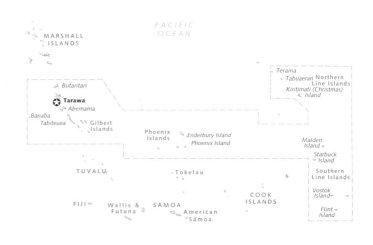

MAP REF: 0.38

2. Can I see your passport? A border guard investigates a Demilitarised Zone building Tony Wheeler

3. Ballroom decor at the Reconstruction Station in Pyongyang Tony Wheeler

4. Waterfalls at Rimyongsu, where underground streams spectacularly burst through basalt rock Tony Wheeler

5. A coordinated crowd of women in blue, representing winter, at the Arirang Mass Games Tony Wheeler

Continuing to defy the odds stacked heavily against it, North Korea is a land where ancient myths bend to modern political reality, where dictator Kim Jong Il runs the only brand around and is also believed to control the weather. Few are allowed into the hermit state, and then only under constant escort, leaving the country free of commercial tourism and ensuring that the lives of ordinary North Koreans remains as mysterious to outsiders as that of its leader. Behind the propaganda, rumour and weirdness are the real story; the fascination is in finding the truth.

BEST TIME TO VISIT
May, for May Day and the Arirang Mass Games, or any time free of famine

ESSENTIAL EXPERIENCES
Feeling the full force of North-South tension along the Demilitarised Zone at Panmunjeom

Taking in pristine mountain views in the stunning resort of Kumgangsan

Walking (with minders) amid Pyongyang's architectural wealth, and grabbing a few solo moments shopping in Department Store No 1

Revisiting the past at the ancient Korean capital of Kaesong

Exploring the far north and Korea's highest peak and holy mountain Paekdusan

GETTING UNDER THE SKIN
Read widely – there's not a lot of factual material in print or on the web, and people are rarely ambivalent about North Korea

Listen to the beat of the marching feet of the world's fifth largest army

Watch *Forever in Our Memory*, a 1999 film that deals with the starvation of up to three million North Koreans during the 1990s

Eat *bibim naengmyeon* (cold noodles), or the Korean menu on any tour

Drink *soju* (rice wine) or *nokcha* (green tea)

IN A WORD
Juche (self-reliance)

TRADEMARKS
The Great Leader (the late Kim Il Sung) and his son, The Dear Leader (Kim Il Jung, AKA The Great Leader; Confused? So are we.); cult of personality; the 38th parallel; Cold War 21st century style: kidnapping, nuclear tests, rapprochement, border tension

SURPRISES
There's an Internet café (just one); the current Great Leader has only uttered six words in public ('Glory to the people's heroic military'), and is said to own 20,000 movies

I have a fascination with cities and countries that seem to exist at a 90-degree angle to reality. In the world today North Korea is undoubtedly the best example of the phenomenon, and when George W Bush – himself a denizen of a strange universe – decided to skewer North Korea on his axis of evil I simply had to go.

—Lonely Planet's *Korea*

1. Hooping it up at a mass gymnastics display at Pyongyang   Tony Wheeler

6. Soldiers at the Arirang Mass Games: if wars were won by whose army dances the best, the North Koreans would win hands down   Tony Wheeler

MAP REF: I,33

2. Ribbons ripple through the air during a Farmers' Dance John Elk III

3. A bearded gentleman rugs up in *hanbok* (traditional dress) against the winter Juliet Coombe

4. Seoul's bright lights dazzle the shopping districts Jeff Yates

5. Meticulously weaving a traditional basket in the Korean Folk Village John Elk III

6. A new broom sweeps the path outside the temple at Haeinsa Richard I'Anson

LEFT 1. A serene Buddha statue surveys Songnisan National Park, known for its blend of temples and hiking trails John Banagan

An Asian economic tiger, South Korea is a mosaic of old and new: rural folk villages and DVD mini-cinemas, ancient stone pagodas and rock music bars, buzzing modern cities and feudal-era fortresses, densely forested mountains graced by some of Asia's finest Buddhist temples. It's a compact and little-explored country, where Asian traditions, Western fashions, Confucian ideals and democratic ideas mingle to form an identity based equal parts on language, national pride and a fondness for nature's beauties.

BEST TIME TO VISIT
September to November (autumn)

ESSENTIAL EXPERIENCES
Rubbing shoulders with the locals at one of Seoul's boisterous traditional markets

Wandering through Gyeongju, the ancient capital of the Silla kingdom

Early-morning jostling at Busan's hectic fish market

Hitting the beach at Daecheon, for the best sand and seafood on the west coast

Exploring the past by visiting Jikjisa, a temple dating back to the 5th century

Hiking around spectacular Sereoksan National Park

GETTING UNDER THE SKIN
Read *Yi Sang's Wings*, an allegory of adultery, colonialism and the absurdity of life; Rhie Won-Bok's *Korea Unmasked*, which details Korean history, culture and sociology

Listen to Park Dong-jin, leading voice of the *pansori*, traditional storytelling through music

Watch *Chihwaseon* (Painted Fire), by director Im Kwon Taek, about a famous 19th-century painter; Park Chan-wook's *JSA (Joint Security Area)*, a thriller about tensions on the border between North and South Korea

Eat *bulgolgi* (sweet marinated beef cooked at the table), *bi bim bap* (stir-fried meat, rice, veggies, red pepper paste and fried egg) and *kimchi* (a fiery pickled cabbage concoction traditionally buried during winter to ferment)

Drink *soju* (clear potato-based alcohol which packs a heck of a kick), or for something more soothing try *nok cha* (green tea)

IN A WORD
Annyeong haseyo (hello, informal)

TRADEMARKS
Big city Seoul; seafood and rice; the 38th Parallel; Confucious drinking in Itaewon; young salary-mad workers; the land between Japan and China

SURPRISES
The youngest person in the party *always* pours the drinks; when exchanging money, use your right hand — the left signals disrespect

Korea is probably the most Confucian nation in Asia. The middle-aged office worker who jumps the queue to pay for a Coke at the 7-Eleven does not even register your presence because you have not been introduced. Once contact has been established, everything changes. Courtesy is highly valued and most Koreans will go out of their way to be pleasant and helpful. And you should return the favour — be polite and smile, even when bargaining over prices in the market.

— Lonely Planet's Korea

MAP REF: J,33

2. Observing the remains of Gathering Station 14, bombed during the Gulf War Christine Osborne

3. Iconic Kuwait Towers, Kuwait City's most distinctive landmark Chris Mellor

4. Phoning home from the middle of the desert Izzet Keribar

5. A visitor to the Kuwait Museum shows off his traditional headgear Izzet Keribar

LEFT 1. Festively decorated water reservoirs outside Kuwait City Izzet Keribar

With the 1990–91 Gulf War a fading memory, Kuwait is once again the prototypical Persian Gulf oil state. Walking around Kuwait City, it is hard to imagine the destruction of just a decade ago. There has been an obsessive, meticulous re-creation of the country's pre-invasion appearance. Liberation brought a new kind of openness to Kuwaiti life and for those looking for a relaxed entry into the Muslim world, Kuwait offers opportunities to wander around souks, mosques and other sandy traces of bygone Bedouin days.

BEST TIME TO VISIT
May (spring) or October (autumn) — or in the early 18th century when Kuwait was nothing more than a few tents clustered around a fort

ESSENTIAL EXPERIENCES
Taking in the views of the Sief Palace from the Kuwait Towers in Kuwait City

Sampling Islamic art at the Tareq Rajab Museum in Kuwait City

Buying Bedouin goods at Sadu House in Kuwait City

Strolling through the public gardens in Al-Ahmadi

Wandering among the archaeological ruins on Failaka Island

GETTING UNDER THE SKIN
Read Thomas Friedman's *From Beirut to Jerusalem*, an excellent read for anyone wishing to more fully understand the causes and effects of the region's strife

Listen to *Stars of Kuwait*, a complete taste of Kuwaiti music

Watch *Fires of Kuwait* by David Douglas — shot in Kuwait after the Iraqi war. It follows a number of teams who fought to extinguish the hundreds of burning oil wells

Eat *fuul* — broadbean paste made with garlic, olive oil and lemon; *falafel* — spiced, fried chickpea balls; *khobz* — Arabic flat bread; *hummus* — chickpea paste with garlic and lemon

Drink coffee — served Arabic-style

IN A WORD
Gowwa (hello, informal)

TRADEMARKS
The oil industry; mosques; Kuwait Towers; Bedouin culture; colourful souks; cloth weaving; museums; coffeehouses; delicious Arab food; archaeological sites; the remarkably easygoing feel of Kuwait City

SURPRISES
The temple and archaeological ruins on the island of Failaka Island; informal gatherings *(diwaniya)*, usually at someone's home, where Kuwaitis gather to chat

The problem of land and, to a lesser extent, seaborne mines has pretty well put what used to be a bustling water-sports culture in Kuwait into the deep freeze. Mines have also put an end to organised desert safaris and 'wadi bashing'.

— Lonely Planet's *Bahrain, Kuwait & Qatar*

MAP REF: I,24

2. Russian-style apartment buildings dominate Toktogula Road in Karakol Anthony Plummer

3. Tash-Rabat Caravanserai, a fortified traveller's inn dating from the 15th century, once a popular stop on the old Silk Road in central Kyrgyzstan Bradley Mayhew

4. A horse-riding hero wearing a denim jacket and a Kyrgyz hat in Jailoo, south of Kochkor Anthony Plummer

5. Roadside assistance at Lake Song-Kol where a bogged car is towed by hardy horses Bradley Mayhew

What Kyrgyzstan lacks in gracious buildings and fancy cakes, it makes up for with nomadic traditions such as laid-back hospitality, a healthy distrust of authority and a fondness for drinking fermented mare's milk. It is perhaps the most accessible and welcoming of the former Soviet Central Asian republics, and boasts the region's most dramatic mountains – the central Tian Shan and Pamir Alay ranges.

BEST TIME TO VISIT
April to early June (spring) and September to October (autumn)

ESSENTIAL EXPERIENCES
Hiking in the rugged Ala-Archa Canyon, within sight of the region's highest peak

Soaking in the thermal springs and spas of Lake Issyk-Kul and wildlife watching for big cats, ibex, bear and wild boar

Stopping off at Karakol, famous for its apple orchards, Sunday market and backstreets full of Russian gingerbread-style cottages

Travelling through the Kyrgyz Fergana Valley via the hair-raising Bishkek-Osh Road

GETTING UNDER THE SKIN
Read Chinghiz Aitmatov's novel *Djamila*, which tells of Kyrgyz life and culture

Listen to Kyrgyz traditional music played on a mixture of *komuz* guitars, a vertical violin known as a *kyl kyayk*, flutes, drums, mouth harps (*temir komuz*, or *jygach ooz* with a string) and long horns

Watch Aktan Abdykalykov's *Besh Kumpyr* (Five Old Ladies)

Eat homemade *beshbarmak* (large flat noodles topped with lamb or horse meat or both and cooked in vegetable broth) or snack on samsa (a meat pie with flaky puff pastry baked in a tandoori oven)

Drink *kymys* (a mildly alcoholic drink of fermented marc's milk) or settle for a cup of green tea

IN A WORD
Salam (hello)

TRADEMARKS
Horse sausages; teahouses; yurts; mountains; felt rugs; nomads; horse riding

SURPRISES
Bishkek, the capital, is named after a wooden plunger – a *bishkek* is a churn used to make fermented mare's milk; the name Kyrgyz is one of the oldest recorded ethnic names in Asia, going back to the 2nd century BC in Chinese sources

Kyz-kumay (kiss-the-girl) involves a man who furiously chases a woman on horseback in an attempt to kiss her. The woman gets the faster horse and a head start and if she wins gets to chase and whip her shamed suitor. This allegedly began as a formalised alternative to abduction, the traditional nomadic way to take a bride.

– Lonely Planet's *Central Asia*

1. Squinting into the sun, a happy family poses for a portrait outside their summer yurt Anthony Plummer

6. Graves of nomads form the shape of a yurt for shelter in the afterlife Bradley Mayhew

MAP REF: I,27

2. Working the rice paddies on Khong Island Bernard Napthine

3. A young girl passes blue doors in the restored city of Luang Prabang Martin Lladó

4. Lavishly dressed women carry offerings to Vientiane's Pha That Luang Juliet Coombe

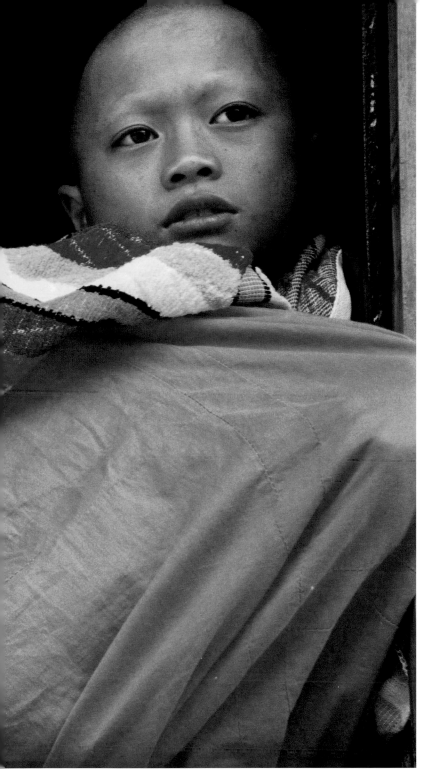

1. Novitiate monks peek out of a window Martin Lladó

Life in laid-back Laos is languid and leisurely: watching the morning sun light up the mighty Mekong River, wandering through aromatic markets and kicking back with a beer in hand. It's the simple pleasures that make a visit to this enigmatic country a delight, and what Laos lacks in in-your-face attractions is made up for with lush surrounds, friendly folk and gastronomic treats. The casual grandeur of Unesco World Heritage–listed Luang Prabang and small-town feel of the capital, Vientiane, make Laos one of the highlights of Southeast Asia.

BEST TIME TO VISIT
November to February, as Laos knows how to turn up the sweltering heat and torrential downpours are a speciality

ESSENTIAL EXPERIENCES
Circumnavigating Vientiane's revered Pha That Luang stupa

Shopping nirvana at Luang Prabang's night market

Floating down Nam Song in Vang Vieng till dusk

Fine dining at one of Luang Prabang's atmospheric eateries

Cooling off under the Kuang Si waterfall, near Luang Prabang

GETTING UNDER THE SKIN
Read *Bamboo Palace* by Christopher Kremmer – part travelogue, part mystery, it chronicles the lost dynasty of Laos

Listen to expat Paris-based troupe, Molam Lao

Watch *Bombies*, a documentary probing the legacy of the US carpet bombing campaign inflicted on Laos

Eat *fõe*, noodle soup in any variety; *tam màak hung*, deliciously laden spicy papaya salad

Drink Bolaven Plateau brew for coffee aficionados; light and tasty Beer Lao; *lào-láo*, a clear yet fiery rice alcohol that's more of an acquired taste

IN A WORD
Pai talat (to the market)

TRADEMARKS
Longtail boats; rice; Buddha-filled pagodas and wats; café culture; rural bandits; unexploded ordnance

SURPRISES
Laos has one of the lowest population densities in Asia – around 18 people per sq km (about 11 per sq mi); by the end of the Vietnam War, Laos had the dubious distinction of being the most bombed country in the history of warfare

Laos is beset by economic hardship and instability. In 2003, the US signed a Bilateral Trade Agreement with Laos, ending a trade embargo that had been in place since the communists took power in 1975, while the government set a goal to haul itself out of the Least Developed Country bracket by 2020.

— Lonely Planet's *Southeast Asia*

5. Vang Vieng's markets are the place to haggle for groceries Sara-Jane Cleland

MAP REF: L,31

2. Patches of snow cling to the roof of a building overlooking the Filharmonijas Laukums Jonathan Smith

3. Well-preserved buildings line a cobbled street in the Old City of Riga, founded in 1201 Steve Raymer

1. An elderly woman in Riga bears bunches of flowers for a lucky beneficiary   Steve Raymer

Latvia may be sandwiched between Estonia and Lithuania, but its capital, Riga, is the biggest and most vibrant city in the Baltics. Great day-trip destinations surrounding Riga include the coastal resort Jurmala, the Sigulda castles overlooking the scenic Gauja River Valley, and the Rastrelli Palace at Rundale. Latvia's less-travelled roads are equally rewarding, from the dune-lined coast and historic towns of the Kurzeme region in the west of the country to the remote uplands of the east.

BEST TIME TO VISIT
April to September (spring to summer)

ESSENTIAL EXPERIENCES
Visiting Rastrelli's lavishly Baroque Rundale Palace outside Riga

Swinging across the Gauja River Valley in a cable car

Strolling in the land of the Livonian people at Cape Kolka

Beachcombing for washed-up amber along Latvia's Baltic coast

Burrowing in the Riezupe sand caves near Kuldiga

Wandering through Riga's massive Central Market

GETTING UNDER THE SKIN
Read Latvia's national epic, *Lacplesis* (The Bear Slayer), written by Andrejs Pumpurs in the mid 19th century and based on traditional Latvian folk stories

Listen to AutoBuss Debesis, art rock with a Latvian twist

Watch *Homeland*, a documentary by Juris Podnieks that captures the tumultuous events of the early 1990s

Eat *piragi*, meat pasties baked in the oven – Latvia's answer to fast food

Drink the infamous Balzams, a thick, jet-black, 45% proof concoction – it's best served with coffee or mixed with equal parts vodka

IN A WORD
Sveiks (Hi, or even Goodbye)

TRADEMARKS
Vibrant Riga; drinking sessions; scientists; sports-loving people; singing and dancing troupes

SURPRISES
Pig's snout is a traditional Christmas dish; Riga is over 800 years old; Latvia is a remnant of the Holy Roman Empire; Latvia became a member of the European Union in May 2004

Cobbled streets, chocolate-box collections of brightly painted houses and a trio of medieval Old Towns sufficiently historic to be included in Unesco's World Heritage list are among the huge trove of treasures… Whole sweeps of history and a myriad of legends and myths little known outside the immediate region hide behind each castle, folk costume, forest and lake.

– Lonely Planet's *Estonia, Latvia & Lithuania*

4. Fish caught in Lake Lubans hang to dry outside a house in Idena   Niall Benvie

MAP REF: F,22

2. The so-called Temple of Bacchus at Baalbek Mark Daffey

3. Rebuilding Beirut means thinking modern while preserving history Bethune Carmichael

4. Looking up to street posters in Tyre Bethune Carmichael

5. Restoration work continues at Khan al-Franj (Inn of the Foreigners) Bethune Carmichael
LEFT 1. Palatial ruins of the Ottoman-era bathhouse Hammam al-Jadid Clint Lucas

Lebanon's modest borders pack in a powerful mix of cultures and traditions: mountain ski resorts and bucolic valleys, Roman ruins and Islamic architecture, bikini-clad beachgoers and women in head-to-toe chadors. The years of civil war and destruction are finally over, and the Lebanese, famed for their commercial skill, great food and appreciation of a good party, are hard at work to regain their status as the Middle East's commercial centre. Beirut, once the Paris of the Middle East, is a bustling, cosmopolitan city intent on making a comeback.

BEST TIME TO VISIT
June to mid-September – or before 1918 to experience the reign of the Ottoman Empire

ESSENTIAL EXPERIENCES
Watching the sunset at Pigeon Rocks, Beirut's most famous natural attraction

Spending a day wandering around the extraordinary Roman ruins at Baalbek

Driving along the magnificent scenic route to the Biblical Cedars

Wandering through the ancient ruins at Byblos

Discovering Mameluk architecture and medieval markets in Tripoli

Basking in the splendour of the palace at Beiteddine

GETTING UNDER THE SKIN
Read William Dalrymple's *From the Holy Mountain*, a funny, thought-provoking account of the author's journey in the footsteps of a 6th-century monk

Listen to *Fairuz Chante Zaki Yassif*, performed by Fairuz and composed by Zaki Yassif, the father of Lebanese folk music

Watch *Le cerf-volant* (The Kite) by Randa Chahal Sabag, about a love affair between a Lebanese girl and an Israeli soldier

Eat *kibbeh* (spiced minced lamb in a fried bulgur-wheat shell); *baklava* (syrupy-sweet filo pastries)

Drink *jellab,* a sweet drink made with raisins and pine nuts; *arak* on ice with a splash of water

IN A WORD
Ahalan was sahalan (hello; literally 'welcome and welcome')

TRADEMARKS
Dramatic landscapes; delicious food; ancient cities; sunny beaches; Mt Lebanon Range; crusader castles; temple complexes; picturesque port towns; olive groves and vineyards

SURPRISES
A world-famous arts festival is held every July in Baalbek; there are amazing trekking opportunities; Lebanon is the biblical 'land of milk and honey'

The cake shops in Lebanon look so tempting with their vast array of cookies and pastries. Most of the pastries are specialities of the region and are unfamiliar to many visitors. All of them are totally delicious and worth trying, even if you don't have a particularly sweet tooth.

– Lonely Planet's *Lebanon*

MAP REF: J.23

221

2. Green hills form a gentle backdrop to the magnificent Maletsunyane Falls in Maseru Kim Wildman

3. Stirring for safe passage, a Gwa Gwa woman prepares a sugary offering to ensure good luck for travellers Di Jones

4. Sharing a joke with a Basotho boy Di Jones

5. Children play in the cool waters near Qacha's Nek village Di Jones

6. Dazzling flowers known as Red Hot Pokers bloom at the heels of a grinning mountain trekker on the road to the Ribaneng Falls Di Jones

LEFT 1. Wrapped comfortably in oilskins, a woman and her horse-riding husband stand at the edge of Makhaleng valley Di Jones

Appropriately dubbed 'the kingdom in the sky', Lesotho is a mountainous country landlocked in the heart of South Africa. Its forbidding terrain and the defensive walls of the Drakensberg and Maluti ranges gave both sanctuary and strategic advantage to the Basotho (the people of Lesotho), who forged a nation while playing a key role in the manoeuvres of the white invaders on the plains below. Lesotho is an often surprising combination of rapidly developing modernity and ancient culture. It has managed to avoid many of the recent wars and much of the political instability that has plagued most of the African continent.

BEST TIME TO VISIT
May to September, to avoid the rains

ESSENTIAL EXPERIENCES
Spending a night in a Basotho village on the edge of townships surrounding Maseru

Hiking along the top of the Drakensberg escarpment

Climbing Thaba-Bosiu (Mountain At Night), where King Moshoeshoe the Great established his second mountain stronghold

Riding sure-footed Basotho ponies through the rugged and beautiful interior

Driving the spectacular road between Leribe and Katse over the Maluti Mountains

Following in the fossilised footsteps of dinosaurs near Quthing

GETTING UNDER THE SKIN
Read *Stories By and About Women in Lesotho*, edited by K Limakatso Kendall, containing tales told orally by Southern Sotho women and providing insights into women's thoughts and decision-making processes in Lesotho

Listen to the *lekolulo*, a flute-like instrument played by herd boys; the *thomo*, a stringed instrument played by women; and the *setolo-tolo*, a stringed instrument played with the mouth by men

Eat *frikkadel* (fried meatball) or *koeksesters* (small doughnuts dripping in honey)

Drink locally made *joala* (sorghum beer) or maize beer

IN A WORD
Dumela (hello)

TRADEMARKS
Poverty; landlocked by South Africa; rainmaking rituals; mountains; the 'kingdom in the sky'

SURPRISES
The Basotho are traditionally buried in a sitting position, facing the rising sun and ready to leap up when called; the famous Basotho pony is the result of crossbreeding between short Javanese horses and European full mounts

Much of the folklore puts common sense into practice: toasting fresh rather than stale bread is bad (because it causes rheumatism); when working at straining beer, take an occasional drink (or your hands will swell); a spider in a hut should not be molested (it's the strength of the family); a howling dog must be silenced immediately (or it will bring evil).

— Lonely Planet's *South Africa, Lesotho & Swaziland*

SOUTH AFRICA

Oxbow
Jonathane
Peka
Pitseng
Mothae
Teyateyaneng
Sefikeng
Seshote
Motsitseng
Maseru
Mokhotlong
Mazenod
Marakabei
Motsekuoa
Semonkong
Malealea
Matebeng
Sekake
Mpiti
Mekaling
SOUTH AFRICA
Ralebona

MAP REF: R,23

2. Kpelle tribeswomen harvesting rice Jacques Jangoux

3. Buckets of smiles, a grinning child carries a pail of water Robert Harding World Imagery

4. A potter decorates earthenware bowls before firing them Jacques Jangoux

5. The smiles and stares of two young Kpelle boys Jacques Jangoux

6. A pygmy hippopotamus bears its ugly fangs R. Kurtz
LEFT 1. An adolescent boy is daubed in white for a ritual that celebrates coming-of-age Thomas S England

Diamond-rich Liberia is on the north Atlantic coast of West Africa, bordered by Sierra Leone, Guinea and Côte d'Ivoire. It's in recovery from seven years of bitter civil strife, which was brought to an end in 1997 with open presidential elections. A regional peace initiative means one day travellers will again be able to explore this equatorial country, bask on its beautiful beaches, trek across verdant hillsides and explore pockets of magnificent rainforest.

BEST TIME TO VISIT
November to April, in the dry season

ESSENTIAL EXPERIENCES
Spotting elephants, pygmy hippopotamii, chimpanzees and antelopes

Exploring Liberia's stunning rainforest, covering around 40% of the country

Visiting the bustling town of Ganta (Gompa City) in Liberia's mountainous interior

Dining on collard greens and sweet-potato pie at a tiny roadside 'chop bar'

Swimming in the vast Atlantic Ocean at Ellen's Beach, near Monrovia

Experiencing the rich diversity and ceremonial cultures of over a dozen different ethnic groups

GETTING UNDER THE SKIN
Read *Liberia: Portrait of a Failed State* by John-Peter Pham, a sensitive, factual account of African politics and Western intervention

Listen to *Pavarotti & Friends – For The Children Of Liberia*, a collection of extreme musical genres – including Bon Jovi and the Spice Girls – under the uplifting guidance of Luciano Pavarotti

Watch *Liberia: America's Stepchild*, by Liberian filmmaker Nancee Oku Bright, a startling documentary about the settlement of freed American slaves in Liberia and their interactions with the indigenous peoples

Eat goat soup, the national soup, and traditional rice bread made with mashed bananas

Drink ginger beer, *poyo* (palm wine) and strong coffee

IN A WORD
Diamonds for sale

TRADEMARKS
Diamond smugglers; tidal lagoons; lush rainforest; amazing wildlife; rubber plantations; a nation of proud survivors; mangrove swamps; a struggling economy; cassava and sweet potato; a founding member of the United Nations

SURPRISES
Monrovia is one of the wettest capitals in Africa with over 4500mm of annual rainfall and humidity of over 90% – phew!

When is a Rebel Not a Rebel? That is the question people in Liberia had to ask themselves after some yellow T-shirts worn by the Liberian government's 'Navy Rangers' were captured and worn by rebels, causing utter confusion. T-shirts may not seem like decent military dress, but this is a conflict where gangsta-chic is as common as camouflage fatigues, and high-as-a-kite rebels have been known to wear pink bathrobes and shower caps.

– Lonely Planet's *Africa*

MAP REF: N,19

2. Tents gather in an hospitable semicircle at an encampment in the Libyan Sahara Desert Doug McKinlay

3. A massive swell of dunes rolls towards the palm-fringed Dawada Lakes Doug McKinlay

4. An elderly man takes an evening stroll past mud-brick houses in Ghadhames Patrick Syder

5. A cheerful Tuareg man from the Ash Shati' region looks out from under his white headscarf Doug McKinlay

The word is out: Libya is the latest travellers' hotspot, and one of the last unspoilt places on the Mediterranean seaboard. Obscured from Western view for the last 30 years under the government of Colonel Mu'ammar Gaddafi, the country has recently begun courting international tourism. Ripe for discovery are Libya's incredible hospitality, beautiful desertscapes, well-preserved classical ruins, prehistoric rock art and palm-fringed oases.

BEST TIME TO VISIT
November to March for cooler temperatures – or during Libya's golden age in the 2nd century AD

ESSENTIAL EXPERIENCES
Shopping in the bustling medina in Tripoli

Walking through the streets and souks of Benghazi

Viewing the desert architecture and old city at Ghadhames

Exploring the archaeological site at Leptis Magna, regarded as the best Roman site in the Mediterranean

Visiting the preserved Greek city of Cyrene

Hiking through the magnificent Jebel Akhdar mountains

GETTING UNDER THE SKIN
Read Libyan-born and American-raised Khaled Mattawa's *Ismailia Eclipse*, poetry that speaks across both cultural and political borders

Listen to *Marhab* by Masoud, modern Libyan folkloric tunes

Watch *Lion of the Desert* by Libyan filmmaker Moustapha Akkad, about a Libyan Guerilla soldier who tries to stop the invasion of Italian troops during WWII

Eat *cuscus bil-Bosla* – coucous with lamb, beans and tomato; *dolma mshakila* – peppers and zucchinis stuffed with spiced, minced lamb; *shorba bilhout* – spiced fish soup; delicious, sweet local dates

Drink sweet mint tea or the excellent local mineral water

IN A WORD
Ahlaan wasahlaan (welcome)

TRADEMARKS
Unesco World Heritage–listed sites; ancient Roman and Greek cities; beautiful resort towns; local souks and medinas; Islamic culture; historic mosques and *hammams*; gorgeous beaches; mud-brick desert architecture

SURPRISES
Stunning oases nestled in the Saharan desert; Tuaregs – the blue men of the desert; the pottery market at Gharian

Libya's not all date palms and deserts, but if shifting sands and camel trains are your thing, it's got desert for days, and a quick jaunt down into the Fezzan will take you boldly where nomad has gone before. For a country that's been all but swallowed by the Sahara, you'll be surprised to see how pleasantly Mediterranean it can be.

— World Guide, www.lonelyplanet.com

1. A local man sits at the crest of a dune in the Ubari Sand Sea while behind him the Unmal Miah Lake shimmers like a mirage Jane Sweeney

6. The honeycombed chambers of a fortified granary store in the Berber village of Kabaw Anthony Ham

MAP REF: K,21

2. A vineyard flourishes at the foothills of a stony mountain range in Vaduz William Boyce

3. Rows of wooden stakes fringe the roof of a country barn Dave G. Houser

1. Early risers plant fresh tracks in the immaculate snow at the Malbun ski resort Walter Bibikow

Postage stamp-sized Liechtenstein is sandwiched snugly between Austria and Switzerland, Liechtenstein's domineering elder sibling. The Swiss franc is the legal currency and border regulations are necessary only on the Austrian side. A cross-country walk takes on a new meaning here, as Liechtenstein measures a mere 25km north to south and 6km west to east. It's a prosperous place with a high standard of living, low taxes, numerous banks, the wealthiest royal family in Europe, its own stamps and an enviable unemployment rate of around 1.3%.

BEST TIME TO VISIT
December to April for winter sports, May to October for hiking

ESSENTIAL EXPERIENCES
Having your passport stamped to earn bonus bragging points

Tackling the rugged hiking trails that wind through stunning Alpine scenery

Exploring tiny Vaduz, which sits below historic Vaduz Castle

Whizzing down the Malbun resort's ski runs

Collecting stamps at the Postage Stamp Museum in Vaduz

GETTING UNDER THE SKIN
Read *Secrets of the Seven Smallest States of Europe: Andorra, Liechtenstein, Luxembourg, Malta, Monaco, San Marino and Vatican City* by Thomas Ecchardt, which outs Liechtenstein from its historical closet

Listen to Vaduz-born classical composer Joseph Gabriel Rheinberger (1839–1901)

Watch films from countries with less than 10 million inhabitants at the Vaduz Film Festival, held every August

Eat filling soups, cheeses, and Alp-fortifying food such as *rösti* (fried shredded potatoes) and *wurst* (sausage)

Drink local, rarely exported, wine

IN A WORD
Vilcch chöi mer üs mal zum Briefmärkele träffe? (maybe we could swap stamps sometime?)

TRADEMARKS
A copycat Switzerland; wine producers; obsessive philatelists; a tax haven for enthusiastic entrepreneurs; the Alps; a retreat for expats; tiny mountain villages; crisp air; banks; ski-runs and hiking routes

SURPRISES
Dentures are an important export; there's no military service – the 80-strong army was disbanded in 1868; bank customers can no longer deposit money anonymously

Despite its small size, Liechtenstein has two political regions (upper and lower) and three distinct geographical areas: the Rhine valley in the west, the edge of the Tirolean Alps in the southeast, and the northern lowlands. A third of the population is foreign residents.

— Lonely Planet's *Western Europe*

4. The fairytale Gutenberg castle perched on a wooded hill Dennis Hallinan

MAP REF: H,21

2. Vilnius presents a frosty vista from Gedimino Hill Jonathan Smith

3. The famous Hill of Crosses in Siauliai, where devotional crucifixes bristle from the tombstones Jane Sweeney

1. Look at me! The dramatic silhouette of a statue beneath the Belfry of St John's in Vilnius Tom Cockrem

Rebellious, quirky and vibrant, Lithuania owes much to the rich cultural currents of central Europe. It once shared an empire with neighbouring Poland that stretched from the Baltic almost to the Black Sea. Its capital Vilnius boasts a Baroque Old Town that is the largest in Eastern Europe and praised as the 'New Prague'. Lithuania's natural treasures also glitter – from the forests of the south to the magical Curonian Spit and the Nemunas Delta on the coast.

BEST TIME TO VISIT
May to September (spring and summer)

ESSENTIAL EXPERIENCES
Wandering through the winding streets of Vilnius and peering into hidden courtyards

Exploring the Curonian Spit, an isolated thread of sand composed of dunes and lush pine forests inhabited by elk, deer and wild boar

Savouring fish freshly smoked to an old Curonian recipe

Visiting the old Lithuanian capital of Trakai – a quiet town in an attractive area of lakes and islands dotted with old wooden cottages

Soaking up the curative powers of Druskininkai's mineral springs

GETTING UNDER THE SKIN
Read Antanas Skma's semi-autobiographical novel *Balta drobule*, which pioneered the use of stream of consciousness in Lithuanian literature

Listen to the avant-garde jazz of the Ganelin Trio

Watch *Koridorius* (The Corridor) by director Šarcnas Bartas or *The Necklace of Wolf's Teeth* by Algimantas Puipa

Eat *zeppelin cepelinai*, an airship-shaped parcel of thick potato dough, filled with cheese, *mesa* (meat) or *grybai* (mushrooms). It comes topped with a sauce made from onions, butter, sour cream and bacon bits. You also might like to try smoked pig's ears (or not).

Drink the local beer Utenos or potent *stakliskes*, a honey liqueur

IN A WORD
Làbas (hello)

TRADEMARKS
Winning independence from the Soviet Union; Baltic states; Stalin World; Eurovision Song Contest

SURPRISES
When visiting a Lithuanian, bring an odd number of flowers – even-numbered bouquets are for the dead! Never shake hands across a doorway, as it is believed to bring bad luck.

Described as the 'Mecca of Lithuania', the sight of thousands upon thousands of crosses covering the Hill of Crosses has inspired many pilgrimages. Large and tiny, expensive and cheap, wood and metal, the crosses are devotional, to accompany prayers, or finely carved folk art masterpieces. Others are memorials, tagged with flowers, a photograph or other mementoes in memory of the deceased, and inscribed with a sweet or sacred message.

– Lonely Planet's *Estonia, Latvia & Lithuania*

4. Pedestrians tramp over the snow heaped beneath the pillars of Parliament in the capital Izzet Keribar

MAP REF: G,22

2. A whimsical monument to nonviolence outside a European Union building in the capital Martin Moos

3. The stark exterior of Grand Theatre de la Ville de Luxembourg in Luxembourg City Bruce Yuan-Yue Bi

4. Like a vision from a dream, the illuminated Castle of Vianden glimmers in the night Martin Moos

Lilliputian Luxembourg may not be big enough to contain the letters of its name on a map of Europe, but it makes up in snazz what it lacks in size. It has a wealth of verdant landscapes crisscrossed by rivers and dotted with the sort of rural hamlets that most people associate with fairy tales. Luxembourg's people are justifiably proud of their heritage: the nation's motto is inscribed everywhere throughout Luxembourg City, the capital – *Mir wëlle bleiwe wat mir sin* – 'We want to remain what we are'. After a visit, you're sure to hope they do.

BEST TIME TO VISIT
March to June, for the most pleasant weather

ESSENTIAL EXPERIENCES
Feeling claustrophobic in Luxembourg City's fortress casements, a honeycomb of damp chambers and connecting tunnels hewn from the belly of the Bock

Taking in the superb panoramas from Citadelle du St Esprit in Luxembourg City

Spending a lazy day visiting the wineries along the Moselle Valley's Route du Vin

Playing 'king of the castle' at Vianden

Hiking among the amazing rock formations in the primeval landscape of the Müllerthal 'Little Switzerland' region

GETTING UNDER THE SKIN
Read *How to Remain What You Are*, a humorous look at Luxembourg ways by George Müller, a local psychologist and writer

Listen to Fluyd, an alternative rap 'n' roll group, and Sascha Ley

Watch the excellent Luxembourgian animation of *Kirikou et la Sorcière*

Eat *judd mat gaardebounen* (slabs of smoked pork served in a thick cream-based sauce with huge chunks of potato and broad beans), *ferkelsrippchen* (grilled spareribs) and *liewekniddelen mat sauerkraut* (liver meatballs with sauerkraut)

Drink Moselle wines labelled *'Marque Nationale du Vin Luxembourg'* (which means the wine has passed various wine-tasting tests)

IN A WORD
Moien (hello)

TRADEMARKS
Home to the most dramatically situated capital city in Europe; dumplings; a tax haven; stunning castles; beautiful china; proud people

SURPRISES
Whitsunday is celebrated with a handkerchief pageant in honour of St Willibrord; the Moselle Valley's wine festival is held from August to November's 'New Wine' celebration in Wormeldange

The north of the country lures outdoors enthusiasts with sylvan settings promising fabulous skiing and hiking. The Moselle Valley, just east of Luxembourg City, is one of Europe's most idyllic wine-producing regions. And the capital is no more than an hour's drive from anywhere else in the country, so you can truly get a sense of the lay of the land without spending aeons running around.

– World Guide, www.lonelyplanet.com

1. The charming village of Esch sur Sure sits at a quiet bend of the meandering river Sure Andy Caulfield

5. The tranquil town of Grund, now a Unesco World Heritage–listed site Bruce Yuan-Yue Bi

MAP REF: H.20

2. Some of Macau's wealth of culinary delights are glimpsed in this steaming food stall on a central street
Lawrence Worcester

3. Fragrant smoke wafts from votary incense at the A-Ma temple Richard I'Anson

4. These delicately prepared dumplings will be eaten in the fun of a traditional Chinese banquet
Oliver Strewe

5. A heavy nose, a floral finish and a fruity cap – the membership criteria for the Wine Society of Macau
Oliver Strewe

6. A devotee lights a candle at the temple of Kwan Yin, goddess of mercy Lawrence Worcester
LEFT 1. An opera singer gazes heavenward for inspiration as her powerful voice fills the concert hall Michael Aw

Macau may be firmly back in China's orbit, but its Portuguese patina makes it a most unusual Asian destination. In contrast to nearby Hong Kong its atmosphere is relaxed and laidback, with Mediterranean-style cafés filled with palm-readers, caged birds and pipe-smokers. Highlights include fabulous architecture, narrow cobbled alleys, grand Baroque churches and balconied colonial mansions. Macau is wooing commerce and tourism like never before, and plans are afoot for all kinds of family-oriented shopping malls and theme parks to counter-balance the peninsula's long-held popularity as a haven for gamblers.

BEST TIME TO VISIT
October to December (winter)

ESSENTIAL EXPERIENCES
Strolling along Praia Grande and visiting the A-Ma Temple

Munching on a bowl of *caldo verde* and a plate of *bacalhau* at one of the Portuguese restaurants in Taipa village

Skywalking around the outer rim of the Macau Tower or climbing to the top of the telecommunications spire

Swimming and basking on the 'black sand' of Hác Sá Beach on Coloane

GETTING UNDER THE SKIN
Read Austin Coates' *City of Broken Promises* – a fictionalised account of the life of 18th-century Macanese trader Martha Merop

Listen to a heady mix of opera, musicals, visiting orchestras and other musical events at the annual two-week Macau International Music Festival held in October

Watch *The Bewitching Braid* by Macanese director Cai Yuan Yuan

Eat the Portuguese-inspired *porco à Alentejana*, a tasty casserole of pork and clams, or the Macanese *galinha africana* (African chicken), a chicken cooked in coconut, garlic and chillies

Drink *vinho verde*, a crisp, dry, slightly effervescent 'green' wine from Portugal that goes down a treat with salty Portuguese food and spicy Macanese dishes

IN A WORD
Nei ho ma? (hello, how are you?)

TRADEMARKS
The former Portuguese colony; the spin of the roulette wheel; great food; a shopping haven

SURPRISES
The Procession of the Passion of Our Lord is a 400-year-old tradition in which a colourful procession bears a statue of Jesus Christ from Macau's St Augustine Church to Macau Cathedral; tourism generates more than 40% of Macau's GDP

Eating – be it Portuguese or Macanese 'soul food', Chinese dim sum or the special treats available from street stalls and night markets – is one of the most rewarding aspects of a visit to Macau.

– Lonely Planet's *Hong Kong & Macau*

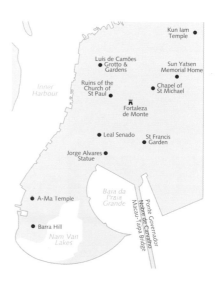

MAP REF: L,32

2. A bronze sun gilds the rippled surface of Lake Ohrid as a fishing boat drifts homeward Jon Davison

3. Glassy lake, mountain and sky are almost indistinguishable through the cypress trees surrounding the Church of Sveti Naum Paul Hellander

4. A comfortable silence reigns in an orthodox reading room Izzet Keribar

Smack bang in the middle of the mountainous Balkan Peninsula, encircled by Greece, Bulgaria, Albania, Serbia and Montenegro, it's no wonder the Former Yugoslav Republic of Macedonia has been a powder keg of Ottoman and Orthodox influences. These days the opportunities for relaxation and exploration are unexpectedly varied: you can sit in a lively café, experience the time-worn Turkish bazaars, gaze at any number of medieval monasteries, wander in space-age shopping centres and marvel at Lake Ohrid's swag of cultural monuments.

BEST TIME TO VISIT
July and August – the best months to catch Macedonia's festivals

ESSENTIAL EXPERIENCES
Wandering through Skopje's Oriental bazaar district

Visiting the City Art Gallery housed in the Daud Paša Baths in Skopje, once the largest Turkish baths in the Balkans

Making a pilgrimage to the 17th-century Church of Sveti Naum at Ohrid

Scrambling through the Ruins of Heraclea at Bitola

Skiing the southern slopes of Šar Planina, west of Tetovo

Hiking in the Pelister National Park

GETTING UNDER THE SKIN
Read *Black Lamb and Grey Falcon* by Rebecca West, a between-the-wars Balkan travelogue

Listen to the Tavitjan Brothers Trio's self-titled album, featuring some of the most famous jazz musicians in Macedonia

Watch Milcho Manchevski's *Before the Rain*, a visually stunning vision of how inter-ethnic war in Macedonia might begin

Eat Turkish-style grilled mincemeat; *burek* – cheese or meat pies; Ohrid trout

Drink *skopsko pivo* – the local beer; *rakija* – the national firewater, a strong spirit distilled from grapes

IN A WORD
Zdravo (hello)

TRADEMARKS
Orthodox churches; splendid mosaics; Lake Ohrid; bazaar districts; smoky cafés and bars; Byzantine monasteries; ski resorts; Roman ruins

SURPRISES
The gnarled, 900-year-old plane tree at Ohrid; the five-day Balkan festival of Folk Dances and Songs, held at Ohrid in early July

The most famous and popular Macedonian folk dance is called Teskoto (The Hard One). It is a male dance for which music is provided by the tapan and the zurla (large pipes). It starts very slowly and gets progressively faster. This dance symbolises the national awakening of the Macedonian people and is performed with dancers dressed in traditional Macedonian costumes.

— World Guide, www.lonelyplanet.com

1. The tiny 13th-century Church of Sveti Jovan Bogoslov Kaneo stands guard over Lake Ohrid Paul Hellander

5. Empty wedding dresses appear to hover threateningly over the heads of women in a Skopje clothing shop Izzet Keribar

MAP REF: I,22

2. An avenue of stately baobabs in Toliara near Morondava Andrew MacColl

3. A swashbuckling girl and her piratey parrot in Fianarantsoa Margie Politzer

4. Traditional henna patterns on the face of a young girl in Nosy Be Olivier Cirendini

5. Pirogues drift into an aimless symmetry off the island of Nosy Nato Olivier Cirendini

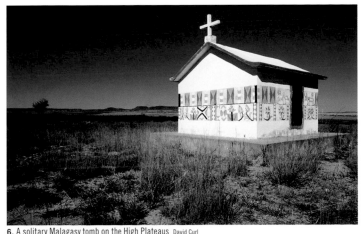

6. A solitary Malagasy tomb on the High Plateaus David Curl

LEFT 1. Vividly dressed village girls with baskets of produce balanced on their heads, on their way to market in the south of Madagascar Chris Barton

Madagascar's teeming fertile forests and geographical isolation have served to preserve and propagate 'nature's design laboratory' in a mix found nowhere else on earth. Sadly, this astounding diversity is threatened by aggressive deforestation. Still, for now, Madagascar's forests are a shimmering, seething mass of a trillion dripping leaves and slithering, jumping, quirky creatures from nature's bag of tricks: lemurs, chameleons, periwinkles and baobabs, aloes, geckos, sifakas and octopus trees.

BEST TIME TO VISIT
April to October (winter) – or for an authentic pirate experience, the 17th century when more than 1000 pirates were based on Madagascar's east coast

ESSENTIAL EXPERIENCES
Kicking back in Fort Dauphin (Taolagnaro), with its windswept coastline and picturesque mountain backdrop

Sailing out to Île Sainte Marie – a former haunt of pirates

Spotting lemurs at Parc National de Montagne d'Ambre

Exploring the lush rainforests of Parc National de Ranomafana

Trekking in the beautiful Masoala Peninsula

GETTING UNDER THE SKIN
Read *Madagascar, Island of the Ancestors* by John Mack, a superb ethnographic overview of Malagasy culture

Listen to Paul Bert Rahasimanana ('Rossy') – check out *Island of Ghosts* or *Bal Kabosy*

Watch Raymond Rajaonarivelo's *Quand les Étoiles Rencontrent la Mer* (When the Stars Meet the Sea), the story of a boy born during a solar eclipse; *Angano...Angano... Tales from Madagascar*, a documentary in the oral Malagasy tradition

Eat *vary hen'omby* (rice served with stewed or boiled zebu) or Malagasy cheeses (made from zebu cow's milk)

Drink *betsa-betsa* (fermented sugar cane juice) or *punch aux cocos* (rum and coconut milk punch)

IN A WORD
Manao ahoana ianao (how do you do?)

TRADEMARKS
Lemurs; pirates; zebu-drawn carts; fourth-largest island in the world; trekking

SURPRISES
Over half of the world's chameleon species are found in Madagascar; according to the *vintana* belief, Friday (which is associated with nobility) is considered a good day to be born, while Thursday is associated with servitude

The seminomadic Bara are a relatively small tribal group based in southwestern Madagascar around Ihosy. Their origins are unclear, although they are considered to be among the most African of Madagascar's tribes. Their culture focuses almost exclusively on the zebu, which is the most important commodity and the major determinant of wealth. According to tradition, a young Bara man must prove himself by stealing zebu – only after he has done this will he be considered a desirable marriage partner. Being imprisoned for zebu-rustling may enhance his appeal even further.

– Lonely Planet's *Madagascar*

MAP REF: Q,24

239

2. A young villager observes the dry landscape of southern Malawi Jerry Galea

3. The inquiring faces of village children in the Nsasje District Jerry Galea

4. A man hoists a basket over his head in southern Malawi Jerry Galea

5. With its hind legs ready to spring, a timid reedbuck stands alone under a brooding sky in Nyika National Park Andrew van Smeerdijk

6. A spirited afternoon game of volleyball outside the Indaba bar in Cape Maclear Dennis Johnson
LEFT 1. A sombre-faced fisherman lost in thought on the banks of a lake Juliet Coombe

The tourist brochures bill Malawi as 'the warm heart of Africa', and for once the hype is true. Malawi's ever-changing landscape takes you from the top of lofty mountains, down steep escarpments, through woodland, farmland and empty grassland, to the shores of a magnificent lake. Nature lovers will adore the national parks and game reserves, mountain hiking and plateau trekking, lake diving and boating – plus the warm welcome, as Malawians tend to be extremely friendly toward travellers.

BEST TIME TO VISIT
Late April to November (the dry season)

ESSENTIAL EXPERIENCES
Paddling across Lake Malawi with the shrill call of fish-eagles floating across the waves

Riding with zebras and antelopes across the rolling plateau of Nyika National Park

Climbing the steep winding paths of Mt Mulanje to cool grassy plateaus speckled with wildflowers

Taking a wildlife drive through Liwonde National Park to spot elephants, antelopes, hyenas and lions

Journeying back in time on the *Ilala* ferry on Lake Malawi

GETTING UNDER THE SKIN
Read Malawian poet Steve Chimombo's highly acclaimed *The Rainmaker*, or Paul Theroux's *Jungle Lovers*, a light and humorous take on 1960s Malawi culture and politics

Listen to Lucius Banda, who plays soft ('Malawian-style') reggae, or Ethel Kamwendo, one of Malawi's leading female singers

Watch *Up in Smoke*, a documentary exploring the effects of the tobacco industry in Malawi

Eat *chambo* (a Lake Malawi fish – a local speciality) or *nsima* (maize porridge – the regional staple)

Drink the locally brewed beer Chibuku

IN A WORD
Moni (good morning)

TRADEMARKS
Baobab trees; Lake Malawi, fish; national parks; trekking; teeming wildlife

SURPRISES
Lake Malawi covers almost a fifth of Malawi's total area; the remains of settlements of modern humans dating back some 100,000 years have been found on the shores of Lake Malawi

Great emphasis is also placed on handshakes. There are various local variations, involving linked thumbs or fingers, or the left hand touching the right elbow, which you'll pick up by observation, but these are reserved for informal occasions (not greeting officials). A 'normal' western handshake will do fine in most situations.

– Lonely Planet's *Malawi*

MAP REF: P.23

2. The Petronas Towers, among the world's tallest structures, dominate the skyline of Kualar Lumpur Simon Bracken

3. Tea pickers carve patterns through crop fields during harvest in the Cameron Highlands Anders Blomqvist

4. Fishing boats float languidly under a radiant sky in Tanjong Bunga Manfred Gottschalk

5. His body illustrated with age and tattoos, an elderly man rests in the Menyang Sedi Longhouse near Lake Batang Ai Tom Cockrem

1. Hide and seek – a young girl peeks through a broken fence near Lake Batang Ai Tom Cockrem

Malaysia is an assault on the senses – a cultural fusion of colours, flavours and dialects combined with sticky tropical heat. It boasts superb beaches, mountains and national parks, plus a heady mix of people – Malay, Chinese, Indian, and the diverse indigenous tribes of Sabah and Sarawak in Borneo. Historical influences loom large in the stately colonial architecture of Georgetown (Penang) and Melaka, and the prosperous nation's love of progress is proclaimed in its gleaming, futuristic buildings.

BEST TIME TO VISIT
May to September (the dry season)

ESSENTIAL EXPERIENCES
Balancing on the creaky canopy walk over Taman Negara National Park

Snorkelling with Technicolor fish in crystal-clear waters off the Perhentian Islands

Sipping a freshly snipped brew of full-bodied Highlands tea in the Cameron Highlands

Climbing the challenging craggy peak of Mt Kinabalu

Haggling for bargains under the bright lights of Kuala Lumpur's night markets

GETTING UNDER THE SKIN
Read Joseph Conrad's *Lord Jim* – adventure on the South China Seas and the real-life story of Raja Brooke of Sarawak; *The Return* by KS Maniam – contemporary Malaysian fiction exploring the Indian Malaysian experience

Listen to traditional Malay *gendang* (drum) music; kampung-style world music by Zainal Abidin; KL alternative rock band Flop Poppy

Watch Mahadi J Murat's *Sayang Salmah* (1995), a taut family drama set in post-independence Malaya; *Guardians of the Forest*, a documentary account of the plight of the indigenous Orang Asli people, directed by Alan D'Cruz (2001)

Eat the stinky but delicious durian fruit; *laksa* (spicy coconut noodle soup)

Drink *air kelapa* (coconut water); *tuak* (Borneo rice wine)

IN A WORD
Jalan-jalan (I'm just travelling around)

TRADEMARKS
Orang-utans; tea plantations; Mahathir Mohamad; colonial remnants; Petronas Towers; jungle tribes; logging and dams; tropical islands; hawker food; gleaming mosques

SURPRISES
Malaysia is well on the way to achieving its goal of becoming a fully industrialised nation by 2020; nine state sultans still reign, and they take five-year turns at being *yang di-pertuan agong* (chief sultan of Malaysia)

Moving from the cities to the more rural, and thus Malay, parts of the country, the laid-back ethos becomes stronger and Islamic culture comes more to the fore, particularly on the east coast of the peninsula. In Malaysian Borneo you'll be fascinated by the communal lifestyle of the tribes who still live in jungle longhouses – here, hospitality is a key ingredient of the social framework.

– Lonely Planet's *Malaysia, Singapore & Brunei*

6. A keymaker in Georgetown, Penang, takes a moment to leaf through a newspaper Anders Blomqvist

MAP REF: N,31

2. Thatched bungalows stretch out into the sea off Dhunikolhu island James Lyon

3. The bow of a *dhoni* boat appears to hover above calm, ethereal waters John Borthwick

4. Cheeky boys splash about in a rubber tube on Maalhoss island John Borthwick

This small Islamic nation of fishing and trading people has a history, culture and language all its own. The Maldives is made up of a string of 1190 tiny islands, most of them measuring less than a couple of kilometres and bobbing only a few metres above sea level. If your idea of paradise is a pristine tropical island with swaying palm trees, white-sand beaches and turquoise lagoons, then the Maldives will not disappoint.

BEST TIME TO VISIT
December to April (the dry season)

ESSENTIAL EXPERIENCES
Swimming in a clear-blue lagoon, strolling on soft white sand and sitting under a coconut tree

Scuba diving to see turtles, mantas and morays, whale sharks, nurse sharks, hammerheads and rays

Exploring the underwater shipwreck *Maldive Victory*, alive with corals and home to trevally, snapper, squirrelfish and cod

Taking a flight over the atolls and watching the free-form patterns of sea, sandbank, reef and island

GETTING UNDER THE SKIN
Read *Mysticism in the Maldives*, which documents Maldivian myths and stories

Listen to popular local bands Mezzo and Zero Degree

Eat *garudia* (soup made from dried and smoked fish, often eaten with rice, lime and chilli) for a main meal and finish off with an *arecanut* (an oval nut chewed with betel leaf, cloves and lime), which is the equivalent of an after-dinner mint

Drink *raa* (a sweet and delicious toddy tapped from the crown of the palm trunk)

IN A WORD
A-salam alekum (hello)

TRADEMARKS
Pristine tropical islands; swaying palm trees; pure white-sand beaches; brilliant aquamarine water; abundant marine life; gloriously coloured coral; peerless diving

SURPRISES
Ancient beliefs survive: the islanders fear *jinnis* – evil spirits that come from the sea, land and sky; the full name of the country is Dhivehi Raajjeyge Jumhooriyyaa

Just a few metres below the surface, it's a world of steep cliffs, big boulders and vast blue voids – a complete contrast to the uniform flatness of the islands and the sea. The water is filled with huge whale sharks, graceful turtles, sluggish sea cucumbers and schools of psychedelic-coloured fish. Soft corals, sea fans, feather stars and sponges decorate the reefs, while little staghorns and colourful polyp patches are colonising the old hard-coral blocks.

– Lonely Planet's *Maldives*

1. Fresh-faced students promenade in their brilliant white school uniforms on the streets of Male' James Lyon

5. A sandy path winds its way through a grove of palm trees Dennis Wisken

MAP REF: N,27

2. The dusty hands of a Dogon hunter grip an old rifle in Mopti
Dan Herrick

3. Long, vividly painted wooden boats known as *pinasse* carry goods and people between Mopti and Timbuktu along the river Niger David Else

4. An indigo-clad Tuareg carpet seller in Timbuktu displays his wares from the top of his head Patrick Syder

5. Desert bloom – a stunning Tuareg woman sits in the sand in the village of Tin Telout John Elk III

1. The Great Market in Djenné comes to life in front of the century-old mud-brick mosque built in the classic Sahel style David Else

From Bamako to Timbuktu, Mali has desert scenery that may have you believing you're on the set of *Lawrence of Arabia*. And there's so much more, from the fringes of the Saharan desert and the great Niger River, to medieval mud-brick mosques and pink-hued sandstone villages. Malians are a proud and enduring people who have suffered through drought and famine of biblical proportions. There is a wealth of talented musicians and great passion among the people for their traditional culture.

BEST TIME TO VISIT
October to February (before the heat) — or in June 1960 when Mali gained independence from France

ESSENTIAL EXPERIENCES
Hunting for bargains in Bamako's pavement market stalls

Trekking through the magnificent Bandiagara Escarpment

Watching a gorgeous sunset at Gao

Photographing the mud-brick houses and mosque at Djenné

Buying colourful handwoven fabrics at the market in Ségou

Making your way through the desert to enigmatic isolated Timbuktu

GETTING UNDER THE SKIN
Read *The Unveiling of Timbuctoo: The Astounding Adventures of Caillie* by Galbraith Welch, an account of the first Western explorer to both reach and return from Timbuktu

Listen to the beautiful and intimate tracks on *Je Chanterai pour Toi* by Boubacar Traoré; Ry Cooder and Ali Farka Touré's *Talking Timbuktu*

Watch *Yeleen* by Souleymane Cissé, depicting the struggle of a young warrior to destroy the corruption of an older society.

Eat fried Nile perch; *poulet yassa* – chilli spiced grilled chicken; *riz yollof* – meat or vegetables cooked with tomato

Drink ginger and hibiscus juices sold in plastic bags

IN A WORD
Merci (thankyou)

TRADEMARKS
Castellated mosques; desert landscapes; the Bambara and Dogon cultures; bustling markets; archaeological ruins; faded French colonial glory; ancient rock paintings; the indigo turbans and robes of the Tuareg; griot music; desert elephants

SURPRISES
The music and dance performances held in local *carrefour* (cultural centres); the riotous football matches; the villages carved into mountain cliffs

The most captivating event on the Mali calendar is the crossing of the cattle at Diafarabé. Every year during December, in a tradition that goes back 160 years, Diafarabé gears up to cope with a sudden influx of cattle and herders as they converge on the river bank. It's a time for celebrations and festivities as herders are reunited with friends and family after several long months in the desert.

— World Guide, www.lonelyplanet.com

6. A young girl crouches at the foot of a tree in a village by the river Niger David Else

MAP REF: L,19

2. The Megalithic Mnajdra temple complex, built to follow the sun's alignment, dates to 3600-2500 BC Juliet Coombe

3. A colourful *luzzu* fishing boat sports an 'eye of protection' Patrick Syder

4. This domed church and its Maltese Cross preside over the water's edge Patrick Syder

5. A fisherman and his boat posing by St Julian's Harbour Eoin Clarke

At first glance Malta appears to be steeped in the past. Ancient temples, the oldest free-standing structures in existence, traditions dating back over 2500 years and buses that could have been around when Malta gained independence in 1964 – it all makes you wonder if the country should be declared a living museum. Though Malta has a rich history it also offers beaches, bars, bustling Mediterranean life, friendly locals, a passion for *festas*, water sports and excellent opportunities for scuba diving.

BEST TIME TO VISIT
February to June (before the heat) – or any time outside 1942 when the country was bombed for 154 days and nights continuously

ESSENTIAL EXPERIENCES
Wandering round the magnificent fortified capital of Valletta, built by the Knights of St John

Enjoying the view overlooking Malta from the city of Mdina

Experiencing a festa, lasting up to five days and including fireworks, the parade of the patron saint, brass bands, food, drink and general celebration

Scuba diving at the Azure Window, a giant rock arch in the cliff surrounding the Inland Sea on the island of Gozo

Swimming at the Blue Lagoon, one of the best bathing spots in the Mediterranean

GETTING UNDER THE SKIN
Read Francis Ebejer's *For Rozina… A Husband*, based on Maltese village life and comprising a collection of short stories; *The Kappilan of Malta* by Nicolas Monserrat tells of a priest's experiences during WWII

Listen to Charles Camilleri's *Il Weghda* – the first opera written in Maltese, and the Beangrowers' *Beangrowers* – a pop/electro/rock/punk mix

Watch Ridley Scott's *Gladiator*, one of the many films shot in Malta; the 1953 movie *The Malta Story*, which plays out events leading up to the island being awarded the George Cross in 1942; the blockbuster *Troy* starring Brad Pitt and Eric Bana

Eat *timpana* – oven-baked macaroni with egg, meat and tomatoes; *mqaret* – deep-fried pastries stuffed with chopped, spiced dates

Drink Kinnie – a soft drink flavoured with bitter oranges and aromatic herbs

IN A WORD
Kif inti? (how are you?)

TRADEMARKS
Churches; ancient buildings; crazy drivers; British tourists; crusading knights; the Maltese Cross; pedestrianised Valletta

SURPRISES
There are no permanent water features on Malta; the country didn't invent Maltesers; it's one of the most densely populated countries in the world

Gozo is one of the contenders for the title of Calypso's Isle – the mythical island described in Homer's Odyssey *where the nymph Calypso seduced the hero Odysseus and kept him captive. If the cave above Ir-Ramla on Gozo was really Calypso's hideaway, then it's no wonder that Odysseus was keen to get home. The view may be pretty and the island delightful, but it's a long, hot and scratchy climb up from the beach, and the cramped living quarters leave a lot to be desired.*

— Lonely Planet's *Malta & Gozo*

1. Malta rivals Venice for the romantic beauty of the gondola Chris Hermes

6. Rising above the buildings of Mosta, this church claims one of the world's largest unsupported domes, almost 40 metres across Eoin Clarke

MAP REF: J,21

2. Bliss infuses the face of a girl drinking coconut milk straight from the source Oliver Strewe

3. A bronzed snorkeller emerges from the waters of Likiep Atoll Christian Aslund

4. Locals take time out for a game of volleyball on Kwajalein Atoll Christian Aslund

1. A traditional beach barbecue on Likiep Atoll Christian Aslund

The Marshalls are made up of more than one thousand flat coral islands of white-sand beaches and turquoise lagoons. Like other Pacific paradises there's spectacular diving, lush tropical greenery and beautiful beaches. The flipside is that many of the Marshallese still struggle with the after-effects of the 20th-century's Atomic Age. Bikini Atoll is the most famous of the nuclear-testing sites of the 1960s, though inhabitants of other islands also suffer from radiation poisoning. Many islands remain too contaminated to be resettled or visited.

BEST TIME TO VISIT
Diving is at its best May to October, when the water is calmest, though water temperatures are bathlike year-round

ESSENTIAL EXPERIENCES
Deep-sea fishing off Longar Point on Arno Atoll

Witnessing the night-time pyrotechnics of missile-testing on Kwajalein Atoll, the world's largest coral atoll

Relaxing on Majuro Atoll's chilled-out beaches

Swimming and fishing off Mejit Island

Discovering history on Maloelap Atoll among the twisted wrecks of WWII bombers

GETTING UNDER THE SKIN
Read *Man This Reef* by Gerald Knight – translated legends of an elderly Marshallese storyteller

Listen to local boy band, County Light – their debut album *Jambo* combines English and Marshallese songs

Watch shocking documentaries about Bikini Atoll including Dennis O'Rourke's definitive *Half Life*

Eat fresh seafood

Drink coconut milk straight from the source

IN A WORD
Yokwe yuk (love to you – the traditional greeting)

TRADEMARKS
Bikinis; warmly welcoming Marshallese; 'secret' US bases; WWII wrecks, stunning but uninhabitable beaches; big game fishing

SURPRISES
Visiting the traditional small village of Laura on Majuro Atoll; camping out on the outer islands in absolute serenity

The Marshall Islands consist entirely of slender coral atolls and islands sprinkled with coconuts, pandanus and breadfruit trees. Few other crops grow in the atolls' salty sand, so the Marshallese long ago turned to the sea for their resources. They became, of necessity, expert fishers and navigators.

– Lonely Planet's *South Pacific*

5. Sun, sand and a comfortable armchair. Who could ask for more? Oliver Strewe

MAP REF: N,37

2. Martinique's richly hued mountain ranges are a study in contrast Walter Bibikow

3. A hurricane sky darkens the bay Jean Robert

4. This fishing boat provides a focal point for beachgoers Jean Robert

Martinique is a slice of France set down in the tropics, with islanders wearing Paris fashions and breakfasting on croissants. But the *zouk* music pouring out of bars and nightclubs are a reminder that Martinicans have a culture of their own, solidly based on West Indian Creole traditions. French may be the official language, but most locals speak Creole, which retains traces of the many tongues spoken by African slaves. Martinique's large towns feel like modern suburbs, but thankfully nearly a third of the island is forested.

BEST TIME TO VISIT
February to March (early spring)

ESSENTIAL EXPERIENCES
Enjoying the cosmopolitan society of Fort-de-France, with its blend of French and Creole cultures

Exploring Saint-Pierre's ruins, caused by the 1902 volcanic eruption

Soaking in the sun on the vast stretches of beach at Les Salines

Cruising the Route de la Trace, a scenic rainforest drive across the mountainous interior

GETTING UNDER THE SKIN
Read *The Collected Poetry of Aime Cesaire*, the force behind the Black Pride phenomenon known as *négritude*; *Texaco* by Patrick Chamoiseau and *Malemort* by ÉSdouard Glissant are also excellent reads

Listen to *Shades of Black* by zouk band Kassav'

Watch *Sugar Cane Alley*, by Euzhan Palcy, documenting the love and sacrifice of a poor black family living on a sugar plantation in Martinique in the 1930s

Eat *accras* (fish fritters) or delicious French pastries

Drink *ti-punch* (a mixture of white rum, sugarcane juice and a squeeze of lemon) or the local beer, Lorraine

IN A WORD
Bonjour (hello)

TRADEMARKS
French cuisine; lush mountains; volcanoes; sugar plantations; *zouk* music

SURPRISES
Josephine Bonaparte was born in Martinique; Paul Gauguin spent five months on Martinique in 1887

In the small towns of Martinique the term 'family' is a broad one. So it is no surprise that a family dinner at Christmas time might involve up to 50 guests. In addition to blood relatives and relatives by marriage, close friends and neighbours are likely to show up. And all of them hungry.

— Lonely Planet's *World Food Caribbean*

MARTINIQUE CAPITAL FORT-DE-FRANCE POPULATION 425,966 AREA 1,100 SQ KM OFFICIAL LANGUAGE FRENCH

1. The crowd is in motion at the Carnival   Photolibrary

5. La Diamant hosts this poignant memorial to drowned African slaves   Walter Bibikow

MAP REF: M,13

2. A camel caravan picks a path through the dunes near Chinguetti in the Adrar region Olivier Cirendini

3. The enchanting greenery of the oasis near Terjit bursts from the surrounding dry rock Anthony Ham

4. Shy children hide behind one other in the wide open desert spaces of Trarza Eric Wheater

Mauritania's biggest attraction is the very desolation that keeps so many people away. In this mysterious, wild, confounding country resources are scarce and sand is plentiful. Among the vast, blank, shifting dune-fields and strange, flat-topped mountain ranges, the only fertile land is found in the oases and along a narrow strip bordering the Senegal River. Set in this severe landscape is a deeply traditional Islamic republic, inhabited by warm, yet reserved, humorous people, measuring out endless amounts of hospitality in glasses of tea with ten sugars.

BEST TIME TO VISIT
December to March, when it's cooler (but still hot)

ESSENTIAL EXPERIENCES
Navigating the empty sea of Saharan dunes by camel

Exploring the ruins of Koumbi Saleh, legendary capital of the medieval empire of Ghana

Lingering in Chinguetti – the seventh-holiest city of Islam

Visiting Nouakchott's wharf and fish market, Port de Pêche

Succumbing to the enchantment of the old quarter of Ouadâne

Counting two million sandpipers in Parc National du Banc d'Arguin

GETTING UNDER THE SKIN
Read Michael Asher's recounting of the first west-to-east camel crossing of the Sahara in *Impossible Journey: Two Against the Sahara*

Listen to the stunning combination of Arabic melodies and African percussion by Diva Dimi Mint Abba

Watch Abderrahmane Sissako's poignant *Hermakano* (Waiting for Happiness), set in Nouâdhibou

Eat at a *méchui*, a traditional nomad's feast, where an entire lamb is roasted over a fire and stuffed with cooked rice (cutlery optional)

Drink glasses of strong, sweet mint tea

IN A WORD
Salaam aleikum (hello)

TRADEMARKS
Endless sand; oases; desertification; birdlife; 'controlled democratisation'

SURPRISES
Only in 1980, when there were an estimated 100,000 Haratin slaves in Mauritania, did the government finally declare slavery illegal, although there are regular round-ups of antislavery activists; Mauritania boasts the longest, slowest, dustiest train in the world

The old quarter of Ouadâne is one of the most enchanting semighost towns of the Sahara. As you arrive across the sands or plateau from Atâr or Chinguetti, the stone houses seem to tumble down the cliff like an apparition, and they change colour depending on the time of day. From the base of the town, the lush gardens of the oasis stretch out before the desert again takes hold.

– Lonely Planet's *West Africa*

1. Heavily wrapped locals trudge along the sandy road between Nouâdhibou and Nouackchott Jane Sweeney

5. A young Mauritanian girl dressed in rich purple cloth Olivier Cirendini

MOROCCO
ALGERIA

ATLANTIC OCEAN

Ain Ben Tili

Bîr Moghrein

Western Sahara

Zouérat

Nouâdhibou

Atâr   Ouadâne

MALI

Nouâmghâr

Nouakchott   Tichit

Oualâta

Rosso

Kiffa   Tintâne   Néma

SENEGAL

MAP REF: L.18

2. A *séga* dancer shakes her booty in Belle Mare Patrick Horton

3. Thatched umbrellas cast cool discs of shade on an idyllic beach near Trou d'Eau Douce Jean-Bernard Carillet

4. A picturesque rural scene near the oddly named town of Flic en Flac Jean-Bernard Carillet

1. A mountain range soars above verdant palm-fringed valleys John Hay

Mauritius boasts endless sugar-cane plantations, dramatic mountains, a vibrant cultural mix and some of the finest beaches and aquamarine lagoons in the Indian Ocean. The island has a distinct Indian flavour, seasoned with African, Chinese, French and British elements. You can enjoy a dish of curried chickpeas or a Yorkshire pudding on the terrace of a French café, sipping imported wine or a thick malty ale while listening to Creole music and the conversation of locals in any number of tongues.

BEST TIME TO VISIT
July to September (winter)

ESSENTIAL EXPERIENCES
Lazing on the long, casuarina-fringed beach of Belle Mare

Diving offshore, especially at the northern end of the island

Hunting for bargains in the downtown market in Port Louis

Strolling around the beautiful Sir Seewoosagur Ramgoolam Botanical Gardens at Pamplemousses

Hiking in the Black River Gorges National Park – a must for nature lovers

GETTING UNDER THE SKIN
Read the romantic novel *Paul et Virginie* by Bernardin de St Pierre, or *Petrusmok* by well-known author Malcolm de Chazal

Listen to Ti-Frère, the most popular séga singer, or Creole singer Jean Claude-Monique

Eat *rougaille* (a Mediterranean dish of tomatoes, onions, garlic and any kind of meat or fish) or *daube* (stew)

Drink *lassi* (a yogurt and ice-water drink) or *alouda glacé* (a syrupy brew of agar, milk and fruit syrup)

IN A WORD
Tapeta! (cheers!)

TRADEMARKS
Home to the extinct dodo; sugar plantations; coconut palms; pamper-happy beach resorts; Indian-fusion cuisine

SURPRISES
Undersea walks are becoming increasingly popular in Mauritius – participants don lead boots and diving helmets and stroll along the seabed feeding the fish, while oxygen is piped in from the surface

The cornerstone of Mauritian Creole cooking is the carri, a rich, spicy onion sauce that owes a lot to Indian cooking. This is one dish that is best sampled in the home, or in the kitchen of a small guesthouse, where every cook creates their own personal blend of herbs and spices. Once you've tasted a home-cooked carri poisson (fish curry), other meals will seem bland.

– Lonely Planet's *Mauritius, Réunion & Seychelles*

5. Giggling sisters make their way to school in Mahébourg Jean-Bernard Carillet

MAP REF: Q,26

257

2. A human skull adorns a tomb in the town of Muna, Yucatán
Jeffrey Becom

3. A villager drags an obstinate pig past a vibrant Tlacotalpan house Jeffrey Becom

4. Hanging loose during siesta time in Chichicapa Jeffrey Becom

5. The ancient Mayan temple of Kukulcán dwarfs a group of visitors in Chichén Itzá Greg Elms

1. Bright shades and dark shadows converge in a street in Real del Monte Jeffrey Becom

6. The face of an elderly *campesino* in San Blas Christian Aslund

Like its native jalapeño peppers and agave tequila, Mexico embodies a spicy, fiery passion for *la vida*. This same spirit overflows from the country's vibrantly colourful art and music, and its complex culture, history and geography. Mexico's charm is its mix of modern and traditional, the clichéd and the surreal, the ancient and the brand-new. True to the country's contradictory nature, the attitude towards the US, its neighbour to the north, is a combination of both uncertainty and longing.

BEST TIME TO VISIT
October to May, to avoid extreme temperatures

ESSENTIAL EXPERIENCES
Navigating your way through massive Mexico City, especially the Museo Nacional de Antropología and the world's largest open-air market

Eating fish tacos at sunset on the beach in Zipolite

Exploring the awe-inspiring ruins at Teotihuacán, Palenque and Monte Albán

Being immersed in the Mayan world of the Yucatán

Exploring Baja's long coastline and rugged interior

Snorkeling at Isla Mujeres and Cozumel

GETTING UNDER THE SKIN
Read eyewitness accounts of the Spanish arrival in the 'new world' such as *History of the Conquest of New Spain* by Bernal Díaz del Castillo; *The Labyrinth of Solitude* by Octavio Paz is a poetic exploration of Mexican myths and identity

Listen to Vicente Fernandez' tear-your-heart-out *ranchera* ballads, Los Tigres del Norte and Café Tacuba — pioneers of *rock en español*

Watch Mayan peasants fleeing north for a new life in *El Norte*; a taste of magical-realism romance in *Like Water for Chocolate*; the raw edge of Mexican cinema's nuevo wave in *Amores Perros*

Eat a *comida corrida* (the daily special set menu offered in the markets), chocolate *mole*, sweet *tamales* with milky *atole*, staples like tortillas, beans and chillies, *tunas* (prickly pear cactus fruit), *nopales* (cactus leaves)

Drink *jugos naturales*, especially the bloodlike *vampiro* fruit juice (beet and carrot); all three alcohols from the maguey plant: tequila, mezcal and the less alcoholic *pulque*; *cerveza* (beer); spicy Mexican hot chocolate

IN A WORD
¡Que le vaya bien! (may things go well for you!)

TRADEMARKS
Mariachis; beaches and coastal resorts; trying to get to the US; Diego Rivera and Frida Kahlo; *telenovelas*; cliff divers in Acapulco; the phrase *mañana*; revolutionary heroes (from Pancho Villa to Subcomandante Marcos); border towns; margaritas; Día de los Muertos skeletons

SURPRISES
Seeing pre-Hispanic ruins in the metro stations; the Olmecs were the first people to extract chocolate from cacao beans – 3000 years before anyone else; the Caesar salad was invented in Tijuana

The old expression 'You are what you eat' takes on new meaning here where cuisine is, above all, mestizaje (literally, a mixture). Like the nation itself, it was born of the fusion of native and Spanish cuisines.

– Lonely Planet's *Mexico*

MAP REF: K,9

2. The Sleeping Lady mountain range reclines by glassy waters in Kosrae Ned Friary

3. A snorkeller investigates what lies beneath the palm fronds of Satawal Atoll Casey Mahaney

4. The river carves a green corridor through the rainforests of Pohnpei Michael Aw

5. In a blur of grass skirts, traditional dancers on Yap boogie to frenzied beats Casey Mahaney
LEFT 1. Glistening in the sun, a girl whistles through her hands on the island of Yap Michael Aw

There's something to be said for a country that has tried to outlaw ties and baseball caps. Despite being firmly tied to the USA's economic and political apron strings, each of the four island states has maintained its own culture: Kosrae remains a casual backwater; Pohnpei a jungle paradise; bright, bubbly Chuuk attracts divers with its sunken WWII wrecks; and unconventional Yap is a traditional centre, famous for its massive stone money.

BEST TIME TO VISIT
Temperatures hover around 81°F (27°C) year-round, but it's a little less humid December to June

ESSENTIAL EXPERIENCES
Diving the sunken Japanese fleet resting in Chuuk lagoon

Bashing through thick rainforest interiors or snorkelling the fringing reef of Kosrae

Staying amongst the hibiscus flowers and jungle hillsides on Pohnpei

Rocking on at Nan Madol, Pohnpei's ancient stone city

Embracing traditional life in Yap, where some people still wear loincloths and everyone has a bulge of betel nut in their cheek

Collecting seashells on Nukuoro, an uninhibited Polynesian haven

GETTING UNDER THE SKIN
Read *Islands Islands: A Special Good,* by Bernadette V Wehrly – a collection of poems, songs and legends

Listen to Randall Mathias' album *Little Refonuwach*, a blend of contemporary and traditional Chuukese melodies

Watch *The Paradise Islands, Micronesia* – a video designed to show off the islands as a tourist destination

Eat (or rather chew) *buw* (betel nut), sometimes with tobacco added on Yap

Drink *sakau* (kava), a narcotic drink made from the roots of pepper shrubs, which is hugely popular on Pohnpei

IN A WORD
Mogethin (Yapese), *Kaselehia* (Pohnpeian), *Ran annim* (Chuukese) – greetings from the respective islands

TRADEMARKS
Giant stone money; red-stained lips from betel nut chewing; diving in underwater maritime 'museums'; bountiful seafood feasts; dark jungle interiors; friendly villagers; empty beaches

SURPRISES
Micronesian societies are made up of clan groupings, with descent traced through the mother (except on Yap, where descent is patrilineal); the head clan on each island can trace its lineage back to the island's original settlers

The residents of the FSM have eight major indigenous languages between them; no two states have the same native tongue. They communicate with each other in English, the language of their most recent colonial administrator.

— Lonely Planet's *Micronesia*

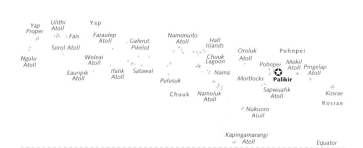

MAP REF: M,35

2. Punk's not dead in Moldova Dan Herrick

3. The majestic Soroca Fortress dates from the 15th century
Dan Herrick

4. When caught in the right light, the All Saints Church of Chişinău blends seamlessly into the sky Dan Herrick

1. His three sons: a farmer and brood horse around on the way home Brother Luck

5. A honey vendor plies his trade at the Kishinev covered market Jeff Greenberg

One of Europe's smallest yet most divided nations, Moldova is a country of multiple personalities. The nation claims some of the most fertile soil in the former Soviet Union with forests and vineyards stretching to every corner of its landlocked borders. Yet the natural splendour of Moldova conceals a population torn by political and ethnic tensions. Civil strife has given rise to two break-away republics: Transdniestr and Gaugauz. With a history as colourful as its landscape, Moldova is an intriguing place to visit; a post-Soviet enigma waiting to be unveiled.

BEST TIME TO VISIT
May to August, or whenever you can – Moldova's Kafkaesque bureaucracy makes obtaining a visa a virtual lottery

ESSENTIAL EXPERIENCES
Strolling along the leafy boulevards of the capital Chişinău, stopping to smell the roses at the 24-hour flower stalls

Finding a taste of the Orient by bargaining your way up and down the exotic central market

Heading underground to the subterranean wine village at Cricova and sampling Moldova's most successful export: dry white Sauvignons and gaudy sparkling reds

Getting a feel for the austerity of religious life at the magnificent 13th-century monastery of Orheiul Vechi carved into a remote cliff face

GETTING UNDER THE SKIN
Read Tony Hawkes' travelogue *Playing the Moldovans at Tennis*, the product of an unlikely bet involving the Moldovan football team; for a deeper cultural perspective read Charles King's *The Moldovans: Romania, Russia and the Politics of Culture*

Watch *The Last Month of Autumn*, winner of the Cannes Grand Prix in 1967, a poetic tale of an elderly Moldovan peasant and his family which has come to represent the national spirit

Eat *mamaliga*, a maize porridge served with cheese, cream and diced fried meat; in Gagauz try the very savoury *sorpa*, a spicy soup made from ram's meat

Drink Sauvignon, Cabernet and Muscat wines produced in abundance in local vineyards, and be sure to sample local varieties such as Feteasca, Black Rara and Moldova

IN A WORD
La revedere! (goodbye)

TRADEMARKS
Fine wine; sunflowers; tin-pot republics; oriental carpets; statues and memorials; national pride

SURPRISES
The separatist republic of Transdniestr created its own state currency by sticking a postage stamp of Suvorov, a local war hero, on obsolete Russian roubles

Local traders [in Chişinău's central market] flog carpets from Turkey while wrinkled pensioners desperately clutch a bizarre collection of bras, T-shirts and not-so-sexy knickers. Porters scurry around with trolleys to carry goods away, cars honk like crazy as they madly try to squeeze through the bustling crowds, women spit out sunflower seeds and old men huddle in groups haggling for the best bargain.

— Lonely Planet's *Romania & Moldova*

MAP REF: H,23

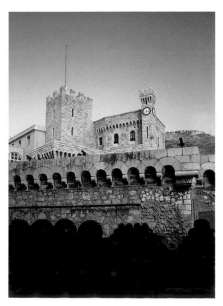

2. With its cannons and cannonballs, the Prince's Palace is an imposing sight David Tomlinson

3. Monaco's architecture oozes grace and presence David Tomlinson

1. A harbour view of the city of dreams: Monte Carlo Neil Setchfield

Although it's more a pre-breakfast stroll than a country, Monaco packs a lot of living into a little land. Most of the people who dwell here come from somewhere else, drawn by the sun, glamorous lifestyle and – most importantly – tax-free income. This is the playground of Europe's elite, a country where Lady Luck might clean you out at the casino one day and put you on the Grimaldi guest list the next. It's a glittering, preening, swanking opportunity for people-watching that shouldn't be passed up by amateur anthropologists.

BEST TIME TO VISIT
April/May and September/October (spring and autumn)

ESSENTIAL EXPERIENCES
Losing money in the over-the-top splendour of the Monte Carlo Casino

Visiting the Musée Océanographique, probably the best aquarium in Europe, with 90 seawater tanks and a display of living coral

Wandering around Monaco's Palais du Prince, which was built in the 13th century

Checking out the spectacular views from the Jardin Exotique, which has 7000 varieties of cacti and succulents

Sailing off Monaco in a glass-bottomed boat

GETTING UNDER THE SKIN
Read Peter Mayle's *Anything Considered*, a novel about Monaco featuring monks, crime and truffles; *The Bridesmaids: Grace Kelly and six intimate friends*, in which Judith Balaban Quine persuades Grace's best buddies to spill the beans

Listen to the prize-winning Monte Carlo Philharmonic

Watch Grace Kelly in the Hitchcock classic *To Catch a Thief* – she met Prince Rainier while filming; *Golden Eye*, with Pierce Brosnan as 'Bond, James Bond' and location shots including the Grand Corniche and Monte Carlo Casino

Eat finger food (if you want to compete with the wannabe starlets on Monte Carlo's beach)

Drink martinis or mineral water

IN A WORD
Très chi-chi

TRADEMARKS
Princess Grace; the casino; the Formula One Grand Prix; endless gossip about princesses Caroline and Stephanie; a tax-free haven; Ferraris

SURPRISES
James Bond really does live in Monaco (well, Roger Moore does); the citizens of Monaco (known as Monégasques) only number about 5000 out of the total population; Monaco's territory only covers 1.95 sq km

Money is safe in Monaco and so are the people who have it. The police presence in Monaco is striking (don't even think about running a red light), and their perpetual vigilance is aided by TV cameras posted on nearly every corner. Street crime is virtually unknown, but Monaco's see no evil, hear no evil banking system has come under criticism from French regulators for tolerating money laundering.

– Lonely Planet's *France*

4. Get ready to rumble when the Grand Prix comes to town Pascal Rondeau

MAP REF: H,20

2. Eat my dust – the horse races at the Nadaam Festival stir things up Bradley Mayhew

3. Happiness is your own reindeer Justin Jeffrey

4. A weather-worn Kazakh in his fox-fur hat
Bradley Mayhew

5. Monks on wheels – a group of Buddhists perform an impromptu ritual on the Mongolian Steppes
Graham Taylor

6. Three boys mounted on tough ponies, the local equivalent of a school bus Graham Taylor
LEFT 1. A wrestler warms up before his bout by dancing *devekh* (eagle dance) Graham Taylor

Mongolia has always stirred up visions of the untamed: Genghis Khan and his hordes, and wild horses galloping across the Steppes. Even today, outside of Ulaan Baatar you may get the feeling you've stepped into another century rather than another country. The 'Land of Blue Sky' is a place where Siberian forests, rolling Steppes, the vast Gobi Desert, glacier-wrapped mountains and crystal-pure lakes meet. It is also one of the last unspoiled travel destinations in Asia.

BEST TIME TO VISIT
May to October, to avoid the cold

ESSENTIAL EXPERIENCES
Exploring the museums and monasteries of Ulaan Baatar, which offer a fascinating glimpse into the culture of pre-Soviet Mongolia

Riding a horse along the Steppes

Camping out under the stars in the Gobi Desert

Visiting a *ger* – the large white felt tents symbolic of Mongolia's nomadic heritage

Fishing in the vast beautiful lake Khövsgöl Nuur, with water so pure you can drink it

GETTING UNDER THE SKIN
Read *The Secret History of the Mongols*, recording the life and deeds of Genghis Khan

Listen to *Spirit of the Steppes: Throat Singing from Tuva & Mongolia*, featuring *khoomi*, the unique vocal artform with no analogue in the West

Watch *The Story of the Weeping Camel*, about a camel who abandons her calf – the surprise hit of film festivals in 2004

Eat mutton: mutton with noodles, mutton with rice, or mutton disguised as something clsc

Drink *airag*, fermented mare's milk, or *süütei tsai*, salty tea

IN A WORD
Za (a catch-all term said at the conclusion of a statement)

TRADEMARKS
Ghengis Khan; savage hordes; *gers*; horses; archery; barbecues and hotpots; scantily clad wrestlers; endless plains

SURPRISES
No-one was more surprised than the Mongolians when the Soviet Union collapsed, leaving them without an international patron, and spectacularly broke

Mongolians sing to their animals: there are lullabies to coax sheep to suckle their lambs, croons to control a goat, to milk a cow or imitate a camel's cry – there are far more Mongolian songs about the love of a good horse than the love of a good woman.

– Lonely Planet's *Mongolia*

MAP REF: H,31

2. The ancient village of Ait Benhaddou, redolent with the romance of *The Arabian Nights* David Wall

3. Oriental arches recur like a hall of mirrors at the 800-year-old Tin Mal Mosque Prayer hall in Tiznit John Elk III

4. Vibrant as a desert bloom, a Berber woman stands out in the lunar landscape of the High Atlas Mountains Sara-Jane Cleland

5. An elaborate shadow falls across a window shutter at Le Jardin de Majorelles, an ornamental garden in Marrakesh Amerens Hedwich

6. Steam wafts invitingly from food stalls at the market in Place Djemaa el-Fna, Marrakesh John Brettell
LEFT 1. Two boys from the Er-Rachidia region bask in the reflected glow of the desert sun on the Merzouga dunes Izzet Keribar

Tangier, Casablanca, Marrakesh…just the names of these cities stir a hint of spice in the nostrils. Morocco has been thoroughly mythologised, and for good reason – the light is shimmering, the art extraordinary, and the region's history comes alive in its medieval cities, Roman ruins, Berber kasbahs and Islamic monuments. If you can survive the touts it's also heaven for shoppers, with open-air markets throughout the country piled high with rugs, woodwork, jewellery and leather – said to be the softest in the world.

BEST TIME TO VISIT
October to April for pleasant temperatures countrywide

ESSENTIAL EXPERIENCES
Indulging in Moroccan café culture – fresh croissants, mint tea and olives all round

Trekking in the mountains and sleeping at a home-stay to enjoy the legendary Berber hospitality

Exploring the medinas of Fès and Marrakesh – two of the world's largest intact medieval towns

Visiting the Roman ruins and mosaics at Volubilis

Soaking in a *hammam* (traditional bathhouse) – every town has at least one

Wandering past the snack stalls and entertainers of Marrakesh's Djemaa el-Fna

GETTING UNDER THE SKIN
Read *Year of the Elephant* by Leila Abouzeid, or Leonora Peet's *Women of Marrakesh*, in which Peets gets about as close as a non-Muslim can to the lives of local women

Listen to Berber group Master Musicians of Joujouka

Watch *Le Coiffeur du Quartier des Pauvres* by Mohammed Reggab, an insight into the plight of the poor in a working-class suburb of Casablanca. The classic *Lawrence of Arabia* includes scenes filmed in the fabulous kasbah of Aït Benhaddou.

Eat *seksu* (couscous) with a *tagine* (a vegetable and lamb casserole)

Drink sweet mint tea or fresh orange juice (with cinnamon or orange-flower water)

IN A WORD
Ssalamu 'lekum (hello)

TRADEMARKS
Mint tea; Berbers; Fès; couscous; quality rugs; Bogart and Bergman in *Casablanca*

SURPRISES
The last Barbary lion, a species indigenous to Morocco and used in ancient Roman amphitheatres for disposing of Christians, died in captivity in the 1960s

Arab hospitality is legendary and invitations may well be extended to the home. This is perfectly normal in Morocco and you may find that an invitation is earned after just a brief conversation with the driver of a taxi, with a young man or woman in the hammam (bathhouse), or sitting next to an old man on the bus. This is a tremendous opportunity to experience something of real Moroccan culture. 'Dine and feed your guests even if you are starving' goes the proverb, and the generosity you are shown can be nothing short of astonishing.

– Lonely Planet's *Morocco*

MAP REF: J.19

2. Fishermen mend their colourful nets outside the Catholic church on Ilha de Moçambique David Else

3. A pedal-powered peddlar outside his shop on Ibo Island Matt Fletcher

4. Handmade clay pots, a speciality of Ponta da Barra, for sale by a dusty roadside Tim Rock

5. Work and weather unravel the shirt of a dhow fisherman in Inhambane Tim Rock

6. Commuters come and go during peak hour at a transit station in Maputo Tim Rock
LEFT 1. A young student of Islam studies in the sunlight outside a mosque in Vilankulo Nick Ray

While Mozambique has had more than its share of difficulties – not least of which was a long, horrific civil war – the atmosphere is upbeat, and reconstruction has proceeded at a remarkable pace. The country's modern face reflects a unique blend of African, Arabic, Indian and European influences – its cuisine is spicier, its music more tropical, and its pace more laid-back than its formerly British neighbours. Mozambique's coastline is one of the longest on the continent, with endless stretches of white-sand, palm-fringed beaches and unexplored offshore reefs.

BEST TIME TO VISIT
June to August, when rainfall and temperatures are at their lowest

ESSENTIAL EXPERIENCES
Visiting Pemba, a coastal town at the mouth of a huge bay with a great beach, some interesting buildings and a lively atmosphere

Exploring Ilha de Moçambique (Mozambique Island), the northern half of which has been declared a Unesco World Heritage–listed site

Swimming at the Bazaruto Archipelago National Park

Seeing the grand Zambezi River dammed by the Barragem de Cahora Bassa – set in stunning scenery at the head of a magnificent gorge

Lazing on the long, beautiful beaches of Tofo and Barra

GETTING UNDER THE SKIN
Read *Dumba-Nengue – Histórias trágicas do Banditismo* by politician, journalist and environmentalist Lina Magaia

Listen to Léman's *Automy dzi Txintxile* (Changes of Life) and *Katchume* by Kapa Dêch

Watch *Borders of Blood* and *Mueda, Memory and Massacre*

Eat *matapa* (cassava leaves cooked in a peanut sauce, often with prawns) in the south and *galinha á Zambeziana* (chicken with a sauce of lime juice, garlic and hot pepper) in Quelimane and Zambézia province

Drink *sura* (palm wine) or *nipa*, a local brew made from the fruit of the cashew

IN A WORD
lixile (good morning)

TRADEMARKS
Friendly people; guerrilla war; poverty; beautiful beaches; land mines

SURPRISES
Large mammals believed to be extinct or on the verge of extinction in Mozambique include the black rhino, white rhino, giraffe, roan antelope and the African wild dog

If you are offered a gift, in many parts of the country it is considered polite to accept it with both hands, sometimes with a slight bow or, alternatively, with the right hand while touching the left hand to the right elbow. If you receive with only one hand use the right one, and always give things with the right hand.

– Lonely Planet's *Mozambique*

MAP REF: Q,23

2. The dramatic silhouette of a tree is etched against the red morning sky as a boat enters the waters of Taungthaman Lake Anders Blomqvist

3. A barefoot monk embarks on the long walk over Taungthaman Lake on the magnificent U Bein's Bridge Antony Giblin

4. Temple ruins scattered like boulders amid the cultivated plains of Bagan, Mandalay Bernard Napthine

Myanmar (Burma) still wears its traditional longyi even as its neighbours abandon their saris and sarongs for Levis and miniskirts. Its holy men are more revered than its rich or its famous, and in the countryside, where rice paddies are still farmed using water buffalo, it might be the 16th century as easily as the 21st. These romantic images are a traveller's dream, but they exist in the presence of oppression and hardship. Myanmar is ruled by a harsh military regime, and human rights abuses are widespread, despite resistance by Aung San Suu Kyi and other democracy activists. Many travellers choose not to travel to Myanmar because of the current political situation there.

BEST TIME TO VISIT
November to February (the cool season) – or when the military regime shuts up shop

ESSENTIAL EXPERIENCES
Taking a trip to Bagan, where thousands of ancient temples rise spectacularly out of a vast, treeless plain

Joining the pilgrimage to Kyaiktiyo, a shining golden boulder stupa perched on a mountaintop cliff

Drifting on pristine Inle Lake, home to floating villages, water gardens and monasteries

Browsing the rollicking night market (and dodging the fruit bats) in riverside Pathein

GETTING UNDER THE SKIN
Read *Freedom from Fear & Other Writings* – essays by and about Aung San Suu Kyi; George Orwell's *Burmese Days* – the classic novel of British colonialism; Paul Theroux's *The Great Railway Bazaar* – a funny account of the author's train trip through 1970s Burma

Listen to traditional rhythmic Burmese music or original compositions by Burmese rocker Zaw Win Htut

Watch John Boorman's *Beyond Rangoon*, which dramatised the 1988 pro-democracy uprising and its brutal suppression; Kon Ichikawa's *The Burmese Harp,* a beautiful 1950s black & white film

Eat *thouq* (spicy salad with lime juice) or *peh-hin-ye* (lentil soup)

Drink Mandalay Beer or *htan ye* (fermented palm juice)

IN A WORD
Bama hsan-jin ('Burmese-ness', a quiet, modest and cultured quality)

TRADEMARKS
Golden buddhas; jade; opium; Aung San Suu Kyi; ethnic embroidery; the military regime; the road to Mandalay

SURPRISES
Myanmar's other famous dissidents (with jail time to prove it) are side-splitting comedians The Moustache Brothers; Myanmar's opium crop is rivalled only by Afghanistan's

For most Burmese, Buddhism is the guiding principle, and life centres around the monastery. A typical Burmese values meditation, gives alms freely, and sees his or her lot as the consequence of sin or merit in a past life. The Burmese value the quiet, subtle and indirect over the loud, obvious and direct. They also love a good laugh, and puns are considered a high form of humour.

— Lonely Planet's *Southeast Asia*

1. Laden with goods, a barge eases its way through the gloomy morning mist in Nyaungshwe Anders Blomqvist

5. Wearing stoic expressions three novice monks stand at one of the famous oval windows at the Shwe Yaunghwe monastery, Inle Lake Antony Giblin

MAP REF: L.30

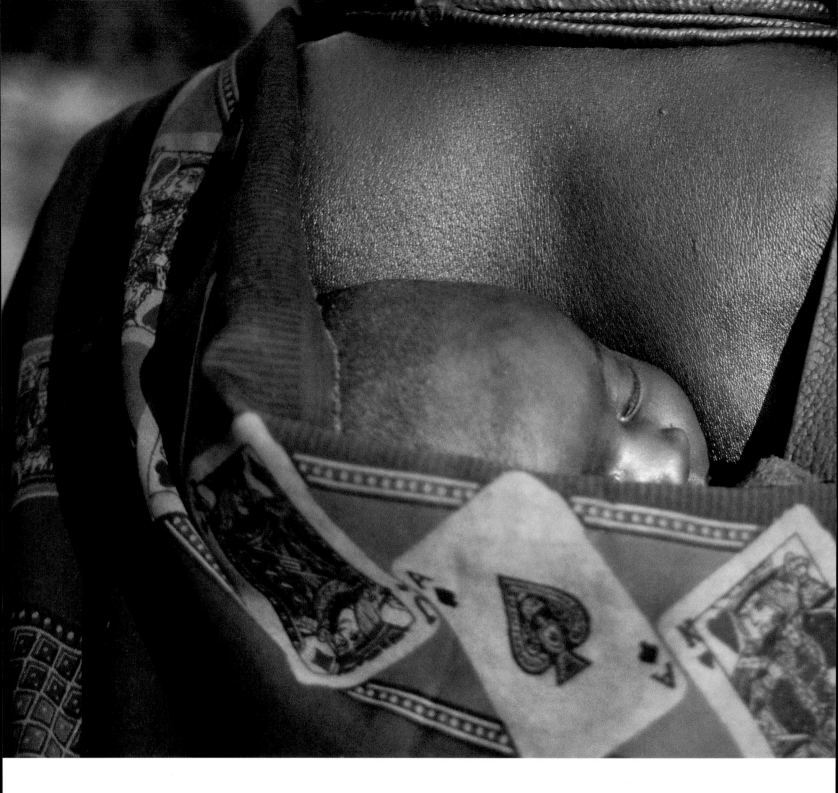

2. With stealth, cunning and a charming smile, a Kalahari man stalks his prey through the dry grass Dennis Jones

3. A small regiment of Himba children stands to attention in the village of Okangwati in Kunene Manfred Gottschalk

4. A zebra crossing in Etosha National Park, Kunene
Dennis Jones

5. The crest of a desert wave – one of the massive Sossusvlei sand dunes of Central Namibia Daniel Birks

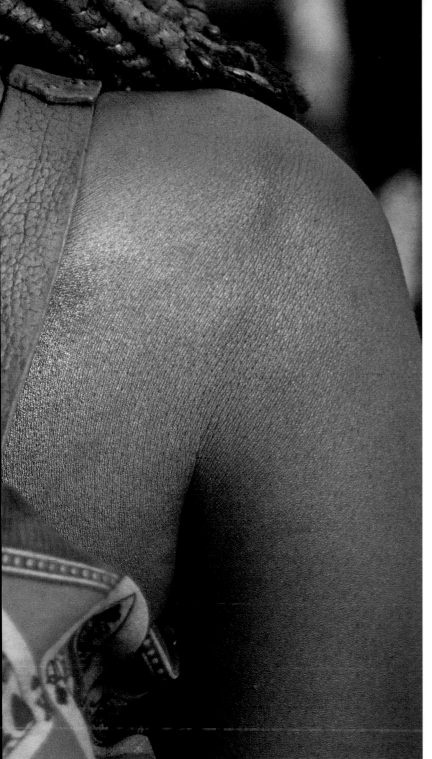

It's hard to imagine how the German colonisers of Namibia coped with the unlimited elbow room, vast deserts and annual quota of 300 days of sunshine, but that's exactly what draws travellers nowadays. Wedged between the Kalahari and the chilly South Atlantic Ocean, it's a land of deserts, seascapes, wildlife reserves, ancient rock art, gentle bushwalking terrain and an exhilarating sense of sheer boundlessness.

BEST TIME TO VISIT
May to October (the dry season)

ESSENTIAL EXPERIENCES
Wandering around Windhoek, Namibia's attractive capital city

Camping at Etosha National Park, one of the world's best wildlife-viewing venues

Heading to the 'dune sea' of the Namib Desert, home to the country's enigmatic emblem, the dunes of Sossusvlei

Driving through Khaudom Game Reserve, a wild and hard-to-reach park packed with wildlife

Luxuriating in the hot springs at Ai-Ais in the Fish River Canyon

Soaking up the European vibe of Swakopmund, Namibia's most German town

GETTING UNDER THE SKIN
Read *Born of the Sun*, the largely autobiographical first novel by local author Joseph Diescho

Listen to Namibia's renowned ensemble the Cantare Audire Choir

Watch *Sophia's Homecoming*, which tells the story of an Owambo woman who goes to work as a domestic in Windhoek

Eat a cooked breakfast with bacon and *boerewors* (farmer's sausage)

Drink the light and refreshing Windhoek Lager, or try a traditional brew such as *mataku* (watermelon wine)

IN A WORD
Hallo (hello)

TRADEMARKS
Sand dunes; diamond mining; German beergardens and coffee houses; vast deserts; limitless sunshine; rock art; wonderful wildlife

SURPRISES
The word of elders should not be questioned and they should be accorded utmost courtesy; in areas where individual sand dunes are exposed to winds from all directions, a formation known as a star dune appears

The most poignant thing about rock art is that it remains in the spot where it was created. Unlike in a museum, sensitive viewers may catch a glimpse of the inspiration that went into the paintings. In Namibia, you'll find examples of the genre in rock overhangs all over the country, but the most renowned sites are at Twyfelfontein, Spitzkoppe and the Brandberg, all in North-Western Namibia.

– Lonely Planet's *Namibia*

1. Riding in style, a Himba baby snoozes against its mother's back Adrien Vadrot

6. Hardy quiver trees take root in rocky terrain John Borthwick

MAP REF: Q,21

2. A divine sunset tempers the industrialism of phosphate loading Simon Foale

3. The entrancing beauty of Anibare Bay always catches the breath Philip Game

1. One of them has to catch it...local kids play Aussie Rules football Mark Baker

Nauru was once the rich kid of the Pacific, wealthy through phosphates. But now the stocks of bird poop have been exhausted, mining has utterly destroyed the landscape, and the island survives on handouts from Australia in return for hosting a detention centre for asylum seekers. With fresh water, vegetables and power in short supply, and a new detention centre being built on Christmas Island, Nauru's future is in the balance.

BEST TIME TO VISIT
March to October, to avoid the cyclone season

ESSENTIAL EXPERIENCES
Slumbering under shady palms at Anibare Bay, Nauru's best beach

Deep-sea fishing off Yaren

Shuddering at Nauru's 'topside' in the central plateau – a burning wasteland of searing white rock, bizarre coral pinnacles and ugly, deep pits

GETTING UNDER THE SKIN
Read *Nauru: Phosphate and Political Progress* by Nancy Viviani, an authoritative history of the mining that has crippled the island

Listen to the strange cry of the noddy bird

Watch *The Reef: Our Future, Our Heritage*, a documentary about the deteriorating reefs around the island

Eat Chinese food, common on the island

Drink *demangi*, the island's traditional take on fermented toddy

IN A WORD
Kewen (gone, dead)

TRADEMARKS
Mined-to-exhaustion plateaus; a quick-fix asylum for Australia's refugees; wealthy islanders with guano-stained wallets; satellite TV in most homes; weightlifting world champions pumping iron in every gym

SURPRISES
Nauruans still hunt on the bald plateau for black noddy birds, often using stereos that play taped pre-recorded bird calls; most meals served on the island consist of imported junk food

Most traditional customs, dances and crafts have been completely subsumed by Nauru's all-encompassing focus on phosphate. No-one on Nauru knows how to make handicrafts anymore, except for a few of Nauru's most aged citizens.

— Lonely Planet's *South Pacific*

4. Nauru's worked-out phosphate fertiliser fields have a distinctive lunar quality Tim Graham

Anna Point

Ewa Anetan

Baiti

Anabar

Uaboe

Nibok Ijuw

Phosphate Stockpile

Denigomodu

Anibare

Buada

Aiwo *Buada Lagoon* *Anibare Bay*

Meneng

Boe Menen House *Meneng Point*

Yaren Government House

Parliament House

PACIFIC OCEAN

MAP REF: O.37

2. The Sadhu of the Lake – as if summoned by higher powers, a sword-bearing Hindu holy man materialises from a pool of flowers, Kathmandu Bill Wassman

3. The jagged edge of Mt Machhapuchhare rises into the empty morning sky in Annapurna Richard I'Anson

4. Wisdom creases the kind face of an elderly woman in Ghandruk Richard I'Anson

5. A mahout (elephant keeper) prepares a take-away lunch of molasses and rice for his herd in Royal Chitwan National Park Anders Blomqvist

1. The imperious figure of a Rai tribeswoman sitting amidst the exotic vegetation of Sagarmatha province Bill Wassman

Draped along the heights of the Himalaya, Nepal's sublime scenery, time-worn temples and peerless walking trails leave visitors spellbound. Rich in spirituality and spectacular scenery, the country is the quiet cousin of neighbouring powerhouses China and India. Nothing compares to being amongst some of the world's tallest peaks for a natural high, but while there are grand feats to be enjoyed in Nepal, part of the country's appeal lies in simple pursuits: witnessing age-old rice harvesting or relishing the cultural cul-de-sac of Bhaktapur.

BEST TIME TO VISIT
October to November, for balmy days and crystal-clear visibility

ESSENTIAL EXPERIENCES
Being stuck in traffic amid bikes, cows, cars, beggars, pilgrims and vendors in Kathmandu

Taking on the high tides of Bhote Kosi for the ultimate white-water rafting adventure

Pondering the universe in Buddha's tranquil birthplace, Lumbini

Being amused by Swayambhunath's tribes of garrulous monkeys

Navigating a boat on Pokhara's sublime lake, Phewa Tal

Riding an elephant on safari in Royal Chitwan National Park

Pushing your body to the limits on an extended trek, whether it's in the all-encompassing Langtang or once-in-a-lifetime Mt Everest region

GETTING UNDER THE SKIN
Read *Tenzing and the Sherpas of Everest* by Judy and Tashi Tenzing, a compelling tale about Nepal's national hero

Listen to *Nepal: Ritual and Entertainment,* all-encompassing Nepalese sounds from damai ritual music to panchai baja ensembles

Watch *Darpan Chhaya,* an emotionally charged musical highlighting the Nepalese fascination with all things romantic, patriotic and theatrical

Eat *dal bhaat tarkari* – it's what you get if you combine lentil soup, rice and curried vegetables, and is the staple Nepalese diet

Drink a refreshing *lassi* (curd and water in any number of flavours) or *chang*, a hearty Himalayan brew made from barley

IN A WORD
Namaste (hello/goodbye)

TRADEMARKS
Maoist rebels; prayer flags; *om* chanting; chai tea; mandalas; shopping for Buddhas

SURPRISES
Nepal's most significant celebration, Dasain (October), involves the biggest animal sacrifice on the calendar; always remove your shoes before entering a Nepali home

At once a time machine and a magic carpet, Nepal sweeps you along crooked, timeworn streets flanked by irregular, multi-roofed pagodas, stupas and stone sculptures, and into rooms cluttered with horror-eyed masks, spinning prayer wheels, trippy thangka scrolls and Tibetan carpets. Muttered chants, esoteric tantric hymns and Nepalese music hang in the air, whether it be the twang of a four-stringed saringhi or the plaintive notes of a flute.

— World Guide, www.lonelyplanet.com

6. The village of Panauti rises and shines in the glow of early morning, Bagmati province Mark Andrew Kirby

MAP REF: K.28

2. Den Hague's ivy-covered, red-shuttered cop shop Zaw Yu

3. Unesco World Heritage—listed windmills at Kinderdijk Chris Mellor

4. A mannequin set in a sultry pose attracts attention in a shop window Izzet Keribar

5. Kids imagining life as a cannonball in the courtyard of Nederland's Scheepvaartmuseum, Kaltenburgerplein Martin Moos

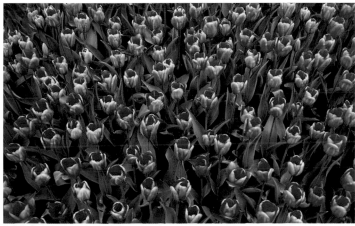

6. Tulip fever lives on in Amsterdam Chris Mellor

LEFT 1. One of Amsterdam's 550,000 bikes – the preferred mode of transport – parked in front of a graffiti mural Richard Nebeský

One of the chief pleasures of the Netherlands is its lively contrast between pragmatic liberalism and the buttoned-up, just-so primness of a culture founded on Calvinist principles. In Dutch society, ostentation is anathema and fuss of any kind is regarded as undignified. The towns are surrounded by canals and castle walls, the endlessly flat landscape which inspired the nation's early artists still stretches unbroken to the horizons, and the dykes still occasionally threaten to give way.

BEST TIME TO VISIT
April to September (spring through summer), for tulips and picnic weather

ESSENTIAL EXPERIENCES
Exploring Amsterdam's many neighbourhoods, from red-light sleaze and bohemian chic to stately grandeur

Visiting Hoge Veluwe National Park, the country's largest, which also houses works by Van Gogh, Picasso and Mondriaan in the Kröller-Müller Museum

Riding a bicycle around the Randstad region to see the spectacular bulb fields, which explode into colour between March and May

Wandering around the labyrinth of tunnels on Maastricht's western outskirts

GETTING UNDER THE SKIN
Read *The Diary of Anne Frank*, a moving journal that describes her life in hiding in Nazi-occupied Amsterdam; *The Fall* by Albert Camus, an existential monologue that uses Amsterdam's canal system as an analogy for the rings of Hell

Listen to Tiësto, the undisputed trancemeister, or for something more highbrow, pianist Ronald Brautigam

Watch *Stromenlied* (Song of the Rivers) by acclaimed documentry filmmaker Joris Ivens

Eat *stamppot* (potatoes mashed with kale, endive or sauerkraut, and served with smoked sausage or strips of pork) or *Vlaamse frites* (chips with mayonnaise) for a quick snack

Drink Heineken beer or try Dutch gin *(jenever)*, which is often drunk with a beer chaser; the combination is known as a *kopstoot* ('head butt')

IN A WORD
Een pils/bier, alstublieft (a beer, please)

TRADEMARKS
Bikes; dykes; windmills; clogs; tulips; red-light district; pot smoking; Van Gogh

SURPRISES
Dutch ovens were invented in Pennsylvania; the Dutch are reputedly the tallest people in the world

The country is crowded and Dutch people tend to be reserved with strangers. On the trains, you'll notice that passengers sit to maintain the greatest distance between each other. The Dutch treasure their privacy because it is such a rare commodity. Still, they're far from antisocial – their inbred gezelligheid (conviviality) will come out at the drop of a hat. Expect chummy moments at the supermarket.

– Lonely Planet's *The Netherlands*

MAP REF: G,20

2. Palm fronds adorn the sky above a traditional Kanak house in Grande Terre, North Province Jean-Bernard Carillet

3. A weird and wonderful wood-carved palisade in Vao Jean-Bernard Carillet

4. A corridor of blue stretches out to the horizon between the white shores of Ouvéa lagoon in the Loyalty Islands Jean-Bernard Carillet

1. Washing day on Lifou Island where colourful Kanak dresses line up to dry in the sun Vincent Talbot

Kanaks and *café au lait,* blackbirding and barrier reefs, Melanesian massacres and *menus du jour* – New Caledonia exemplifies that one person's bread is another person's *pain.* It's still very much a colony of France, and the motherland has sent in the marines more than once to keep the local population from rioting. Political unrest aside, New Caledonia attracts divers and tourists who flock to experience the Pacific with a taste of France.

BEST TIME TO VISIT
May to October, to avoid the cyclones and mosquitoes

ESSENTIAL EXPERIENCES
Canoeing down a river by moonlight through a drowned forest in Parc de la Rivière Bleue

Watching the sun set across a tranquil lagoon from anywhere along Ouvéa's white-sand beach

Sailing in the glittering bay around Île des Pins

Delving into the architectural masterpiece that is Noumea's Jean-Marie Tjibaou Cultural Centre

Scuba-diving the world's second-largest reef

Discovering the tiny raised coral atoll of Tiga with deserted beaches and great diving

GETTING UNDER THE SKIN
Read Jean-Marie Tjibao's *Kanaké – the Melanesian Way,* an insight into Kanak culture featuring colour photographs, poems and legends

Listen to OK! Ryos, a Mare band known for their harmonies and soaring vocals – try *Wa Coco,* their 'best of'

Watch *Le Bal du Gouverneur,* a romance set in 1950s New Caledonia

Eat *bougna,* a delicious combination of taro, yam, sweet potato, banana, and pieces of chicken, crab or lobster cooked in banana leaves in a ground oven

Drink *kava* sold from private houses called *nakamal*

IN A WORD
Kanaks traditionally refer to themselves as Ti-Va-Ouere ('Brothers of the Earth')

TRADEMARKS
Dispossessed Kanak community; French tourists in abundance; idyllic grass huts on the beach; colonial strife; stunning beaches; clan societies

SURPRISES
New Caledonia's economy centres around mining and metallurgy; cricket has been the favourite sport of Kanak women since the missionaries introduced it to the Loyalty Islanders in the 1850s

Traditionally, the Kanaks had a very sensible relationship with the environment, considering it their garde-manger *(food safe). This contrasts greatly with modern-day attitudes and practices. Mining, smelting, urbanisation around Noumea, bushfires and feral cats and dogs are the predominant dangers to nature in New Caledonia.*

– Lonely Planet's *South Pacific*

5. Soaked and smiling, a young girl of Lifou Island Peter Hendrie

MAP REF: Q,37

2. Cruising for a bruising, a snowboarder prepares for a spectacular wipe-out in the Cardrona ski fields, Otago Grant Somers

3. Under a forbidding cloak of cloud, a volcano broods in Tongariro National Park Dennis Johnson

4. Virgin snow sheathes the peak of Mt Taranaki, a dormant volcano in the North Island Chris Mellor

5. Nosy neighbours greet each other with a traditional *hongi* in Rotorua Anders Blomqvist

1. A fine mist rises above the bubbling surface of the appropriately named Champagne Pool, Waiotapu Thermal Reserve Simon Bracken

One could be forgiven for thinking that Mother Nature decided to take her best features and exhibit them all in this South Pacific island nation. All the classics are there – awe-inspiring Alps, plunging fjords, expanses of pristine beach, dense rainforests, active volcanoes – but what makes this such a stellar performance is the sheer concentration of it all. Top it off with lively indigenous culture, cosmopolitan cities and a people with a distinctly Kiwi lust for life, and you know this is one special country.

BEST TIME TO VISIT
November to April, when the weather is warmest

ESSENTIAL EXPERIENCES
Traversing the South Island on the TranzAlpine train

Throwing yourself off something high – bungee jumping is as compulsory here as seeing the Eiffel Tower in Paris

Enjoying a gourmet feast of fresh fish and chips on a deserted Northland beach

Seeing the marine life off the coast of Kaikoura

Spending a culture-filled weekend in one of the cities – the Polynesian bustle of Auckland, creative current of Wellington or European feel of Christchurch

GETTING UNDER THE SKIN
Read Witi Ihimaera's *The Whale Rider* – a moving insight into the spirituality, tradition, and culture of the Maori people

Listen to Salmonella Dub's *Killer Vision*, which displays influences quintessential to the new wave of New Zealand music

Watch Peter Jackson's *Lord of the Rings* trilogy – the stunning landscape dominates the films

Eat whitebait – a seasonal delicacy; hu hu grubs – slug-like and not for the faint-hearted, but delicious off the grill

Drink a 'boutique beer' – independent breweries are providing delicious variations on the traditional varieties

IN A WORD
Sweet as, bro

TRADEMARKS
Sheep; Maori; the All Blacks; clean and green; nuclear-free; extreme sports; the end of the earth; Middle Earth; Neil Finn; Janet Frame; pohutukawa blossoms

SURPRISES
Not everyone plays rugby; there's a thriving food and wine culture; much more than just two islands

The cries echo across the sheltered bay, reverberating from steep cliff sides. It is not hard to imagine Captain Cook on his sailing vessel, moored silently in this same cove, with the same sounds haunting the ship's crew; or for that matter the Maori on their quests for pounamu, greenstone, which they value so much. Little has changed since the forests re-colonised the carved out glacial valleys after the ice age ten thousand years ago.

– *Kiwi Tracks*, © Andrew Stevenson, 1999; Lonely Planet Travel Literature

6. Polished by tidal waters, sleek boulders and rock formations create an otherworldly atmosphere on the West Coast Ruth Eastham & Max Paoli

MAP REF: T,38

2. Macho *muchachos* wrestle on the paving stones of Léon
Eric Wheater

3. The little women of Río San Juan fitted out for their First
Communion Margie Politzer

4. A blinkered beast of burden plods through the vibrant streets of Granada Alfredo Maiquez

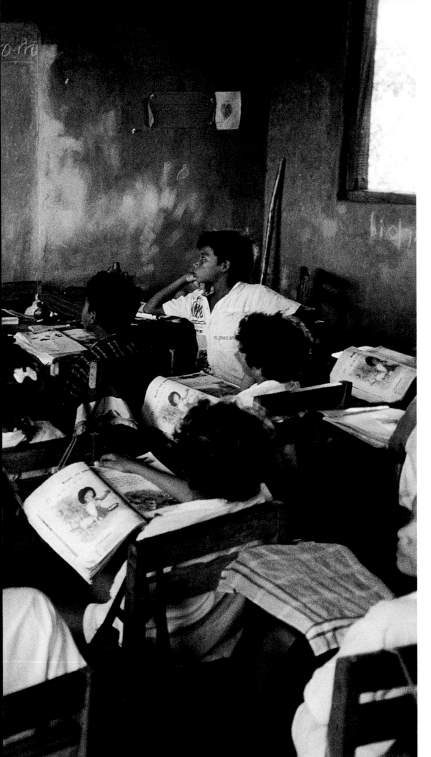

1. A teacher competes for the undivided attention of her pupils in a village school Eric Wheater

Tucked between Costa Rica's mammoth ecotourism scene and Honduras' dazzling displays of indigenous history, Nicaragua is all too often ignored by travellers. Their loss. The warm, inclusive pride of the Nicaraguan people suffuses the country with an intoxicating energy that captivates visitors. For the cognoscenti, Nicaragua is inspiring landscapes, colonial beauty, weeklong parties, stunning wildlife, beautiful beaches, rollicking reggae and long nights spent with friends in the plaza – all rolled up in a neat little package that carries a discount price tag.

BEST TIME TO VISIT
June to March, to avoid the dusty end of the dry season – or in the 13th century, before the Aztecs arrived

ESSENTIAL EXPERIENCES
Watching the moon rise over the cathedral in colonial Granada

Climbing the volcanoes on Isla de Ometepe and cooling off by swimming in the Lago de Nicaragua

Kicking back in a beach hammock in San Juan del Sur

Spotting a quetzal at the Reserva Natural Miraflor

Buying handicrafts at Masaya's Mercado Viejo

Enjoying perfect snorkelling off Little Corn Island

GETTING UNDER THE SKIN
Read Rubén Darío's *Stories and Poems* – masterpieces by the founder of Spanish modcrnism; Salman Rushdie's *The Jaguar Smile: A Nicaraguan Journey* – revealing personal experiences of a visit

Listen to Duo Guardabaranco's *Antología* of collected pop works; Los Mejia Godoy's *Loving in Times of War* – legendary Nicaraguan brothers sing folk

Watch *Nicaragua Was Our Home* – a documentary about Miskito Indians and Sandinistas that purportedly influenced Reagan's foreign policy; *Alsino and the Condor* – a boy's struggle to escape the realities of his war-torn homeland

Eat *baho* – beef, yucca, plaintains and vegetables slowly simmered; *sopa de albondiga* – cornmeal-ball soup

Drink Flor de Caña rum; *pinolio* – dissolved ground corn (add sugar!)

IN A WORD
¡Va pue'! (all right!)

TRADEMARKS
Contras and Sandinistas; dusty farms and towns; rickety buses with chickens; earthquakes and hurricanes; US intervention in politics

SURPRISES
Amazing biodiversity, there are no ruins, the unique Caribbean culture on the Atlantic coast, the friendliest people in Central America

I'd spent my days being lectured by former Sandinista rebels and meeting three-year-old orphans, my nights getting loaded on Flor de Caña rum and dancing with gorgeous Nicaraguan men. It was an overly romantic 23-year-old leftist's dream come true.

– 'How I Learned to Stop Worrying and Love Nicaragua', *On the Road*, www.lonelyplanet.com

5. A cavalcade of cowgirls salute the crowd at a rodeo in Estelí Eric Wheater

HONDURAS

Puerto Cabezas

Ocotal

Guasaule

Somotillo

Matagalpa

Caribbean Sea

Corinto

León

Boaco

Managua

Juigalpa

Bluefields

Masaya

Granada

Lago de Nicaragua

Monkey Point

Rivas

Isla de Ometepe

PACIFIC OCEAN

San Carlos

San Juan del Norte

COSTA RICA

MAP REF: M,10

2. Swords come out for celebration during a Ramadan festivity in Niamey Eric Wheater

3. Beautiful Wodaabé bachelors line up to be admired at the annual Salt Festival in Agadez Antony Giblin

4. A devotee hangs hip outside the Grande Mosquée of Niamey Oliver Strewe

5. Two builders prepare all-natural construction materials by soaking them in the waters near Diffa Oliver Strewe

6. A baby in a pouch enjoys a spot of traditional dancing in Maradi Oliver Strewe

LEFT 1. Tuareg women in Niamey robed in traditional blue and black mantles Eric Wheater

Niger sits precariously on the edge of the Sahara, a barren windswept land ravaged by drought and colonial conquest, yet somehow surviving against the odds. It's a country of aristocratic desert nomads, skilled artisans and a race of tall, lithe people so physically beautiful that even the men enter beauty contests. With unmissable sights like the stark beauty of the Ténéré Desert and the ancient caravan town of Agadez, Niger is a vital element of the Saharan experience.

BEST TIME TO VISIT
November to February, when it's cooler

ESSENTIAL EXPERIENCES
Exploring the labyrinthine old mud-brick quarters of Zinder and Agadez

Enjoying the bustle and colour of Zinder's weekly market

Searching for wildlife in Parc National du W

Hearing the stories of the Tuareg around the campfire or beneath the rock art of the Aïr Mountains

Watching the sun set over the mighty Niger River from a pirogue in Niamey

Seeking out the silent gravitas of deserted villages and vast sand dunes of the Ténéré Desert and Djado Plateau in the Sahara

GETTING UNDER THE SKIN
Read *In Sorcery's Shadow: A Memoir of Apprenticeship Among the Songhay of Niger* by Paul Stoller – a very readable, often humorous, and detailed account of his fieldwork among the Songhay of Niger

Listen to the impassioned vocals and masterful musicianship of Yacouba Moumouni in his album *Alatoumi*

Watch *The Sheltering Sky*, directed by Bernardo Bertolucci, which was filmed in Niger

Eat dates, yoghurt, rice, mutton, rice with sauce, couscous and ragout

Drink tea or a Flag beer

IN A WORD
Bonjour (hello)

TRADEMARKS
Desert nomads; camels; uranium mining; dinosaur bones; the Tuareg; the Fulani

SURPRISES
There are five principal tribal groups: the Hausa, Songhaï-Djerma, Wodaabé, Tuareg and Kanouri; camel racing is a favourite Tuareg sport

To win the attention of eligible women, single men participate in a 'beauty contest'. The main event is the Yaake, a late-afternoon performance in which the men dance, displaying their beauty and charm. Dressed to the hilt, they form a line with blackened lips to make the teeth seem whiter, lightened faces, star-like figures painted on their faces, braided hair, elaborate headwear and all kinds of jewellery. Tall, lean bodies, long slender noses, white even teeth and white eyes are what the women are looking for.

– Lonely Planet's *West Africa*

MAP REF: L.21

2. Muskets bristle amongst a rabble of celebrating men at the Durbar Festival, Kano Jane Sweeney

3. Traditional mud huts huddled on stilts in Sokoto Jane Sweeney

4. A well-attired woman of Katsina David Wall

5. Pink-and-yellow cloth frames the face of a woman in Zaria
Guy Moberly

1. Ornately dressed Hausa-Fulani horsemen pay annual homage to the Emir in Kano Jane Sweeney

6. Street scenes of Kano Jane Sweeney

In Nigeria hundreds of different peoples, languages, histories and religions all sit shoulder to shoulder in a hectic, colourful and often volatile republic. It is a country struggling to contain the sum of its parts within a democratic framework. A chronic crime problem, religious intolerance, large-scale unemployment and overcrowding in poor living conditions regularly push the rule of law to the brink. Despite this, there is still an unfaltering optimism among Nigerians that their proud nation will indeed make it to the party.

BEST TIME TO VISIT
December to March

ESSENTIAL EXPERIENCES
Viewing wildlife at Yankari National Park

Club-hopping in Lagos

Visiting the ancient mud-walled city in Kano

Shopping for rare books at the Onitsha Writers' Market

Exploring the Niger Delta

GETTING UNDER THE SKIN
Read anything by Nobel Prize winner Wole Soyinka, internationally acclaimed writer Chinua Achebe or Ben Okri, a crowd-pulling favourite on the Western literary circuit

Listen to world-renowned musician, the late Fela Kuti, whose eclectic fusion of traditional Yoruba call-and-response chanting with freestyle jazz (Afrobeat) was always in demand. Other favourites are king of juju music Sonny Ade, the granddaddy of afro-reggae, Sonny Okosun and soul singer, Sade.

Watch *A deusa negra* (Black Goddess) by Nigerian director Ola Balogun

Eat *egusi* (a fiery-hot yellow stew made with meat, red chilli, ground dried prawns and green leaves) or palm-nut soup (a thick stew made with meat, chilli, tomatoes, onions and palm-nut oil)

Drink palm wine (a favourite drink all over Nigeria, especially in the south where the palm trees grow wild)

IN A WORD
Sannu ('hello' in Hausa)

TRADEMARKS
Fantastic music; money scams; masochistic travellers; violence; corruption; oil-rich economy; Niger Delta

SURPRISES
Nigeria is home to 20% of Africa's entire population; *juju*, the native magic that was the original basis for Caribbean voodoo, is still an important element in many tribal cultures

Many tribal groups still produce fine sculptures and masks. The best known are those made by the Yoruba, whose small twin figures, ibeji, are world famous. The Yoruba also carve figures of the many deities and cults that make up their religion. A figure with a carved double axe balanced on its head represents Shango, the god of thunder. A kneeling couple portray Eshu, the representative of Olurin, the supreme or sky god. For the cults of epa and gelede, masks are carved with elaborate superstructures incorporating human and animal groups.

– Lonely Planet's *West Africa*

MAP REF: M,21

2. Caution: Reindeer Crossing – a buck traverses an icy road in Arctic Norway David Tipling

3. The Antmands Dottir bar promises warmth and wine to a local in Tromsø Christian Aslund

4. A local sniffs the wax on a visiting surfer's board in the coastal village of Unstad in Lofoten Christian Aslund

5. Autumn colours fringe the foothills near Skjak Anders Blomqvist

1. Pale northern light beams down on bronzed bodies in Stryn Christian Aslund

Europe's 'wild west', Norway has a ruggedly beautiful frontier character, with easy access to wild outdoor country and forested green belts circling even the largest cities. Its mountains, fjords and glaciers are highly prized, along with its cultured cities, unspoiled fishing villages and rich historic sites, from Viking ships to medieval churches. North of the Arctic Circle, the population thins, the horizons grow wider, and seals, walruses and polar bears sun themselves on ice floes.

BEST TIME TO VISIT
May to September (late spring to summer)

ESSENTIAL EXPERIENCES
Being overawed by the grand fjords of Arctic Norway, which dwarf anything in the south

Wandering the streets of colourful, historic Bergen

Visiting the virtually intact 9th-century *Oseberg* Viking ship and museum in Oslo

Touring the stave churches at Borgund, Heddal and Urnes

Viewing the midnight sun from Nordland

Spotting walruses, polar bears and whales in the high Arctic

GETTING UNDER THE SKIN
Read *A Doll's House* by quintessential Norwegian dramatist Henrik Ibsen, or Jostein Gaarder's bestseller *Sophie's World*

Listen to composer Edvard Grieg or indigenous Sami artist Ailu Gaup

Watch *The Pathfinder*, based on a medieval legend and presented in the Sami language, or Anja Breien's *Jostedalsrypa*, about a 14th-century girl who survived the Black Death

Eat *lapskaus* (a hearty meat stew with vegetables) or *lutefisk* (dried cod soaked in potash lye)

Drink the national spirit, *aquavit* (or *akevitt*) – a potent potato and caraway liquor. The standard Norwegian beer is pils lager.

IN A WORD
Vær så god (an all-purpose expression of goodwill)

TRADEMARKS
Vikings; fjords; the aurora borealis; stave churches; skiing; the midnight sun; whaling

SURPRISES
Lemmings don't throw themselves off cliffs in mass suicide; the legal drinking age is 18 years for beer and wine, but 20 for spirits

Trolls come in all shapes and sizes, some large some small, but nearly all have four fingers and toes on each hand and foot, as well as long, crooked noses and bushy tails. It's believed that trolls can live for several hundred years and are credited with having produced both Þór's hammer and Oðinn's spear. They also have a penchant for harassing billy goats and despising the sound of church bells. They're known to get irritable and may anger easily but they're generally kind to humans.

– Lonely Planet's *Norway*

6. A lonely rowing boat floats beneath a heavy sky in the town of Flåm Brent Winebrenner

MAP REF: E,21

2. Robes billowing in the hot breeze, a group of men stand outside a shop in Sharqiya, Al Ashkara Christine Osborne

3. After sorting their first catch, fishermen in Mutrah prepare to launch off again Chris Mellor

4. Dressed for devotion, four men march past a Burami mosque Chris Mellor

5. A weathered local man in his workshop in the historical town of Bahla Clint Lucas

1. A donkey and scooter share a car park outside a building in Nizwa Christine Osborne

Previously regarded as the hermit of the Middle East, Oman is slowly coming out of its shell. One of the more traditional countries in the region, it has become more outward-looking in recent years. Once an imperial power that jostled with both Portugal and Britain for influence in the Gulf, its development since 1970 is striking, given that its oil reserves are greatly limited. An ever-increasing number of travellers are discovering its friendly people, dramatic mountain landscapes and vast unspoilt beaches.

BEST TIME TO VISIT
Mid-October to mid-March, to avoid the monsoon season

ESSENTIAL EXPERIENCES
Visiting the Omani–French Museum in Muscat
Browsing through the early-morning fish market in Mutrah
Visiting the dramatically sited forts of Nakhal and Jabrin
Bargain-hunting at Nizwa's colourful *souq*
Exploring the archaeological sites around Salalah
Discovering Wadi Ghul, the Grand Canyon of Arabia
Hiking and caving in the Hajar Mountains

GETTING UNDER THE SKIN
Read Phillip Ward's *Travels in Oman: On the track of the Early Explorer*, a combination of modern travelogue and historical traveller accounts

Listen to *Symphonic Impressions of Oman* by Lalo Scifrin, performed by the London Symphony Orchestra, which captures the mood, scenery and traditions of Oman

Eat *balaleet* – a popular breakfast dish of sweet vermicelli with egg, onion and cinnamon; *machboos* – slow-cooked meat and rice with onion, spices and dried limes

Drink *laban* – salty buttermilk; cardamom-infused yoghurt drinks

IN A WORD
Tasharrafna (nice to meet you)

TRADEMARKS
Impressive forts; sandy beaches; beautiful mountain scenery; vibrant bazaars; groves of frankincense trees; men in bright blue *dishdashas* (shirt dresses); ancient ruins; traditional dance and music; silver jewellery; desert motoring; remote villages

SURPRISES
Camel racing is a traditional sport, as is bull-butting – pairing Brahmin bulls to fight (no injury or bloodshed is involved); nomadic Bedouin tribes still live in the interior

Every spring the sultan spends several weeks driving around the country on a 'meet the people tour'. This is covered extensively on Omani TV. A few minutes viewing one of the reports will show you the extent to which the day-to-day life of the average Omani living in a town in the interior or a fishing village on the coast is close to what it would have been centuries ago.

– Lonely Planet's *Oman & UAE*

6. Men flock to the market on the edge of the desert in Sanaw Christine Osborne

MAP REF: L,26

2. A room with a view or two – visitors gaze through the marble grille of the Shish Mahal (Palace of Mirrors) at Lahore Fort Bradley Mayhew

3. Bus drivers break for morning tea at the Rajah bazaar in Punjab John King

4. A young boy dwarfed by the towering doorways of the Badshahi Mosque, Lahore Richard I'Anson

5. Old timers hang out in Peshawar's old city district
Richard I'Anson

Media impressions of Pakistan are a jumble of Islamic fundament-alism and martial law, while for overland travellers the country is often seen as the last hurdle before reaching India. In fact Pakistan offers some of Asia's most mind-blowing landscapes, extraordinary trekking, the spectacular Karakoram Highway, a multitude of cultures, and a long tradition of hospitality. It's the site of some of the earliest human settlements and the crucible of two of the world's major religions: Hinduism and Buddhism.

BEST TIME TO VISIT
November to April in the south (when it's cooler), May to October in the north (before winter sets in)

ESSENTIAL EXPERIENCES
Trekking among giants in Baltistan, where the Karakoram erupts in an unequalled display of peaks and twisting glaciers

Experiencing an emotion-charged cricket match at Karachi

Exploring the ancient site of Moenjodaro, relic of an Indus Valley civilisation

Soaking up the frontier atmosphere of Quetta, a desert outpost with buzzing bazaars

Rambling through the tangle of twisting alleyways in Lahore's Old City en route to the historic Lahore Fort

GETTING UNDER THE SKIN
Read *Pakistan: The Eye of the Storm*, by former BBC correspondent Owen Bennett-Jones; Salman Rushdie's *Shame*, whose characters are a metaphor for Pakistan

Listen *Nusrat Fateh Ali Khan*, the revered Qawwali singer, who has collaborated on soundtracks for *Dead Man Walking* and *The Last Temptation of Christ*

Watch The second film in the *Earth*, *Fire* and *Water* trilogy, directed by Deepa Mehta and depicting the tragic upheaval of Partition

Eat meat and vegetable curries; hot and spicy samosas

Drink fresh fruit juices, milky tea, buttermilk flavoured with pistachios

IN A WORD
Ap khairiyat se hai? (how are you?)

TRADEMARKS
Trekking the Karakoram Highway; totally obsessed cricket fans; Shoab Akhtar, the world's fastest bowler; General Musharraf; nuclear weapons; oily, spicy curries

SURPRISES
In the tribal areas bordering Afghanistan federal law applies only to the roads and 10 yards on either side – elsewhere tribal law applies

Sindh, dubbed the 'Land of Uncertainties', is also a land of verdant patches of sheesham and pipal trees, colourful parrots, darting kingfishers, and white herons precariously perched on the backs of waddling water buffaloes. In the hot season the landscape shimmers and its earthy browns, reds and greys verge on creamy-white. In autumn the coastline is suffused with colour, the sky and sea tinted with magical crimson hues.

– Lonely Planet's *Pakistan*

1. The majestic mausoleum of Bibi Jawindi looms over passers-by in Uch Sharif, Punjab Bradley Mayhew

6. The killer peak of K2 viewed from Gondogoro La John Mock

MAP REF: K,27

2. A well illustrated chief's house with painted gables and a steeply pitched thatched roof Michael Aw

3. An orange-fin anemone fish lights up the surroundings Michael Aw

The Republic of Palau is becoming a byword for an underwater wonderland, showcasing Micronesia's richest flora and fauna, both on land and beneath the waves. It's a snorkeller's paradise, with an incredible spectrum of coral, fish and sumo-sized giant clams. There's a good chance this bounty will survive, as Palauans are active on environmental issues, particularly regarding overtourism, overfishing, erosion, litter and pollution.

BEST TIME TO VISIT
September to July, avoiding stormy August

ESSENTIAL EXPERIENCES
Sailing through the twisty maze of the Rock Islands

Keeping a respectful distance from a traditional *bai* (men's meeting house) on Micronesia's second-largest island, Babeldaob

Climbing Malakal Hill on Koror Island for great views of the Rock Islands

Diving into history around Peleliu, the WWII-ravaged paradise

Chowing down on outstanding seafood including mangrove crab and lobster at Koror's smorgasbord of eateries

GETTING UNDER THE SKIN
Read Arnold H Leibowitz's *Embattled Island: Palau's Struggle for Independence*, a US-friendly take on Palau's postwar political history

Listen to *Natural...*, the first album by the Paluan band, InXes

Watch *Palau – The Enchanted Islands*, a scuba adventure by filmmaker Avi Klapfer

Eat cassava, betel nut, tuna, sushi, lobster

Drink abundant and fresh coconut milk

IN A WORD
Alii (hello)

TRADEMARKS
Giant clams; maverick politicians taking on Uncle Sam; red-mouthed betel-nut chewers; WWII wrecks and ruins; storyboard art; outrigger canoes

SURPRISES
The draft Palauan constitution of 1979 – it created the world's first nuclear-free state... until the US asked for amendments; the thousands of crab-eating macaques on Angaur island

Palau's unique art form is the storyboard, a smaller version of the carved legends that have traditionally decorated the beams and gables of men's meeting houses. The carving style was suggested in 1935 by Japanese anthropologist Hisakatsu Hijikata, who viewed the smaller boards as a way to keep both the art form and legends from dying out. Today, many of the storyboard scenes depicted have an element of erotica.

— Lonely Planet's *Micronesia*

1. Viewed from above, the islands of Palau present a vision of pristine splendour Michael Aw

4. Threads of local history are woven into the tales enacted in Yapese dancing Casey Mahaney

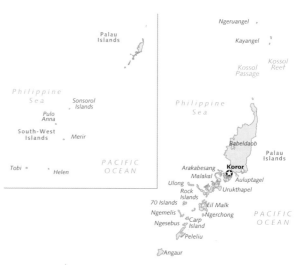

MAP REF: N,34

299

2. A congregation of holy men gather in formation Hanan Isachar

3. Altar boys walk out of church Hanan Isachar

4. This boy carries a staff in procession Hanan Isachar

5. Children peer inquisitively down on the crowd below Hanan Isachar

6. Just another stroll for two local women Hanan Isachar

LEFT 1. A line of palm trees snakes from the Monastery of St George of Koziba, creating a splash of green in the cliffs of Wadi Qelt Brett Shearer

Today 'Palestine' is two territories of Israel: Gaza in west Israel, on the shores of the Mediterranean Sea, and the West Bank bordering Jordan. It's the birthplace of Christ, the Holy Land of the medieval Crusades, a landscape of striking contrasts and a travel agent's worst nightmare. Despite ongoing efforts by the UN, the long-fought struggle for independence, characterised by terrorism, has resulted in a land ravaged by violence. The religious significance of the area to Arabs, Jews and Christians, combined with its strategic location, has made the Palestinian Territories among the most hotly disputed bits of real estate in the modern world.

BEST TIME TO VISIT
September to November and March to May are best, but check the political climate rather than the temperature

ESSENTIAL EXPERIENCES
Visiting the Byzantine mosque at Hisham's Palace in ancient Jericho, the world's oldest town

Experiencing the kitsch 'mangerfication' of Bethlehem by taking a trip to Shepherds' Fields and a look at Milk Grotto Chapel – a shrine to the Virgin Mary's lactations

Floating in the eerie tranquillity of the Dead Sea

Observing the enchanting old quarter of Nablus and its impressive minaret skyline
Swimming in the natural spring of Wadi Qelt, a nature reserve near Jericho

GETTING UNDER THE SKIN
Read *Gaza: Legacy of an Occupation* by Dick Doughty and Mohammed El-Aydi, which gives an emotive, gritty view of Palestinian life in the Strip. And of course, the Bible is an informative travelogue

Listen to tinny Arabic pop VERY LOUDLY from street-traders' cassette decks

Watch the Palestinian version of a 'road trip' movie, *Route 181 – Fragments of a Journey to Palestine-Israel*. Directed by Michel Khleifi (Palestinian) and Eyal Sivan Route (Israeli), it charts the UN-imposed borders decided in Resolution 181, 1947

Eat a street-stall *swharma* (grilled meat sliced from a spit and served in pita bread)

Drink juice made from tamarind, dates and almonds

IN A WORD
Al-hamdu lillah 'al as-salāma (thank God for your safe arrival)

TRADEMARKS
Birthplace of Christ; armed checkpoints; Yasser Arafat; massive concrete 'peace walls' covered with razor wire; Palestine Liberation Organization (PLO); Turkish baths; heart-starting stovetop coffee; suicide bombers; mosques; minarets; searing, dry heat

SURPRISES
Cash, what's that? In Palestine people buy everything, right down to their morning coffee, with a credit card. Occasionally, though, you might stumble on a coin bearing the name Palestine, dating from the Ottoman Empire or British Mandate period.

The water of the Dead Sea is laden with minerals. It is 33% solids, contains 20 times as much bromine as sea water, 15 times as much magnesium and 10 times as much iodine. Bromine, a component of many sedatives, relaxes the nerves; magnesium counteracts skin allergies and clears bronchial passages; iodine, which is essential to good health, has a beneficial effect on thyroid functions.

– Lonely Planet's *Israel & the Palestinian Territories*

MAP REF: J,23

2. Houses jumbled at unusual angles along the main street of Bocas del Toro on Isla Colón Andrew Leanne Walker

3. Teribe children play in the lush surroundings of the remote village of Sicyic in Bocas de Toro Province Scott Doggett

4. A stone angel watches over the sky line of Panama City Alfredo Maiquez

Its name may be synonymous with a canal and a hat, but this little-visited isthmus nation has some of the finest birdwatching, snorkelling and deep-sea fishing in the Americas. Proud Panama celebrates its Spanish heritage with frequent and colourful festivals, seasoned with the influences of the seven remaining indigenous groups and the West Indian culture of its black population. It's difficult to leave the country without feeling you're in on a secret the rest of the travelling world has yet to discover.

BEST TIME TO VISIT
Mid-December to mid-April (the dry season)

ESSENTIAL EXPERIENCES
Birdwatching at Cana, deep in the heart of Parque Nacional Darién

Watching a huge ship nudge its way through the Panama canal

Sampling the coffee in the cool mountain town of Boquete

Diving with the sea turtles on Archipiélago de Bocas del Toro

Photographing the Spanish colonial architecture of Península de Azuero

Hiking through Parque Nacional Volcán Barú in search of the elusive quetzal

GETTING UNDER THE SKIN
Read *When New Flowers Bloomed*, a collection of stories by women writers from Panama and Costa Rica. *Tekkin' a Waalk* by Peter Ford includes a stroll along Panama's Caribbean coast.

Listen to Panamanian folk music on Samy and Sandra Sandoval's *Grandes Exito*

Watch the Academy Award-winning documentary *The Panama Deception* by Barbara Trent, which investigates the US invasion of Panama

Eat *sancocho* (the national dish: a spicy chicken and vegetable stew) or *carimañola* (a deep-fried roll of *yucca* filled with chopped meat)

Drink *chicheme* (a delicious concoction of milk, sweet corn, cinnamon and vanilla) or *seco* (distilled from sugar cane, served with milk and ice)

IN A WORD
Vamos, pues (let's go)

TRADEMARKS
The umbilical cord between Central and South America; the world's most famous shortcut; Manuel Noriega; Swiss banks; corrupt politicians; Panama hats

SURPRISES
The Kuna Indians of the San Blas Archipelago run the 378 islands as an autonomous province, with minimal interference from the national government. They maintain their own economic system, language, customs and culture, with distinctive dress, legends, music and dance.

The madness of Carnaval peaks on Shrove Tuesday with the biggest parade of all. Floats of all sizes rule the avenue, separated by bands of gaily dressed people walking slowly in themed formations – not the least conspicuous of which is the traditional formation of transvestites. Most of them carry a razor in each hand as a warning to macho types that a punch thrown at them will not go unanswered.

– Lonely Planet's *Panama*

1. A Choco Indian family posing on the porch of their home in Darién Alfredo Maiquez

5. A girl and her parrot out for a stroll in Bocas del Toro Andrew Leanne Walker

MAP REF: M,11

2. A mother and child walk through their village in the early morning mist, Sepik region Michael Gebicki

3. Twilight game – two girls keep a balloon in the air, Kirawina Island Michael Gebicki

4. A Christian mother and child attending church in Madang Jerry Galea

5. A lone fisherman punts home as dusk settles near Maliwai John Borthwick

6. Traditional dancers shake it up in grass skirts and matching anklewear Liz Thompson

LEFT 1. A Southern Highlands man includes a woolly hat in his traditional headdress Jerry Galea

Kundus and *garamut* drums beat out dizzying rhythms in the sweet sticky heat. The sound of insects rings in the air, and frogs and geckos bark as night falls, silenced only by a sudden deluge of tropical rain. The vegetation surrounding you is on growth hormones – an overproductive superabundance of greenery. This is PNG, a raw, remarkably untamed land, filled with great mountain ranges, mighty rivers and stunning beaches, and five million people living much the way they have for thousands of years.

BEST TIME TO VISIT

June to September is cooler, drier and takes in the majority of the provincial celebrations and Highlands *sing sings*

ESSENTIAL EXPERIENCES

Standing atop snowflecked Mt Wilhelm on a clear morning, taking in both north and south coasts of the world's second-biggest island

Attending a Highlands *sing sing* to watch tens of thousands of people gather bedecked in *bilas* (finery) of body-paint, masks and headdresses of bird-of-paradise feathers

Snorkelling over the teeming reef-life – millions of fish in impossible colours, giant clams, monster gropers and WWII shipwrecks

Travelling up the mighty Sepik River into the powerhouse of Pacific art

Visiting the ghost town of Rabaul, buried in Tuvurvur's volcanic ash

GETTING UNDER THE SKIN

Read biologist Tim Flannery's *Throwim Way Leg*, an account of his many field trips into the interior's remotest parts in search of tree-kangaroos

Listen to Telek's *Serious Tam* CD (Real World), showcasing the extraordinary voice and music of Rabaul's most famous son

Watch Robin Anderson and Bob Connelly's cinematic triptych *First Contact, Joe Leahy's Neighbours* and *Black Harvest*, an outstanding exposition of Highlanders' first encounters with the outside world and their emergence into modern times

Eat fresh fish, lobster and market gardeners' produce

Drink SP Lager

IN A WORD

Em nau! (fantastic! right on!)

TRADEMARKS

Penis-gourds; betel nut; *sing sings*; tropical islands; bilum bags; tribal art; laid-back 'PNG time'; beautiful beaches; Kokoda Trail; Asaro mud men; yam worship; rascals

SURPRISES

Women suckling pigs, *umus* (underground ovens), shell-money, shark-calling, ancestor worship, altitude sickness, birds-of-paradise, bats

You raise your gaze a few degrees and you see the rim of the old caldera with its five volcanos, one still smoking, and you remember where you are. Beneath the earth under your feet there are made roads, a sewerage system, parks and ovals, but above that everything has been laid to waste. It's black at night and the unnerving quiet is only broken by the wind and the scavengers moving through its bones. Slowly, very slowly, people are coming back to Rabaul.

– Lonely Planet's *Papua New Guinea*

MAP REF: 0.35

2. A Paraguayan family shares a joke Pablo Corral Vega

3. An employee of the General López Steam Railway takes a smoke break Jeremy Horner

The tourist trail largely bypasses this small subtropical country, landlocked in the heart of South America, and therein lies much of Paraguay's charm. Travellers who visit with an open heart and mind are rewarded with unspoilt natural beauty, an abundance of wildlife and some of the friendliest and most unaffected people in the world. Conversing in a blend of Spanish and Guaraní that epitomises the country's unique cultural interweaving, the Paraguayans are most certainly the highlights of this *Paraíso Perdido* (Paradise Lost).

BEST TIME TO VISIT
May to September (winter) — or before 1865 when Paraguay lost over a quarter of its national territory in the disastrous War of the Triple Alliance

ESSENTIAL EXPERIENCES
Surviving a squashed ride in one of Asunción's wooden-floored buses

Catching a game of *fútbol* (soccer) with all the accompanying hysteria

Visiting the Jesuit Missions of Trinidad and Jesús — impressive colonial remains where missionaries and Guaraní Indians once lived and learned harmoniously together

Exploring the vast, thorny wilderness of the Chaco — host to exotic and endangered animals and birds

Heading up the Río Paraguay on a local passenger boat

GETTING UNDER THE SKIN
Read Augusto Roa Bastos' *Son of Man*, which ties together several episodes of Paraguayan history, or for travel literature try *At the Tomb of the Inflatable Pig: Travels Through Paraguay* by John Gimlette

Watch Hugo Gamarra's *The Gate of Dreams* about Augusto Roa Bastos' life and literature; Claudio MacDowell's *The Call of the Oboe*, set in a forsaken Paraguayan village; Enrique Collar's *miramenometokéi: Espinas del Alma* (Thorns of the Soul), about a girl marked by family secrets — one of Paraguay's few national productions, set in modern-day Asunción and its outskirts

Listen to harp and guitar-based folk music and its interpretations by guitarists such as Agustín Barrios Mangoré and Berta Rojas

Eat *chipa* (cheese-bread sold everywhere); *sopa paraguaya* (cornbread); freshly boiled *mandioca* (cassava); *borí borí, sooyo sopy* and *locro* (typical stew-like soups that bear the brunt of many local jokes)

Drink *tereré* (ice-cold *yerba mate* — herbal tea, best shared with the locals), Pilsen (the watery national beer), *caña* (sugarcane alcohol)

IN A WORD
Mba'eichapa? (how are you?)

TRADEMARKS
Jaguars in the jungle; dictators, corruption and contraband; duty free electronic goods; handicrafts; horse-drawn carts; red-dirt roads that turn into rivers in tropical rains

SURPRISES
The German-speaking Mennonite community in dusty Filadelfia; Nueva Australia, named after a short-lived attempt by Australians to set up Utopia in Paraguay

Paraguay is South America's 'empty quarter', a country little known even to its neighbours. PJ O'Rourke summed it up bluntly when he wrote 'Paraguay is nowhere and famous for nothing' — and then, on a short visit to cover elections, promptly fell in love with the place. You might well do the same.

— World Guide, www.lonelyplanet.com

1. Brazilian *vaqueiros* in repose before leading a herd of cattle from Paraguay to Cuiaba Stephanie Maze

4. One of Paraguay's many bustling fruit and vegetable markets Peter Guttman

BOLIVIA

BRAZIL

The Chaco

Fortín Toledo

Loma Plata

Filadelfia

Eastern Paraguay

Asunción ⊛ Nueva Australia

Itaguá Piribebuy

ARGENTINA

Villa Florida

Santa Mariá

San Ignacio Guazú

MAP REF: R,13

2. The 500-year-old city of Machu Picchu, a dazzling survivor of the Inca kingdom Mark Daffey

3. Aymará women weaving mats by the shores of Lake Titicaca Eric Wheater

4. Ready to roll – an Aymará boy about to race his old bicycle tyre Eric Wheater

5. Two colourfully garbed Aymará girls share a joke Eric Wheater\

1. The soaring knife-edged peaks of Alpamayo dramatically slice into the sunset in Cordillera Blanca Grant Dixon

If Peru didn't exist, travel guide books would have to invent it. It's a land of lost cities and ancient ruins, brooding Andean peaks and trashy urban beaches. It's dense jungles and overcrowded cities, mysterious Incan rites and Roman Catholic masses, practising shamans and dashboard Virgin Marys, Shining Path guerillas and ex-shoeshine-boys for president. It's like the whole world in a snowdome.

BEST TIME TO VISIT
June to August (the dry season)

ESSENTIAL EXPERIENCES
Arriving at Huayna Picchu, above Machu Picchu, just as the sun rises

Sinking into the hot springs at Aguas Calientes after hiking to Machu Picchu

Getting a bird's-eye view of the Nazca Lines

Visiting the islands of Lake Titicaca

Hiking in the Cordillera Blanca

Walking through Cuzco over ancient cobblestones and past walls built by the Incas

GETTING UNDER THE SKIN
Read *The Bridge of San Luis Rey,* by Thornton Wilder, an examination of 18th-century colonial Peru

Listen to *Afro-Peruvian Classics: The Soul of Black Peru,* on David Byrne's Luaka Bop label

Watch *Fitzcarraldo,* directed by Werner Herzog and featuring a particularly maniacal Klaus Kinski in an epic film about an obsessed opera lover who wants to build an opera in the jungle

Eat *ceviche* – fresh seafood marinated in lemon juice and chilli peppers, and served with corn on the cob or *yucca*

Drink Inka Kola, bubble-gum flavoured fizz; *chicha morada,* a non-carbonated sweet drink made from purple corn; papaya fruit juice

IN A WORD
La noche es larga (the night is long)

TRADEMARKS
Pan pipes; quirky hats; religious iconography; Incan ruins; llamas; the Andes; colourful textiles; old black Dodges with Madonnas painted on the side; jungles; mysterious biomorphs and geoglyphs etched into the land; 16th-century Spanish architecture and artefacts

SURPRISES
Snow and skiing, sand boarding, multiple petticoats under brightly coloured taffeta dresses, village squares filled with schoolchildren and marching bands

Puno is often said to be the folklore capital of Peru, boasting as many as 300 traditional dances and celebrating numerous fiestas throughout the year. Although they often occur during celebrations of Catholic feast days, the dances usually have their roots in preconquest celebrations often tied in with the agricultural calendar.

– Lonely Planet's *Peru*

6. Glamour llamas in the freezing Alto Plano region Wes Walker

MAP REF: P.12

2. Kids surf the nets in Tamontaka Eric Wheater

3. Public transport is slow but reliable in Santo Tomas, Mindanao Island Eric Wheater

4. Mt Mayon rises dramatically above rice paddies in Albay John Pennock

5. Every hour is peak hour in the Blumentritt district of Manila John Pennock

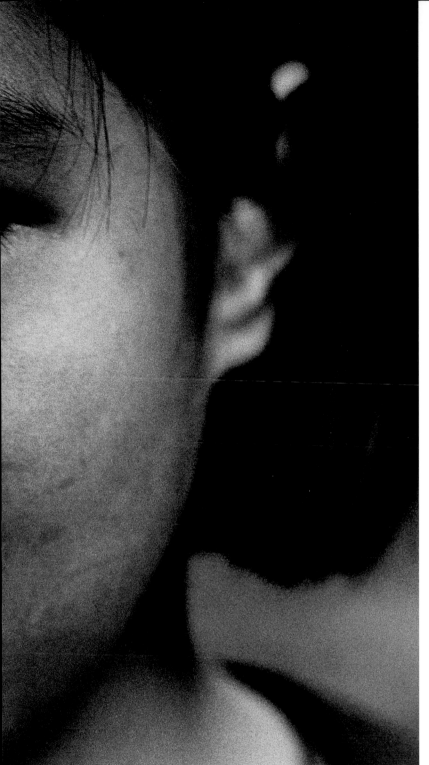

Closer to Spain and Mexico via the fabled galleon trade, and some say to Hollywood by way of its showbiz politics, the Philippines remains Southeast Asia's destination of surprises along routes less travelled. There are more than 7000 shimmering islands to choose from, plus endless fiestas, but the best thing is the sense that there are still discoveries to be made. With so many islands and comparatively few visitors, the Philippines is one of the last great frontiers in Asian travel.

BEST TIME TO VISIT
September to the middle of May (the typhoon off-season) — or before Magellan arrived in 1521

ESSENTIAL EXPERIENCES
Landing on Boracay beach by boat

Absorbing the 17th-century atmosphere of Unesco World Heritage–listed Vigan

Joining in the Mardi Gras fun at Iloilo's Dinagyang festival

Rubbing elbows with Pontius Pilate and Barabbas at Crucifixion re-enactments in Pampanga

Losing one's sanity in Manila but finding reasons to return

GETTING UNDER THE SKIN
Read *Great Philippine Jungle Energy Cafe*, a magical novel by the award-winning Alfred A Yuson, or Pico Iyer's bittersweet insights in the Philippines chapter of his travelogue *Video Nights in Kathmandu*

Listen to *Anak* (Child), the international hit by Freddie Aguilar

Watch *Back to Bataan*, a wartime film about WWII, starring John Wayne and Anthony Quinn, with a Filipino cast

Eat *dinuguan*, a thick, black soup made of pig's blood with either pork or chicken entrails

Drink *guyabano* juice, a refreshment made from the soursop fruit

IN A WORD
Okey, pare ko (It's cool, man)

TRADEMARKS
Jeepneys; San Miguel beer; *barong* shirts; Latin-souled Asians with Californian accents; Imelda Marcos' shoes; ultra-hospitable people

SURPRISES
Guimaras Island, for its delectable mangoes, ethereal islets and Trappist monastery where you might meet T-shirted and denim-clad monks

Somewhat alarmingly for many foreign visitors, Filipinos often deep-fry their meat and fish and also love to eat pork fat, again preferably deep-fried. Though some dishes may not appeal to you, don't pass up the chance to try lechon baboy, *a spit-roasted pig served with a rich liver sauce. It's often jokingly referred to as 'my heart attack' or 'young man's food'. (If you eat too much of it, you'll certainly die young.)*

– Lonely Planet's *Diving & Snorkelling Philippines*

1. Curiosity and confidence, enduring character traits of the nation witnessed in the expression on a child's face Oliver Strewe

6. And that's the man who stole my floral shirt! A colourful mob of Ati-Atihan Festival celebrants on Panay Island John Pennock

MAP REF: M,33

2. The grave of John Adams, mutineer and founding colonist
Wolfgang Kaehler

3. Foamy waves crash against rocky outcrops on Pitcairn
Island's rugged coast Leonard Zell

4. Christian's Cave set on a sheer cliff face above palm groves Wolfgang Kaehler

Beautifully green and lush, and with a population you could easily seat in a city bus, tiny Pitcairn is most famous as the hideaway settlement for the notorious HMS *Bounty* mutineers. Ironically, more than 200 years later, it's one of the last remnants of the British Empire that Fletcher Christian and his gang rebelled against. With points of interest with names like John Catch-a-Cow and Bitey Bitey, the antiquated language of the mutineers' descendants is an attraction in itself.

BEST TIME TO VISIT
April to October (the dry season)

ESSENTIAL EXPERIENCES
Catching up with the HMS *Bounty* mutineers on Pitcairn – there are several relics, along with Fletcher Christian's cave

Beachcombing by the beautiful lagoon on Ducie Atoll

Birdwatching on Henderson Island with its unique *makatea* (raised coral island) geology

Reading pre-European history in the mysterious Polynesian petroglyphs carved into the rocks at Down Rope

GETTING UNDER THE SKIN
Read *Fragile Paradise* by Glynn Christian (Fletcher's great-great-great-great-grandson), an investigation of the mutiny and the mutineers' fate on Pitcairn

Watch the original film about the mutiny, *In the Wake of the Bounty* (1933) – filmed in Pitcairn, Tahiti and Australia, and starring a young Errol Flynn, or any of the three later versions, starring Clark Gable, Marlon Brando and Mel Gibson respectively as the good guy.

Eat breadfruit, the miracle fruit the HMS *Bounty* was sent out to collect

Drink water

IN A WORD
Whutta-waye? (How are you?)

TRADEMARKS
Fletcher Christian descendants; beaches that you'd jump ship for; coral atolls; pirate hideaways; beautiful Tahitians; seafaring language

SURPRISES
The people of Pitcairn really are descendants of the original HMS *Bounty* mutineers and their Tahitian companions: HMS *Bounty* family names – Adams, Young and Christian – are still common

The island's curious array of place names confronts the visitor immediately on arrival at the Bounty Bay landing. The accurately named Hill of Difficulty is the steep trail that leads up to Adamstown, perched 120m above the sea on the Edge...Heathen idols were found and cast into the sea at Down the God, and the intriguingly named Little George Coc'nuts was a coconut grove owned by George Young, son of mutineer Ned Young...Right in Adamstown you find a spot with the dire name, Where Dick Fall. A little further to the west, below Christian's Cave, the cliffs must be particularly dangerous since the map lists: Where Dan Fall, Johnny Fall and the succinct Tom Off. It's no better on the west coast, Where Warren Fall, or the east coast, Where Freddie Fall. But the south coast has the most enigmatic and worrying warning of all – Oh Dear.

– Lonely Planet's *South Pacific*

1. Mutiny at court – a child plays on the anchor of the notorious HMS *Bounty*, laid to rest outside the court house building Wolfgang Kaehler

5. The oldest house standing on Pitcairn Island, with Christian's Cave in the backgound Wolfgang Kaehler

Oeno
Island

Henderson
Island

Ducie
Atoll

Adamstown

Pitcairn
Island

SOUTH
PACIFIC
OCEAN

MAP REF: R,6

2. A castle in the sky towers over the hillsides of Nowy Wisnicz in the Carpathians Krzysztof Dydyński

3. Snow blankets a spruce forest in the foothills of the Tatra Mountains Krzysztof Dydyński

4. Colourful gabled buildings stand like dolls' houses along the old town square of Jelenia Gora Krzysztof Dydyński

5. A mural on the Witkacy Theatre features a striking image of the artist and philosopher who leant the venue its name in Zakopane Krzysztof Dydyński

6. Lock up your grandfathers — feisty folk singers let it rip at a music festival in Kazimierz Dolny Krzysztof Dydyński
LEFT 1. A street scene in the old quarter of Warsaw, frozen in the frame of a pale blue archway Izzet Keribar

Poland is a country of striking contrasts: contemporary city slickers fill the capital, Warsaw, while in the countryside horse-drawn carts negotiate peaceful lanes where the new millennium is just a rumour. Nestled in the heartland of Europe, Poland has been both a bridge and a front line between eastern and western Europe. Today the country has bounced back from the turmoil of the 20th century and reinvented itself as a must-do fixture on every traveller's map.

BEST TIME TO VISIT
May to June (late spring) and September to mid-October (autumn) — or the 16th century, Poland's golden age

ESSENTIAL EXPERIENCES
Seeing Warsaw change before your eyes

Exploring Krakow's beautiful old town and staying up late to hit the cellar bars

Strolling around Gdansk's historic streets and then heading to the haunting sands of the Baltic coast

Hiking and climbing the Tatras, home to some of Europe's finest mountain scenery

Visiting Auschwitz and praying that such tragedies never happen again

GETTING UNDER THE SKIN
Read *The Heart of Europe: A Short History of Poland* by Norman Davies, a readable, fascinating insight into the development of the nation

Listen to Krzysztof Komeda's jazz piano compositions, icons of Polish culture

Watch anything by Roman Polanski, Poland's most famous film export — try *Knife in the Water,* his first feature film

Eat *bigos* (sauerkraut with a variety of meats) and *pierogi* (stuffed dumplings), both essential to your Polish experience

Drink *wódka* (vodka), the drink of choice — *zubrówka* (bison vodka) is flavoured with a blade of bison grass, a local wild herb

IN A WORD:
Na zdrowie! (cheers!)

TRADEMARKS
Lech Walesa and striking shipbuilders; Pope John Paul II; bleak Communist architecture; heroic goalkeepers and toasts of *wódka* to all of the above

SURPRISES
The country has some of Europe's best mountain, coastal and lake scenery; Poland is staunchly Catholic

Every hour the hejnał (bugle call) is played on a trumpet from the higher tower of St Mary's Church in Krakow Market Square to the four quarters of the world in turn. Today a musical symbol of the city, this simple melody, based on five notes only, was played in medieval times as a warning call. Intriguingly, it breaks off mid-bar. Legend links it to the Tatar invasions; when the watchman on duty spotted the enemy and sounded the alarm, a Tatar arrow pierced his throat mid-phase, the tune has stayed that way thereafter. Since 1927, the hejnał has been played on Polish radio every day at noon.

— Lonely Planet's *Poland*

MAP REF: G,22

2. Dusk tinges the harbour at Ferragudo in unusual hues of pink and blue Paul Bernhardt

3. A swarthy sea dog treats both himself and his fish with the curative combination of salt and sun Jeff Greenberg

4. Washing day in Loule, Algarve Jeffrey Becom

5. An elderly widow in Lisbon dressed in the sombre clothes characteristic of her age Bill Wassman

1. Shoppers stride past the magnificent blue-and-white tiled walls of the Capela das Almas in Porto John King

Savouring life slowly is a Portuguese passion, and much of the best pleasures are humble: traditional folk festivals; simple, honest food drowning in olive oil; music that pulls at the heart strings, recalling past love and glory; and markets overflowing with fish, fruit and flowers. The landscape is wreathed in olive groves, vineyards and Unesco World Heritage sites, while Portugal's delightfully laidback capital, Lisbon, is an architectural time warp, with Moorish, medieval, Manueline and Art Nouvea riches.

BEST TIME TO VISIT
Mid-June to September (summer)

ESSENTIAL EXPERIENCES
Enjoying the nightlife of Bairro Alto, Lisbon

Exploring the revitalised medieval district of the Alfama in Lisbon

Sunbathing on the sandy beaches of Costa da Caparica

Discovering Neolithic standing stones in the wild countryside near Évora, Elvas and Castelo de Vide

Wandering around the beautifully preserved hill-top villages of Monsaraz and Marvão

GETTING UNDER THE SKIN
Read *Fernando Pessoa & Co: Selected Poems by Fernando Pessoa,* a collection of work by Portugal's greatest poet. Nobel Prize winner José Saramago's *O Evangelho segundo Jesus Cristo* (The Gospel According to Jesus Christ) is a unique reinterpretation of the biblical gospels.

Listen to *O Melhor* by Amália Rodrigues, who brought *fado* (bittersweet Portuguese folksongs) international recognition, or *Film* by rock band The Gift

Watch *O Fantasma* directed by João Pedro Rodrigues, which recounts the tale of a sex-obsessed trash collector, or Wim Wenders' *A Lisbon Story*

Eat *sardinhas asadas* (charcoal-grilled sardines) or *pasteis de nata* (custard tarts)

Drink *vinhos* (wine) or tawny port

IN A WORD
Tudo bem (All's good)

TRADEMARKS
Cork plantations; golf courses; Lisbon nightlife; football fanatics; wild ocean beaches; late-bottled vintage port; the Lisbon earthquake of 1755

SURPRISES
Many historians believe that it was Portuguese explorers who first reached Australia, some 250 years before its 'official' discovery by Captain James Cook; some 15 thousand million corks a year come from Portugal – around 60% of world output

The cockerel motif that you see all over Portugal has its origins in a 16th-century 'miracle'. According to the story a Galician pilgrim on his way to Santiago de Compostela was wrongfully accused of theft while passing through Barcelos. Though pleading his innocence, he was condemned to hang. In his last appearance at the judge's house the pilgrim declared that the roast cockerel on the judge's dinner table would stand up and crow to affirm his innocence. The miracle occurred, the pilgrim was saved and the cockerel gradually became the most popular folk-art motif in the country.

— Lonely Planet's *Portugal*

6. Festival decorations strew the town of Campo Maior with dappled shadows Carlos Costa

MAP REF: I,19

2. Palm trees reach out to the ocean on Isla Verde Greg Johnston

3. A passing nun adds the finishing touch to a Spanish colonial tableau in old San Juan Alfredo Maiquez

1. Too cool for school, a pair of girls size up an accordian player at the Castillo de San Cristóbal Lou Jones

Puerto Rican culture is a mixture of Spanish, African and Taíno traditions topped with a century-thick layer of American influence – and consequently nothing in Puerto Rico is one-dimensional, from architecture to political identity. Spanish is the island's main language, but people also use many English, Amerindian and African words. Roman Catholicism reigns, but is infused with spiritualism and folkloric traditions. The music keeps time with African *la bomba* and also 'Nuyorican' salsa that hails from émigrés in New York. Puerto Rico is uniquely a part of, and apart from, the US and the rest of the Caribbean.

BEST TIME TO VISIT
To avoid crowds and inflated prices, come during hurricane season (May-November) – but keep an eye on weather reports!

ESSENTIAL EXPERIENCES
Drinking *café con leche* near dawn after a night of dancing

Taking sunset walks at El Morro when the evening breeze picks up

Enjoying the lush rainforest at El Yunque

Swimming in the bioluminescent bay at Vieques

Lazing in a hammock or dipping into the crystalline waters on Culebra

Sampling fine rums native to Puerto Rico

Winter whale-watching or surfing in Rincón

Wandering through Ponce's historic district brimming with *criollo* architecture

GETTING UNDER THE SKIN
Read Rosario Ferre's revisionist stories in *Sweet Diamond Dust*. Christina Duffy Burnett's *Foreign in a Domestic Sense* is an examination of American imperialism.

Listen to *coquís*, Puerto Rico's native frogs; the infamous sounds of Tito Puente and Willie Colon; the compilations *Viva Salsa* and *Salsa Superhits* by Fania Records

Watch the acclaimed *West Side Story* which represents stateside Puerto Ricans of the day. See Rachel Ortiz' heartfelt documentary *Mi Puerto Rico*.

Eat plantain dishes like *mofongos* and *tostones*, *sofrito* and *asopao de pollo* (traditional meals), *carrucho* (conch), *tembleque* (coconut pudding)

Drink piña coladas, *Cuba libres*, *mojitos* or any other rum drink, *batidos* (milkshakes) made with *mamey* (a sweet, fragrant fruit) or *guanábana* (soursop)

IN A WORD
Ay, bendito! (Poor thing/What a shame/Oh dear!)

TRADEMARKS
Living *la vida loca*; the 51st state; the rhythm and rhyme of Nuyorican poets; Bacardi rum cocktails

SURPRISES
The immensity of the cruise ships that come and go like mobile cities; the incongruity of using the US dollar

Puerto Rico is where four centuries of Spanish Caribbean culture come face to face with the American convenience store. This leads to some strange juxtapositions – parking lots and plazas, freeways and fountains, skyscrapers and shanties – but it's all apiece with the Caribbean's hybrid history.

— World Guide, www.lonelyplanet.com

MAP REF: L,13

4. Patriotism is about wearing your banner on your balcony at Casa Borinquen in Old San Juan John Neubauer

2. Stark lines and contrasts mark the geometry of a mosque in Doha Mark Daffey

3. The rippled surface of a sand dune swells effort-lessly into an inland sea near Khor al-Adaid Mark Daffey

4. In the harbour of Al-Khor, a fishing dhow looks towards a distant mosque Mark Daffey

5. Bedouin men chilling on a wall Christine Osborne

6. The modern architecture of the Barzan Tower challenges classical styles in the foreground at the Corniche, Doha Mark Daffey

LEFT 1. Wild camels traverse the forbidding sand dunes of Jarayan al Batnah Mark Daffey

Best known for being unknown, Qatar has a habit of falling off the world's radar – in fact, it only started issuing tourist visas in 1989. Foreign maps of Arabia drawn before the 19th century don't show the Qatar peninsula, and most people in the West don't even know where it is. Fewer still can pronounce it (somewhere between 'cutter' and 'gutter'). Travel to this thumb-shaped country in the Persian Gulf and you'll find a a land of ritzy hotels, ancient rock carvings, enormous sand dunes and distinctive architecture. You can catch troops of traditional dance performers wearing costumes resplendent with jewellery. There's the opportunity for amazing desert excursions, or if greenery and shade are what you're after, you can stroll along the lovely 7km coastal corniche in Doha.

BEST TIME TO VISIT
November to March for milder weather – or during the Stone Age when the inhabitants of the region experienced a more forgiving climate than today

ESSENTIAL EXPERIENCES
Marvelling at the sea turtles at the Aquarium in the Qatar National Museum in Doha

Looking at a restored traditional Qatari house at the Ethnographic Museum in Doha

Taking in the amazing view of the ocean from the mosque in Al-Khor

Wandering through the ancient fort at Al-Zubara

Watching the locals haggling at the markets

GETTING UNDER THE SKIN
Read *Arabian Time Machine: Self-Portrait of an Oil State* by Helga Graham, a collection of interviews with Qataris about their lives, culture and traditions

Listen to *The Music of Islam: Volume 4*, recorded in Qatar and featuring traditional melodies played on the *oud*, a traditional stringed-instrument

Watch *Qatar: A Quest for Excellence* made by Greenpark Productions, exploring the life and culture of Qatar through evocative visual images and music

Eat *labneh*, a kind of yoghurt cheese often made from goat's milk; *matchbous*, rice served with spiced lamb or *wara enab*, stuffed vine leaves

Drink *qahwe*, spiced Turkish coffee; or fruit juices

IN A WORD
Salaam (hello)

TRADEMARKS
Traditional houses; the Arabian oryx; sand dunes; ancient forts; traditional Bedouin weaving; old watchtowers; palm-lined seashores; rambling souks; easygoing people; sandstorms; fierce heat; Islamic culture; coastal towns; historical museums

SURPRISES
Aladdin's Kingdom – the only amusement park in the gulf with a serious roller coaster; camel races at Al-Shahhainiya, a popular sport

Qatar is primarily a Bedouin culture, and the tribal ethos is still strong in modern society. Bedouins (being nomads) had a culture traditionally based on poetry and song rather than buildings or art. However, the practical art of weaving has produced some beautiful Bedouin artefacts. Traditional Qatari dress is characterised by gold or silver embroidery, known as al-zari or al-qasab.

– World Guide, www.lonelyplanet.com

MAP REF: K,25

2. Some of the hottest items on sale at the market in St Paul
Olivier Cirendini

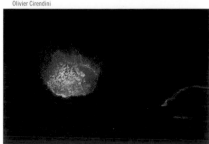

3. The scalding crater of the Piton de la Fournaise broods and
boils Olivier Cirendini

4. Street beats and bright bandanas at a festival in St Louis Jean-Bernard Carillet

Réunion is so sheer and lush, it looks as if it has risen dripping wet from the deep blue sea – which it effectively has, being the tip of a massive submerged prehistoric volcano. The island is run as an overseas *département* of France, making it one of the last colonial possessions in the world. French culture dominates every facet of life, from the coffee and croissant in the morning to the bottle of Evian and the carafe of red wine at the dinner table. However, the French atmosphere of the island has a firmly tropical twist, with subtle traces of Indian, African and even Chinese cultures.

BEST TIME TO VISIT
May and June

ESSENTIAL EXPERIENCES
Hiking the three extraordinary cirques, the active Piton de la Fournaise volcano, and Piton des Neiges – Réunion's highest peak

Soaking up the breathtaking and varied scenery, from austere mountains to intriguing amphitheatres

Mixing in with the colourful cultural melting pot *à la Réunionnais* of Creoles, Europeans, Indians and Chinese

Feasting on the delicious diversity of food, from traditional Creole curries to *haute cuisine française*

Strolling down Le Barachois, a seafront park lined with cannons and cafés

GETTING UNDER THE SKIN
Read Catherine Lavaux's *La Réunion: Du Battant des Lames au Sommet des Montagnes*

Listen to Compagnie Creole, a Caribbean group originally from Réunion but now based in Paris

Eat *carri poulpe* (octopus curry) and, if you want to spice up your meal, add some *rougaile* (a spicy tomato, ginger and vegetable chutney)

Drink *rhum arrangé* (a mixture of rum, fruit juice, cane syrup and a blend of herbs and berries) or a bottle of French red wine

IN A WORD
Bonjour (hello)

TRADEMARKS
Volcanoes; trekking; lush forests; bad beaches; fantastic food; a French colony

SURPRISES
Early settlers developed a taste for the apical bud of the palmiste palm (unfortunately once the bud is removed, the palm dies); the Plaine-des-Palmistes, a green plateau filled with flowers, was stripped bare in a few generations; there are still people searching for the treasure of pirate Olivier Levasseur (or 'La Buse' – the Buzzard) in Mauritius, the Seychelles and Réunion

In keeping with the French love of perfume, Réunion has long been the garden of the great fragrance houses of Paris. The mainstays of the essential-oil business are geranium, vetiver and the evocative ylang-ylang, which you can often smell in the night air all over the island.

– Lonely Planet's *Mauritius, Réunion & Seychelles*

1. The jagged peaks of the Bras des Merles in the awesome Cirque de Mafate watch over a hiker's paradise of swirling mists and tumbling waterfalls Deanna Swaney

5. A tide of heavy cloud washes around the peak of La Roche Ecrite Olivier Cirendini

MAP REF: Q.26

2. Tiny barns dot the gently rolling slopes in the green countryside Diana Mayfield

3. Forest workers and their wives travel on flat bed wagons along the Vișeu de Sus railway Colin Shaw

4. Headscarves and brightly coloured striped aprons are the traditional garb for this part of the Maramureș Diana Mayfield

5. A man climbs the stairs to his Sighișoara apartment Diana Mayfield

Romania is the Wild West of Eastern Europe, a country where tourism means you and a horse and cart. But it's certainly chasing the dreams of the West. Straddling the rugged Carpathian Mountains, Romania offers an extraordinary kaleidoscope of cultures and sights, including majestic castles, medieval towns, superb hiking and skiing; and Bucharest has a charm all of its own. Romania's greatest asset is its diversity, whether you want to stray off the beaten tourist track or stay well and truly on it.

BEST TIME TO VISIT
May and June, followed by September and early October.

ESSENTIAL EXPERIENCES
Descending underground to a cave or salt mine in Transylvania, Crişana or Banat

Sharpening your fangs and practising saying 'I vant to suck your blurd' at Dracula's castle in Bran

Experiencing 'cart-rage' when trying to overtake a horse-drawn cart on a winding mountain road

Slapping on some smelly, curative mud on the Black Sea coast

Braving a vigorous drinking session of 60-proof moonshine *palincă* (brandy) with exuberant locals

Marvelling at the striking baroque architecture at Braşov and castle-spotting at Râsnov

GETTING UNDER THE SKIN
Read Norman Manea's *The Hooligan's Return: A Memoir*, relating the return of this accomplished author to his homeland in the late 1990s

Listen to Pasărea Colîbrî, a very popular contemporary band with great folk-inspired soft rock and pop tunes

Watch *Cold Mountain*, directed by Anthony Minghella and starring Nicole Kidman and Jude Law, which was filmed at the Carpathian Mountains

Eat *ciorbă de burtă*, a lightly garlicky soup made of tripe

Drink wine, wine and more wine – among the best are Cotnari, Murfatlar, Odobeşti, Târnave and Valea Călugărească

IN A WORD
Bună (hello)

TRADEMARKS
A film-set for cheap horror flicks; mountain festivals; Dracula and all things Transylvanian; Queen Marie of Romania; imposing castles; medieval villages; wine producers; rolling green countryside; a country that's ripe for discovery

SURPRISES
Romania is usually in the top five countries in the world for having the highest marriage rates.

Romanians tend to be down-to-earth, don't waste time on false niceties, and like people who are open but also pragmatic and forthright. They have a Latin temperament and are often strong-minded, charming, stubbornly proud and staunchly aware of their roots. Most take great pride in their country's rich natural heritage and folk culture. Befriend any Romanian and within hours an expedition to the mountains will be mapped out for you.

— Lonely Planet's *Romania & Moldova*

1. An eerie glow on the cobbled streets of Sighişoara, the birthplace of Vlad Ţepeş whose gruesome exploits partially inspired the Dracula legend   David Greedy

6. Arges valley near Poienari and the defensive fortress of Vlad Ţepeş   Colin Shaw

MAP REF: H,22

2. The distinctive Soviet architecture of the colossal Hotel Rossiya in Moscow Jonathan Smith

3. The famous Trans-Siberian snakes through a winter wonderland Martin Moos

4. Figures traverse the frozen surface of the River Neva in St Petersburg Steve Kokker

1. Elegant furs and an amiable smile are the uniform of this cabin attendant on the Irkutsk to Moscow express Simon Richmond

Winston Churchill famously described Russia as a 'riddle wrapped in a mystery inside an enigma', and this remains an apt description of a place most outsiders know very little about. A composite of the extravagant glories of old Russia and the drab legacies of the Soviet era, Russia is a country that befuddles and beguiles but never bores.

BEST TIME TO VISIT
May to October

ESSENTIAL EXPERIENCES
Experiencing imperialist extravagance at the Hermitage in St Petersburg

Sweating it out in a *banya* – the combination of dry sauna, steam bath and plunges into ice-cold water is a regular feature of Russian life

Taking one of the world's great train journeys across Siberia

Learning to drink vodka the Russian way

Paying your respects to Lenin's mummified body in Red Square

Gazing at the crystal-clear blue waters of Lake Baikal from an old wooden cottage in lovely Listvyanka

GETTING UNDER THE SKIN
Read Tolstoy's *War and Peace,* if you're feeling brave, otherwise have a go at Dostoevsky's *Crime and Punishment*

Listen to anything by Tchaikovsky or Rachmaninoff

Watch the Oscar-winning *Burnt by the Sun,* a poignant treatment of the Stalinist purges

Eat *bliny* (pancakes with savoury or sweet fillings) and, of course, caviar

Drink vodka – what else?

IN A WORD
Za vashe zdarov'e! (to your health!)

TRADEMARKS
Vodka; corrupt billionaires; Soviet-era architecture; *babushkas* in scarves; queues; dachas; shopping at GUM; *matryoshka* dolls; cabbage and cabbage

SURPRISES
It's actually relatively easy to get a visa; St Petersburg is a beautiful city of canals, sometimes known as the 'Venice of the North'

The world's largest country encompasses all the pleasure and pain of the human condition, with the last decade's social and economic revolutions giving a dynamic – and disastrous – spin to Russian lives… It's precisely the Russian people's endearing combination of gloom and high spirits, rudeness and warmth, secrecy and openness that makes journeying through their country such a different experience.

– Lonely Planet's *Russia & Belarus*

5. The candy-striped Chesma Church in St Petersburg built for Catherine the Great as a resting place on the road to her country residence Steve Kokker

MAP REF: F.28

327

2. Gaudy shopfronts in the capital, Kigali Doug McKinlay

3. A reconstruction of the ancient palace of the Mwami (King) in Nyanza Ariadne Van Zandbergen

4. Nyakarimbi, a village known for its artists – creators of brilliant cow dung paintings in geometric designs Ariadne Van Zandbergen

5. Pretty in green, a muslim girl of Cyangugu Ariadne Van Zandbergen

1. Holding the house together, a woman stands at the entrance to a homestead in Nyanza Ariadne Van Zandbergen

Rwanda is often called *Le Pays des Milles Collines* (the Land of a Thousand Hills) for the endless mountains in this scenically stunning little country. Nowhere are the mountains more majestic than the peaks of the Virunga volcanoes in the far northwest of the country, forming a natural frontier with Congo (Zaïre) and Uganda. Hidden among the bamboo and dense jungle of the volcanoes' forbidding slopes are some of the world's last remaining mountain gorillas. A beautiful yet brutalised country, Rwanda is all too often associated with the horrific genocide that occurred here in 1994, but the country has taken giant strides towards recovery in the years since.

BEST TIME TO VISIT
Any time except mid-March to mid-May when the long rains set in

ESSENTIAL EXPERIENCES
Visiting the rare mountain gorillas in the dense forest of Parc National des Volcans

Soaking up the sun, sand and stunning scenery at Gisenyi, on Lake Kivu, Rwanda's answer to the Mediterranean

Tracking down huge troops of colobus monkeys in Nyungwe, the country's largest tropical rainforest

Exploring one of Africa's best ethnographical and archaeological museums in Butare, Rwanda's intellectual capital

Checking out the nightlife in Kigali

GETTING UNDER THE SKIN
Read *We Wish to Inform You That Tomorrow We Will Be Killed with Our Families* by Phillip Gourevitch, a brilliant account of the killings and how the international community failed Rwanda in 1994 and beyond

Listen to the queen of Rwandan music, Cecile Kayirebwa

Watch *Gorillas in the Mist* – the story of Dian Fossey's years with the mountain gorillas of Rwanda and her battle with the poachers and government officials

Eat *tilapia* (Nile perch), goat meat and beef brochettes

Drink the local beers, Primus and Mulzig, or try the local firewater, *konyagi*

IN A WORD
Muraho ('hello' in Kinyarwanda) – use unsparingly

TRADEMARKS
The horrific 1994 genocide; Dian Fossey; volcanoes; dense jungles; gorilla tracking; mountains

SURPRISES
Tiny, landlocked Rwanda has 340 people per square kilometre; there are thought to be around only 700 mountain gorillas left in the world today

In Rwanda and Burundi, the period of colonial rule was characterised by the increasing power and privilege of the Tutsi people. The Belgian administrators found it convenient to rule indirectly through Tutsi chiefs and their princes, and the Tutsi had a monopoly on the missionary-run educational system. The result was the aggravation of long existing tensions between the Tutsi and Hutu peoples, igniting the spark that was later to explode in the 1994 Rwanda genocide.

– Lonely Planet's *East Africa*

6. A boy launches his dugout canoe for a day's fishing on the lake, Gisenyi Ariadne Van Zandbergen

MAP REF: 0.23

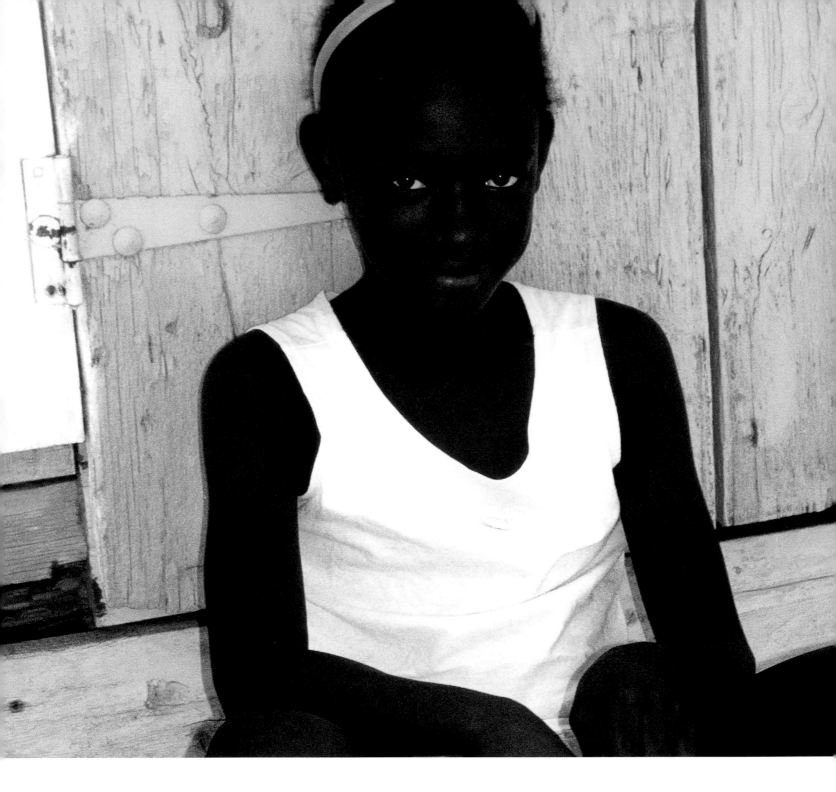

2. Time to paint the house blue again soon Richard Cummins

3. An essential mode of transport in Charlestown Colin Shaw

4. The catch of the day dries out in front of Bloody Point Restaurant Wayne Walton

5. The citadel's interior makes an inviting retreat in Brimstone Hill Fortress National Park Richard Cummins

The islands of St Kitts and Nevis are two of the sleepiest places in the Caribbean, and one of the few countries in the region where agriculture is still a larger part of the economy than tourism. The islands have mountainous interiors, patchwork cane fields, salt ponds and deeply indented bays. The culture of the islands draws upon a mix of European, African and West Indian traditions. While three quarters of the population live on St Kitts, both islands are small, rural and lightly populated.

BEST TIME TO VISIT
Year-round

ESSENTIAL EXPERIENCES
Staying in cosy, atmospheric plantation inns

Strolling the expansive coconut-lined Pinney's beach on Nevis

Enjoying St Kitts' southeast peninsula, with its fine scenery and beaches

Exploring Brimstone Hill Fortress National Park with its historic significance and coastal views

Diving amongst rays, barracuda, garden eels, nurse sharks, sea turtles, sea fans, giant barrel sponges and black coral

Wandering around the seaside village of Old Road Town to see vintage sugar cane trains hauling loads of freshly cut cane from the fields to the mills

GETTING UNDER THE SKIN
Read *Historic Basseterre: The Story of its Growth* by Sir Probyn Inniss recounts the growth of the capital. Read Sir Fred Phillips' memoirs *Caribbean Life and Culture: A Citizen Reflects* for a more personal account.

Listen to West Indian and African influenced music

Eat fresh fish and seafood until bursting point

Drink Cane Spirit Rothschild (CSR), a clear sugar cane spirit, by itself or with Ting, a grapefruit soft drink

IN A WORD
Put your feet up

TRADEMARKS
Sugar; snorkelling; laid-back attitude; plantation estates; fine beaches; cricket

SURPRISES
The federation of the two islands forms the smallest nation in the Western Hemisphere. While Kittitians and Nevisians amicably coexist – they share essentially the same culture, and most Nevisians live on St Kitts – they are fierce rivals. Their annual cricket match is an intense affair.

St Kitts' southeast peninsula is wild, unspoiled and dotted with white-sand beaches. The scenery has a certain stark beauty, with barren salt ponds, grass-covered hills and scrubby vegetation. The main inhabitants are green vervet monkeys, which you may see bounding across the road, and a few wild deer.

– Lonely Planet's *Eastern Caribbean*

1. A young girl smiles for the camera from outside a doorway in Basseterre, the capital of St Kitts
Wayne Walton

6. Palm trees watch yet another fuschia and red sun set over the Caribbean – gin and tonic anyone?
Bill Bachmann

MAP REF: L,13

2. The interior of the Cathedral of the Immaculate Conception depicts colourful biblical scenes Richard Cummins

3. This woman carries brooms to market
Michael Lawrence

4. A portrait of a smiling girl Michael Lawrence

5. There's never a dull moment when strolling down Brazil St Richard Cummins

6. A fisherman sits on a jetty, tending his boat Michael Lawrence
LEFT 1. Rainforest in the Morne Coubaril Plantation near the Caribbean coast with the peak of Petit Piton looming behind Michael Lawrence

Resort developments on St Lucia have made this high, green island one of the Caribbean's trendy package-tour destinations, but it's still a long way from being overdeveloped. Bananas are still bigger business than tourism in this archetypal island heaven, and much of the island is rural: small coastal fishing villages give way to a hinterland of banana and coconut plantations folded within deep valleys topped by rich, mountainous jungle. The rugged terrain continues offshore in a diving heaven of underwater mountains, caves and drop-offs.

BEST TIME TO VISIT
January to April

ESSENTIAL EXPERIENCES
Hobnobbing with the yachties at Marigot Bay

Playing pirates on Pigeon Island, a base used by 'Wooden Leg' de Bois for raiding passing Spanish galleons

Keeping your eyes peeled in the Frigate Islands Nature Reserve for frigate birds, herons, and (gulp!) boa constrictors

Holding your nose to investigate the stinky Sulphur Springs bubbling mud and gases from underground volcanoes

Heading for the extremes on Moule à Chique, the island's southernmost point, with views of the Maria Islands and St Vincent

GETTING UNDER THE SKIN
Read Derek Walcott's *Collected Poems, 1948-1984*, an anthology by St Lucia's favourite son and Nobel Prize winner

Listen to calypso, reggae and dub, especially at a Friday night 'jump-up' party

Watch the many movies that have used St Lucia as a backdrop including *Superman II* and the 1967 original *Doctor Dolittle* with Rex Harrison

Eat West Indian and Creole dishes from across the Caribbean

Drink the local beer, Piton, brewed in Vieux Fort

IN A WORD
Bon jou – good day (in Kwéyòl, which the French Creole islanders sometimes use)

TRADEMARKS
Pirate hideouts; yachties recruiting for their next voyage; pristine beaches; impenetrable jungles; the Pitons towering over the island; bananas aplenty

SURPRISES
In these idyllic surroundings, swimming isn't always a good idea as Bilharzia (schistosomiasis) is endemic to St Lucia (but only in freshwater)

St Lucia has a mix of English, French, African and Caribbean cultural influences, which are manifested in many ways. For instance, if you walk into the Catholic cathedral in Castries, you'll find a building of French design, an interior richly painted in bright African-inspired colours, portraits of a black Madonna and child, and church services delivered in English.

– Lonely Planet's *Eastern Caribbean*

CARIBBEAN
SEA

Castries

Anse La Raye

Canaries

Soufrière

Micoud

Choiseul

ATLANTIC
OCEAN

Vieux Fort

MAP REF: M,13

2. Aerial of coconut palms covered with volcanic ash, on a plantation on the island of St. Vincent Nathan Benn

3. Aerial view of volcanic landscape to the north of the island of St Vincent Yann Arthus-Bertrand

4. Shopping for fresh vegetables on Union Island in the Grenadines Wes Walker

1. Man with model boats Peter Guttman

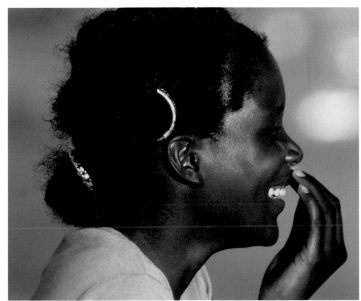

5. A young woman on the island of Bequia laughs Peter Guttman

St Vincent & the Grenadines form a multi-island nation well known to wintering yachties, aristocrats and rock stars, but off-the-beaten path for most other visitors. The 30 islands and cays that comprise the Grenadines reach like stepping stones between St Vincent and Grenada and are surrounded by coral reefs and clear blue waters. Fewer than a dozen are inhabited, and even these are lightly populated and barely developed. St Vincent and the Grenadines share traditional West Indian culture, giving it a multi-ethnic twist of African, Black Carib, French and British influences.

BEST TIME TO VISIT
January to May

ESSENTIAL EXPERIENCES
Trekking up St Vincent's La Soufrière volcano and passing through banana estates and rainforest before reaching the scenic summit

Enjoying the pristine beaches and reefs of the Tobago Cays

Diving to find colourful sponges, soft corals, great stands of elkhorn coral, branching gorgonian and black corals, and a few sunken wrecks

Relaxing on the black-sand surf beaches of St Vincent's Atlantic coast

Drinking with Mick Jagger in Mustique

Hanging out with lizards after climbing Fort Duvernette

GETTING UNDER THE SKIN
Read the history of St Vincent's Black Caribs in *Wild Majesty: Encounters with Caribs from Columbus to the Present Day* by Peter Hulme and Neil Whitehead

Listen to reggae, calypso, steel bands and local boy made good, Kevin Lyllle

Watch *Pirates of the Caribbean*, which was mostly shot at St Vincent's

Eat *bul jol* (roasted breadfruit and saltfish with tomatoes and onions) and feast on the plentiful tropical fruits

Drink the locally distilled Captain Bligh Rum or the local lager, Hairoun

IN A WORD
Pass me the sunscreen, please

TRADEMARKS
Rock stars and royalty; tropical island paradise; exclusive resorts; yachts; volcanoes

SURPRISES
Mick Jagger lived on Mustique; the sweet, juicy St Vincent orange is ripe while still green

Bequia's shipbuilding heritage lives on through local artisans who build wooden scale models of traditional schooners and Bequian whaling boats. The boats are crafted to exact proportions, painted in traditional colours and outfitted with sails and rigging… Most of the models are made for custom orders, replicas of visiting yachts made for their owners. One of their best-known works was a model of the royal yacht, HMS Britannia, which was presented to Queen Elizabeth II during her 1985 visit.

– Lonely Planet's *Eastern Caribbean*

MAP REF: M,13

2. The Fuipisia Falls cascade from the jungle wall on the Edenic trail of the Mulivaifagatola River Mark Daffey

3. Painting himself into a corner, a man crouches on corrugated iron roof Peter Hendrie

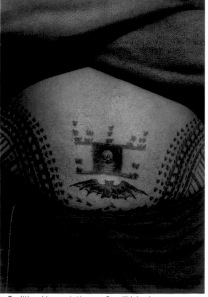

4. Traditional tummy tattoos on Savai'i Island Peter Hendrie

5. Tangled in a net of shadows, a young adventurer crosses the canopy walkway in the Falealupo Rainforest Reserve
John Borthwick

1. Released from church, children prepare to sully their Sunday best in Apia Will Salter

6. Cheerful churchgoers at the entrance to the Vaiusu Catholic Church, Upolu Island Peter Hendrie

Samoa is so laid-back it's only a *kava* session away from being comatose. Palm-fringed beaches, booming white surf and lush rainforests wreathed in misty clouds make it the kind of place that Hollywood location scouts go gaga over. The Samoan Islands comprise two entirely separate entities: the independent country of Samoa and the US territory of American Samoa. Over the years it's been visited by trading ships and served as a bolt hole for the homeless riffraff of the seas – ex-whalers, escaped convicts, bawdy traders and retired pirates. After such a tumultuous history, this is a place that has earned a little time in the sun.

BEST TIME TO VISIT
May to October, when the weather is perfect and the events calendar is full

ESSENTIAL EXPERIENCES
Spending the night in a 225-year-old banyan tree amid fruit bats and birds on Falealupo Peninsula

Playing a game of *kirikiti* – a home-grown Samoan version of cricket

Discovering Pulemelei Step Pyramid, Polynesia's largest and most mysterious ancient monument

Gazing into Olemoe Falls, Samoa's most beautiful waterfall and tropical pool

Staying at Aggie Grey's legendary hotel (Aggie was supposedly the model for Bloody Mary in James Michener's Pulitzer Prize–winning novel *Tales of the South Pacific*)

Blowing your mind at Alofa'aga Blowholes, one of the world's largest marine blowholes

Getting volcanic at Sale'aula Lava Field, a vast expanse of black basalt formed by flowing lava enveloping a buried village

GETTING UNDER THE SKIN
Read *Where We Once Belonged* by Sia Figiel, a local author's first novel about dispossession in modern Samoa

Listen to world-renowned Samoan hip hop such as the Boo Ya Tribe and King Kapisi

Watch *Fa'a Samoa: The Samoan Way*, an amusing video portraying everyday life in Samoa

Eat a traditional Polynesian feast cooked in an *umu* (below-the-ground oven)

Drink *kava*, the ceremonial drink made from the ground roots of pepper plants

IN A WORD
Malo or *Talofa* – traditional greetings

TRADEMARKS
Hefty rugby-playing locals; crazed *kava* ceremonies; palm-fringed beaches; ornate traditional tattoos; volcanoes periodically blowing their tops; Robert Louis Stevenson

SURPRISES
The International Dateline makes Samoa the last place on earth to see the sun set and means many travellers arrive the day before they left

Falealupo Peninsula figures prominently in local legend. The natural beauty of the area belies the dark significance it holds for Samoans, who believe that the gateway to the underworld of the aitu *(spirits) is found at the place where the sun sets in the sea.*

— Lonely Planet's *South Pacific*

MAP REF: P.1

337

2. Uniformed guard outside the fortress of La Rocca Lucio Bonini

3. Bright poppies colour the foreground of San Marino Lucio Bonini

1. The castle-fortress perched on the northern peak of Monte Titano has a commanding view of the surrounding landscape Herr Muller Peter/Mediocolor

It might be geographically part of Italy, but the Most Serene Republic of San Marino is miraculously the world's oldest surviving republic. If you're into the experience of extreme kitsch, this is the place for you – it's packed to the gills with 'genuine reproductions' of medieval relics. A dozen or so kilometres inland from Rimini, it's not much bigger than two or three suburbs strung together but has its own distinctive flavour and proud identity, boasting three grand fortresses and some of the most stunning views of the Adriatic.

BEST TIME TO VISIT
July to September for the best weather

ESSENTIAL EXPERIENCES
Paying a visit to the Basilica del Santo – the heart and spirit of both the city and the republic

Taking a panoramic stroll to the Cesta, the highest of the fortresses

Roaming unhindered around La Rocca, the First Tower

Descending into the deep dungeon in the tower fortress Montale

Wandering around the richly, carved stone Palazzo Publico

Marvelling at the views from the Piazza della Libertà

Walking in the relative calm and quiet of the Appennines

GETTING UNDER THE SKIN
Read *Secrets of the Seven Smallest States of Europe: Andorra, Liechtenstein, Luxembourg, Malta, Monaco, San Marino and Vatican City* by Thomas Ecchardt

Listen to *Live in San Marino*, by Lino Patruno & His Jazz Star of Italy   an excellent album of popular jazz standards recorded live in the republic

Watch Darryl Zanuck's *The Prince of Foxes*, filmed in San Marino (he 'rented out' the entire republic!)

Eat brioche for breakfast, pasta with *carciofi* (artichokes), mushrooms or *vongole* (clams), grilled seafood or *bustrengo* (a sweet cake made with polenta, apples, honey, raisins and lemon zest)

Drink frothy cappucinos or *grappa* (spirits distilled from grape residue)

IN A WORD
Buongiorno (literally 'good day')

TRADEMARKS
Stamp and coin collecting; stupendous fortresses; rampant postcard production; the smell of frankincense and myrrh on holy days; Mount Titano; bell towers; amazing architectural design; jam-packed streets full of tourists

SURPRISES
The Museo di Auto d'Epoca – a museum of cars, both old and new; Chiesa di San Francesco – the oldest building in the republic

If you're looking for something a little extra while you're there, you might want to coincide your visit with the 'Medieval Days with Antique Crossbow Competition', because, really, what's a castle and three fortresses without a crossbow or two. Failing that you could wait till 3 September when the Sammarinese brush off the crossbows again to celebrate National Independence Day.

– World Guide, www.lonelyplanet.com

4. The coats of arms of four of the Republic's nine districts are displayed above the archways of the entrance to San Marino's parliament building William Hume

MAP REF: H,21

2. These dugout canoes have beached themselves Grazyna Bonati

3. Go bananas at the market Grazyna Bonati

4. This pupil eagerly awaits the next lesson Grazyna Bonati
LEFT 1. Children wash at a stone trough Grazyna Bonati

Never heard of this little slice of the Caribbean in the Gulf of Guinea? You're not the only one. The two islands of São Tomé and Príncipe comprise the smallest country in Africa, and one of the newest. These sleepy islands boast miles of deserted beaches, crystal-blue waters, rolling hills, jagged rock formations and lush rainforests. The Portuguese may have left little infrastructure after independence in 1974, but they did leave a strong cultural legacy. Portuguese (as well as Forro, a form of Creole) is spoken throughout the islands and Roman Catholicism is the major religion.

BEST TIME TO VISIT
June and September

ESSENTIAL EXPERIENCES
Swimming at the secluded white-sand beaches with a lush jungle backdrop on the East Coast

Exploring São Tomé town — a friendly, quiet capital city with scenic side streets and colonial architecture

Snorkelling on the true tropical paradise of Príncipe

Straddling the equator at Ilhéu das Rolas

Sipping on some of the best coffee you'll ever taste

Visiting the pleasant town of Trindade in the island's interior where you can see the Waterfall Cascadas de São Nicolau nearby

Hiking through rainforest and birdwatching

Kicking back and relaxing under the palm trees

GETTING UNDER THE SKIN
Read *Former Portuguese Colonies* by Herb Boyd which includes an historical overview of São Tomé and Príncipe

Listen to Gilberto Gil Umbelina, the most famous popular recording artist from São Tomé and Príncipe

Eat fantastic fresh fish and a wonderful assortment of fresh fruit

Drink excellent coffee or the local beer, Creola

IN A WORD
Olá (hello)

TRADEMARKS
Where is this place?

SURPRISES
The illiteracy rate on the islands is 90%. The islands became the biggest sugar producers in the world shortly after the Portuguese founded the town of São Tomé in 1485.

Outside the capital most São Toméans still live very simple island lives, with agriculture and fishing being the main occupations. There's a bit of activity early in the morning when the boats come in and the fish are distributed, a bustling market later in the morning and then a lazy siesta — a chance to avoid the afternoon heat and drink some imported boxes of vino. In the evenings people gather wherever there's a TV set and a generator.

– Lonely Planet's *Africa*

MAP REF: N.20

2. The Diwan, or meeting room, of Madaïn Salah is a sight to be admired Tony Wheeler

3. These locally made baskets and ceramic bowls are sold in Najran Basket Souq Tony Wheeler

4. The 875 foot Faisaliah Tower in Riyadh was designed by renowned architect Sir Norman Foster Tony Wheeler

5. These traditional balconies and decorative façade in Jeddah's old town make a pretty sight Chris Mellor

1. The lion tomb is an imposing sight at the Al-KhuraibbaTombs near Al-Ula Tony Wheeler

Once an exclusive club for the chosen few, such as pilgrims bound for Mecca, oil sheiks from Texas, contract workers from everywhere else, and the odd asylum-seeking dictator, Saudi Arabia now welcomes visitors on special visas. The cost is stiff, the restrictions intimidating, but the thrill of just being there is unbeatable. Delights for the intrepid, moneyed traveller include ancient souks in urban landscapes, antiquities half-buried in the desert, a biblical sea and the heady taste of Arabian hospitality.

BEST TIME TO VISIT
November to February

ESSENTIAL EXPERIENCES
Exploring the spectacular rock tombs of Medain Salah

Witnessing the sword dance *ardha*

Sculpture-spotting along Jeddah's corniche

Judging the camel beauty contest near Hafar al Batin

Sighting dugongs in the Red Sea around the Farasan Islands

Admiring rock art around Najran

Visiting the ancient Masmak Fortress in Riyadh

GETTING UNDER THE SKIN
Read *Sandstorms, Days and Nights in Arabia*, Peter Theroux's memoir of the Middle East, or the delightful coffee-table book *The Kingdom of Saudi Arabia*

Listen to *Arabian Masters*, featuring Umm Kolthum, Fairouz, Abdel Halim Hafez, and other Arabic singers and musicians

Watch *Lawrence of Arabia*, David Lean's 1962 epic, not quite Saudi Arabia (shot in Jordan) but many similarities

Eat with your fingers (but never with the left hand). Try a boiled young camel on steaming rice.

Drink cardamon-flavoured coffee

IN A WORD
Is-salaam 'alaykum (Peace be upon you)

TRADEMARKS
Old *souqs* and camel markets; Aramco (Arabian American Oil Company); dates and carpets; millions of expatriate workers in thousands of construction sites and camps; bearded men in robes greeting one another with hugs and kisses; Mecca and Medina

SURPRISES
Stumbling onto a back lot in Jeddah, where, according to the locals, one will find the tomb of Eve; for women, wearing an all-encompassing *abaya* is essential for visiting Saudi Arabia

The most romanticised group of Arabs is no doubt the Bedouin (also called Bedu). While not an ethnic group, they are the archetypal Arabs – the camel-herding nomads who travel all over the deserts and semideserts in search of food for their cattle. From among their ranks came the warriors who spread Islam to North Africa and Persia 14 centuries ago.

– Lonely Planet's *Middle East*

6. The Auto Cube is one of many modern artworks in Jeddah Chris Mellor

MAP REF: K,24

2. These punters enjoy a drink in Edinburgh's The Honeycomb
Jonathan Smith

3. It may be called Greensleeves, but the dresses are red
Jonathan Smith

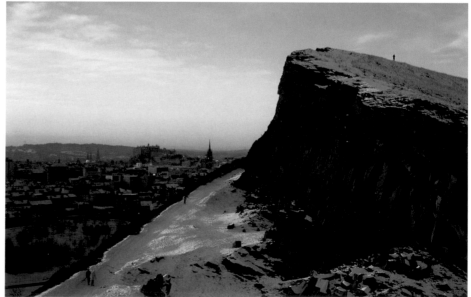

4. The magnificent Salisbury Crags give a different perspective on Edinburgh   Neil Wilson

1. The desolate ruins of Dunnottar Castle, Stonehaven Graeme Cornwallis

Given the long list of influential Scottish inventors and scientists, you would think that the Scots would have come up with something to tame the weather. But, as comedian Billy Connolly said, 'there's no such thing as bad weather, only the wrong clothes'. Weather aside, Scotland, like a fine malt, is a connoisseur's delight – a complex mix of history, culture and arts, festivals galore, feisty people and a wild and beautiful landscape – it should be savoured slowly.

BEST TIME TO VISIT
May to September – or before the Act of Union in 1707 when the English stayed south of the border

ESSENTIAL EXPERIENCES
Taking in the magnificent view of the Firth of Forth from the top of Edinburgh Castle

Viewing the aurora borealis on a clear winter's night from the shores of Loch Tay

Walking around Neolithic homes at Skara Brae, Orkney, built before the Egyptians thought of pyramids

Climbing Ben Nevis to experience the remote beauty of Scotland's Highlands

Hitting a very small ball into a very small hole, with a very tall flag in it, at St Andrews

GETTING UNDER THE SKIN
Read anything by Robert Burns, or *Trainspotting* by Irvine Welsh, for an incomparable but often incomprehensible insight into Scotland

Listen to the Proclaimers or check out The Corries for true Scottish folk

Watch *Whisky Galore*, adapted from Compton MacKenzie's novel of the same name. MacKenzie is known for the adage 'Love makes the world go round? Not at all! Whisky makes it go round twice as fast'.

Eat haggis, *neeps* and *tatties* (haggis, turnips and potatoes) or try some *cranachan* (whipped cream flavoured with whisky, and mixed with toasted oatmeal and raspberries)

Drink whisky, Deuchars IPA (beer) or Irn-Bru (soft drink)

IN A WORD
Och aye tha noo (how are you?/I'm fine; the meaning is not very easy to translate)

TRADEMARKS
Hogmanay and *ceilidhs*; castles, kilts and tartanalia; Highland Games; bagpipers; haggis; deep-fried Mars Bars; whisky; serious drinkers; heart disease; independence; *mingin'* weather; the Loch Ness Monster; Sean Connery

SURPRISES
More redheads are born in Scotland compared to the rest of the world. Some of the oldest mountains in the world can be found in the Highlands of Scotland

Barr's Irn-Bru, which commands 25% of the Scottish fizzy-drinks market, is 'Scotland's other national drink'. Scots swear by its efficacy as a cure for hangovers, which may account for its massive sales. Tasting notes: Colour is a rusty, radioactive orange. Nosing reveals a bouquet of bubble gum and something vaguely citrussy, maybe tangerine? Carbonation is medium, and mouth-feel…well, you can almost feel the enamel dissolving on your teeth.

– Lonely Planet's *Edinburgh*

5. A thoughtful Highland Cow licks its chops in Inverness-shire Neil McIntyre

MAP REF: F.19

2. A herd of Roan antelope approach a pair of stately baobab trees in Reserve de Bandia Ariadne Van Zandbergen

3. The former Maison des Esclaves (Slave House), now a museum and memorial to the horrors of the transatlantic slave trade, Île de Gorée David Else

4. A young girl of Dakar looks after her baby brother Eric Wheater

5. Children playing on the beach at Yoff Eric Wheater

6. A child cavorts in front of a crumbling colonial building in St Louis David Else

LEFT 1. A pointy-shoed pedestrian hits the pavements of St Louis Eric Wheater

Lush Senegal is known for its great natural beauty and gorgeous tropical climate. Surrounded by desert, it offers a rich landscape, great beaches for soaking up the sun and some excellent scuba diving opportunities. Dakar, its capital city, is raw, crowded and exciting, and more favoured by travellers than many of the other larger African cities. Senegal has a rich musical culture with many internationally recognised musicians. Best of all is a slow wander through its streets.

BEST TIME TO VISIT
November to February — or in the 13th-14th centuries when the Djolof kingdom flourished

ESSENTIAL EXPERIENCES
Experiencing West African culture at Dakar's IFAN Museum

Basking in the sun on the beaches of Cap Skiring

Soaking up the atmosphere in Kaolack

Viewing the grand houses of the old European quarter in island St Loius

Spotting pink flamingos in the Parc National de la Langue de Barbarie

Purchasing trinkets at the Marché St-Maur in Ziguinchor

Driving through Niokolo-Koba park to see hippos, baboons, buffalo and more

Admiring the wild, breathtaking scenery of the Siné-Saloum Delta

GETTING UNDER THE SKIN
Read God's Bits of Wood by Senegalese writer Sembene Ousmane, the story of adversity faced by strikers on the Dakar-Niger train line in the 1940s

Listen to the amazing voice of Senegal's most famous singer Youssou N'Dour on Eyes Open

Watch Safi Faye's Mossane, the story of a beautiful young girl promised to an arranged marriage but carrying on a secret, chaste love affair

Eat maffé saloum (beef cooked with peanuts, tomato, yams and carrots) or yassa (chicken cooked with olives, lemon and onions)

Drink bissap juice, a popular local drink with lots of zing, or spicy ginger juice

IN A WORD
Asalaa-maalekum (greetings, literally 'peace' in Wolof)

TRADEMARKS
The Wolof and Mandinka tribes; a thriving groundnut industry; beautiful mosques; lively fishing communities; colourful bird-life; vibrant markets; mangrove swamps; gorgeous handicrafts; amazing wildlife; excellent beaches; marabouts (holy men); tasty cuisine; good beer

SURPRISES
Stunning tapestries at the famous, cooperative-run Manufactures Sénégalaises des Arts Décoratifs in Thiès; the Maison des Esclaves (Slave House) on Gorée Island

Tiny Gorée Island, about 3km (2mi) east of Dakar, is a wonderfully peaceful place with about 1000 inhabitants, no asphalt roads and no cars. You'll find colonial-style houses with wrought-iron balconies, an old town hall, decent beaches and Le Castel, a rocky plateau that offers good views of the island and Dakar and is now occupied by a bunch of ganjafied drum junkies.

— World Guide, www.lonelyplanet.com

MAP REF: M,18

2. Wild and woolly musicians pipe traditional tunes Lee Foster

3. The tiled rooves of the walled town of Kotor resplendant in the afternoon sun Patrick Horton

4. Woman in traditional red headscarf Lee Foster

5. The Ostrog Monastery near Nikšić, clasped in the stony fissure of a cliff face in Montenegro Patrick Horton

1. Gazing over the Adriatic, the former fishing village Sveti Stefan in Budva now attracts high fliers and high prices Patrick Horton

6. A line of washing adds character to a cheery mural in Kotor Patrick Horton

Serbia and Montenegro still suffer an ignominious reputation as Balkan bullyboy cultivated by former leader, Slobodan Milošević, but this does the country a great injustice. The heart of former Yugoslavia has another history, an alter ego that reveals a widespread passion for the virtues of high culture, recreation and having a damn good time. Montenegro is a feast of beautiful Adriatic beaches set against spectacular coastal mountains, Kosovo serves up a dish of traditional Ottoman villages, while Belgrade is a multicultural hotpot of architecture and refinement, leaving Novi Sad as a jazzy brew of pedestrian promenades and outdoor cafés along the Danube.

BEST TIME TO VISIT
August to October (summer) – or any time before the Euro hordes rediscover this land that tourism forgot

ESSENTIAL EXPERIENCES
Dancing at dawn in Novi Sad's baroque citadel during the Exit music festival
Wandering around the Old Town in Kotor's walled medieval city
Taking in the stunning views of Kotor Fjord on the hairpin drive to Cetinje
Sunbaking with the beautiful people on any of Budva's fine beaches
Basking in views of the Danube from Belgrade's Kalemegdan Citadel

GETTING UNDER THE SKIN
Read Tim Judah's *The Serbs: History, Myth and the Destruction of Yugoslavia*, a comprehensive and thoroughly readable account of Serbia's part in Yugoslavia's demise. Ivo Andrić's novel *Bridge on the Drina* foresaw the region's disasters of the 1990s

Listen to Blehmuzika – brass music influenced by Turkish and Austrian military music. Darkwood Dub provides more contemporary electro-fusion styles

Watch Emir Kusturica's *Underground* – a heady, chaotic film dealing with Yugoslavia's history. Danis Tanović's superb satire *No Man's Land* spotlights the absurdity of Yugoslavia's internal warring

Eat a *mešano meso* (mixed grill) – a mountain of grilled meat for the carnivorously inclined. It comprises *ćevapčići* (mini sausages made from minced pork, beef or lamb), *pljeskavica* (large, spicy hamburger steak) and *ra njići* (pork or veal shish kebab with onions and peppers)

Drink the terribly good Montenegrin beer brew, Nikšićko Pivo. Local cognac, *vinjak*, and the ubiquitous plum brandy, *šljivovica*, are good for stripping your throat lining

IN A WORD
Nema problema (No problem)

TRADEMARKS
Piano accordions; eastern-bloc hairstyles; nationalist fervour; meat…meat and more meat; Soviet fashion; war-torn countryside

SURPRISES
Europe's deepest fjord; widespread Turkish (Ottoman) influences; loads of jazz; gorgeous beaches; superb lakes and National Parks

Novi Sad's attractions are simply wandering the pedestrian streets, such as Dunavska, with their strings of smart boutiques and lively outdoor cafés, and visiting Petrovaradin Citadel.

— Lonely Planet's *Eastern Europe*

MAP REF: H,22

2. A young girl takes a break from shopping Jeff Greenwald

3. Green as far as the eye can see on Mahe Island John Hay

1. Unusual granite formations on Anse Source D'Argent beach lend La Digue Island the ambience of a lost world Ralph Hopkins

Among the 115 coral islands that make up the Seychelles are some of the most idyllic island getaways in the Indian Ocean, or indeed the world. Here you will find the luxuriant, tropical paradise that appears in countless advertisements and glossy travel brochures. But however seductive the images, they simply can't compete with the real-life dazzling beaches and crystal-clear waters of Praslin and La Digue, or the cathedral-like palm forests of the Vallée de Mai. There are more shades of blue and green in the Seychelles than it is possible to imagine

BEST TIME TO VISIT
March to May and September to November

ESSENTIAL EXPERIENCES
Lazing on some of the most beautiful beaches on the planet

Exploring the secluded islands for sensational snorkelling, diving and marine life

Meandering through the wild and wonderful vegetation of Praslin's Valleé de Mai

Relaxing on La Digue – renowned for its laid-back ambience, idyllic beaches and friendly folk

Visiting Aldabra, one of the world's largest coral atolls and the original habitat of the giant land tortoise

Hunting for hidden pirate treasure on the eerie and mystical large granite island of Silhouette

GETTING UNDER THE SKIN
Read *Aldabra Alone* by Tony Beamish, which looks at life among the giant tortoises during an expedition to the Aldabra group

Listen to Creole pop and folk musician Patrick Victor

Watch Jacques Cousteau's documentary *The Silent World*, much of which was shot on Assumption Island

Eat *carri coco* (a mild meat or fish curry with coconut cream) and *nouga* (a sweet, sticky coconut pudding) for dessert

Drink the local lager, Seybrew, or try a fresh fruit juice

IN A WORD
Bonzour. Comman sava? ('Good morning. How are you?' in the local language)

TRADEMARKS
Palm-fringed beaches; land tortoises; coral atolls; upmarket resorts; diving enthusiasts

SURPRISES
Giant tortoises are endemic to only two regions in the world: Seychelles and the Galápagos Islands; the famously erotic nut of the *coco de mer* palm grows only on the female tree and can weigh up to 20kg

Most Seychellois are Catholic and the majority are avid churchgoers. But there is also a widespread belief in the supernatural and in the old magic of spirits known as gris gris. *Sorcery was outlawed in 1958, but there are quite a number of* bonhommes *and* bonnefemmes di bois *(medicine men and women) practising their cures and curses and concocting potions for love, luck and revenge.*

— Lonely Planet's *Mauritius, Réunion & Seychelles*

4. A liner cruises under a pearly sky off Aldabra Atoll Ralph Hopkins

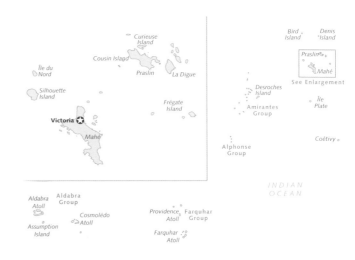

MAP REF: P.25

2. Three girls waiting at the crossroads for travellers to stop and buy bananas near Rogberi Vanessa Wruble

3. Traditional circle huts in a village near the northern town of Binkolo Vanessa Wruble

4. Fetching water from the well in Koidu Vanessa Wruble

5. Men fix their boat on the banks of the prosaically named River No 2 Vanessa Wruble

6. Drummers from the Cultural Village in Freetown Vanessa Wruble
LEFT 1. A young girl from Masonga Eric Wheater

Despite its rich diamond mines, Sierra Leone's development has been challenged by political instability since independence in 1961. Throughout the 1990s it was gripped by a savage civil war between the government and Revolutionary United Front. Freetown, pumped full of international aid, has a happy-go-lucky and vibrant atmosphere and Freetown Peninsula has some of west Africa's most magical beaches. In the interior are lush landscapes, jungle and reserves abundant with wildlife.

BEST TIME TO VISIT
November to April, but in the future when stability is restored

ESSENTIAL EXPERIENCES
Splashing and partying at the stunning beaches – brilliant white sand backed by thick jungle

Admiring spectacular views from Mt Bintumani, West Africa's highest point

Reflecting on history at Freetown's famous 500-year-old cotton tree, under which slaves were sold until 1787

Diving and snorkelling in the crystal waters near Banana Islands

Spotting elephants, pygmy hippos and rare bongo antelopes at Outamba-Kilimi National Park

Being charmed by Sierra Leone's wonderfully friendly people

GETTING UNDER THE SKIN
Read *Blood Diamonds: Tracing the Deadly Path of the World's Most Precious Stones* by Greg Campbell

Listen to *A Chapter of Roots* by Sierra Leonean singer/songwriter Freddy Shabaka, or the Brooders playing a jammin' mix of roots, rock and reggae

Watch the disturbing and moving documentary, *Cry Freetown*, filmed by award-winning local cameraman Sorius Samura after the battle of 1999

Eat groundnut stew (meat and ground-peanut stew); pepper soup; steamed yam; and roasted corn

Drink light and fruity *poyo* (palm wine) and local Star beer

IN A WORD
Which way to the beach?

TRADEMARKS
Gem smugglers; hot and humid equatorial weather; diamond mines; colourful markets; a country with indomitable spirit recovering from civil war; chaotic traffic jams; beach, beach and more beach; rare wildlife; okra-based meals

SURPRISES
At a Sierra Leone market you can buy anything, from enormous saucepans to always-handy monkey skulls

The Mende and Tenne operate a system of secret societies responsible for maintaining culture and tradition. If you see young children with their faces painted white, you'll know that they're in the process of being initiated. Masks are an important feature of some groups' ceremonies and are highly prized (copies are made for tourists, but local cloth is often a better buy).

— Lonely Planet's *Africa on a Shoestring*

GUINEA

Kabala

Kambia

Makeni

Kono (Koidu-Sefadu)

Lungi
Lunsar
Freetown

Kailahun

Shenga
Bo
Kenema

Bonthe

ATLANTIC OCEAN

LIBERIA

Sulima

MAP REF: M,18

2. The tactile walls of Esplanade – Theatres on the Bay, dubbed 'the durians' by locals Glenn Beanland

3. Impassive mannequins remain unfazed by hefty pricetags on Orchard Road, Singapore's shopping nirvana Glenn Beanland

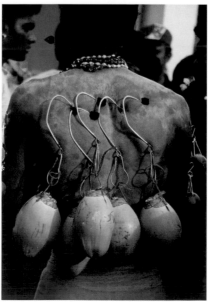

4. Body-piercing made even more painful by dangling pawpaws at the Thaipusam Festival Susan Storm

5. A modern Singaporean girl checks her look before taking on the busy streets Tom Cockrem

1. Behind the scenes at a *wayang kulit* (shadow play) puppet show which usually re-tells tales from the Hindu epic the *Ramayana* Glenn Beanland

Many people (including a fair few Singaporeans) dismiss the island-city of Singapore as the McDonald's of Southeast Asia – blandly efficient and safe, boringly unadventurous and overwhelmingly corporate. It's true that Singapore has traded in its steamy rickshaw image for towers of concrete and glass, but a sultry heart still beats beneath the big-city surface. This is an undeniably Asian city with a unique mix of Chinese, Malay and Indian traditions, where fortune tellers, calligraphers and temple worshippers are still a part of everyday life.

BEST TIME TO VISIT
February to October, during the dry season

ESSENTIAL EXPERIENCES
Discovering the region's arts and culture at the Asian Civilisations Museum

Exploring Little India – on Sunday evening it's like the set of a Bollywood musical

Tucking into a bowl of noodles or melting over a bowl of curry at a hawker-style food centre

Watching the fabulously glitzy drag diva cabaret shows at the Boom Boom Room

Taking in the sky-high views on the cable-car ride to the granddaddy of amusement parks, Sentosa Island

Eyeballing beasties at Singapore's excellent zoo, or after dark on the Night Safari

GETTING UNDER THE SKIN
Read *Foreign Bodies* and *Mammon Inc* by Hwee Hwee Tan – two modern morality tales about Singaporean youth. Suchen Christine Lim's *Fistful of Colours* captures the tensions between modern and traditional Singapore

Listen to Chinese opera, or local bands the Boredphucks and Force Vomit

Watch Eric Phoo's *Mee Pok Man*, internationally acclaimed as a truly Singaporean film, and Tay Teck Lock's *Money No Enough*, which was a huge local box office hit

Eat Hainanese chicken-rice (Singapore's signature dish) or *kaya* toast (toast with egg and coconut topping)

Drink Tiger beer or a healing herbal tea in Chinatown

IN A WORD
Kiasu ('afraid to lose' – Singaporeans are very competitive)

TRADEMARKS
Orchard Road shops; Changi airport; hawker-stall food; litter-free streets; Singapore Slings at Raffles Hotel; efficient public transport; Lee Kuan Yew; rogue traders; Changi Prison; Hello Kitty

SURPRISES
It's not all concrete – gardens and greenery are everywhere; despite their modern manners, many Singaporeans are deeply religious and superstitious

Feng shui, the Chinese technique of manipulating or judging the environment, dictates much of what you see in Singapore – from the five-fingered shape of the Suntec City mall to the angle of the Hyatt Regency Hotel's front doors. Pronounced 'fung shway', and literally meaning 'wind-water', the art of geomancy taps into unseen currents that swirl around the surface of the earth and are caused by dragons that sleep beneath the ground.

– Lonely Planet's *Singapore*

6. Bright lights and lanterns illuminate North Bridge Road to celebrate Chinese New Year Richard l'Anson

MALAYSIA

Woodlands

Ji Kayu

Changi

Jurong

Queenstown

Bedok

Singapore

Jurong

Strait of Singapore

Strait of Singapore

Southern Islands

MAP REF: N,31

2. Bojnice Castle presides over the fairytale township
Richard Nebeský

3. Caught wearing the same outfit, Slovak girls dance up a storm Martin Moos

4. Velvet locomotion – a train speeds towards the High Tatra Mountains Martin Moos

5. A restored façade in Bardejov, a township that time-capsules Gothic and Renaissance architecture Richard Nebeský

1. A Slovakian-style boutique hotel – a gypsy caravan rests near Spiš Mark Daffey

6. Cheap downhill thrills – skiing in the Low Tatras attracts cash-strapped Western Europeans Richard Nebeský

Slovakia, the Czech Republic's less glamorous partner, emerged dishevelled and sleepy after the 'Velvet Revolution' of 1989. Although it's now holding its own in a rebuilding Eastern bloc, there's a refreshing absence of Prague-style glitz and glamour. It is a land of real spirit, where folk traditions have survived the domination of foreign rulers and where a plethora of castles and chateaux pay testament to untold wars and civil conflicts. Strike up a conversation at a bar and you'll find an intelligent, engaging and friendly person at the other end.

BEST TIME TO VISIT
May to June (for sunny weather) – or before Bratislava becomes sold as 'the new Prague'

ESSENTIAL EXPERIENCES
Roaming the crumbling ruins of Spiš, Slovakia's largest castle

Discovering Levoca, a medieval walled town and a treasure-chest of Renaissance architecture

Wandering, wining and dining in the bustling, renovated old town of Bratislava

Luxuriating in the spa at Bardejovské Kúpele after exploring the *skansen* (open-air museum) in the spa's foothills

Exploring the caves of Slovak Karst

Following the crowd to Bojnice, the most visited chateau in Slovakia

GETTING UNDER THE SKIN
Read the brilliant village tales of Bozena Slancikova and the poetry of Ivan Krasko

Listen to Dezider Kardoš's second symphony, *Hero's Ballad*, and Jana Kirschner

Watch seminal vampire chiller *Nosferatu*, set in spooky Orava Castle

Eat *bryndzové halušky* (small potato dumplings, similar to Italian gnocchi, topped with sheep's cheese and a sprinkling of fried bacon bits) and cakes that would be three times the price in a Viennese cake shop

Drink homemade *slivovice* (plum brandy) and Zlatý Ba ant (Golden Pheasant beer) made in Hurbanovo

IN A WORD
Ahoj (hello)

TRADEMARKS
The poor sister of the Czech Republic; Stalinist architecture; high-rise apartment blocks; farmers; villages; mountains

SURPRISES
The largest meteor ever to hit Europe landed near the East Slovakian town of Zboj in 1866, its flight was visible from the High Tatras, over 200km away

For the majority of foreign tourists, the High Tatra mountains are Slovakia's biggest attraction – and with a splendidly jagged and snow-patched central massif rising abruptly out of a green plain, it's easy to see why. It's also Slovakia's most diverse wildlife area – home to brown bears, wolves, lynxes and other wild cats, marmots, otters, golden eagles and mink. One animal protected even outside national parks is the chamois, a mountain antelope, which was for a time near extinction but is now making a comeback.

– Lonely Planet's *Czech and Slovak Republics*

MAP REF: H,22

2. Fierce dancers dressed as Kurent, a mythical figure said to chase away winter and usher in spring, Kurentovanje festival, Ptuj Martin Moos

3. A lantern casts a stark shadow against a bright wall in Maribor Martin Moos

4. Ljubljana's 17th-century Franciscan Church of the Annunciation rises like a wedding cake above the Triple Bridge Neil Wilson

5. Ghostly church spires in the twilight, Ljubljana Damien Simonis

1. Slovenia welcomes Pope John Paul II Bojan Brecelj

It's a tiny place, about half the size of Switzerland, and numbers less than two million people, but Slovenia (Slovenija) is blessed with rich resources and natural good looks. Persistently peaceful, Slovenia has been doing just fine since breaking from Yugoslavia, and its many delights belie its small stature: the Venetian harbour towns on the Adriatic coast and the *Sound of Music* scenery of the Julian Alps, the concert halls of Ljubljana and the countless opportunities for adventure in its national parks. And just to place it for you, Slovenia is bordered by Italy, Austria, Hungary, Croatia and the Adriatic Sea.

BEST TIME TO VISIT
May to September for summer sun

ESSENTIAL EXPERIENCES
White-water rafting on the turquoise rapids of the Soča River
Daydreaming while boating on the fairytale Lake Bled
Marvelling at the world-renowned Lipizzaner horses strutting their stuff at Lipica
Attempting to conquer the dramatic Predjama Castle
Partying Slovenia-style at the Kurentovanje festival in Ptuj

GETTING UNDER THE SKIN
Read *Questions about Slovenia* by Matja Chvatal – this explains the differences between Slovenia, Slovakia and Slavonia, describes what *koline* (pig-slaughters) are, and pinpoints the things that make Slovenes laugh. *Slovenia: My Country* by Joco nidarši č is a heartfelt but never cloying paean to the photographer's homeland

Listen to anything by Vita Mavric – a classic Slovene chanteuse, or *Pulover Ljubezni – Jumper of Love* by Terra Folk, modern Slovene folk music

Watch Maja Weiss's *Varuh Meje*, which follows the journey of three young women on a break from college who take a perilous journey down the Kolpa River, crossing national, political, and sexual boundaries

Eat *likrofi* – ravioli of cheese, bacon and chives; *gibanica* – a rich dessert consisting of layers of flaky pastry with fruit, nut, cheese and poppy-seed filling topped off with cream

Drink *ganje* – a strong brandy or *eau de vie* distilled from a variety of fruits but most commonly apples, plums and cherries. *Zlata Radgonska Penina* is an excellent sparkling wine based on Chardonnay and Beli Pinot

IN A WORD
Dober dan (good day/hello)

TRADEMARKS
Fairytale castles; virgin forests; cobalt-blue rivers; adventure-mad locals

SURPRISES
Slovenia is NOT Slovakia; this tiny country has produced several world ski champions; and it has been making high-quality wine since the time of the Romans

Slovenia has been dubbed a lot of things since independence from Yugoslavia in 1991 – 'Europe in Miniature', 'The Sunny Side of the Alps', 'The Green Piece of Europe' – and, though they may sound like blurbs, they're all true.

– Lonely Planet's *Slovenia*

6. A man steers a boat through the gentle waters of Lake Bled, Gorenjska Jon Davison

MAP REF: H,21

2. A spear-fisherman prepares to strike off Sikaiana Atoll
Simon Foale

3. Mother and child leave their stilted, thatched home on Ghizo Island Peter Hendrie

1. Floating in a dugout canoe, a group of carefree local boys enjoy paddling near Ghizo Island   Peter Hendrie

The Solomons was once the world's most dangerous place – cannibalism, head-hunting and warfare were rife, and foreign visitors were usually killed upon making landfall. Today the islanders are laid-back and friendly, and they inhabit a stunning archipelago of coral atolls, lagoons and reefs that sees almost no tourists. Ancient arts are still practised and WWII wreckage is strewn across the country. Pristine beaches give way to dense tropical jungle, while people till their village gardens the way they have for thousands of years.

BEST TIME TO VISIT
July to November (the drier season)

ESSENTIAL EXPERIENCES
Riding a boat across Marovo Lagoon

Chillin' on Uepi Island for a few days and snorkelling in the lagoon

Seeing Malaita's lagoons where artificial islands support hundreds of villagers

Visiting skull caves – macabre and fascinating shrines to ancestor worship

Watching a shiver of reef-sharks hunting fish in a frenzy of boiling water

Diving over the WWII wreckage from the famous Battle of Guadalcanal

GETTING UNDER THE SKIN
Read *Ples Bilong Iumi – The Solomon Islands, the Past Four Thousand Years* by Sam Alasia et al. *Lightning Meets the West Wind – The Malaita Massacre* by Keesing & Corris relates the story of a district officer's killing by Kaiwo tribesmen in 1927.

Watch Terrence Malick's *The Thin Red Line*, a grim war film based on James Jones' 1963 novel about the WWII battle for Guadalcanal

Eat crayfish and coconuts, mangoes and other tropical fruits (the islanders were eating sweet potatoes long before it was fashionable)

Drink Honiara's own Solbrew beer – 'lets get fresh!'

IN A WORD
Apinun! (good afternoon)

TRADEMARKS
Spear-fishing from outrigger canoes; deep-sea fishing; snorkelling and scuba diving; fresh fish at Honiara market; tide shifts under stilt-house villages; getting around by boat; incredible friendliness

SURPRISES
Great T-shirt art, skull caves and ossuaries; blonde-haired Melanesians; the sound of falling coconuts; weird wares in trade stores; night-time coconut-crab spotting; racing flying fish in trade boats; *very* early morning mass; crowds gathering at grass airstrips

The notorious head-hunter Ingava ruled from a coral-walled fortress on Nusa Roviana until it was destroyed in 1892. His tribe had a dog, Tiola, as its totem and worshipped at a rock carved in its likeness before going head-hunting. Remains of the Dog Rock are still there. The fortress was up to 30m wide, and 500m of the coral walls still remain. There's a giant's cave nearby.

– Lonely Planet's *South Pacific*

4. A Malaita Islander plays a traditional bamboo panpipe   Peter Hendrie

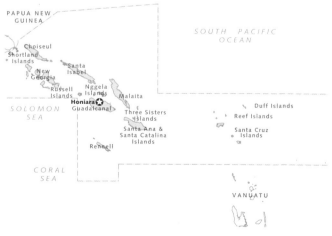

MAP REF: P.36

2. Two local boys chat with Australian troops at a newly constructed windmill Claver Carroll

3. An overloaded mule carts brushwood into town Richard Mills

1. A group of young men, pleased to see their local watering hole start trading for the day   Claver Carroll

Situated in the Horn of Africa, Somalia has had a long history of internal conflict that continues to this day. It also has some of the longest beaches that Africa has to offer, plateaus and mountains, a continuously hot climate and a rich nomadic culture. The friendly people, often dressed in long, flowing robes, are regal and striking. Despite a high rate of criminal activity, there is a growing sense of hope for a more peaceful future.

BEST TIME TO VISIT
From July to August or from January to February for the dry season

ESSENTIAL EXPERIENCES
Buying henna and frankincense on the streets of Mogadishu
Observing the rich culture in Hargeisa
Splashing in the reportedly shark-free waters of Gezira beach
Visiting the tannery at Brava
Journeying in the beautiful mountains from Hargeisa to Berbera
Watching herders bringing their livestock to the watering hole at Liboi
Staying right on the beach in the old Arab town of Merca
Wandering amongst the friendly people of Berbera

GETTING UNDER THE SKIN
Read *Aman: The Story of a Somali Girl* by Janice Boddy and Virginia Lee Barnes, a first-person account of the story of a Somalian girl's life

Listen to *Waaberi 'New Dawn'* by Maryam Mursal and the Waaberi ensemble – gentle singing and sounds from one of Somalia's greatest treasures

Watch *Black Hawk Down* by Ridley Scott, an account of the flawed events surrounding a US military combat mission in Somalia

Eat a breakfast of fried onions and sheep liver with bread, *baasto* (spaghetti) or rice with sauce, or *soor* (porridge made from sorghum)

Drink fresh mango or papaya juice

IN A WORD
Ma nabad baa? (greeting; literally 'Is it peace?')

TRADEMARKS
A large rural population; goats and camels; lively teahouses; tasty, traditional food; women with hennaed hands and feet; wide valleys; street traders; chewing *khat*; tropical fruit; beautiful old Arab towns; colourful robes; magnificent sunsets

SURPRISES
Camel trading at the livestock market; the satin-draped green Sheik Madar's tomb in Hargeisa; goat herds on the runway at Mogadishu airport

Founded in the 10th century AD by Arab immigrants from the Persian Gulf, Mogadishu had its heydey in the 13th century. It was then that the mosque of Fakr al Din and the minaret of the Great Mosque were built. The city's wealth was based on trade across the Indian Ocean with Persia, India and China, which is what attracted the Portuguese during the 16th century.

— Lonely Planet's *Africa on a shoestring*

4. Rocking out the crustaceans – musical men use large shells as instruments   Claver Carroll

MAP REF: M,25

2. A family of elephants gather at a water hole Richard I'Anson

3. Catching the curl at Noordhoek, one of Cape Town's best surfing beaches Paul Kennedy

4. A Zulu woman flaunts her traditional earplugs and elaborate headress, which indicates her marital status Mitch Reardon

5. A Zulu chief proffers visitors to his village a pipe Richard I'Anson

1. Rhino on the storm – a white rhino examines the horizon at Hluhuwe-Umfolozi National Park   Mitch Reardon

6. Sunsets over the quiver trees on the plains of South Africa   Carol Polich

A huge variety of landscapes, climates and cultures are crammed into Africa's southern tip – there are 11 official languages, for a start. It's a truly spectacular, friendly and rewarding place for all visitors, offering something for even the most experienced of travellers. You can find yourself sipping a superb wine on majestic Table Mountain, catching a perfect wave on an unspoilt subtropical beach, tracking a lion on an African safari, or exploring for diamonds in the vast flat expanses of Kimberley.

BEST TIME TO VISIT
February and March for warm, sunny weather

ESSENTIAL EXPERIENCES
The stunning views from the top of Table Mountain, overlooking the 'fairest cape' of them all

Learning to surf in the warm waters of KwaZulu-Natal

Touring along the spectacular garden route to go whale-watching in Hermanus

Visiting the 'Big Hole' diamond mine in Kimberley

Exploring the spectacular Drakensberg Mountains

GETTING UNDER THE SKIN
Read Nelson Mandela's autobiography, *Long Walk to Freedom*. A truly compelling book, and a compulsory read of the epic life story of the man who won freedom for his people

Listen to the South African national anthem, a uniting chant containing words from 4 of the 11 official languages

Watch *Cry Freedom*, Richard Attenborough's powerful film detailing the moving story of black activist Steve Biko, or *Egoli*, the most popular soap opera showing a modern, multicultural and vibrant South Africa

Eat a *braai* (barbecue), with local meats including *boerewors* (hearty farmers sausage). *Biltong* (dried and cured meat) is also a favourite throughout the country

Drink some of the best wines in the world from the Cape Winelands, or the local brew, Castle Lager

IN A WORD
Howzit…

TRADEMARKS
Cape Town; rugby Springboks; Biltong; Table Mountain; *braai*; beaches; diamond and gold mines; the township of Soweto; Kruger National Park; Nelson Mandela

SURPRISES
With such climatic diversity, it's guaranteed to be summer somewhere in South Africa all year round; the Kruger National Park has the greatest diversity of animals in the whole of Africa, and is the size of Wales

South Africa is one of the world's best kept secrets, and is among the most beautiful, amazing and unique countries you could wish to visit. It has a history that can only be described as operatic in its tragedy, and yet a triumphant spirit prevails. There is no denying that poverty, violence and AIDS are all part and parcel of the past and future of South Africa, but the sense of pride across all communities is almost tangible. The overwhelming friendliness of the people is probably the most vivid memory that you'll take home.

– Lonely Planet's South Africa, Lesotho & Swaziland

MAP REF: S,22

2. Symbolic billboards of bulls guard the hillside Damien Simonis

3. A detail of Galathea's tower, part of the Teatre-Museu Dalí, Figueres Martin Lladó

4. Joan Miró's vibrant *Dona i Ocell* sculpture, housed at the Parc Joan Miró in Barcelona Damien Simonis

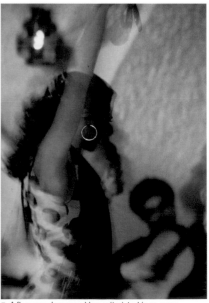

5. A flamenco dancer and her guitarist whip up some nightclub action Barbara Van Zanten

1. This picturesque clifftop bell tower resides at Guadalest in the Alicante region David Tomlinson

6. Appreciative art lovers flock to the Museo del Prado Guy Moberly

Spain has been the home of some of the world's great artists and has museums and galleries to match. In the cities, narrow twisting old streets suddenly open out to views of daring modern architecture, while spit-and-sawdust bars serving wine from the barrel rub shoulders with blaring, glaring discos. There are endless tracts of wild and crinkled sierra to explore, as well as some spectacularly rugged stretches of coast. Culturally, the country is littered with superb old buildings, from Roman aqueducts to Gothic cathedrals, and almost every second village has a medieval castle.

BEST TIME TO VISIT
May, June and September

ESSENTIAL EXPERIENCES
Exploring the amazing, whimsical architecture of Gaudí's Parc Güell in Barcelona

Bargain-hunting in El Rastro flea market in Madrid

Partying through the night during Valencia's Las Fallas

Pouring over the fascinating Romanesque relics of medieval Aragón at Huesca and San Juan de la Peña

Visiting the wonderful Museo Guggenheim in Bilbao

Sipping summertime *cañas* (beers) and enjoying the magnificent views to the Sierra de Guadarrama at Las Vistillas

Driving around and getting lost in the alpine countryside of the Navarran Pyrenees

Walking the Camino de Santiago to Santiago de Compostela

GETTING UNDER THE SKIN
Read the 17th-century novel *Don Quijote de la Mancha* by Miguel de Cervantes, or *For Whom the Bell Tolls*, a terse tale of civil war by Ernest Hemingway

Listen to Andrés Segovia, who established classical guitar as a genre, or flamenco guitarist Paco de Lucia

Watch Pedro Almodóvar's *Todo Sobre Mi Madre* (All About My Mother), which portrays the lives of an improbable collection of women

Eat home-cooked paella, or *fabada asturiana* (a heavy white-bean–based stew)

Drink red wine from the Ribera del Duero region or a Voll Damm beer

IN A WORD
Buenos días (good day)

TRADEMARKS
Flamenco; bull-fighting; drunken Brits on Ibiza; Picasso; football; the Spanish Inquisition; the Running of the Bulls festival

SURPRISES
In Catalunya devil and dragon figures run through the streets spitting fireworks at crowds during the *correfoc* (fire-running). Leading *gaiteros* (bagpipers) are heroes in Galicia

Especially around the Fiestas de San Isidro, the chulapos and manolas of Madrid come out of the woodwork. The gents dress in their traditional short jackets and berets and the women in mantones de Manila, and put their best feet forward in a lively chotis. What is all this? The mantón de Manila *is an embroidered silk shawl, which few people now wear, except during fiestas. The* chotis *is an oldtime working-class dance not unlike a polka.*

— Lonely Planet's *Spain*

MAP REF: I,19

2. Vibrant water lilies in bloom outside Kandy Anders Blomqvist

3. A novice monk pauses from his daily chores for a smiling snap Dallas Stribley

4. Balancing act – the stilt-fishermen of Weligama cast their lines into the perilously high tide Dallas Stribley

Marco Polo dubbed Sri Lanka the finest island in the world, and visitors continue to be seduced by the heavy warm air, the endless rich green foliage, the luxuriant swirls of the Sinhalese alphabet, the multicoloured Buddhist flags, and the variety of saris, fruit, jewellery and spices on sale in the markets. Sri Lankan festivals announce themselves with sparkling lights strung over town clock towers and bazaar alleys.

BEST TIME TO VISIT
December to March (the driest time of the year) – or around the 7th century, to flog your wares to the Arab traders.

ESSENTIAL EXPERIENCES
Sharing the first rays of the morning sun with pilgrims at the summit of Adam's Peak

Lazing the day away on the beach in sleepy Mirissa

Wandering through tea plantations in the hills around Nuwara Eliya

Getting up close to the young elephants at Pinnewala Elephant Orphanage

Climbing the spectacular rock fortress of Sigiriya

Experiencing a *puja* (offering of prayer) at the Temple of the Tooth in Kandy

Attempting to spot an elusive leopard in Yala West National Park

GETTING UNDER THE SKIN
Read Michael Ondaatje's *Running in the Family*, a humorous account of returning to Sri Lanka after growing up there in the 1940s and '50s

Listen to www.labaila.com, web-streamed Sri Lankan radio from Los Angeles

Watch Prasanna Vithanage's *Death on a Full Moon Day*, a film about a father who refuses to accept the death of his soldier son

Eat coconut *sambol*, a hot accompaniment to curry made of grated coconut, chilli and spices

Drink *arrack*, the local spirit, which is usually fermented from coconuts or palm trees

IN A WORD
Ayubowan (may you live long)

TRADEMARKS
Beautiful beaches lined with palm trees; tea plantations; coconuts; friendly, smiling faces, elephants; rice and curry; batik; three-wheelers winding in and out of traffic; good cricketers and enthusiastic supporters; Kandyan dancers

SURPRISES
Buddhist temples that depict images of Hindu gods; serious traffic accidents are rare despite the apparent lack of road rules

The nation stops when Sri Lanka's First Eleven play cricket. Workers take leave from their workplaces for the day or afternoon, transistor radios reveal the score in the corner of the office, crowds gather around television screens in the Singer stores, radios blare on buses with coverage in Sinhala, Tamil and English. Almost everyone follows the game, men and women. And if Sri Lanka wins, fire crackers sound around the neighbourhood.

– Lonely Planet's *Sri Lanka*

1. Women engage in the back-breaking harvest of tea near Nuwara Eliya Anders Blomqvist

5. In the early morning light train tracks snake into the capital, Colombo Dallas Stribley

MAP REF: N,28

2. With the Kassala Hills as a stunning backdrop, a camel train progresses through Eastern Sudan
Eric Wheater

3. Majestic Madhi's Tomb, re-built in 1947 to commemorate the nation's greatest Muslim leader Damien Simonis

4. A boy bears grain around the souq, Kassala
Eric Wheater

5. A man re-thatches his home in hope of rain in the dry northern region around Kassala Eric Wheater

6. Two brilliantly dressed girls pose for a portrait against a mud-brick wall Eric Wheater
LEFT 1. A goat-seller shows off one of the herd's finest at a hectic market in Omdurman, Khartoum Eric Wheater

The ancient Egyptians knew Sudan as the Land of Cush – a source of ivory, gold, spices and incense. It was power and the promise of great hidden treasures that made Sudan – the largest country in Africa – the object of invasion and exploration for much of its long and tumultuous history. This land that stretches from the Sahara to the Red Sea to the swamps of the Sudd, is a diverse and fascinating melange. Yet today much of it remains unexplored – one of the last frontiers of travel.

BEST TIME TO VISIT
November to March (the dry season)

ESSENTIAL EXPERIENCES
Riding the ferris wheel in Khartoum, from where you can see the two Niles, Blue and White, meet and meld after their lengthy journeys from the African hinterland

Visiting the pyramids and hieroglyphs of Meroe, all that remains of Africa's southern-most pharaohs

Losing yourself in the atmospheric *souqs* (markets) and camel markets of Omdurman

Getting dizzy from the spinning of the whirling dervishes of Halgt Zikr

Wandering the melancholy ruins of abandoned Suakin, once a thriving Red Sea port full of coral houses

GETTING UNDER THE SKIN
Read Tayeb Salih's *Season of Migration to the North*, a compelling tale of a Sudanese man torn between the West and his homeland; or *Emma's War* by Deborah Scroggins, the true and moving story of a British aid-worker who married a Sudanese warlord

Listen to Abdel Gadir Salim's *Merdoum Kings* – big band arrangements of Sudanese songs

Eat *fuul* (stewed brown beans), *ta'amiya* (the local equivalent of felafel), and fresh Nile perch

Drink *shai* (tea), always served sweet and sometimes with mint, or coffee scented with cardamom and cinnamon

IN A WORD
Tamam (good, well or right)

TRADEMARKS
Bedouin in flowing robes; the untouched beauty of the Red Sea coast, Khartoum, a great city at the confluence of rivers amid the desert; Dinka, Nuer and Nuba tribespeople – tall and proud

SURPRISES
Diverse landscapes and accompanying diverse cultures from the arid north to the lush and mountainous south; overwhelming hospitality – a national point of pride

People, on meeting, always carry out some form of greeting, even if relatively short, and the most common is to enquire if all is tamam *(well). The reply is almost inevitably a beaming smile and a convincing 'tamam!' To an outsider perhaps a little oppressed by the evident difficulties of daily life for most Sudanese, it is testimony to these people's capacity to be satisfied with what life gives, however little it may seem to a Westerner.*

– Lonely Planet's *Egypt & the Sudan*

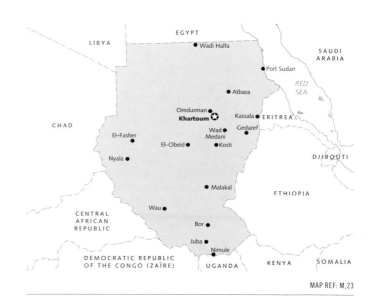

MAP REF: M,23

2. Nervous young dancers prepare for ceremonial dancing to honour the king in Mbabane Richard I'Anson

The smallest country in the southern hemisphere is also one of the most easygoing — laid-back Swazis are more likely to celebrate for fun than demonstrate for reform. A progressive and hands-on attitude towards wildlife preservation has endowed it with a striking bunch of national parks. Black and white rhinos, elephant, and more recently lions, have been reintroduced into the collection of national parks and game reserves. In the rich and vigorous culture of the Swazi people, significant power is vested in the monarchy. The kingdom is highly conservative, and in many ways illiberal, but it works and has popular support.

BEST TIME TO VISIT
June to August

ESSENTIAL EXPERIENCES
Walking around the Malolotja Nature Reserve — one of Africa's most enchanting wilderness areas

Wildlife-watching in the excellent private Mkhaya Game Reserve

Bunking down in a beehive hut in Mlilwane Wildlife Sanctuary

Witnessing the spectacular annual Umhlanga dance and Incwala ceremony in the Ezulwini Valley, Swaziland's royal heartland

Shooting white-water rapids, including a 10m waterfall, on the Usutu River

Shopping for Swazi arts and crafts, including stunning tapestries

GETTING UNDER THE SKIN
Read *The Kingdom of Swaziland* by D Hugh Gillis, a history of the kingdom

Listen to gospel singer France Dlamini

Watch anything by film pioneer Hanson Ngwenya

Eat fantastic seafood — seafood kebabs, seafood curry, grilled trout with almonds…

Drink home-produced beer, often made from sorghum or maize

IN A WORD
Sawubona (hello in Swati; literally 'I see you')

TRADEMARKS
Casinos; sugar cane; speed bumps; lions; rare black rhinos

SURPRISES
Mkhulumnchanti is the name of the Swazis' deity; respect for both the aged and ancestors plays a large part in the complex structure of traditional Swazi society; most Swazis rely at least partly on traditional medicine: there are two types of practitioners, the *inyanga* (usually a man) and the *sangoma* (usually a woman)

The identity of the Swazi nation is partly maintained by a tradition of age-related royal military regiments. These regiments provided the military clout to hold off invaders during the difaqane and have helped to minimise the potentially divisive differences between clans, while emphasising loyalty to the king and nation. Annual rituals such as the important Incwala or 'first fruits' ceremony and Umhlanga (Reed) dance have the same effect of bolstering national identity.

— Lonely Planet's *South Africa, Lesotho & Swaziland*

3. Sun-like floral forms and bold colours dominate local art, Ezulwini Valley Richard I'Anson

4. A *sangoma* (traditional spiritual doctor) fixes his patients with an examining gaze Ariadne Van Zandbergen

5. A Swazi woman sits outside a traditional 'beehive' hut Ariadne Van Zandbergen

Piggs Peak

Mhlume

⚜ **Mbabane**
Lobamba

Siteki   MOZAMBIQUE

Manzini

Mankayane

Big Bend

Hlathikulu

Nhlangano

SOUTH AFRICA

Lavumisa

MAP REF: R.23

6. Women gather for a village meeting amid the austere landscape of Ezulwini Valley Ariadne Van Zandbergen

LEFT 1. Let's go bowling — a hungry Swazi boy drinks his morning porridge from a traditional clay bowl
Ariadne Van Zandbergen

2. A toothy child grins from under a sensible woollen hat
Bo Jansson

3. Flames roar at a Walpurgis bonfire honouring the return of spring, a celebration dating back to the Viking era, Vejbystrand Anders Blomqvist

4. Pale blue light filters over the Bjorkliden ski fields in Norrbotten Christian Aslund

Sweden is a land of contradictions that make an unexpectedly pleasing whole. Starkly beautiful lake and forest landscapes contrast with stylish, modern cities; the country is as famous for its Viking-era sites as it is known for its cutting-edge technology; even the flat, relatively balmy south contrasts with the mountainous, Arctic north. It's a place where you can get away from it all in quiet forests or be right in the thick of things in busy towns.

BEST TIME TO VISIT
Late May to late July if you want sunshine; December to March if you want to ski

ESSENTIAL EXPERIENCES
Drifting around Stockholm and its archipelago by boat

Skiing Dalarna's slopes or watching Vasaloppet, the world's biggest cross-country skiing race

Ambling around the historic town of Lund

Taking advantage of *allemansrätten* (public right to the countryside) and hiking Sweden's superb forest

Exploring the ruins of Visby's chuches

Touring the glassworks of Glasriket (Kingdom of Crystal) in Kalmar

GETTING UNDER THE SKIN
Read Charlotte Rosen Svensson's *Culture shock! Sweden: A Guide to Customs and Etiquette* for an accurate guide to Swedish cultural behaviour

Listen to ABBA, Roxette or Ace of Base, if that's your thing. Or give the Hives, Millencolin or Sami folk-music, known as *yoik*, a spin

Watch anything by Ingmar Bergman, or *Mitt Liv Som Hund* (My Life as a Dog)

Eat a lot of fish and the ubiquitous potato — try *sill och nypotatis* (pickled herring and new potatoes), *pytt i panna* (fried diced potatoes, sausage and onion served with diced beetroot and a fried egg), *kötbullar och potatis* (Swedish meatballs and potatoes), *Janssons frestelse* (baked potato, onion, cream and anchovy dish), and, if you're really brave, *surströmming* (fermented herring, stinky and not for the faint hearted)

Drink *kaffe* (coffee), which the Swedes love and do surprisingly well, but they love their aquavit and their *öl* (beer) even more. Try Absolut vodka, and Spendrups or Pripps beer

IN A WORD
Jättebra! (fantastic!)

TRADEMARKS
Beautiful blondes of both genders; Saabs and Volvos; cheap but impossible-to-assemble furniture; ABBA; Vikings; tennis players; meatballs and schnapps; sexually liberated socialists; Ericsson; skiing

SURPRISES
Not all Swedes are blonde; Sweden is not completely covered in snow in winter; alcohol can only be bought through the state-run alcohol retailing monopoly, Systembolaget; in summer it is hot enough to swim

The city of Stockholm might have been arranged by some divine hand to serve as a canvas for the rarefied northern European light. Whether it's the coldest wash of blue-white in winter or the amber hues of an autumn afternoon, light is the defining element of the city.

1. The peak of a farmhouse roof peers over a bright yellow field on the Kulla Peninsula Anders Blomqvist

5. Cows kick back in comfort in rural Vejbystrand Anders Blomqvist

MAP REF: E,21

2. Birch trees bloom with late-autumn colour in the Graubünden countryside Martin Moos

3. Half-timbered façades distinguish the rustic architecture of Kloster St Georgen in the preserved township of Stein am Rhein Martin Moos

4. Icono-tastic – Switzerland's most photographed mountain, the Matterhorn, reflected in a tranquil lake Gareth McCormack

1. Youngsters make the most of a wintery day by skating on frozen Lake Zürich Martin Moos

It's not much of a problem finding scenes of devastating beauty in Switzerland. The clichés are all here: soaring peaks, tumbling waterfalls, sparkling lakes, quaint rural houses and, of course, cows grazing contentedly in their verdant Alpine meadows. Towns and cities offer picture-perfect medieval centres and colourful parades and festivals. Trains wind through the mountains and, to complete this tourist fairytale, everything runs, well, like clockwork.

BEST TIME TO VISIT
Anytime

ESSENTIAL EXPERIENCES
Getting in amongst it in the Alps — by train, funicular, cable car or postal bus, or on foot, skis, snowshoes or dog sled

Relaxing in a centuries-old Roman spa

Wine tasting inside a glacier atop Klein Matterhorn

Rising above it in a hot-air balloon

Following Lord Byron's footsteps through Château Chillon

Sleeping in the straw of a farmer's empty barn in summer

GETTING UNDER THE SKIN
Read Johanna Spyri's *Heidi* – the classic children's story of an orphan girl living in the Swiss Alps, and Anita Brookner's *Hotel du Lac* – a novel centred on a group of out-of-season hotel guests around Lake Geneva

Listen to Appenzeller Echo – a traditional Swiss group, featuring yodelling and Alphorn, or Yello – groundbreaking '80s electronica

Watch Alain Tanner's *Messidor* – a grim feminist road-movie (think *Thelma & Louise* with Alps) or Krzysztof Kieslowski's *Three Colours: Red* – the story of a relationship between a model and a judge, set in Geneva

Eat *rösti* (fried, shredded potatoes) and chocolate

Drink Rivella (lactose-based soft drink) or absinthe (wormwood grows in the Val de Travers)

IN A WORD
Röstigraben (literally '*rösti* trench'); refers to the cultural divide between German- and French-speaking Switzerland

TRADEMARKS
Clocks; banks; cows; mountains; edelweiss; fondue; blondes; Swiss Army knives; Matterhorn; mercenaries

SURPRISES
Diverse architecture (La Chaux-de-Fonds is Le Corbusier's home town); Valais cow fights; snow golf

Walking around St Moritz Dorf is like gate-crashing an F Scott Fitzgerald dinner party – the Jazz Age improvising around the same old tune after all these years… Whether you enjoy this show of wealth could hinge on your reading habits. Fans of PG Wodehouse will find 3D versions of their favourite characters, but students of Das Kapital may be less than amused.

– Lonely Planet's *Switzerland*

MAP REF: H,21

5. On the way up – in January Château d'Oex hosts its annual hot-air balloon festival Mark Honan

2. A local shepherd girl tends her flock near the Phoenician temple of Amrit Wayne Walton

3. Tea for two brewed fresh and sweet in the Souq al-Hamidiyya, Damascus John Elk III

4. Reverential worshippers pray at Sayyida Ruqayya Mosque, Damascus Clint Lucas

5. Two smiling friends reunited in the walled city of Tartus Wayne Walton

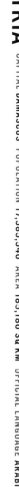

Syria's location at a geographical crossroads has resulted in a history that is rich and varied. From the ancient cities of Alexander the Great and the Romans, to the castles of the Crusaders and the bustle of modern-day Damascus and Aleppo, Syria is truly unique. Full of hidden treasures and surprisingly easy to get around, Syria is a gem for travellers looking to get off the beaten track and go somewhere on a budget.

BEST TIME TO VISIT
March to May (spring)

ESSENTIAL EXPERIENCES
Experiencing the sun setting over the ruins of Palmyra, an ancient Roman city in a desert oasis

Taking in the sweeping views from the impregnable battlements of Crac des Chevaliers

Haggling for authentic Bedouin jewellery in Aleppo's Ottoman-era souk

Visiting the early Christian monastery where Simeon the Stylite perched on a pillar for 32 years

Escaping the bustle of Damascus' streets to the tranquil porticos of the Umayyad Mosque

Catching a performance at Bosra's superbly preserved Roman theatre

GETTING UNDER THE SKIN
Read Agatha Christie's *Come Tell Me How You Live* – a light-hearted picture of archaeology and life in the desert in the mid-20th century

Listen to Farid al-Atrache – the Arabic Sinatra, a famous crooner of the 1940s and '50s – or George Wasouf, the country's biggest pop export

Watch *Dreams of the City*, an evocative fictional study of Damascus, and *The Nights of the Jackal*, an engrossing study of the impacts of war and westernisation on a family in a small Syrian village

Eat *mahalabiyeh* – a dessert similar to a blancmange, laced with orange-blossom essence, almonds and pistachios

Drink *chai* (tea), served in small glasses and incredibly sweet

IN A WORD
Marhaba (hello)

TRADEMARKS
Call to prayer; hair-raising taxi rides; men in *galibeyahs*; women in *abayas*; Carlos the Jackal; ancient ruins; posters of the president

SURPRISES
Syria has the oldest continually occupied cities in the world; families with 10 children or more get free public transport for life; vintage American cars in good condition fill the streets

Even today it is easy to imagine yourself in the era of Burton, when the West was first getting to discover the ancient East. Many of Syria's amazing sights are visited by far more sheep than people, and there is a definite Indiana Jones quality to hitching a ride to some half-uncovered temple poking from the undergrowth on some far removed hillside. This is not going to last.

– Lonely Planet's *Syria*

1. Camel guides await visitors to Palmyra, an excavated city dating back to the 2nd century AD John Elk III

6. Impressively atop a plateau, the old Arab fort of Qala'at ash Shmemis dominates the surrounding plains
Nick Tapsell

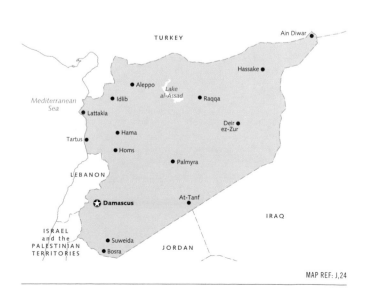

MAP REF: J,24

381

2. Children dive from a roof into an idyllic lagoon on Tahiti Paul Kennedy

3. Palms and parishioners – the church dominates island life on Fakarava Atoll Jean-Bernard Carillet

4. Displaying traditional *tatau* (tatoo) patterns, which pre-date Christian colonisation Gary Steer

5. A young boogie-boarder rides the wave of popularity that is making body boarding the rage throughout Polynesia Paul Kennedy

LEFT 1. Young dancers preparing to dance a welcome to disembarking visitors at Pape'ete harbour Tony Wheeler

Ever since French explorers landed on the island in the 18th century, Tahiti has almost singularly represented the tropical-paradise myth for Europeans. It's French Polynesia's biggest, most famous and historically interesting island, but the glossy pictures in travel agents' windows are almost certainly of other unspoilt French Polynesian islands. People come to French Polynesia to live it up in stylish resorts, scuba dive in lagoons teeming with tropical fish, gorge on the unique mix of French and Polynesian cuisine and, basically, experience a little French chic mixed with South Pacific charm.

BEST TIME TO VISIT
The drier, cooler months from June to October, or in July for the *Heiva i Tahiti* festivities

ESSENTIAL EXPERIENCES
Approaching the impossibly beautiful, rugged coastline of the Marquesas under sail

Gazing at the amazing *tiki* and other archaeological artefacts at Hiva Oa

Snorkelling the gorgeous lagoon at Bora Bora

Partying in Pape'ete

Daydreaming on Mo'orea, an accessible yet still traditional island

Browsing and bargaining at Marché du Pape'ete on a busy Sunday

GETTING UNDER THE SKIN
Read *The Marriage of Loti*, by Pierre Loti, a romance that reinforced the romantic myth of Tahiti.

Listen to *Echo Des Iles Tuamotu Et De Bora Bora*, an authentic slice of Paumotu music by Marie Mariteragi.

Watch the 1962 remake of *Mutiny on the Bounty*, starring Marlon Brando as Christian – much of this film was shot in Tahiti.

Eat from *les roulottes*, the cheap roadside snack bars.

Drink a local Maitai, a distinctively Polynesian take on the cocktail (there's a hefty wallop of coconut liqueur in every drink).

IN A WORD
Aita pe'a pe'a (no problems)

TRADEMARKS
Paul Gauguin's depictions of island beauty; green mountains leaping from sapphire lagoons; surfing championships; *tiki* ornaments hanging over every dashboard; colourful *pareu* (fabric) worn by men and women; lascivious dancing that outraged missionaries

SURPRISES
Even the 'always-smiling' Tahitians get the 'blues' (a mood they call *fiu*), when they can seem distant or incommunicative

It's common to speak of Tahiti as if it were the whole colony; in fact it is merely the largest island, the site of the capital (Pape'ete) and the only international airport (Faa'a).

– Lonely Planet's *South Pacific*

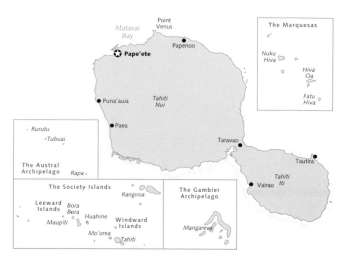

MAP REF: Q,4

2. Trainspotting in Taipei – the MRT (Mass Rapid Transit) speeds over gridlocked traffic Martin Moos

3. A brief hike from Tienhsiang leads to a stunning pagoda in Taroko Gorge Martin Moos

4. Young girls about to dance in the Double 10th Day parades, Taipei Alain Evrard

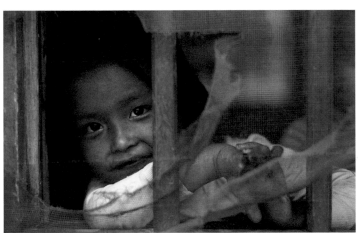

5. A child practises people-watching through a torn mesh screen Eric Wheater

6. Scootering around town, a mother and child ride Taiwan's favourite metropolitan transport Martin Moos

LEFT 1. A peaceful elderly man completes a Buddhist ceremony in Tainan, a bastion of traditional culture Martin Moos

Taiwan is a modern industrialised megalopolis clinging to the fringes of an ancient culture; a string of teeming cities at the foot of a glorious mountain range. It's traditional noodles from a 7-Eleven, aboriginal tribes in miniskirts and a day of temple rituals followed by waterslide rides. If you step outside chaotic Taipei, you'll discover why Taiwan is known as Ilha Formosa, 'the beautiful island'. Mountain peaks puncture a sea of clouds, slick black volcanic rock wraps the coastlines and waterfalls shroud themselves in mist. Taiwan is a computer-generated Chinese watercolour.

BEST TIME TO VISIT
Autumn weather from September to November is the most pleasant

ESSENTIAL EXPERIENCES
Discovering the finest collection of Chinese artefacts in the world at Taipei's National Palace Museum

Indulging in the pleasures of Tainan, famous for fine weather, wonderful food and a multitude of riotously colourful temples

Being overawed by Toroko Gorge, one of the world's great natural spectacles: sheer limestone and marble cliffs towering over a fast-flowing jade-green river

Taking the spectacular scenic road that winds up the east coast of Taiwan between the mountains and the sea

GETTING UNDER THE SKIN
Read *Harmony in Conflict* by Richard Hartzell, an often-recommended primer for Westerners thinking about living in Taiwan

Listen to Mando-pop, the soothing, soft pop schmaltz with Mandarin lyrics, epitomised by singers S.H.E. and Sun Yan Zi

Watch *Betelnut Beauty* by Lin Cheng-sheng – a raw film dealing with the mean streets of Taipei and the city's second-most notorious occupation (the betelnut vendor)

Eat anything you can find on the mainland, as well as Taiwan's own Fujian-Taiwanese cuisine. The adventurous must try 'stinky tofu': ubiquitous in Taiwanese food stalls

Drink the national brew, Taiwan Beer – it won second prize at the Brewing Industry International Awards 2002, and it's pretty cheap, too

IN A WORD
Wei? (used when answering your mobile phone)

TRADEMARKS
Sabre-rattling with the PRC; English teaching; Chiang Kai-shek; 'made in...'

SURPRISES
Taiwan's aborigines are only 2 per cent of the population. They are most numerous in the mountainous regions in the east of the island, where they still preserve vestiges of their original Australoid culture (with many making a living from tourism).

If you want to understand Taipei, just cross the street. The little green men on the 'walk' lights don't just flash; they're animated, ambling amiably as displays above them count down the seconds until the light changes back to red. As you cross, the street alongside you turns into a river of trucks, buses and cars, and motorscooters too numerous to count. In those last crucial seconds, the little green man goes into double-time. That's Taipei in a nutshell.

—Lonely Planet's *Taiwan*

MAP REF: K,32

385

2. An Afghan woman cooks in a refugee camp Shamil Zhumatov

3. Portrait of a Tajik elder at the Nauruz celebrations near Dushanbe Robert Harding World Imagery

4. This Tajik woman sells traditional pancakes at the market Shamil Zhumatov

5. A man poses in the doorway of a yurt Nevada Wier

6. In the village of Dzharteba, a man carries a sack of flour on a donkey, greeting a cyclist going the opposite way Alexander Demianchuk

LEFT 1. A Tajik family tuck into a typical meal of mutton, tea and bread Robert Harding World Imagery

A Persian-speaking outpost in a predominantly Turkic region, Tajikistan is the odd man out in Central Asia. The country is a patchwork of self-contained valleys and regional contrasts, forged together by Soviet nation-building and shared pride in a Persian cultural heritage that is claimed as the oldest and most influential in the Silk Road region. That Tajikistan was the most artificial of the five Soviet-fashioned Central Asian republics is tragically illustrated by the bloody way it fell apart as soon as it was free of Moscow rule.

BEST TIME TO VISIT
April to June or September to November

ESSENTIAL EXPERIENCES
Driving from Khojand to Dushanbe through a vertical world of towering peaks with jaw-dropping high-altitude lakes and deserts

Hiking in the Fan Mountains

Visiting the turquoise Iskander-Kul lake

Being overwhelmed by the Wakhan Corridor, a remote and beautiful valley peppered with forts, Zoroastrian ruins and spectacular views of the Hindu Kush

Wandering in Istaravshan's backstreets and attending the Tuesday bazaar

GETTING UNDER THE SKIN
Read works by Tajikistan's most popular living writer, Taimur Zulfikarov, or *Kim* by Rudyard Kipling – the story of the Raj during the 19th-century cold war between Russia and Britain in which the region became embroiled

Listen to *Falak*, a popular form of melancholic folk music, often sung *a capella*

Watch *The Beginning and the End* directed by Tajikistan's Sayf Rahim

Eat *Krutob* (a wonderful rural dish of bread, yogurt, onion and coriander in a creamy sauce) or snack on a *nahud sambusa* (chickpea samosa).

Drink the sickly sweet cola and luminous lemonades manufactured in Dushanbe or Khorog

IN A WORD
Assalom u aleykum (peace be with you)

TRADEMARKS
Mountains, civil war, the Silk Road, Persian culture

SURPRISES
Sogdian, the lingua franca of the Silk Road widely spoken in the 8th century, is still heard in the mountain villages of the Zeravshan Valley; most Tajiks are Sunni Muslims, but Pamiri Tajiks of the Gorno-Badakhshan region belong to the Ismaili sect of Shia Islam, and therefore have no formal mosques

Traditional Tajik dress for men includes a heavy, quilted coat (chapan), tied with a sash that also secures a sheathed dagger, and a black embroidered cap (tupi), which is similar to the Uzbek doppilar. Tajik women could almost be identified in the dark, with their long, psychedelically coloured dresses (kurta), matching headscarves (rumol), striped trousers worn under the dress (izor) and bright slippers.

— Lonely Planet's *Central Asia*

MAP REF: I,27

2. A Barabaig girl wears a goatskin garment distinctive of her tribe Ariadne Van Zandbergen

3. A game warden protects the endless plains and diverse wildlife of the Serengeti National Park Dennis Johnson

4. Stocking up on food before a long train journey Greg Elms

5. A Maasai woman wears the multicoloured beaded fan neckwear Ernest Manewal

1. Flamingos are a splash of colour on Lake Magadi Steve Davey

Dig below the heat and dust, and Tanzania will take your breath away – literally if you dare to climb Kilimanjaro. The Great Rift Valley, Ngorongoro Crater, Lake Victoria, the Serengeti and Zanzibar are legendary. Fearless explorers, proud warriors and mighty beasts have roamed across this unassuming land, but history and politics have not always been kind and successive self-serving rulers have left their mark. Crumbling façades reflect the crumbling economy, and today Tanzania is a fascinating land of eclectic contradictions, remaining faithful to its heritage while bravely struggling to adapt to the present.

BEST TIME TO VISIT
Late June to October – or before 1498, when the first European arrived

ESSENTIAL EXPERIENCES
Conquering altitude, cold and fatigue on Kilimanjaro

Rediscovering some of the world's oldest hominid fossils

Wandering lost in the alleys and mayhem of Zanzibar's Stone Town

Basking in a superb Serengeti sunset

Succumbing to the beating drums on a steamy African night

Forgetting time under the billowing sail of an ancient *dhow*

Seeing the mass migration of wildebeest

GETTING UNDER THE SKIN
Read Emily Said-Ruete's *Memoirs of an Arabian Princess* – an autobiographical glimpse into the life of a Zanzibari princess who eloped to Europe

Listen to *Music from Tanzania & Zanzibar*, Vol 2 by various artists – a reflection of Zanzibar's Afro-Arab culture

Watch the spectacular IMAX documentary *Kilimanjaro – To the Roof of Africa* directed by David Breashears

Eat *pilau* (a tasty meat and rice dish full of the Spice Island's aromatic produce) or *ugali* (a bland staple made from maize or cassava flour, eaten with a sauce)

Drink *konyagi* – a potent white-rum-style drink

IN A WORD
Hakuna matata (no worries, not a problem)

TRADEMARKS
Cunning baboons; mosquito nets; the Big Five; fragrant spices; Arabian palaces; wildlife safaris; endless dusty plains; traditional Maasai; grinning children; white beaches

SURPRISES
Some local buses don't break down; large bottoms are considered beautiful

The word mzungu, *meaning 'white person' – and beloved of screeching urchins all over East Africa – was coined in the days of the early European explorers. It comes from the Kiswahili verb* kuzunguka: *'to wander around aimlessly, like a mad person'. The Swahili word for a hangover* kuzungu-zungu *('my head's going round and round') comes from the same root. Travellers wandering around aimlessly and nursing hangovers? Not much has changed...*

– Lonely Planet's *Africa*

MAP REF: 0,24

6. A black rhinoceros surveys the stark Ngorongoro National Park David Else

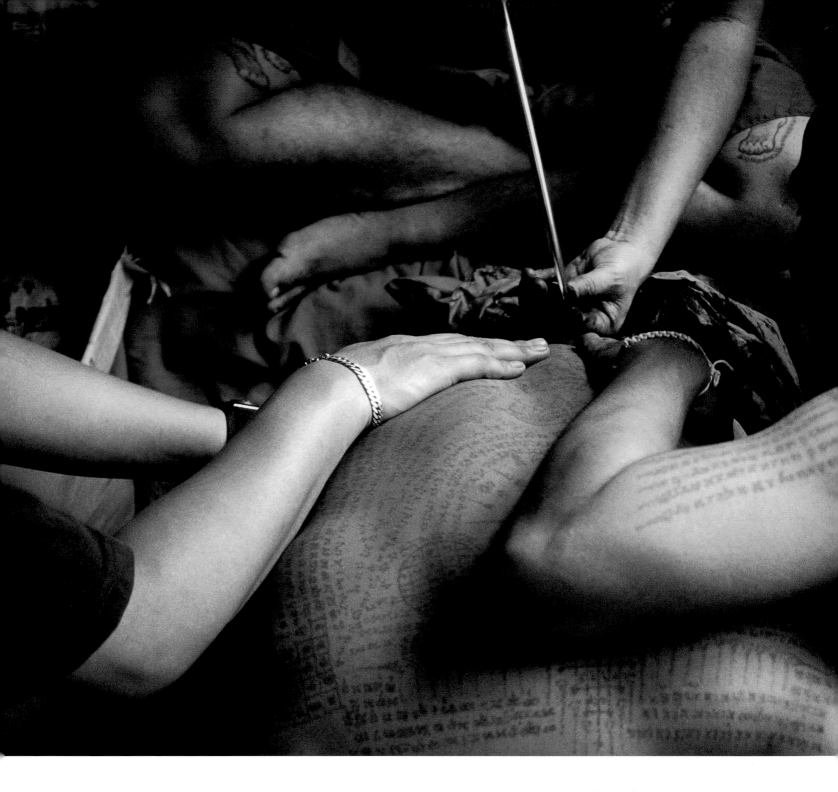

2. Young monks begin early morning prayers in Nong Khai
Richard I'Anson

3. A blurred boy flies his kite down the street on the predominantly Muslim island of Ko Panyi Dominic Arizona Bonuccelli

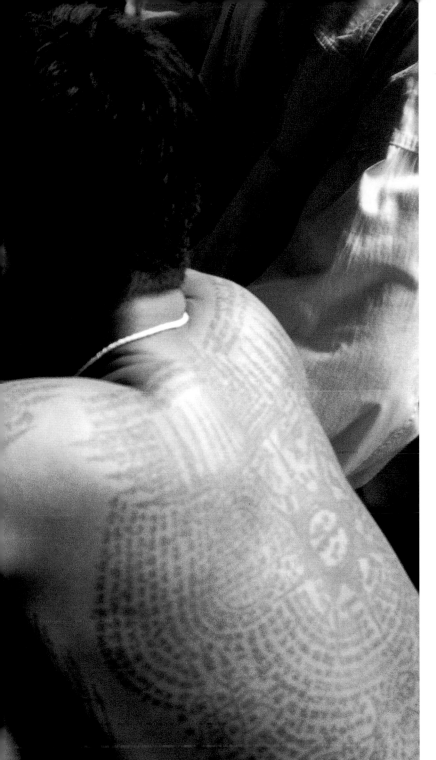

1. A tattooist monk carves emblems of luck and protection into the flesh of another monk while his helpers hold the subject down Joe Cummings

Thailand is the total package: jaw-dropping natural beauty, eye-catching architecture, an intricately woven culture and downright fabulous cuisine. Southeast Asia's most accessible and instantly appealing country gets under your skin. Your taste buds start to crave their daily dose of *phàt thai* noodles, your senses revel in the neon-lit delights of Bangkok, and artfully dodging traffic becomes second nature. Whether you're barefooting it on a budget or going five-star ritzy, dive in!

BEST TIME TO VISIT
Thailand is a year-round destination, but the rainy season falls between June and August

ESSENTIAL EXPERIENCES
Visiting Thailand's former capital, Ayuthaya, which lives up to its World Heritage Listed status

Chilling out in delightful Chiang Mai before trekking in the Golden Triangle region

Dancing under the full moon to thumping electronic beats on Ko Pha-Ngan

Escaping to Thaleh Ban National Park, satisfying any naturalist

Exploring all things exotic in Thailand's turquoise waters

Shopping: anywhere, anytime

GETTING UNDER THE SKIN
Read Chart Kobjitti's *Pan Ma Ba* (Mad Dog & Co) — an account of Thailand's *farang* (foreigner) scene. Stir-fry up a storm with David Thompson's sumptuous *Thai Food*.

Listen to Carabao's *Made in Thailand*, a *pleng pue cheevit* (song for life) classic

Watch the sweet essence of Thai culture in *Fan Chan* (My Girl)

Eat *tôm yam kûng* (spicy prawn and lemongrass soup) or taste sensational *mîang kham* (an appetiser of coconut, ginger, lime, peanuts and dried shrimp)

Drink sugar cane juice or rice whisky

IN A WORD
Mai pen rai (it's all right/nevermind)

TRADEMARKS
Technicolor Thai silk; Bangkok pollution; nomadic hair-braiders; exquisite beaches; noisy *túk túks*; Singha beer; heartwarming hospitality; pampering spas and silky pools

SURPRISES
In Thai, the word for 'meal', *méu*, is a close homonym with the word for 'hand', and Thais extend a hand towards a bowl of noodles or a banana leaf-wrapped snack with amazing frequency; every Thai house, office building or rice field has to have a spirit house to go with it — a place for *phrá phum* (earth spirits) native to this site to live in

Food lies very close to the heart of khwaam pen thai (Thai-ness)...To truly appreciate Thai culture you must understand and appreciate the food. If you become comfortable with both, perhaps you will become kin jai (eat heart)... Finally you may come to understand what Thais mean when they are ìm jai (full heart), an expression that fuses culinary satisfaction with general contentment.

— Lonely Planet's *World Food Thailand*

MAP REF: L.30

4. Heavy trading at the Damnoen Saduak Floating Market, Ratchaburi Province Chris Mellor

2. A well-dressed monk lights ritual incense in the town centre Bernard Napthine

3. Mass transit for the faithful – a group of monks are taken across Lhasa in a truck Richard I'Anson

4. Girls visiting Sera Monastery Richard I'Anson

5. Keeping the faith – a villager holds up an image of the exiled Dalai Lama Richard I'Anson

Tibet is a land of stark, arid beauty, where snowcapped mountains guard sacred turquoise lakes, and centuries-old monasteries are pervaded by the smell of yak-butter lamps, the chanting of mantras by monks in saffron robes, and the prostrations of the pious. Throughout the country, faded, wind-torn prayer flags flutter from the roofs of whitewashed brick-and-mud homes. While the Chinese occupation remains an intrinsic and oppressive part of everyday life, the unwavering faith of the Tibetans gives them strength to protect their culture and heritage.

BEST TIME TO VISIT
May, June, September and October

ESSENTIAL EXPERIENCES
Cleaning away all the sins of your lifeftime by walking the circuit of Mt Kailash

Gazing up at the Potala, an architectural masterpiece and structural centrepiece of Lhasa

Spending a low-oxygen night at Rongphu Monastery, the world's highest monastery

Views from high mountain passes that are literally and figuratively breathtaking

Bumping along the Friendship Highway, which, despite its name, is not hospitable or fast

Witnessing raucous monastic debates — despite occasional looks of terror, the monks generally seem to enjoy them

GETTING UNDER THE SKIN
Read Mary Craig's *Tears of Blood: A Cry for Tibet*, a riveting account of Tibet since the Chinese takeover, or Heinrich Harrer's *Seven Years in Tibet*, an engaging account of Harrer's sojourn in Tibet during the mid-20th century

Listen to *Chö*, by Choying Drolma & Steve Tibbets, a stunning introduction to Tibetan religious music; or *Freedom Chants from the Roof of the World* by the Gyuto Monks

Watch *Himalaya*, directed by Eric Valli, an epic story of Tibetan herders, with an all Tibetan cast and spectacular cinematography; *Kundun*, directed by Martin Scorsese, beautifully chronicles the life of His Holiness the Dalai Lama until his exile from Tibet

Eat *tsampa*, a dough of roasted-barley flour and yak butter mixed with water, tea or beer; *momos* are small dumplings filled with meat or vegetables

Drink yak-butter tea — drink it hot, because it's even worse cold; or *chang*, a fermented barley beer

IN A WORD
Tashi delek! (in Tibetan, used as a greeting, literally 'good fortune')

TRADEMARKS
Pious pilgrims and saffron-clad monks; spiritual home of the Dalai Lama; Chinese occupation; yak meat and *momos*; Han immigration; high altitude and low oxygen; sky burials

SURPRISES
Tibetans stick their tongues out to show respect; thumbs up is a sign of begging

Buddhism permeates most facets of Tibetan daily life and shapes the aspirations of Tibetans in ways that are often quite alien to the Western frame of mind. The idea of accumulating merit, of sending sons to be monks, of undertaking pilgrimages, of devotion to the sanctity and power of natural places are all elements of the unique fusion between Buddhism and the older shamanistic Bön faith.

— Lonely Planet's *Tibet*

1. Street sharks — local hustlers play a mean game of pool on the quiet streets of Lhasa Craig Pershouse

6. The Potala remains Lhasa's architectural highlight Richard l'Anson

MAP REF: J,29

2. Umbrellas sprout amongst a crowd gathering for a festival at the stadium in Sansanne Mango Kim Wildman

3. Wearing their wares on their heads, local women march to market in Vogan Kim Wildman

4. What are you looking at? The curiosity of a young boy in the village of Klouto Kim Wildman

5. An elderly Muslim man smiles in silence, Lomé Craig Pershouse

LEFT 1. A tray of wooden bowls hovers above a girl's head in the Ketao market as she pauses for a moment's refreshment Craig Pershouse

Tiny Togo, a thin sliver of land wedged between Ghana, Burkina Faso and Benin, is blessed with deserted beaches, a fascinating culture and friendly people. Upcountry are beautiful hills and plateaus, while the region around Kpalimé, near the Ghanaian border in the southwest, is particularly scenic and is known for its butterflies. The famous fortress-like mud-brick houses of the Tamberma people can be seen in the Kabyé region, a place that has withstood the onslaught of modernisation.

BEST TIME TO VISIT
Mid-July to mid-September

ESSENTIAL EXPERIENCES
Hiking the beautiful hill country surrounding Kpalimé, well known for its butterflies

Gazing at the extraordinary *tata* compounds, built without tools, in the Tamberma Valley

Browsing through the bewildering collection of traditional medicines and fetishes on offer at the Marché des Fétishes in Lomé

Discovering the crumbling colonial charm of Aného, the former capital, set on a picturesque lagoon

Enjoying Lake Togo's water sports, including windsurfing and water-skiing

Having fun bargaining with Mama Benz, the smart wealthy women traders of Lomé's Grand Marché

GETTING UNDER THE SKIN
Read the autobiography *An African in Greenland* by Tété-Michel Kpomassle, who was raised in a traditional Togolese family

Listen to Bella Bellow for a musical hybrid of traditional music fused with the contemporary sounds of West Africa, the Caribbean and South America

Watch Togolese director Anne-Laure Folly's *Femmes aux yeux ouverts* (Women with Open Eyes), which explores the problems facing women in West Africa

Eat *koklo mémé* (grilled chicken with chilli sauce) or *abobo* (snails cooked like a brochette)

Drink *tchakpallo* (fermented millet with a frothy head) or palm wine

IN A WORD
Un-lah-wah-lay ('good morning' in Kabyé, one of the major indigenous languages)

TRADEMARKS
Beaches; fetishes; clay houses of the Tamberma; voodoo; great food

SURPRISES
The Ewe consider the birth of twins a great blessing, but the Bassari consider it a grave misfortune; of the Togolese population, 59% are animists

Many of the Ewe's funeral rites and conceptions of afterlife and death have a strong animist element. According to the Ewe, once a person dies their djoto (reincarnated soul) will come back in the next child born into the same lineage, while their luvo (death soul) may linger with those still living, seeking attention and otherwise creating havoc. Funerals are one of the most important events in Ewe society and involve several nights of drumming and dancing, followed by a series of rituals to help free the soul of the deceased and influence its reincarnation.

— Lonely Planet's *West Africa*

MAP REF: M,20

2. A woman paints a traditional tapa on Tongatapu Island
Deanna Swaney

3. Against the setting sun, figures wade in the shallows at low tide to gather shellfish off Tongatapu beach Peter Hendrie

1. All pens and pony tails, rows of students from the Nuku'alofa Girls High School prepare for class
Peter Hendrie

Since Captain Cook first landed here, Tonga has charmed travellers with its wild feasts, friendly people and awe-inspiring natural beauty. The modern world has crept into the kingdom with LA gangster wear more common than traditional waist mats on the streets of Tongatapu. Still the islands remain peaceful and visually spectacular with rainforest crater lakes and volcanic peaks.

BEST TIME TO VISIT
May to October is the best time to visit as summer (November–April) is the hurricane season

ESSENTIAL EXPERIENCES
Gorging yourself at a Tongan feast, especially on Tongatapu and Vava'u

Dodging the spray at the Mapu'a 'a Vaca Blowholes, Tongatapu – a 5km stretch of geyser-like blowholes with fountains of seawater up to 30m high

Stumbling through unexplored tropical rainforests and limestone caves on 'Eua

Spotting breeding humpback whales who call the ocean around Ha'apai and Vava'u their boudoir

Climbing eerie, uninhabited (but still active) volcanoes that rise out of the ocean on Tofua and Kao

GETTING UNDER THE SKIN
Read *Tonga Islands: William Mariner's Account* by Dr John Martin, published in 1817 and still one of the best books on pre-Christian Tonga

Listen to *Dance Music of Tonga – Malie! Beautiful*, a sampler of various artists of traditional music

Watch *The Other Side of Heaven*, a Disney story of a 1950s missionary preaching in Tonga

Eat a genuine Tongan feast served in an *umu* (underground oven), taro and sweet potato, roasted suckling pig, chicken, corned beef, fish and shellfish

Drink *kava* (Piper methysticum), the all-purpose forget-your-cares-and-stare-at-the-sunset tipple that's widely available

IN A WORD
Malo e lelei (hello)

TRADEMARKS
Friendly indigenous people; migrating humpback whales; kings and queens ruling an island paradise; *tapa* adorning the walls of every building; packed churches on Sunday

SURPRISES
Despite the sackloads of tourist dollars whale-watching brings in, Tonga has a prominent whaling lobby that believes hunting the sea mammals is a long-honoured part of Tongan culture. The king, however, outlawed whaling in the 1970s.

From Captain Cook to Paul Theroux, Tonga has beguiled, charmed and frustrated travellers who have tried to get under the skin of this enigmatic kingdom. Sometimes warmly friendly, sometimes reserved and insular, it defies sweeping description despite being one of the Pacific's most homogeneous societies.

— Lonely Planet's *South Pacific*

4. Two shy girls hide behind a tree on Lifuka Island Patrick Horton

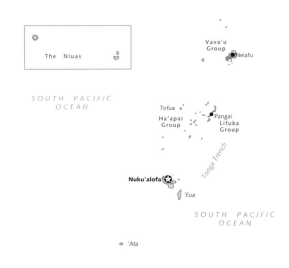

MAP REF: Q.1

2. Bawdy Trinidad Carnival mas bands perform on stage David Sanger

3. A green honeycreeper sings on a branch in the Trinidad and Tobago rainforest Tom Boyden

4. It's a hard life at Tobago's famous Pigeon Point Doug Pearson

5. The creation of a new steel pan (drum) inside the Blue Diamonds panyards, Port-of-Spain Andrew Marshall

1. Dancers strut their stuff in a swirl of colour and electrifying movement at Trinidad Carnival Peter Adams

Tobago and its twin island, Trinidad, are the Caribbean's odd couple. 'Little sister' Tobago is relaxed, slow-paced and largely undeveloped. Trinidad is a densely populated, thriving island with a cosmopolitan population and strong regional influence. It's famous for hosting the loudest and wildest Carnival in the Caribbean, whereas on Tobago the reefs are calm and protected and the beaches are good.

BEST TIME TO VISIT
Mid-April to mid-December, or go two days before Ash Wednesday for Carnival

ESSENTIAL EXPERIENCES
Partying the night away at Port-of-Spain's spectacular Carnival festival

Swimming and snorkelling at palm-fringed, white-sand beaches on Tobago

Spotting birds at Trinidad's Caroni Swamp

Diving at Buccoo Reef off Tobago

Exploring Trinidad's wild and rural east coast – a mix of lonely beaches, rough Atlantic waters and mangrove swamps

GETTING UNDER THE SKIN
Read *A House for Mr Biswas* by VS Naipaul – dig deep into the country's multi-ethnic culture by reading this vivid portrait of life as an East Indian in Trinidad

Listen to long-time king of calypso, The Mighty Sparrow

Watch *Hosay Trinidad*, about the observance of Shi'ite Muharram rites on Trinidad

Eat *callaloo* (a thick green soup made with okra, onions, spices and the leaves of the dasheen plant, onions, peppers and seasoning) or head to a beachside eatery for a shark & bake (a sandwich made with a slab of fresh shark and deep-fried bread)

Drink ginger beer or sorrel (made from the blossoms of a type of hibiscus and mixed with cinnamon and other spices)

IN A WORD
Carnival!

TRADEMARKS
Twin islands; cricket matches; white-sand beaches and glass clear water; bird-watching enthusiasts

SURPRISES
The oddest attraction in Trinidad is Pitch Lake, a continually replenishing lake of tar, which is the world's single largest supply of natural bitumen; Tobago has only 4% of the country's population

The lead up to Carnival begins with a weekend of resting and relaxing, saving up the energy needed for the ensuing festivities. Someone in the neighbourhood might make a braf (a sort of fish stew) and you'll take your only regular meal for the next 48 hours. Come Monday or Juve Tuesday (Shrove Tuesday) the party begins in earnest. In the predawn hours, the sounding of a whistle and the banging of a lapo cabway (single sheep-skin drum) ushers in the beginning of Carnival. By the time the sun comes up, entire streets have been closed and many people don't bother to go to work. Bosses don't mind, they're out in the streets too! Schools don't even bother opening.

— Lonely Planet's *World Food Caribbean*

6. Excited revellers dance in the streets during the atmospheric Trinidad Carnival David Sanger

MAP REF: M,13

2. Knocking on heaven's door – the superb craftsmanship of a door in Tunis Christopher Wood

3. A hive of stairways and storage holes make up the *ghorfas* of Medenine, a building used to store grain Adrien Vadrot

4. A girl smiles generously from beneath her flashy garments at the Sahara Festival, Kebili Craig Pershouse

5. Suspicious eyes peer narrowly from the distinctive blue headscarf of a Tuareg man in Douz Craig Pershouse

1. Death-defying horsemen display astonishing skill and courage at a festival in Douz Craig Pershouse

6. Boats bob at their moorings at the harbour of Bizerte Jane Sweeney

Tunisia is an ancient land moving to a modern beat where millennia of history come alive: in the astonishing Roman colosseum at El-Jem; in the ancient cities of Dougga and Sufetula; in charming medinas surrounded by crenellated walls; and in the fairytale architecture of the Berbers. In Kairouan, the fourth-holiest city in Islam, foundation myths and towering mosques connect Tunisia to the heart of Islam. Infinitely hospitable, Tunisians have their feet firmly planted in tradition while rushing headlong into the modern world.

BEST TIME TO VISIT
Mid-March to mid-May

ESSENTIAL EXPERIENCES
Exploring the archaeological site of Carthage, rich in mythology and sea views

Navigating the mirages of the Chott el-Jerid causeway

Bathing in the hot springs of Ksar Ghilane as the sun sets over the dunes

Ambling the cobbled lanes of Le Kef

Spelunking the underground Roman villas of Bulla Regia

Gazing at the Mediterranean from the village of Sidi Bou Saïd

Haggling with Kairouan's skilled carpet salesmen

GETTING UNDER THE SKIN
Read Mustapha Tlili's novel *Lion Mountain*, or *Pillar of Salt* by Albert Memmi

Listen to the El-Azifet Ensemble, fine purveyors of *malouf*, a traditional Arab-style music form

Watch the backgrounds of international films such as *Star Wars* and *The English Patient* (both set in Tunisia)

Eat couscous with vegetables and harissa sauce (a fire-red chilli concoction made from crushed dried red peppers, garlic, salt and caraway seeds)

Drink coffee, mint tea or, for an alcoholic tipple, try *boukha* — a gloopily sweet, aromatic spirit made from distilled figs, served at room temperature or chilled, and often mixed with Coke

IN A WORD
Bari kelorfik (thank you — a blessing)

TRADEMARKS
Carthage; the Land of the Lotus Eaters; the Sahara Desert; pristine white-sand beaches

SURPRISES
Tunisian proverbs include: 'Good reputation is better than wealth' and 'High prices attract buyers'; Tunisia was the first predominantly Islamic independent state to ban polygamy (1956); Ibadism as practised in Jerba is one of Islam's smallest sects, found elsewhere only in the M'Zab Valley in central Algeria and in Oman

Tunisia is baseball caps and straw hats; mobile phones ringing in the midst of the ancient, serious and exuberant art of conversation; men overflowing with testosterone who don't shirk from wearing jasmine behind the ear; a nation proud of its modernity and filled with men grumbling about how women are favoured and how dangerous it is — for the women, you understand — to give them such freedom.

—Lonely Planet's *Tunisia*

MAP REF: J,21

2. At the altars of cleanliness — men relax on heated marble in the Galatasaray Baths, Istanbul Jeff Greenberg

3. Rose tea for the taking at a street market in Bosphoros Greg Elms

4. A wizened beadseller and his daughter, Istanbul Izzet Keribar

5. Towering monuments of commerce dominate the Istanbul skyline Izzet Keribar

6. Dwellings, churches and fortresses carved into the dreamlike volcanic rock formations of the Göreme Open-Air Museum Diana Mayfield

LEFT 1. Lost in spiritual contemplation, a man sits amid the stately Rüstem Paşa Camii Mosque in Istanbul Izzet Keribar

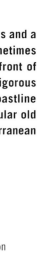

TURKEY

CAPITAL ANKARA POPULATION 68,109,469 AREA 780,580 SQ KM OFFICIAL LANGUAGE TURKISH

Turkey is Asia's foothold in Europe, a melting pot of cultures and a bridge between continents. It is modernising rapidly – sometimes so fast you'd swear you can actually see it happening in front of your eyes. It's secular and Western-oriented and boasts a vigorous free-enterprise economy. The cuisine is to die for, the coastline a dream, and many Turkish cities are dotted with spectacular old mosques and castles. To top it off, Turkey remains the Mediterranean coast's bargain-basement travel destination.

BEST TIME TO VISIT
Spring (late April to May) and autumn (late September to October)

ESSENTIAL EXPERIENCES
Haggling your way to a bargain in the Grand Bazaar in Istanbul

Floating over the spectacular landscape of Cappadocia in a hot-air balloon

Taking in the history of the eerily peaceful Gallipoli Peninsula

Exploring Ephesus, the best-preserved ancient city in the eastern Mediterranean

Letting yourself be scrubbed clean and invigoratingly massaged in a *hamam* (steam bath)

Wandering the cobbled lanes of the beautifully preserved Ottoman city of Safranbolu

Sailing the blue waters of Turkey's southwest coast in a traditional *gûlet* (wooden yacht)

GETTING UNDER THE SKIN
Read Irfan Orga's *Portrait of a Turkish Family*, which tells of a family struggling to survive the collapse of the Ottoman Empire and the birth of the Turkish Republic

Listen to Tarkan, the undoubted king of Turkish pop for much of the 1990s and early 2000s

Watch Peter Weir's *Gallipoli* – an Australian's account of the Anzac experience during the Gallipoli campaign of WWI

Eat Turkish bread – no Turkish meal would be complete without it. *Pide* or flat bread is the most famous variety

Drink *raki* – a clear, strong spirit made of grapes infused with aniseed

IN A WORD
Merhaba! (hello!)

TRADEMARKS
Turkish delight; the place where East meets West and commercialism meets tradition; kebabs in a dozen different varieties; whirling dervishes; delicious Turkish bread; *raki*; carpet sellers; tea offered in a shop immediately prior to a sales pitch

SURPRISES
Turkey has its very own pop industry and it's hugely successful; it gets so cold in some parts of the country that you can ski in winter

Turks are passionate about food – they write love songs to yoghurt, ballads about fish sandwiches and poems that imagine battles between pastry and pilav. Turks have fun with food too. Their ice-cream is so supple it can be used as a skipping rope, a to-die-for eggplant dish is called 'the priest fainted' and plump meatballs are dubbed 'woman's thighs'.

– Dani Valent, *World Food Turkey*

MAP REF: I,23

2. The mausoleum of Sultan Tekesh stands majestically beside the Kutlug Timur minaret tower, Koneurgencho John Noble

3. A man and his mule prepare to cross the road (with minaret and mausoleum in the background) Martin Moos

4. Cheerful children gather outside a traditional yurt in the wide open spaces around Darvaza Martin Moos

The most curious of the Central Asian republics, Turkmenistan resembles an Arab Gulf state without the money. Most of the country consists of an inhospitable lunar-like desert called the Karakum, which conceals unexploited oil and gas deposits. Turkmenistan is sparsely populated and its people, the Turkmen, are only a generation or two removed from being nomads. Turkmenistan is as much a culture as a country, since the Turkmen have never formed a real nation and have allowed their cities to become predominantly populated by other peoples.

BEST TIME TO VISIT
Spring (April to June) and autumn (September to November)

ESSENTIAL EXPERIENCES
Staying in a traditional yurt in the village of Darvaza and going to the nearby Darvaza Gas Craters – an enormous inferno like a volcano at ground level

Visiting the vast Karakum desert

Enjoying some of the best scenery in the country at the Kugitang Nature Reserve – complete with dinosaur footprints and incredibly deep caves with stalactites

Taking a tour around the historic city of Merv – a huge site of vast complexity, which juxtaposes time scales and cultures

Avoiding the thousand plus indigenous species of insects, spiders, reptiles and rodents – including cobras, large black scorpions, tarantulas and prehistoric-looking monitors – at the Repetek Desert Reserve

GETTING UNDER THE SKIN
Read works by Turkmen poet Magtymguly Feraghy. *Sacred Horses: The Life of a Turkmen Cowboy* by Jonathon Maslow is a good, if abrasive, account of this naturalist's visits to the Karakum desert

Listen *City of Love* by Ashkhabad, a five-piece Turkmen ensemble

Eat *diorama* (bread with pieces of boiled meat and onions), *shashlyk* (lamb kebab) and *plov* (rice, meat and carrots)

Drink *chal* (fermented camel's milk) for breakfast in the desert, and tea, which you'll be offered at every juncture throughout the day

IN A WORD
Salam aleykum ('peace be with you' in Turkmen)

TRADEMARKS
'Bukhara' rugs; camels; deserts; hardcore trekkers; yurts; the personality cult of leader President Turkmenbashi (Turkemenbashi translates as 'leader of the Turkmen')

SURPRISES
Merv is Turkmenistan's only Unesco World Heritage site; the Karakum desert has recorded air temperatures of over 50°C (122°F), and the surface of the sand sizzling at a soul-scorching 70° (158°F)

The Turkmen people are a highlight of the country. Friendly, curious and with a great sense of humour, they can make even the bleakest parts of the country great fun. Turkmen are generally very traditional and family-oriented without being overly conservative. Despite Sovietisation, women who live outside Turkmenistan's towns are generally homemakers and mothers, and the men the breadwinners.

– Lonely Planet's *Central Asia*

1. The influence of traditional architectural styles is evident in the alluring designs of a high-rise housing façade Jane Sweeney

5. Her hand heavy with jewellery, a bride in a dazzling veil covers her face Jane Sweeney

MAP REF: I,26

2. Local boys fish for their dinner as the sun slowly sinks into the Atlantic Ocean, Grand Turk Nick Hanna

3. A green turtle explores Turks and Caicos' watery underworld Steve Rosenberg

Oddly named, a little misshapen and often covered with cactus and thorny acacia trees, this archipelago is the often-neglected stepsister to the neighbouring Bahamas. But this is the Caribbean, so this British crown colony still has many charms. Several islands are fringed with exquisite beaches and for divers there are several hundred miles of coral reef that make it a hot destination.

BEST TIME TO VISIT
Mid-April and July (avoid sweltering August to November)

ESSENTIAL EXPERIENCES
Bonefishing at Sapodilla Bay or on South Caicos

Dodging the resort crowds at Providenciales and lazing on incredible beaches

Picnicing with iguanas and flamingos on West Caicos

Hiking the well-designed paths of Middle Caicos

Exploring the underground caverns of Conch Bar Caves National Park, complete with lagoons, stalactites and stalagmites, colonies of bats and petroglyphs by Lucayan Indians

Wall diving or windsurfing off Grand Turk

Shaking up the Salt Cay, a fascinating blend of historic buildings and amazing beaches

GETTING UNDER THE SKIN
Read J Dennis Harris's *A Summer on the Borders of the Caribbean Sea*, a classic 19th-century travelogue. *Water and Light* by Stephen Harrigan is a splendid memoir by a Texan about diving off Grand Turk

Watch *Extraordinary People*, a TV documentary about a world-record attempt at free diving off Turks and Caicos

Eat conch, which can often be better than in the Bahamas

Drink rum – in a cocktail, shot or slipper

IN A WORD
TIs or Belongers (the islanders' names for themselves)

TRADEMARKS
Shady expats living off 'investments' or involved in 'exports'; lavish resorts; cocktails sipped in casinos; excellent birdwatching; terrific year-round tans; excellent diving

SURPRISES
Technically, the Turks and Caicos (like the Bahamas) lie outside the Caribbean Sea; they are washed on the north and east by the Atlantic and on the south and west by the Gulf Stream

The islanders are as devoutly religious as their northern neighbours. This doesn't stop some from philandering or having a tipple, for example, on Sunday, when the pubs (strictly speaking) aren't serving: 'We might be drinking, but we are conscious of our religion'

– Lonely Planet's *Bahamas, Turks and Caicos*

1. Game on! Neighbourhood children while away the hours playing their version of stickball, South Caicos Island Phil Schermeister

4. Children bid farewell to their elementary school in a colourful graduation ceremony Phil Schermeister

MAP REF: L,12

2. Lining up for a laugh, primary school children loiter on the edge of Niutao Island Peter Bennetts

3. The impossibly idyllic Tepuka Islet set like an emerald between sea and sky Peter Bennetts

4. A proctective grandmother looks after the children in an airy house on Funafuti Atoll Peter Bennetts

If you want to disappear for a while, head to Tuvalu. On average, it receives fewer than a thousand tourists a year, so you're likely to have the beach to yourself. The tiny group of islands, however, are seriously endangered by rising sea levels caused by global warming, so you'd better be quick.

BEST TIME TO VISIT
May to September, when the easterly trade winds spring up

ESSENTIAL EXPERIENCES
Joining in a game of soccer on Funafuti's pitch, which doubles as the airport landing strip

Snorkelling in Funafuti Marine Conservation Area to gawp at tropical fish and cavorting turtles

Wreck-spotting on Nanumea Atoll for remains of several US landing craft and a B-24 bomber

Worshipping at the only remaining pre-Christian altar buried in the bush of Nukulaelae Atoll

Training in the Tuvaluan martial art of wielding the *katipopuki* (hardwood spear) on the island of Niutao

GETTING UNDER THE SKIN
Read *The People's Lawyer* by Philip Ells – an amusing and insightful account of a young Voluntary Service Overseas lawyer's spell in Tuvalu, or *The Happy Isles of Oceania – Paddling the Pacific*, by the notorious Paul Theroux

Listen to *Tuvalu: A Polynesian Atoll Society* – a good sampler with chants from several different islands

Watch *Pacific Women in Transition*, featuring a Tuvaluan woman adapting to the changes of modern life on the island

Eat your fill of seafood at a *fatele*, the mega-feast that always involves dancing

Drink *toddy*, the fermented coconut sap that delivers an alcoholic kick

IN A WORD
Se fakamasakoga fua o fai se fatele (any excuse for a *fatele*)

TRADEMARKS
Fine-sand beaches on clear seas; indigenous dot.tv millionaires; first-rate snorkelling around atolls; isolation; rising sea levels

SURPRISES
Although Tuvalu literally means 'cluster of eight', there are nine islands in the nation; the highest point on Tuvalu is just 4.6m (15ft) above sea level

The greenhouse effect is the issue that dominates Tuvalu's future. In fact there's a very real possibility that as the greenhouse effect takes a grip on the world's climate over the next century, Tuvalu could cease to exist altogether.

– Lonely Planet's *Time and Tide: the Islands of Tuvalu*

1. The late Honourable Ionatana Ionatana, former prime minister of Tuvalu, and his son wading together on Funafuti Atoll Peter Bennetts

5. Land surfing on a slippery boat ramp off Nukufetau Atoll Peter Bennetts

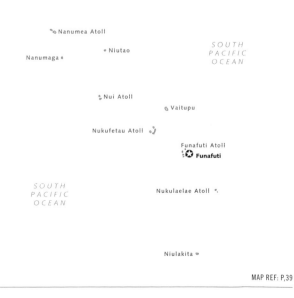

Nanumea Atoll

Niutao

Nanumaga

SOUTH PACIFIC OCEAN

Nui Atoll

Vaitupu

Nukufetau Atoll

Funafuti Atoll
Funafuti

SOUTH PACIFIC OCEAN

Nukulaelae Atoll

Niulakita

MAP REF: P.39

2. A herd of Uganda Kob, a rare breed of impala, gathers beneath the mighty Rwenzori Mountains
Ariadne Van Zandbergen

3. With an innocent expression, a boy leans against a broad tree trunk Eric Wheater

4. Two smiling siblings out for a stroll Eric Wheater

5. A pair of mountaineers brave the icy wasteland of Stanley Plateau, Rwenzori National Park Grant Dixon

6. A group of exhausted porters in the Mt Elgon not far from the Ugandan–Kenyan border Andrew Van Smeerdijk
LEFT 1. A boy in simple pink robes leans against a wall in the capital, Kampala Eric Wheater

UGANDA

CAPITAL KAMPALA POPULATION 25,632,794 AREA 236,040 SQ KM OFFICIAL LANGUAGE ENGLISH

Uganda's remarkable transformation from tragic, war-torn nation into one of the fastest growing economies in Africa is drawing increasing numbers of resourceful travellers to the erstwhile 'Pearl of Africa'. Long held synonymous with the horrors of Idi Amin's terrible dictatorship, Uganda once more has plenty to offer. Downtown Kampala has a contagious buzz and bustle, but can be quickly left behind for beautiful mountains, trekking opportunities and some of the few remaining communities of endangered mountain gorillas.

BEST TIME TO VIST
January to February (when the weather is hot but generally dry) or June to September (the dry season)

ESSENTIAL EXPERIENCES
Staying up to enjoy Kampala's vibrant, fast-changing nightlife

Trekking Mt Elgon's cliffs, caves, gorges and waterfalls without another soul in sight

Spectacular wildlife watching at Murchison Falls

Penetrating the Impenetrable Forest (Bwindi National Park), home to half of the world's surviving mountain gorillas

Roaming through the mystical snowcapped Rwenzori 'Mountains of the Moon'

Chilling away a few more 'no-hurry-in-Africa' days in the Ssese Islands

GETTING UNDER THE SKIN
Read *The Last King of Scotland* by Giles Foden, a page-turner chronicling the experience of Idi Amin's personal doctor-turned-confidant; or *The Abyssinian Chronicles* by Ugandan Moses Isegawa, a coming of age story of a boy and of a country during Idi Amin's dark reign and its chaotic aftermath

Listen to *Ngoma: Music from Uganda*, a cultural preservation project by the multi-ethnic Ndere Troupe

Watch *Raid on Entebbe*, the Charles Bronson classic about the Israeli rescue mission of a Palestinian-terrorist hijacked plane

Eat *matoke* (mashed plantains) and groundnut sauce – food for fuel rather than food for fun

Drink Bell Beer, infamous for its 'Great night, good morning!' ad-jingle, or try *waragi*, the local grain-distilled spirit (watch out for the kick!)

IN A WORD
Mazungu! (white man!)

TRADEMARKS
The tragedy of HIV/AIDS (one in five of the population is afflicted); a freshwater lake bigger than Ireland (Lake Victoria)

SURPRISES
In spite of all they've endured, Ugandans are some of the most open and outgoing people in the world; proof that the number of people, pieces of baggage and chickens that can be squeezed into a *matatu* (minibus taxi) is far more than the 14 it was built for

Take your pick from the highest mountain range in Africa – the Rwenzori Mountains; one of the most powerful waterfalls in the world, Murchison Falls; or perhaps the highest primate density in the world in Kibale Forest National Park – Uganda has all this and more. It's a beautiful country with a great deal to offer and sooner or later the tourist hordes will 'discover' its delights – make sure you get here before they do.

– Lonely Planet's *East Africa*

MAP REF: N.23

411

2. Pick up your dinner ingredients from women selling fresh vegetables on the subway steps in Kyiv Ludovic Maisant

3. Ornate, blue interior of the sculpted corbelled dome of the 17th-century Renaissance Boyim Chapel Carol Ann Wiley

4. Dormition Cathedral's onion domes glint impressively in the sun, contrasting with its blue façade Carol Ann Wiley

1. At Leningrad's Kuznetsky Market a woman waits to sell her strawberries at farmers' rates   David Turnley

5. It's hot work on Yalta's waterfront promenade and these two are indulging in ice-cold refreshment, Black Sea coast   Pascal Le Segretain

A country whose national anthem is 'Ukraine Has Not Yet Died' may not seem the most uplifting destination, but Ukraine rewards travellers with hospitable people, magnificent architecture and miles of gently rolling steppes. Nearly every city and town has a centuries-old cathedral, exquisite mosaics, and many have open-air museums of folk architecture. Kyiv is the cosmopolitan capital with bustling streets and an energetic nightlife juxtaposed against glittering onion domes. The food will stick to your ribs, and you'll be humming bandura tunes for weeks.

BEST TIME TO VISIT
April to June

ESSENTIAL EXPERIENCES

Seeing mummified monks by candlelight in the underground passages of the Caves Monastery in Kyiv

Being dazzled by St Sophia Cathedral's sparkling domes in the nation's capital

Discovering Europe's only virgin beech forest at the Carpathian Biosphere Reserve

Living like royalty in Lviv's early-20th-century hotels; don't miss a night at the opera

Enjoying a champagne picnic on Odesa beach (strictly Odesan champagne only!)

Cutting a hole in the icy crust of the Black Sea in winter and catching your dinner

GETTING UNDER THE SKIN

Read *Everything is Illuminated* by Jonathan Safran Foer which recounts this American author's journey to find his family in the Ukraine

Listen to the soaring notes of the all-male Ukrainian Bandura Chorus, a professional orchestra who perform traditional choral and bandura music

Watch *Zemlia* (the Earth), a 1930 classic by Alexander Dovzhenko considered a milestone in cinematic achievement

Eat bowls of soul-warming *borsch*, or the addictive *varenyky* (boiled dumplings served with cheese or meat)

Drink vodka – the word comes from *voda* (water), and translates roughly as 'a wee drop'

IN A WORD
Dobry den' (hello, literally 'good day')

TRADEMARKS

Cossacks; *pysanky* – the beautifully painted eggs; proud singers; lax anti-money laundering laws; ice fishing; pristine, isolated ski slopes; Chernobyl; Soviet architecture; *borsch*; Orthodox churches; rugged mountains; traditional folk culture; icy temperatures; big, furry hats

SURPRISES
Nearly 3000 rivers flow through Ukraine; chicken Kiev was invented in New York

The heart and soul of Ukrainian folk music lies in the legendary bandura *or* kobza *player, made famous by Shevchenko's first book of poems* Kobzar *(The Bard). Kobzar was named after 16th and 17th wandering minstrels whose songs and ballads of heroic tales and poems were narrated to the accompaniment of the* kobza, *a lute-like instrument. Welcomed everywhere, the* kobza *player was the sacred keeper of Ukrainian folklore and Cossack legends.*

– Lonely Planet's *Russia, Ukraine & Belarus*

MAP REF: H,23

413

2. The Arabian Tower of the Jumeirah Beach Resort billows like a sail in Dubai Neil Setchfield

3. artners in brine – two workers at the dhow harbour in Dubai Izzet Keribar

4. A courtyard of palms beneath the ultra-modern Emirates Twin Towers Clint Lucas

5. A dazzling veil adorns the face of a Muslim woman Chris Mellor

Once an obscure corner of Arabia, the United Arab Emirates has transformed itself into an Arabian success story through a mix of oil profits, stability and a sharp eye for business. Visitors are attracted by beaches, deserts, oases, camel racing, Bedouin markets and the legendary duty-free shopping of Dubai – all packed into a relatively small area. Dubai is the Singapore of the Gulf, with bustling harbours, gigantic shopping malls and bold architecture. Each of the seven emirates bears a unique character.

BEST TIME TO VISIT
November to April

ESSENTIAL EXPERIENCES
Mixing with mobile-phone–toting sheikhs, pint-sized jockeys and punters of every nationality at Nad al-Sheba racecourse in Dubai

Exploring the cool date-palm plantations in the heart of Al-Ain

Cross dunes, ride camels and fly falcons at the luxurious Al-Maha Desert Resort

Looking at the enormous waves of peach-tinged dunes at Liwa oasis

Watching a bullfight on a Friday afternoon in Fujairah

Spending a luxurious night at the architecturally renowned Burj Al Arab hotel, built in the shape of an Arabian dhow sail

GETTING UNDER THE SKIN
Read *Arabic Short Stories*, translated by Denys Johnson-Davies, an excellent primer with tales from all over the Middle East

Listen to a performer playing an ancient *oud*, a carefully constructed wooden instrument, which sounds similar to a mandolin

Watch contemporary Arab cinema at the Dubai International Film Festival

Eat *fuul* (paste made from fava beans, garlic and lemon) and felafel (deep fried balls of chickpea paste served in a piece of Arabic flat bread)

Drink copious quantities of strong *shai* (tea) with *na'ana* (mint), and dark muddy *qahwa* (coffee)

IN A WORD
Marhaba (hi)

TRADEMARKS
Wadi-bashing (four-wheel driving around UAE's oases); a duty-free shopper's paradise; the Trucial states; carpet merchants and Bedouin souvenirs; Pakistani, Indian and Iranian expats; international racehorses

SURPRISES
The United Arab Emirates is the cheapest place outside Iran to buy Iranian caviar

The oil-rich emirate of Abu Dhabi has two beautiful oases: the attractively green and orderly Al-Ain and the spectacular contrast of green farms and towering pink dunes at Liwa. Sharjah offers the country's best museums and art gallery, and a magnificent zoo, as well as the charming port of Khor Fakkan. The smaller emirates are quieter – Umm al-Qaiwain is the closest thing to what the fishing and pearling towns of 50 years ago must have been like.

— Lonely Planet's *Oman & the United Arab Emirates*

1. A group of men brandish canes at a tradional dance in Abu Dhabi Chris Mellor

6. Horses race through the desert near Dubai Izzet Keribar

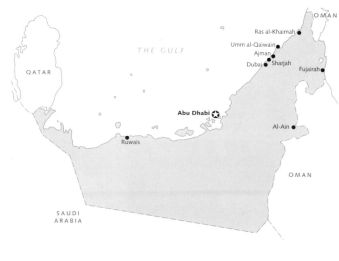

MAP REF: K,25

2. After an oil spill in 2002 this group of penguins have been washed clean and are eagerly returning to their natural habitat, Punta del Este Reuters/Picture Media

3. Ride 'em *gaucho*! A Uruguayan cowboy clings on for dear life at the lively annual Creole Week, Montevideo Andres Stapff

Uruguay may be pint-sized, but it's certainly big-hearted when it comes to attractions. It contains Montevideo, one of South America's most interesting capitals; charming colonial towns like Colonia; the hilly interior (true *gaucho* country); and a cluster of internationally renowned beach resorts.

BEST TIME TO VISIT
December and January, when the beautiful people flock to the beach and are a sight to behold

ESSENTIAL EXPERIENCES
Exploring Montevideo's architectural diversity and multicultural character

Scaling the battlements of the beautiful city of Colonia

Sailing, fishing and basking at Punta del Este on the Uruguayan Riviera

Heading to the quiet interior towns of Tacuarembó, the country's monument to the *gaucho*

GETTING UNDER THE SKIN
Read Juan Carlos Onetti's *Tierra de Nadie* (No Man's Land)

Listen to *La Cumparsita*, one of the best-known tangoes, composed by Uruguayan Gerardo Matos Rodriguez. Uruguayans consider Montevideo to be as much the birthplace of the tango as Buenos Aires.

Eat beef Uruguayans are cow crazy, consuming more beef per capita than almost any other nation. The *parrillada* (beef platter) is standard fare.

Drink *mate*, the brew of choice. Uruguay also produces some excellent wines.

IN A WORD
Tranquilo (chilled out)

TRADEMARKS
The Switzerland of South America; a buffer between rival regional powers; a haven for other country's unwanted rogues; sizzling sun-worshipping humans at Punta del Este

SURPRISES
Many shops and museums in Uruguay close when it rains; Montevideo's late summer carnival includes dance troupes beating out spirited African-influenced rhythms on large drums

Football remains the most popular spectator and participant sport; the most notable teams are Montevideo based Nacional and Peñarol. If you go to a match between these two, sit on the the sidelines, not behind the goal, where fans tend to get rowdy. The rowdiness can carry over onto the streets afterwards.

— Lonely Planet's *Argentina, Uruguay & Paraguay*

1. Is turquoise the new black? Punta del Este Tom Cockrem

4. The giant Hand in the Sand has held many a posing tourist in its grasp, Punta del Este Maurice Joseph

MAP REF: S,14

2. Dense vapour billows endlessly from the smoking vents of Mt Marum volcano on Ambrym Island
Denis O'Byrne

3. A well-dressed willy on Tanna Island where designer denim influences the traditional namba, or penis wrapper   Peter Hendrie

4. Father and son get together at a ritual pig-killing site on Malekula Island   Denis O'Byrne

5. An empty fishing boat at rest in the shallows off Mota Lava Island with the mountains of Vanua Lava in the distance   Denis O'Byrne

6. Villagers on Tanna Island, dressed to impress   Peter Hendrie
LEFT 1. Chief Willie Orion of Salap poses beneath a land dive tower after the big event, Pentecost, Penama   Denis O'Byrne

The *ni-Vanuatu*, as the peoples of Vanuatu are known today, are among the most welcoming people in the Pacific – despite colonialists who came for sandalwood and left with slaves. Vanuatu's fractured terrain of volcanoes and lush forests has produced a kaleidoscope of cultures and more than 100 indigenous languages. After last century's coups, Vanuatu now enjoys its independence. An increasing number of travellers contribute to the local economy by exploring the jungle above and below the water.

BEST TIME TO VISIT
April to October (the southern winter)

ESSENTIAL EXPERIENCES
Witnessing a very old extreme sport as the islanders on Pentecost land-dive to guarantee their yam harvest

Keeping your eyes peeled for dugongs (sea cows) while snorkelling

Watching from the haven of a beach hut on Vila as hundreds of fruit bats cloud the metallic sky before a wild storm

Finding the beach you've always dreamt of, only to discover there's an even better one on the next island (there are 83 islands)

Joining in local volleyball games with the owners of the biggest smiles and blondest afros in the world (*ni-Vanuatu* children)

GETTING UNDER THE SKIN
Read Jeremy McClancy's *To Kill a Bird with Two Stones* – an exceptional history of Vanuatu right up to its independence in 1980

Listen to the *tamtam* or slit drums –still crafted from traditional designs, they were once used to send coded messages between communities

Watch *Finding Nemo* – if you want to see the film that has had a devastating effect on Vanuatu's sea life due to the demand for pet fish

Eat a banana as long as your arm, baked sweet in the oven and sliced like a steak on your plate

Drink *aelan bia* (island beer), otherwise known as *kava*, the becalming brew which most island men imbibe at the end of a long day. Women can drink it at Port Vila's kava bars.

IN A WORD
Tank yu tumas ('thank you very much' in Bislama)

TRADEMARKS
Jungle; local dances; atmospheric drumming; wild boars; carvings and spears; aqua water; snorkelling and scuba diving; big bananas; 'cooking pots'; wild cyclones

SURPRISES
This laid-back place is uptight about magic; the cuisine is well regarded throughout the Pacific

The practice of magic is generally tabu *for women, but most adult men in traditional parts of Vanuatu know a few useful spells. These may be used to further love affairs or produce good crops. A practising magician is employed for more specialist tasks such as raising or calming storms, healing the sick, banishing spirits or controlling volcanoes.*

– Lonely Planet's *Vanuatu*

MAP REF: Q,37

2. Radiant as the sun, the magnificent headdress of a Carnival dancer flashes in the street Mauricio Handler

3. The shopkeeper of a boutique in Tortola leans out of a colourful doorway John Neubauer

1. Loud drums and louder shirts at the Carnival parade in St Thomas Steve Simonsen

Once the hideaway of buccaneers and brigands, the Virgin Islands now attract a more salubrious yachting crew drawn by steady trade winds, well-protected anchorages and a year-round balmy climate. Tourist development has been limited by enlightened environmental policy, and the islands have thoroughly different characters: while the US Virgin Islands have pursued the tourist dollar, the British Virgin Islands are keen to stay limey and out of the limelight.

BEST TIME TO VISIT
The peak tourist season is December to May, but there's dreamy weather year-round

ESSENTIAL EXPERIENCES
Hiking between beaches and great snorkelling sites in the Virgin Islands National Park

Mountain biking around Water Island

Exploring the days when 'King Cane' ruled and sugar was the major crop at the Estate Whim Plantation Museum, St Croix

Retreating to the mountains and beaches of Jost Van Dyke

Getting historical with the largest concentration of colonial buildings in Charlotte Amalie

Chartering a yacht to Anegada – the 'Mysterious Virgin' with a tranquil coral beachfront

GETTING UNDER THE SKIN
Read Martha Gellhorn's *Travels with Myself and Another*, observing the changes between her two visits in 1942 and 1977 to the British Virgin Islands

Listen to a popular Quelbe (a blend of local folk music) group, such as Stanley and the Ten Sleepless Knights

Watch *The Big Blue* set in Hurricane Hole on St John, British Virgin Islands, with lots of atmospheric diving and rich images

Eat a hearty bowl of *callaloo*, the legendary thick green soup

Drink a well-brewed bush tea, believed to cure all your ills

IN A WORD
If yo put yo ear a mango root, yo will hear de crab cough (roughly translated: patience is a virtue)

TRADEMARKS
Wide unspoilt beaches; crystal-clear waters; reggae rhythms; swimming in rum; yachties enjoying an on-deck G&T; flamingos aplenty

SURPRISES
The Virgins aren't owned by Richard Branson – they're both an unincorporated territory of the USA and Crown Colony of the United Kingdom

If you approach the Virgin Islands by sea, it isn't difficult to imagine what might have gone through Christopher Columbus's head in 1493 when he named this unspoilt collection of about 100 islands after the legendary St Ursula and her 11,000 virgins... Here he found peace and plenty as far as the eye could see.

– Lonely Planet's *Virgin Islands*

4. Massive boulders form natural sanctuaries for bathers outside the appropriately named town of The Baths
Mauricio Handler

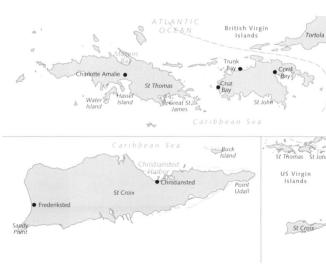

MAP REF: L,13

431

2. The Little Bo-Peep of Tai'zz coaxes her goats uphill
Bethune Carmichael

3. A building in the ancient town of Shaharah perches
precariously above a deep valley Bethune Carmichael

4. Nose wrinkled in the glare of the sun, a local man of Hajja
smiles gently Bethune Carmichael

5. As though lost in time, the stunning buildings of San'a are
slowly illuminated by the morning light Bethune Carmichael

1. Business is slow and stress-free at Cafe Aden in Aden Bethune Carmichael

6. The famous 17th-century limestone bridge of Shaharah spans a deep gorge Bethune Carmichael

Known to the Romans as Arabia Felix – Happy Arabia – Yemen remains the most untouched corner of Arabia. It's here amid the bustling souks, the desert oases, the traditional Arabian architecture and the remote mountain eyries that you feel you might meet Aladdin or Sinbad or any of the characters of the *Arabian Nights*. And while much of Yemen seems untouched by modern events, life continues to unfurl for the locals at a languid pace.

BEST TIME TO VISIT
October to March (when the daytime temperatures are pleasant and the rain infrequent) – or 950 BC when the Queen of Sheba still held sway

ESSENTIAL EXPERIENCES
Exploring the old quarter of San'a – one of the largest preserved medinas in the Arab world, and home to mud-brick skyscrapers built to a 1000-year-old design

Visiting Al-Makha, the first important coffee port on the Red Sea

Meandering through the covered alleys of the Friday market at Bayt al-Faqih

Marvelling at the ruins of the great dam at Ma'rib, a feat of engineering that watered the desert for 1000 years

Following in the footsteps of Rimbaud in Aden

Enjoying the hospitality of the historic cities of Shibam, Sayun and Tarim in the fertile Wadi Hadramawt

GETTING UNDER THE SKIN
Read Tim Mackintosh-Smith's *Yemen, Travels in Dictionary Land* – wry observations of Yemeni life from a long-time San'a resident

Listen to *Yemenite Songs* by Otra Haza – rhythmic fusion by the well-known Israeli of Yemeni origin

Watch Pier Paolo Pasolini's *Arabian Nights*, a racy adaptation of the age-old tale, which includes scenes shot in Yemen

Eat lentil or lamb *shurba* (soup), or *salta* (a fiery stew of lamb, beans, peppers and coriander)

Drink tea scented with cardamom, or coffee (always sweet) with ginger

IN A WORD
Mumkin ithnayn shai (two teas please)

TRADEMARKS
Frankincense; silver jewellery; date palms; stony villages precariously perched on lofty mountaintops; broadly smiling Bedouin tribesmen sporting bandoliers and *jambiyas* (curved daggers); dhows bobbing on the Red Sea; daily sessions of chewing mildly intoxicating *qat* – a national obsession

SURPRISES
Figs and peaches; deliciously spontaneous approach to life; Yemenis are renowned in the Middle East for their senses of humour

Private gardens [in San'a] hide behind mud walls. There are hectares of them, with entries only from the backyards of the houses or mosques. Travellers can best enjoy these improbable oases from the manzars of palace hotels or by looking over walls. The city used to be self-sufficient in vegetables and fruit; the gardens are actively cultivated to this day. On the southeastern tip of the walled city, the old citadel stands on an elevation, surrounded by massive walls.

– Lonely Planet's *Middle East*

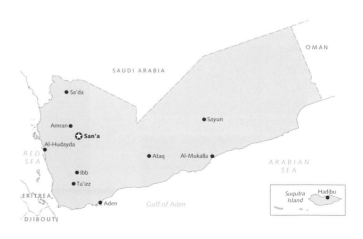

MAP REF: L,25

2. The next Bruce Grobbelaar? Zimbabwean boys play soccer on a dry plain Daniel Birks

3. A schoolgirl takes a cheerful break from classes Eric Wheater

4. A tobacco picker tends her child and crops that contribute to Zimbabwe's biggest export Eric Wheater

5. Traditional healers offer traditional cures outside the National Zimbabwe National Monument, the ruins of a once-great capital Peter Ptschelinzew

LEFT 1. A weary boy manages a smile on the road to Masvingo Richard l'Anson

Zimbabwe is a visually stunning and fascinating place. There's the grandeur of Victoria Falls, incredible wildlife, amazing ruins, the Zambezi River and the unmistakeable warmth and friendliness of the Zimbabwean people. You can spend the night in a tent listening to snuffling hippopotamii in a nearby river, or dance the night away at a percussion jam. Despite internal conflict and ongoing drought, Zimbabwe offers an incredibly rich and diverse range of tours, activities and scenery.

BEST TIME TO VISIT
May to October (dry season) — or before 1980 when Robert Mugabe came to power

ESSENTIAL EXPERIENCES
The incredible displays of art at the National Gallery of Zimbabwe in Harare
Joining a *pungwe*, an all night drinking, dancing and music performance
Taking in the enormous dimensions of the ruins of the ancient city of Great Zimbabwe
Spotting lions, giraffes and zebras at Hwange National Park
Watching a full moon rise over majestic Victoria Falls
Enjoying the natural beauty of Mana Pools National Park
Hiking through the fascinating landscape of the Mavuradonha Wilderness
Visiting the remote sculptors' community at Tengenenge Farm

GETTING UNDER THE SKIN
Read Doris Lessing's *The Grass is Singing*, a critique of race relations in Rhodesia
Listen to *Viva Zimbabwe* by various local artists, a good introduction to Zimbabwean pop music
Watch *Cry Freedom* by Richard Attenborough or *The Power of One* by John G Avildsen, both filmed in Zimbabwe
Eat *sadza ne nyama*, a white maize-meal porridge with meat gravy; grilled trout in the Eastern Highlands; *biltong*, a salty dried meat snack; or gem squash, a type of delicious marrow
Drink *chibuku*, the beer of the masses that's not particularly tasty but has a knockout punch

IN A WORD
Mhoro ('hello' in Shona)

TRADEMARKS
National parks; incredible wildlife; World Heritage sites; remote villages; just about every kind of safari you can think of; the bustle of Harare; mesmerising music; canoeing down the Zambezi River; world-champion soccer player Bruce Grobbelaar

SURPRISES
Being invited to share in a local festivity; the massive bulk of Zimbabwe's biggest tree in the Chirinda Forest Reserve; white-water rafting at Victoria Falls

Stunning Victoria Falls is Zimbabwe's contribution to the world's greatest attractions, and miles and miles of film and videotape are gobbled through cameras here every year. The falls measure a whopping 1.7km (1mi) wide and drop between 90m and 107m (300–350ft) into the Zambezi Gorge. An average of 550,000 cubic metres of water plummet over the edge every minute...

— World Guide, www.lonelyplanet.com

MAP REF: Q,23

A humpback whale glides through the waters off Niue Jenny & Tony Enderby

NIUE (NEW ZEALAND)

CAPITAL **ALOFI**
POPULATION **1700**
AREA **259 SQ KM**
OFFICIAL LANGUAGES **NIUEAN & ENGLISH**

Midway between Tonga and the Cook Islands, which makes it a long way from anywhere, Niue is a classic example of a *makatea* island, an upthrust coral reef. It rises often vertically out of the ocean so there's very little beach, but in compensation there are amazing chasms, ravines, gullies and caves all around the coast. Some of them extend underwater, giving the island superb scuba-diving sites. Like a number of other Pacific nations, the world's smallest self-governing state has been suffering a population decline: today there are more Niueans in New Zealand than on 'the Rock of Polynesia'.

MAP REF: Q,40

Jamestown, nestled snugly in a valley G Renner

SAINT HELENA (UK)

CAPITAL **JAMESTOWN**
POPULATION **7000**
AREA **121 SQ KM**
OFFICIAL LANGUAGE **ENGLISH**

From 1815 until he died in 1821, St Helena had one very famous resident, Napoleon Bonaparte. This very remote island, about halfway between South America and Africa, was where the British shipped the European conqueror after he met his Waterloo. Longwood House, where Napoleon died, is maintained as a museum by the French government. Visitors to the island might also climb the 699 steps of Jacob's Ladder or search out the island's oldest inhabitant, the tortoise Jonathan, which was already thought to be 50 years old when it arrived on the island in 1882.

MAP REF: Q,19

A windswept island church and cemetery yard Wayne Walton

SAINT PIERRE & MIQUELON (FRANCE)

CAPITAL **SAINT-PIERRE**
POPULATION **7000**
AREA **242 SQ KM**
OFFICIAL LANGUAGE **FRENCH**

The French lost Canada to the British after the Seven Years' War in 1763, but 20 years later the British decided to let them keep these two little islands off Newfoundland. Later they changed their minds a couple of times before handing them over permanently in 1815. As the only French territory remaining in North America, the island's main industry, after the dramatic decline of cod fishing off Newfoundland, is tourism. In Montréal you may be able to speak French, drink French wine and eat baguettes, but here you can also spend euros. In the Prohibition era of the 1920s the islands did very well from running booze into the USA.

MAP REF: H,14

SOUTH GEORGIA (UK)

CAPITAL **GRYTVIKEN**
POPULATION **10 TO 20**
AREA **3755 SQ KM**
OFFICIAL LANGUAGE **ENGLISH**

Aptly described as looking like an Alpine mountain range soaring straight out of the ocean, South Georgia's spectacular topography is matched only by its equally spectacular wildlife. The remote island's human population may drop as low as 10 during the long Antarctic winter, but there are two to three million seals, a similar number of penguins and 50 million birds, include a large proportion of the world's albatrosses. Add spectacular examples of industrial archaeology in the shape of the island's half a dozen abandoned whaling stations, plus South Georgia's role as the stage for the final act in Sir Ernest Shackleton's epic escape from the ice, and it's no wonder this is one of the most popular destinations for Antarctic tourists.

MAP REF: V,16

The abandoned Grytviken Whaling Station in King Edward Point Grant Dixon

SVALBARD (NORWAY)

CAPITAL **LONGYEARBYEN**
POPULATION **2500**
AREA **61,229 SQ KM**
OFFICIAL LANGUAGE **NORWEGIAN**

Far to the north of Norway, the archipelago of Svalbard has become a popular goal for Arctic travellers, keen to cruise the ice floes in search of whales, seals, walruses and polar bears. Apart from wildlife there are also some terrific hiking possibilities on the main island where you might encounter reindeer and Arctic foxes. The main town, the engagingly named Longyearbyen, has a long history of coal mining.

MAP REF: B,21

The St Fritiofsbreen glacier in Svalbard Christian Aslund

TOKELAU (NEW ZEALAND)

POPULATION **1400**
AREA **12 SQ KM**
OFFICIAL LANGUAGES **TOKELAUN, ENGLISH & SAMOAN**

Tokelau consists of three tiny atolls, each of them laid out on classic atoll design principles: a necklace of palm-fringed islands around a central lagoon. Off to the north of Samoa, the islands are not only a long way from anywhere, but also a long way from each other; it's 150km from Atafu past Nukunonu to Fakaofo. They're also very crowded: there may be only 1400 people but they've got very little land to share; none of the islets is more than 200m wide and you've got to climb a coconut tree to get more than 5m above sea level. Getting there is difficult even for yachties, as none of the lagoons has a pass deep enough for a yacht to enter.

MAP REF: P,40

Tokelau elders perform a traditional wedding dance Kyle Rothenborg

TRISTAN DA CUNHA (UK)

CAPITAL **EDINBURGH**
POPULATION **300**
AREA **98 SQ KM**
OFFICIAL LANGUAGE **ENGLISH**

Officially a dependency of St Helena, over 2300km to the north, Tristan da Cunha is frequently cited as the most remote populated place in the world. The island is a simple, towering volcano cone, and an eruption in 1961 forced the complete evacuation of the island. The displaced islanders put up with life in England for two years but most of them returned as soon as the island was declared safe in 1963 and went straight back to catching the crawfish which are the island's main export. Nightingale, Inaccessible and two smaller islands lie slightly southeast of the main island.

MAP REF: S,19

The grass-topped cliffs of the northwest coast of Tristan da Cunha G Renner

WALLIS & FUTUNA (FRANCE)

CAPITAL **MATA'UTU**
POPULATION **15,500**
AREA **274 SQ KM**
OFFICIAL LANGUAGES **WALLISIAN, FUTUNAN & FRENCH**

Luckily for Tahiti, Samuel Wallis, its European 'discoverer', didn't attach his name to the island — he was saving it for his subsequent visit to what is now half of another French Pacific colony. The two islands are separated by 230km of open ocean and are remarkably dissimilar. Wallis is relatively low lying with a surrounding lagoon fringed by classic sandy *motus* (islets) while Futuna is much more mountainous and paired with smaller Alofi. The populations are equally dissimilar: Futuna has connections to Samoa while the Wallis links were with Tonga. Wallis has one of the Pacific's best archaeological sites at Talietumu and an unusual collection of crater lakes, while both islands are dotted with colourful and often eccentrically designed churches.

MAP REF: P,39

The striking Sausau Church, Sigave Tony Wheeler

THE TRAVEL BOOK:
A Journey through every Country in the World
September 2005

Published by:
Lonely Planet Publications Pty Ltd
ABN 36 005 607 983
90 Maribyrnong St, Footscray,
Victoria 3011, Australia

www.lonelyplanet.com

Printed by SNP Security Printing Pte Ltd, Singapore

Photographs:
Many of the images in this book are available
for licensing from Lonely Planet Images.
www.lonelyplanetimages.com

ISBN 1 74104 629 7

Lonely Planet Offices

Australia Locked Bag 1, Footscray, Victoria, 3011
tel: 03 8379 8000 fax: 03 8379 8111
email: talk2us@lonelyplanet.com.au

USA 150 Linden St, Oakland, CA 94607
tel: 510 893 8555 TOLL FREE: 800 275 8555
fax: 510 893 8572 email: info@lonelyplanet.com

UK 72-82 Rosebery Ave London EC1R 4RW
tel: 020 7841 9000 fax: 020 7841 9001
email: go@lonelyplanet.co.uk

Publisher: Roz Hopkins
Commissioning Editors: Janet Austin, Laetitia Clapton
Project Manager: Bridget Blair
Print Production: Graham Imeson
Pre-press Production: Ryan Evans
Designer: Daniel New
Design Team: Nic Lehman, Daniel New, Jane Pennells
Image Coordinator: Pepi Bluck
Image Researchers: Claire Gibson, Vallerie Tellini
Editors: Janet Austin, Bridget Blair, George Dunford, Piers Kelly, Martine Lleonart, Nina Rousseau, Simon Sellars
Cartographers: Wayne Murphy, Paul Piaia

Text:
The text in this book is based on Lonely Planet's guidebooks, trade and reference books and website content, which is researched and written by a global team of staff and authors. Content for this book was compiled by:
Zeljko Basic, Kellie Black, Jenny Blake, Lisa Borg, Janet Brunckhorst, Fiona Christie, Laetitia Clapton, Nina Collins, Jay Cooke, Hunor Csutoros, Melanie Dankel, Michael Day, Stefanie Di Trocchio, Sue Dodds, George Dunford, Katie Falkiner, Imogen Franks, Jennifer Garrett, Pablo Garcia Gastar, Marcel Gaston, M Glynn & J Smith, Aimée Goggins, Will Gourlay, Gabrielle Green, Tom Hall (UK), Tom Hall (US), Debra Herrmann, Cameron Holland, Evan Jones, Piers Kelly, Lisa Kerrigan, Emma Koch, Martine Lleonart, Tamar Lowell, Ben Mazey, Louise McGregor, Clare MacKenzie, Rowan McKinnon, Emma McMahon, Annelies Mertens, Rose Mulready, Jen Mundy, Mary Neighbour, Karen Parker, Jolyon Philcox, Sarah Pummell, Nina Rousseau, John Ryan, David Sadler, Ilana Sharp, Wendy Smith, Marg Toohey, Sam Trafford, Marc Visnick, Vivek Wagle, Sarah Wintle, Meg Worby, Rodney Zandbergs

With many thanks to:
Meaghan Amor, Gerilyn Attebery, Douglas Ayling, Judith Bamber, Vicki Beale, Glenn Beanland, Sam Benson, Adam Bextream, Ellen Burrows, Amy Carroll, Rebecca Chau, Fiona Christie, Kate Cody, Jay Cooke, Erin Corrigan, Michael Day, Karina Dea, Barbara Delissen, Brendan Dempsey, Barbara Di Castro, Stefanie Di Trocchio, Heather Dickson, Janine Eberle, Kate Evans, Melissa Faulkner, Imogen Franks, Fayette Fox, Pablo Garcia Gastar, Suki Gear, Cris Gibcus, Robin Goldberg, Will Gourlay, Gabrielle Green, Michala Green, James Hardy, Charlotte Harrison, Jane Hart, Alex Hershey, Errol Hunt, Alice Hunter, Richard I'Anson, Candice Jacobus, Kate James, Laura Jane, Andrew Leggatt, Yukiyoshi Kamimura, Indra Kilfoyle, Emma Koch, Katharine Leck, Jain Lemos, Clare MacKenzie, Claire McKenzie, Kathleen Munnelly, Alan Murphy, David Nelson, Sarah Nichols, Rachael Nusbaum, Stephanie Pearson, Howard Ralley, Andy Riddle, Rachel Roche, John Ryan, Kalya Ryan, Naomi Springall, Lanh Te, Marg Toohey, Sam Trafford, Maria Vallianos, Vivek Wagle, Gerard Walker, Simon Westcott, Tony Wheeler, Tamsin Wilson, Wendy Wright, Rodney Zandbergs, David Zingarelli

All images supplied by Lonely Planet Images with the exception of the following:

Alamy.com
p30 No 1, 2, 3, 4, p31 No 5, p46 No 2, p49 No 2, p78 No 2, 3, p90 No 1, p131 No 5, p170 No 3, p171 No 4, p225 No 2, 3, 4, 5, 6, p229 No 4, p252 No 2, p262 No 1, p277 No 4, p338 No 1, p339 No 4, p376 No 2, p386 No 1, p387 No 3, p399 No 1, 2, 4, p400 No 6, p407 No 2, p419 No 4, p442 No 7, p443 No 12, p144 No 2, 3, p145 No 4

Australian Picture Library/Corbis
p6 No 1, 2, p12 No 2, 3, p14 No 1, 4, p15 No 5, p18 No 1, 2, p46 No 1, p48 No 1, p66 No 1, 2, 3, p67 No 5, p78 No 1, p79 No 4, p91 No 4, p92 No 1, p131 No 6, p162 No 1, 2, p163 No 4, p170 No 2, p218 No 1, 2, p219 No 3, p228 No 2, 3, p306 No 1, 2, 3, p307 No 4, p312 No 1, 2, 4, p313 No 5, p334 No 1, 2, 3, p335 No 5, p358 No 1, p372 No 1, p373 No 2, 3, 4, p387 No 5, p407 No 1, 4, p412 No 1, 2, p413 No 5, p441 No 2, 3, 5

Getty Images
p12 No 1, p13 No 4, p24 No 1, p39 No 4, p47 No 5, p49 No 5, p66 No 4, p232 No 1, p265 No 4, p345 No 5

Impact Photos
p126 No 1, p126 No 2, 3, p127 No 4

Photolibrary.com
p14 No 2, p18 No 3, p19 No 4, p160 No 1, p162 No 3, p170 No 1, p224 No 1, p228 No 1, p248 No 1, p252 No 1, p253 No 5, p443 No 11

Reuters/Picture Media
p7 No 4, p55 No 2, 3, 4, 5, p91 No 2, 3, p93 No 2, 3, 4, p276 No 1, p387 No 2, 4, 6, p418 No 2, 3

Travel Ink
p166 No 1, 2, 3, p167 No 4, p340 No 1, p341 No 2, 3, 4